**Networking
the Enterprise**

Other Related Titles

0-07-060360-X	Spohn	*Data Network Design*
0-07-019022-4	Edmunds	*SAA/LU6.2 Distributed Networks and Applications*
0-07-054418-2	Sackett	*IBM's Token-Ring Networking Handbook*
0-07-004128-8	Bates	*Disaster Recovery Planning: Networks, Telecommunications, and Data Communications*
0-07-020346-6	Feit	*TCP/IP: Architecture, Protocols, and Implementation*
0-07-005075-9	Berson	*APPC: Introduction to LU6.2*
0-07-005076-7	Berson	*Client/Server Architecture*
0-07-012926-6	Cooper	*Computer and Communications Security*
0-07-016189-5	Dayton	*Telecommunications*
0-07-016196-8	Dayton	*Multi-Vendor Networks: Planning, Selecting, and Maintenance*
0-07-034243-1	Kessler/Train	*Metropolitan Area Networks: Concepts, Standards, and Service*
0-07-034247-4	Kessler	*ISDN, 2/e*
0-07-051144-6	Ranade/Sackett	*Introduction to SNA Networking: A Guide for Using VTAM/NCP*
0-07-051143-8	Ranade/Sackett	*Advanced SNA Networking: A Professional's Guide to VTAM/NCP*
0-07-033727-6	Kapoor	*SNA: Architecture, Protocols, and Implementation*
0-07-005553-X	Black	*TCP/IP and Related Protocols*
0-07-005554-8	Black	*Network Management Standards: SNMP, CMOT, and OSI*
0-07-021625-8	Fortier	*Handbook of LAN Technology, 2/e*
0-07-063636-2	Terplan	*Effective Management of Local Area Networks: Functions, Instruments, and People*
0-07-004563-1	Baker	*Downsizing: How to Get Big Gains from Smaller Computer Systems*
0-07-046321-2	Nemzow	*The Token-Ring Management Guide*
0-07-032385-2	Jain/Agrawala	*Open Systems Interconnection: Its Architecture and Protocols: (Revised Edition)*
0-07-707778-4	Perley	*Migrating to Open Systems: Taming the Tiger*
0-07-033754-3	Hebrawi	*OSI Upper Layer Standards and Practices*
0-07-049309-X	Pelton	*Voice Processing*

To order or receive additional information on these or any other McGraw-Hill titles, in the United States please call 1-800-822-8158. In other countries, contact your local McGraw-Hill representative.   **MH93**

Networking the Enterprise

How to Build Client/Server Systems That Work

Richard H. Baker

McGraw-Hill, Inc.

New York   San Francisco   Washington, D.C.   Auckland   Bogotá
Caracas   Lisbon   London   Madrid   Mexico City   Milan
Montreal   New Delhi   San Juan   Singapore
Sydney   Tokyo   Toronto

Library of Congress Cataloging-in-Publication Data

Baker, Richard H.
  Networking the enterprise : how to build client/server systems
that work / Richard H. Baker.
      p.   cm. — (McGraw-Hill series on computer communications)
  Includes index.
  ISBN 0-07-005089-9 :   — ISBN 0-07-005090-2 (pbk.) :
  1. Local area networks (Computer networks). 2. Client/server
computing. I. Title. II. Series.
TK5105.7.B355   1993
658.4'038'028546—dc20   93-2617
                                                                      CIP

    3 4 5 6 7 8 9 0   DOC/DOC   9 9 8 7 6 5 4

ISBN   0-07-005089-9
ISBN   0-07-005090-2 (PBK)

*The sponsoring editor for this book was Jerry Papke and the production
supervisor was Pamela A. Pelton. This book was set in Century Schoolbook
by North Market Street Graphics.*

Printed and bound by R. R. Donnelley & Sons Company.

Contents

Chapter 4. Exactly What Is Client/Server, Anyway?   95

Chapter 5. Like an Old Relation   115

Chapter 6. More than Basic Data   **139**

Chapter 8. The Promise of Open Systems   197

Preface

Reports of the mainframe's death have been exaggerated. But not very much.

Mainframes, minicomputers, and other forms of "big iron" will be around for a while. Some high-volume, transaction-oriented applications will continue to need the processing power of big systems. Mainframes represent large investments, in the systems themselves, in the applications that still run on them, and in the employees who manage them. They will not be easily discarded.

Nevertheless, the trend is clear. It is the enterprise network. When you referred to "the computer," you used to mean a single system in a designated location. Now, the computer is a network that extends to every corner of the organization. This system does not sit in just one place. In a real sense, the enterprise is the network—the enterprise network.

Enterprise networking is the outgrowth of several other closely related movements. One is client/server computing. Information is no longer something to be hoarded in a central computer, like some kind of long-term certificate of deposit. It is a valuable resource. Invest it by making it available to everyone who can use it to support the organization. More than a technology, client/server is a new way to use information.

Downsizing is another important trend. Particularly when networked, smaller computers can handle most of the work formerly assigned to mainframes—and may be able to handle all of it. They also cost a whole lot less. Just like client/server, downsizing is more than its technology. It too represents a new way to use information.

Enterprise networking is neither client/server nor downsizing nor anything else but itself. It is a way to share all the organization's information resources in a single, enterprise-wide network of computer networks. Like its companion movements, it is a new way to use information.

It is also inevitable. Today's business organizations are information-driven. We have developed a new way to use information because we need that new way to use information. Unless we can spread information throughout the organization, its members will be forced to operate under the severe disability of ignorance.

Enterprise networking is not the objective. It is a necessary means to reach that objective. You cannot live without it.

Enterprise networking is an ever-changing, partly completed technology. There are some rough spots. Goals like spreading information on distributed databases are being met more in theory than in practice. The final agreements needed to really open up open systems are bogged down in standards committees. The best internetworking technology is just now finding its way into active service. If needs could cry, the field of network management could produce another Johnstown flood.

All these problems have solutions. This book offers a particularly important perspective that can help you overcome any difficulties. Your objective is to serve your organization by serving its people. If you accept that as your goal, you'll find it easier to find or invent the technology that can get you there.

Spread out as it is, the enterprise network no longer occupies a central location. The new focus is on an important member of your organization: the person who has become known by the unfortunate term *user,* or the even less fortunate term, *end user.* This individual now has a central role in your life. This is a *customer.* The principles of customer service apply just as strongly inside your organization as outside. Your job is to serve your own internal customer.

That's why, as you'll soon notice, this book deals as much with people and with organizational issues as it does with technology. Your job, in the enterprise networking environment, is to serve your organization by serving its internal customers. The technology is just a means to that end.

A country store where I once shopped displayed a poster with several rules for dealing with customers. The sign predated sex-neutral terminology, but it still made a very important final point: *The customer is not an interruption to your work. He is the object of it.*

Richard H. Baker

Make Enterprise Networking Work for You

*To get where you want to go, you have to
know where that is.*

Computer networking used to be a simple idea. There was the computer, a traditional mainframe behind its proverbial glass walls. They called it a host, but by present-day standards it wasn't very hospitable. Cables led out to terminals, called dumb terminals because the computer had all the smarts.

Then came the minicomputer. It was like a mainframe, but smaller. Its purpose was to do for the department what the mainframe had done for the entire company.

Then desktop computers arrived. At first, they were called microcomputers, because they were even smaller than minis. That name never quite fit. These desktop systems were not just miniatures of their larger siblings. They were truly personal computers. When IBM applied that term to its ground-breaking PCs, the title stuck to the entire class.

The PCs soon stretched beyond their purely personal functions. They began to replace the dumb terminals. Add-on terminal emulation boards turned the PCs into so-called smart terminals, or more precisely, not-quite-so-dumb terminals.

Members of the growing PC community also began to network with each other on a little more intelligent basis. At first, they linked their PCs into local area networks, or LANs, each taking in a single office or a small department. These networks' main function was to share expensive resources like laser printers. LANs also began to share other resources like data and application programs. These software resources often ran on high-powered PCs, connected to the LANs in the role of servers.

Serving Clients and Customers

This was a critical change. At first glance, a PC-based server might look like only a smaller version of the large-system host. But remember, PCs are not miniaturized mainframes. They operate in close contact with the people who use them. The host system is a point of control, as well as a source of information. Everything is centralized there. The server directs its attention outward. Its job is to serve its clients. It is no coincidence that this client/server combination exists alongside business practices that emphasize customer service. The ultimate client is a person, the Information Systems (IS) department's internal customer.

Other systems arrive

Meanwhile, somewhere between the PC and the minicomputer, another class of computer was slowly finding a place: the personal workstation with the desktop convenience of the PC, but with the processing power of a larger unit.

Though some workstations run their makers' proprietary operating systems, increasing numbers use *open systems,* often based on the Unix operating system. These open systems are, at least nominally, based on

Host vs. server

- Host
  - Everything's centered here
- Server
  - Everything's centered on the client

Figure 1.1   People, not computers, are at the center of new systems.

generally accepted standards instead of single-source specifications. Unix lends itself to networking. Following the pattern of the LANs, the workstations were networked with companion servers using the same operating systems. Though Unix-based open systems have not yet recorded great market-share statistics, they have attracted enough interest to give them a central position in enterprise networking.

Dealing with diversity

Oh, yes, then there were the people, generally creative types, who brought in yet another type of system: the Apple Macintosh. Many computer professionals wrote off the Macs and their users because they were . . . well . . . different. It also was hard to integrate the Macs into the developing system of networks because they were . . . well . . . different.

That became the problem. It isn't just that the Macs are different. The problem is that all these different types of systems are unlike each other. It was one thing to link some terminals to a mainframe or mini. It was a little harder to hook together networks of similar PCs or workstations, but it could be done. These limited networks only showed the value of using computers to share information. Soon, someone with a PC wanted to swap files with a Mac user, and both wanted access to the data on the mainframe. Networks began to grow—into networks of dissimilar systems and even into networks of networks. These now have evolved into modern enterprise networking.

Today's main networking challenge is not to share a departmental printer, but to share all the resources and all the data in all the enterprise. If a customer service representative in Philadelphia needs information from a mainframe in Seattle, that information should be as readily available as if it were on the service rep's own PC.

To serve this ambitious purpose, today's networks must try to get vastly dissimilar systems to work together, sometimes over incredibly long distances. For many organizations, it is critical that they succeed. Modern organizations run on information, and only a smooth-functioning enterprise network can make all the information available at all locations, all the time.

There have been many reports of successful enterprise networking projects. Modern enterprises run on information. Enterprise networks let people throughout the organization share information and put it to the best possible use. Your organization's ability to compete and survive could depend on its people's ability to find, share, and use information.

There have also been a few reports of unsuccessful enterprise networking projects. People don't like to crow about their failures. They exist, though—evidence that success in even the most worthy of projects is not automatic. It takes work to succeed with an enterprise network. More than that, it takes careful, realistic planning.

The results can be well worth the effort. A successful enterprise network empowers the people who use it. With that power, they can help give the organization important new competitive strength. The key to success is that you map out, then follow, a well-charted route to that goal.

A Goal to Pursue

It makes no sense to set up an enterprise network without a reason, particularly when there are so many good reasons available. There is the cost advantage of smaller systems with higher capacity. Maintenance and personnel costs can be lower, too. Those are just additional benefits that usually come with achieving the major goal: improving your competitive position by giving more people access to more information.

These benefits may seem obvious, and your natural objective is to enjoy them. Even so, the first step in building an enterprise networking plan is to state your objectives. Thomas Jefferson set the example when he opened the Declaration of Independence with a list of self-evident truths.

If you don't state your goals, you can easily get sidetracked. Particularly in an enterprise networking project, it is easy to focus too tightly on technical issues. Someone decides in some way that the organiza-

Wrong reasons to change

- "We have the technology"
- "The boss made me do it"

Figure 1.2 Neither random technology nor unclear goals are good reasons to launch an enterprise network.

tion should buy certain types of hardware and software. That's an easy way to get off the track. Enterprise networking is a technical process, so it's only natural to focus on technical issues. It's easy to lose sight of the reasons you want to use the technology.

Another way to get sidetracked is never understanding the organization's objectives in the first place. Often, you can ask an IS manager why the organization plans to convert, and the answer will be, "Because management wants to."

Enterprise networking is a business venture, not a technical adventure. The questions to ask at the outset are:

- How can the organization respond to rapidly changing conditions?
- How can enterprise networking help it do that?

Tactical vs. Strategic

Most existing computer systems are tactical tools. They help collect the bills, which help make the payroll. They coordinate factory production and foster efficiency measures, like just-in-time delivery. They provide the numbers for reporting and analysis. They use these numbers as a basis for future projections.

All these are tactical functions. They can have great value to an organization. They promote more efficient ways to get products and services to the people who will pay for them.

Enterprise networking can play a role in all these activities. There is a larger role, too, however, and it offers a larger opportunity. That is

Before you risk everything

- How does the organization need to change and adapt?
- How can enterprise networking contribute to that change?

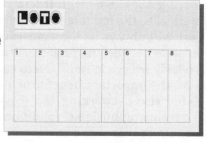

Figure 1.3 Base your plan on business issues, not technical questions.

Tactical to strategic

- Single-purpose tools serve tactical purposes
- An enterprise network promotes organizational strategy

Figure 1.4   Tactical tools help get the job done, but strategic tools promote a well-directed effort.

the ability to transform tactical activities into the foundation of a total business strategy. The network and its components are strategic assets, not just tactical tools.

Networking's role

Ultimately, all employees should have access to the information they need, when they need it, and in a format they can use. When employees have this kind of access, they can become more strategic in their thinking. They won't have to focus entirely on how to schedule processes or get products out the door. They also can think about what those products should be, who will buy them, how to price them, and how to deliver them to the market. This kind of thinking can help set the course of business strategy. Not all users will expand their thinking this way, of course. Still, an enterprise network can support and encourage those who will. It lets your best thinkers make greater contributions to the organization's success.

Cost will always be a consideration, and often a justification, for an enterprise networking project. After all, reduced cost is a tangible benefit nearly everyone in business can appreciate. For this reduced cost, you get the important benefits of a more flexible, responsive enterprise.

Enterprise networking can expand your ability to respond to new and developing business conditions. You can respond faster, too, with more rapid turnaround on developing the applications to capitalize on opportunities. These applications can be up, running, and responding

What users should have

- The information they need
- When they need it
- In a form they can use

Figure 1.5. When users have access to more kinds of information, they expand their thinking and play stronger roles in organizational strategy.

much faster than they could under traditional mainframe practice. The long range goal is not so much immediate cost savings, but to accomplish things like these:

- Increase corporate communication
- Improve access to data
- Create a flexible atmosphere that can respond to change

These are the goals successful enterprise networkers have pursued and achieved.

Practical applications

There are many examples of how enterprise networking can improve an organization's strategic position. Applications like electronic mail (e-mail) improve communication. Client/server techniques and distributed computing provide ways to split applications between various platforms. These provide new ways to retrieve and manipulate data.

At the professional level, standardized application tools, available on PCs, provide the flexibility for rapid change. There are many stories of organizations that have cut application development time and expense by as much as two-thirds.

Two views of the same process

Few IS professionals any longer fit the stereotype of terminally stubborn defenders of the status quo. Surveys show most professionals want to keep up with advancements in their profession. Enterprise networking is exactly the kind of leading edge movement in which they

Enterprise networking goals

- Short term
  - Reduce cost
  - Improve responsiveness
- Long term
  - Improve communication
  - Create flexibility

Figure 1.6   Don't let short-term interests divert you from long-range goals.

are interested. If they appear restrained in joining the trend, it is usually for the sake of maintaining professional standards and traditions.

It is no accident, though, that the stereotype remains. That's because it does fit a significant minority: an influential group that personifies resistance to change. For planning purposes, the conflicting groups can be classified according to how they perceive their roles in life.

Jobs for an enterprise network

- Databases
  - Client/server
  - Distributed
- E-mail
- Application development

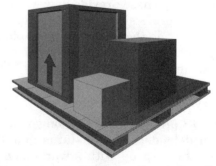

Figure 1.7   The most useful applications create new ways to distribute and use information.

Initial planning checklist

1. In what ways can an enterprise network help make you more competitive?
2. In what ways can networks improve your market position?
3. In what ways can networking make the organization more efficient?
4. Which most accurately expresses your organization's view of an enterprise network?
   - A business opportunity
   - A technical challenge

Members of the traditional group believe, as they were taught to believe, that their function is to deliver resources to the people who need them. Enterprise networking reflects a different perspective: that an IS professional's job is to support the organization by helping users find and create their own computer resources.

These views are not necessarily in conflict. Often, the best way to meet employees' needs for information is to help them develop their own applications or conduct their own database searches. Application development tools now available let them construct useful applications without advanced programming knowledge. There has been a trend toward providing users with these tools. IS primarily plays a supporting role. There also are times when a professional is the best person to serve those needs.

The important thing is that the needs are served. This is a major objective of enterprise networking. User flexibility is an important foundation of enterprise-wide computing. PC applications, the LANs that support them, shared peripherals and information, and interconnections among departments all form the enterprise network.

Working together—with difficulty

To achieve a focus on the business benefits, IS and business management must learn to work together. Given their relationship in the past, this won't be easy. It will be necessary.

There are two conflicting forces at work:

- Many IS professionals still believe standardization and control are too essential to decentralize data management.

- Users, often represented by corporate management, want more access to data, on their own terms and without controls.

To resolve this basic conflict, some organizations have installed mixed systems. IS professionals and users join the process of deciding which applications and resources to distribute among networks. They work together in self-directed teams. IS can maintain a measure of control, placing limits on ad hoc application development. Users have

---

Evaluating the management atmosphere

1. How does top management view computer technology?
   - Does management recognize it as an important strategic asset?
   - What are the concerns about cost and possible problems?
2. When presented with a technological opportunity, does management:
   - Encourage its use?
   - Avoid its use?
3. On whom could you depend to support your case with top management?
   - A visionary leader
   - A leader in training and education
   - A technical expert
4. Who is able to motivate members of middle management?
   - A visionary leader
   - A leader in training and education
   - A technical expert
5. What does management expect for financial justification?
   - By whom?
   - How aggressively should you present your case?
   - How firm must your projections be?

---

more opportunities to make sure the system responds to their needs, not to goals established somewhere else.

Serving the Internal Customer

The employees are the important element in this structure. They are the information system's internal customers. American business has learned to emphasize customer service. It has also learned that you can't effectively serve external customers unless you also support the employees who provide that service. Employees responsible for customer service are the internal customers of other members of the organization. The level of customer service should be just the same internally as it is externally.

IS has many internal customers. They are the users, line managers, senior executives, stockholders, and ultimately the board of directors. By serving these internal customers, IS helps them serve their own internal or external customers.

The value of information

According to reliable estimates, raw materials and other input account for only about 30 percent of the value of a typical industrial product. Information supplies more than 70 percent. Information is an even greater percentage of the value in service organizations that use few raw materials. This means that the most effective sales approach would be to say, in effect, "I'm smarter than the rest. I can get my products to the market faster, and I can deliver a better-quality product—and deliver it on time."

Thus, when a company puts its information in the hands of as many employees as possible, the company literally gets smarter.

Nike has become a leader in athletic shoes. It has done so partly through effective advertising and partly because the firm is geared to respond quickly to marketplace developments. Nike can get new designs into the stores earlier than anyone else. The firm initially installed a mainframe system to run graphics and design applications, but it has since transferred these to PCs. This means Nike can deliver new products with the speed of the athletes in its commercials.

Though the systems support this effort, it is Nike's people who deliver. The system doesn't do the work. It has simply been geared to most effectively support the people and improve their ability to perform.

The system is the user

To put it another way, *the system is the user.* In today's business environment, the user is the primary component. Enterprise networking supports this human element by bringing information directly to people's desktops.

This is much different from traditional practice, where a major goal was to protect data by restricting access to it. Now, it is more important to improve access to data in order to make use of it—and to protect the data at the same time. It is important to protect valuable information, of course, but not at the expense of denying access to people who could use it productively. This can be a difficult transition for IS professionals to make. Like eating oatmeal, it might be the right thing to do, but to some people it still doesn't seem very appealing.

Not everyone needs access to everything. Focus first on getting people who work in tandem to share information with each other. Let managers talk to managers, engineers to engineers, and so on. Once the departmental and functional links have been set up, you can provide internetwork and interdepartmental pathways among groups. These become the core of the finished enterprise network.

Start with something small and simple, not a grand overhaul. The overhaul should be the ultimate goal, but not your immediate one. Build human as well as technical networks between departments. As one consultant said, "It just might happen that you'll get better market response for your next product if R&D actually talks to marketing during the design process. It might be worth a try."

A Systems Approach to Planning

To develop an enterprise networking plan, start by answering questions. These are mostly questions about your organization and what you hope to achieve. Among them:

- What system specifications and file structures do your applications need?
- Do you have or expect a high level of transaction processing?
- How much disk storage capacity will you need? How much more do you think you ought to provide?
- How many sessions will be in progress at once?
- How many users will be logged onto the system simultaneously?

These questions and their answers are preludes to the *systems approach* to an enterprise networking plan. True to its name, this approach systematically identifies, then addresses, the issues and concerns the project will entail. These include:

- Conducting a needs analysis
- Choosing between packaged software and developing a custom code
- Providing for security and disaster recovery
- Maintaining data integrity
- Setting and observing standards

Analyzing the need

A needs analysis is a detailed review of what types of systems and other technology the venture will require. It is not just a technology assessment. It is a process through which you identify the business needs you want to address. Only after you have identified the business need should you worry about the technology available to solve it. You've often heard of forms of computer technology called "solutions." You can't provide a good solution unless you have accurately identified the problem.

A needs analysis should help you identify:

- The current state of your computer and network systems
- How well the existing system meets, or fails to meet, the organization's needs
- How an enterprise network could meet these identified needs
- A preliminary list of goals and priorities
- The systems to be improved or expanded

Elements of a systems approach

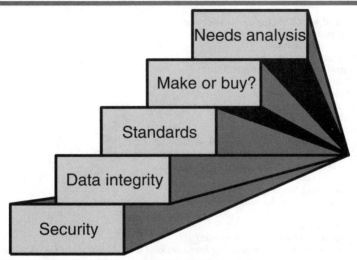

Figure 1.8 A systems approach is a methodical strategy that addresses the major elements of your goals and plans.

Based on this assessment, you can prepare a proposal that will justify the project to senior management and define the standards for success.

Involve users in this process. Start by asking for a list of their information requirements. Almost inevitably, the first report will be a wish list. Give it some respectful attention, then go back to the users and separate their real needs from their wishful thinking.

Only after you've identified the most important needs can you match the technology to the needs. Then, be sure you leave room for the growth that is inevitably going to occur.

Make or buy?

Chances are, you will be creating at least some of your own programming code. Many shrink-wrap applications are available, particularly for PCs. Even so, you may find yourself writing code to supplement or expand these applications. Most database management programs are application development platforms, which will require that you provide some code to use them. So are many spreadsheets and word processors, whose macro facilities are nearly complete programming languages.

Another factor is the availability of better application development tools, and the ability to develop programs on PCs within the networked environment. The newest tools are easier to use, and they can sharply reduce setup time.

Standardization checklist

1. Where and why are standards necessary?
   - User support
   - Integrating services
   - Product selection
   - Uniform network configuration
   - Off-the-shelf applications
   - Application development
2. What are the risks of not standardizing . . .
   - To the organization?
   - To network management?
   - To employees and their departments?
3. At which of these levels should you establish standards?
   - Workstations and their operating systems
   - Network operating systems
   - Cabling and topology
   - Wide area networks and backbones
   - Servers
   - Applications
4. Who will set and enforce the standards?
5. What is the need to alter existing installations that do not meet the standards?

These tools are bringing a major change to programming practice. You no longer have to write reams of code to produce a working application. You can describe many operations with point-and-click operations, and the application itself will write the code to conduct those operations. This is particularly true in Windows-based applications, including database managers, spreadsheets, and word processors. These can call on their extensive programming languages to generate most of the code for an application. The only conventional programming you need do is akin to writing a few macros to customize the application.

As these tools make it easier to address your particular business needs, doing it yourself makes more sense. Even if you don't write applications from scratch, you may write internal macros and other kinds of enhancements to various kinds of shrink-wrap applications.

Observing standards

Few things are more characteristic of the IS profession than its dedication to standards. Some call it an obsession. It has often been a source of conflict. Professionals call for standardization for the sake of data integrity and other worthwhile causes. Users chafe at the same standards, feeling—often correctly—that these inhibit their ability to do their jobs.

Some standards are necessary. The trick is to find out which ones. The GUI, particularly its Windows version, is a notable and widely used standard. It is supposed to present the same type of interface every time, no matter which application is in use.

Windows application developers have created several exceptions. Compare two major Windows word processors, each of which takes a distinctive approach. Microsoft has naturally stuck closely to Windows' uniform approach. Word Perfect has been both praised and condemned for transferring the distinctive characteristics of its character-based products to the Windows version.

Even where exceptions have become the rule, there is enough uniformity to make standardization worthwhile. Though Word Perfect has departed from Windows standards, it is notably uniform within its own product line. People who have learned the mechanics of one Windows application, or one Word Perfect application, need not learn a full new set of commands and functions when they move to new applications from the same families. That means instructors need spend less time teaching mechanics like the use of function keys, and more time teaching better ways to use the application.

Networking technology is another area where standardization can be important. Here, the standards are expansive, not restrictive. They specify ways in which diverse networks, interconnections, and applications can interact with each other, whatever the platforms on which they run. This is also a case where it can often be more important to maintain communication between departments than to require that every department use the same platform.

The approved software list is another form of standardization. Users cite advantages like these:

- Volume discounts. Standardized packages are usually purchased in quantity.

- Reduced support workload. Technicians need only work with a few applications.

- Backup resources. With volume purchasing, it is easy and inexpensive to arrange to have spare software copies on hand to meet unexpected needs.

Advanced users detest approved software lists. They want the freedom to choose their own tools. Sometimes, their position is justified. A different application could help them do their jobs better.

This is another source of conflict, as if you need one. These tactics, alone or in combination, can help resolve it:

- If someone can justify the cost of buying a nonstandard software package, allow it. But warn such users that they're on their own. The company will not offer training or support.

- Use the macro languages available in many standard packages. You can create many functions the users believe they can get only from other programs.

How one firm evaluates software

In selecting software for its approved list, Martin Marietta goes through these steps:

- Decide which products to evaluate, and set priorities for reviewing them.
- Select experts to work with individual products.
- Define the business-related needs the products are expected to meet.
- Obtain evaluation copies.
- Conduct preliminary evaluations that identify the leading candidates for adoption.
- Conduct extensive field tests of the selected final candidates.
- Review the test results and make final recommendations.
- Make selections based on those recommendations.
- Keep records of the review and approval process for use in future evaluations.
- Update the list of approved products and active candidates every three months.

Maintaining integrity

Maintaining data integrity is a major concern of IS professionals. They traditionally have considered this one of their most important responsibilities. They are understandably uneasy with the likelihood that widespread user access will threaten the accuracy and usability of the organization's data resources.

Some companies go so far as to prevent user uploads as a way to keep the core company data pure. It seems simple, but effective: don't allow users to upload data at all. That approach helps keep the data uncorrupted. It is just as effective in screening the core data from necessary updates. The database fails to reflect the research and development users have been doing. It directly conflicts with the major objective of deriving the maximum value from the maximum available data.

There is a better approach, and it lets concerned IS professionals act on their concerns. Establish a dedicated group of professionals who are skilled in both business and system needs. Let them act as gatekeepers to ensure the accuracy of the data that travels up to the server or mainframe. These can be teams of specialists who can monitor uploads and make sure they are not going to foul up everything else in your system. Meanwhile, they can let the database reflect the legitimate changes made at the desktop level.

Maintaining security

Security and disaster recovery are allied with maintaining data integrity. Often, though, they tend to be forgotten, particularly in networked systems. One reason is that it is harder to protect a network than it is an isolated larger system. Another problem is a tendency to think of network resources as inexpensive and easy to replace.

Security is not entirely a matter for security officials or IS professionals. Other people like building managers and electricians also have roles in keeping your resources secure. Include them in your planning. They probably can give you some good ideas about things to do or avoid to make the system more secure.

Justifying the Project

Not all enterprise network projects succeed. Companies that do enjoy success have one thing in common. They have concentrated first on the organization's needs, and on how an enterprise network could meet those needs. They have balanced these against the technological demands and the project's likely costs. The key: start by considering business factors, not technical ones.

Business considerations

No enterprise networking plan can pass any reasonable justification test unless it responds to a business need. Don't do something just because you have the means to do it. Act because you can respond to an identified need and improve your competitive position.

Look for opportunities to gain a future competitive advantage as well as a current-quarter edge. We exist in a highly competitive global economy. A single remark about interest rates can send the stock market into a tailspin the next day. Good news from the Middle East can shoot the market back up again just as quickly. The ideal project puts you in position to respond as quickly as conditions change.

The ability to promote internetworking may seem like a technical consideration, but this too is first a business issue. The technology of internetworking promotes communication. If a plan would promote communication, particularly among diverse elements of the organization, it will enable them to work more closely and to cooperate in a common effort. This, too, improves the organization's ability to compete.

On the other side

Weigh the potential advantages against the cost and difficulty of achieving them. Even a beneficial project may not be worthwhile if the systems would be too complex and hard to manage.

Then, there's the factor called, "If it ain't broke, don't fix it." Beware the false simplicity of that folksy saying. Even good-running systems can often stand improvement. At the same time, don't underrate the value of a system that already works well. It might not be worth the risk of upsetting a delicate balance to try to build in a new project that will give you only a limited return. At least look for a return that is worth the risk.

Don't try to downsize an application that truly requires large-scale computing power. A large system may ultimately evolve into a server role, but it still will be there to run the applications that require its power.

Costs vs. benefits

The traditional form of cost-benefit analysis in data processing compares the cost of computerization with the cost of doing the same job manually.

Enterprise networking requires a different approach. Turn the traditional method around and consider *opportunity cost.* Examine the potential cost savings of converting the application. If there are none, that would end the analysis right there. If there are significant savings, failing to take advantage of them would be a cost. It is the cost of missing an opportunity.

Factors to consider

- Compare:
  - Business need
  - Competitive advantage
  - Opportunity
- With:
  - Complexity
  - Cost

Figure 1.9 When evaluating a potential networking project, compare the business advantages with the technical and financial needs.

Pick a Winner

The universal advice of nearly anyone who has attempted an enterprise networking project is *start small*. Look for an application that involves only a few users, and where the risk of failure is small. This is no time to take chances with vital applications and data. It's much more important that you come up with a winner the first time. You will gain valuable experience, at small risk. Your success will build morale and make doubters less reluctant to participate.

Three are three basic places you can start: an individual or small-group application, a departmental system, or something that extends across the enterprise. It makes sense to start with the smallest possibility that has passed the justification test. You can experiment, you can work at a reasonable scale, and, should you fail, it will be a localized failure.

A single department or user group also can provide a good candidate for the first effort. Here, the users know their needs and are likely to be proficient in using their systems. Many good ideas come from small user groups who can make direct, specific suggestions about how to

Take it from the top

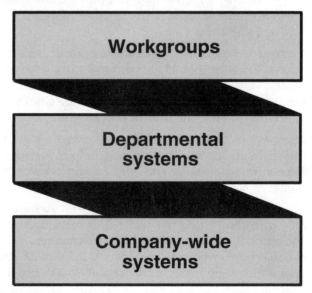

Figure 1.10 Start the networking process with small, workgroup systems. Larger projects require more experience.

meet their needs. These groups also are often under pressure from above to produce more results or solve nagging problems. People in that situation will be anxious to work with you if it means a solution— or better yet an opportunity—will result.

Exception to the rule

Starting small represents conventional wisdom, but there is room for an exception. One leading consultant has advised clients to start with substantial projects instead. Look for an application that will show direct, bottom-line results. That advice is based on the limited budgets many organizations now face. Management may not be willing to spring for a project whose only real benefit would be to show its own feasibility.

If that describes your organization, starting larger can be good advice. Better yet, look for this compromise: a project that is small enough to provide a good demonstration and learning experience, but still can provide enough solid results to be a good investment.

Selection guidelines

Here are some other guidelines for selecting a first project:

- *Be prepared to be flexible.*   The first project will be a learning process, no matter which target you pick. Allow some room for creativity of your development team. Let them explore. Let them find better ways of doing things.

- *Don't restrict yourself.*   Starting small doesn't mean limiting your options. For example, it's all right to work with more than one package at a time. Use the opportunity to learn the ins and outs of two or three packages, though probably no more than that. You can use the experience to pick one that best suits your needs.

- *Target the initial training process.*   Start with a few internal gurus who will run the application and help other users once it's set up. Make sure those folks are trained and are ready to carry the ball whenever the new system comes on line.

- *Let developers and users work together.*   Assign some developers to work with the prospective users. Get some user analysis to guide the development process. Give the professionals an opportunity to talk with the people who are going to have to live with their work. Also, help users understand better what the developers can and cannot provide.

- *Don't pick unnecessary fights.*   Avoid projects that can become battlegrounds for alternate technologies. Pick one where there is a single, clear-cut way to achieve the goal.

Beyond a Good Start

Once you've completed the first project or two, your priorities will begin to change. Now, you will have two main responsibilities:

- To extend the process to larger, more widespread areas that can have greater impact on the organization.
- To help the managers of departments where projects have been completed manage their systems and improve their effectiveness.

The management challenge

Some managers may be unintentionally troublesome. A downsized application should be one that requires less involvement and support from the IS department. That is one source of cost savings, and it will be an opportunity lost if the users can't take charge of their own system.

A few department heads may be slow to do this. You must convince these managers to accept full responsibility for their departmental networks. One clear sign that this is not happening is the department's failure to train its users and maintain necessary records and procedures. The department that is most likely to turn its networking venture into a success is the one that is willing to take responsibility for achieving that success.

Still go slowly

Early success will build confidence, but be careful not to let it build overconfidence. Don't rush into a wholesale makeover. Make changes

How to get a buy-in

- Make managers responsible for success
- Show the benefits of new methods
- Train managers as well as users

Figure 1.11.   Department heads must take responsibility for their own systems.

on a single system, then a single department, and then a single division. A careful approach lets you build on your success to date and helps you gain the support that is necessary for continued success.

Continue to look for appropriate business areas where it might be fruitful to extend the enterprise network. Continue to work within the specific selection criteria you used with the early projects. Expand and amend these criteria as you gain experience. Don't be too quick to assume, though, that you can begin to wing it based on your early success and experience. Continue to maintain a set of criteria against which to evaluate all new proposals and requests. This can save you from the familiar experience of learning from your mistakes.

Remember training

If users are going to accept responsibility for running and using their own systems, you must train them to do so. Start by training a cadre that will support the department's other users.

Often, you'll find computer expertise spread among the users, sometimes in surprising places. It's not unusual for a manager to have gained only limited knowledge of how to operate a desktop computer, while a junior employee has become a self-taught expert on Unix or internetworking.

The problem is not the manager's lack of capacity. Managers and professionals can, and should, learn how to use their own systems. They then can contribute to the development of the company's business. They need to learn only the basics. You need not turn them all into programmers. The object is to empower them to use their own specialized knowledge, backed by the flexibility and information access of the enterprise network.

The new role for MIS

The managers and users of enterprise networks will take on some functions that traditionally have belonged to the Management Information Systems (MIS) staff. That doesn't mean the skilled professionals of this department will have nothing to do. Like the system, though, their jobs will change.

MIS could continue to support the effort, but on a larger scale. Staff members should continue to be the setters of standards, the guardians of the database, and the headmasters of the training program. Instead of acting in the direct role of developing a mainframe system, IS professionals should think of themselves as internal consultants, advising and supporting clients within the organization.

Meanwhile, advances in network technology let you shift development and the operation of computer systems out of the data center and into the user organizations. This will reduce the need for traditional mainframe programmers. It will not eliminate them, though, and it should create new demands for more business-oriented systems professionals to work in partnership with the user community.

From Talk to Action

As they teach in every management school, "Planning is a *good thing.*" The more planning you do before you act, the more successful your action will probably be.

Nevertheless, there are times when excessive planning can be too much of a good thing. You spend so much time planning the transition you never get around to doing the deed. Consultant Cheryl Currid calls this NATO: no action; talk only. To negate this tendency, Currid offers a step-by-step plan for making the move from talk to action:

- *Get top management support.*   Win over the Chief Executive Officer (CEO), Chief Financial Officer (CFO), and anyone else in top management who will listen. Make sure they understand the flexibility and economic benefits of enterprise networking.

- *Be sure you have a willing Chief Information Officer (CIO).*   Like it or not, the information kingdom is about to be transformed. An uncooperative CIO could launch too many missiles and destroy the project

- *Build a winning team.*   Handpick a talented team of volunteers. An enterprise networking project, particularly a company's first one, is likely to be full of unexpected glitches. Form a strongly committed and competent clan. Secure the latitude and resources they need to get the job done.

- *Don't buy cheap stuff.*   Build a strong LAN platform that is Wide Area Network (WAN) -able. Don't fool around. This is not Tinker Toy technology. You'll need an industrial strength LAN and good standards and procedures.

- *Get procedures in order.*   This means backups, security, audits, support, and professional management. If you can't do it yourself, contract with a systems integrator who can.

- *Start assessing the desktop environment.*   You need powerful workstations that can share the processing load of the new applications. Remember, the whole-cost economics of a LAN is different from a mainframe. With LANs and client/server applications, it's what's up front (on the desktop) that counts.

- *Select a strong client/server back-end database.*   The best bet is to pick a database that is robust, supportable, and can be plugged into the network easily.

- *Find the right front-end development tools.*   Chances are you can avoid programming in COBOL or C if you look at the graphics-oriented front-end tools now available. Survey the market and select what you need. Don't be surprised if you end up with a multivendor arrangement between front and back ends. Also, it's no crime to have different tools for users and developers. The beauty of the client/server environment is that you have something for everyone—and it all fits together.

- *Choose a suitable pilot application.*   Survey the current application development project list, and check out the gas guzzlers on the mainframe. Select a project that can be accomplished in a few months; you don't want to wait years for results. Don't take the company's largest database down first. Instead, pull down something that's realistic in size and complexity.

- *Consider outsourcing the mainframe.*   The sooner you go on meter charges for mainframe use, the better. That way, people will realize the benefits of networking right away.

- *Reorganize MIS.*   Start blending the new technology into mainstream MIS, but be sure to play by the new rules, not the old. LANs and client/server computing create some jobs and displace others. Don't try to force-fit a 20-year-old MIS organizational structure onto the new platform.

Other consultants repeat Currid's advice on buying quality hardware, particularly for networking. The computer industry press (of which I am part) has done you a disservice here. The evaluation criteria in product tests have favored the fast and cheap. Higher quality products have been disparaged for their higher prices. Now, after a few years of buying low-priced systems, some users report unusually high breakdown rates.

How Sara Lee proceeded

Based on its experience in multiple business units, Sara Lee has developed a set of procedures that both corporate and MIS management feel can boost a project's success:

- Form a committee of MIS staff members, corporate management, departmental management, and users to define, review, and monitor the project. Many divisions have found this approach to be effective for both short- and long-term planning.

- Identify the applications that are best suited for the network.

- Start with a project that has limited scope, is easy to define and control, and whose success is easy to figure out.

- Don't try to do too much too quickly.

- Identify the work and information flows that are currently in place for the existing system and find out the effect the project will have on those processes.

- Decide who will have the rights and responsibilities of owning the data and will be responsible for maintaining it.

- Clearly identify the project's objectives and quantify the benefits these objectives will provide.

- Get upper management involved in the project from the beginning and secure a commitment from them about its objectives and benefits.

- Make sure the project's rationale is based on strategic business goals rather than political ambitions.

- Regularly review the progress of the project with the multidepartmental committee, making modifications to the plan as the committee deems appropriate.

Don't do this

There also are plenty of mistakes to avoid. Consultant Patrick Corrigan of the Corrigan Group (San Francisco) offers these examples:

- *Do-it-yourself installation.*   Too many companies install their own networks, without sufficient experience or knowledge. Hire a professional well versed in network design and installation. This expert can be a consultant, or an employee who takes responsibility for the entire process.

- *A bargain basement approach.*   Shopping for the cheapest hardware and operating system may ease the initial pain, but bargain shopping will cost you when you run into the inevitable incompatibilities.

- *Using an untested reseller or system integrator.*   Too many people are orphaned by a dealer, Value Added Reseller (VAR), or consultant when things don't go right. Get references, and look for someone who has set up a LAN in a similar environment.

- *Poor planning and design.*   Most networks just happen, says Corrigan. As the network gets bigger and takes on a more critical role, the lack of planning becomes evident. Issues such as user account information, directory structures, and deciding who has access to different types of data should be hammered out when the network is installed. Do it with an eye toward future growth.

- *Unrealistic expectations.*   Most organizations that install networks expect it to be a quick and easy process. Neither is ever true.

- *Assuming everything will work on the first try.* This hardly ever happens, even when you have a professional network installer handling the project.

- *Assuming that anyone can manage the network.* Every network, whatever its size, requires the ongoing attention of a trained network administrator. This administrator must deal every day with problems like backups, application installation and maintenance, management of user accounts, and hardware and software compatibility.

- *Lack of user training.* Users need to be schooled in such issues as dealing with shared peripherals and shared applications. Instead, users often are simply given passwords and shown how to log on to the network.

- *Improper backup.* A major source of trouble for networks of any size is a failure to follow proper backup procedures.

- *Ignoring disaster recovery.* Every company needs a comprehensive disaster recovery plan. This is particularly critical when the business depends on the smooth operation of the network.

Meeting the Human Challenge

Enterprise networks empower employees.
Why, then, do so many employees fear losing
power?

The object of enterprise networking is to spread more information, more opportunities, and more control to the employees. Then they can use their expanding knowledge to improve the organization. If information is power, and it is, that means the employees will gain more power.

This process carries the noble-sounding name of *employee empowerment,* and it not limited to computing. It is a process of giving employees more decision-making responsibility. Empowerment is the key to building successful, responsive organizations, unbound by the structures and strictures of multilevel organization charts.

If you give new power to the employees, that must mean you have to take it from someone else. That doesn't have to be the case, but it's true often enough. That's why some supervisors and managers have staunchly resisted the trend toward employee participation. They fear the loss of their own power, influence and ability to exercise their responsibilities. This is particularly true of managers and supervisors who have learned to regard their subordinates with mistrust and suspicion.

Enterprise networking is just part of that process. With its companion processes, downsizing and client/server computing, enterprise networking supports empowerment. It gives employees better information with which to make better judgments. The resisters include IS professionals who fear the loss of their own power, influence, and ability to exercise their responsibilities. This is particularly true of those who have learned to regard "end users" with mistrust and suspicion.

Don't expect universal gratitude, either, from the employees you are trying to empower. Not everyone welcomes the added responsibility.

Many employees have achieved power, or at least security, in their mastery of traditional methods. They are afraid of losing it. This is particularly true of those who have learned to regard management with mistrust and suspicion.

Enterprise networking is a major technological challenge. That's only part of the problem. The human challenge can be even more difficult. No matter how hard it is to integrate diverse computer systems, it can be infinitely harder to integrate the mistrustful and suspicious people who run and use them.

Today's Workers Are Different

The end user no longer exists. Today's intelligent information worker is not at the end of anything, but at the center. Changes in the understanding of a network and its purposes reflect changes in the understanding of the people who use the network. A modern employee is a much different person than the one who used to punch keys at a terminal. Compared with traditional users, the new networked employee is likely to be:

- A professional or a manager
- A more valuable person
- More mobile
- Assigned to a different type of job

Forget about the "end user"

- Today's employees are:
  - Professional
  - Valuable
  - Mobile
  - Versatile

Figure 2.1   The user is not the least important element, but the most important.

The professional

There has been a fundamental change in the types of people who use computers. The network not only serves a client system, but a human client—an internal customer. Information professionals have had to adapt. Consider the types of people you might have found sitting at terminals a few years ago. Some would have been programmers, of course. Many would have been data entry clerks. Others would have been engineers, accountants, or others with specialized needs. It would have been rare to find either executives or secretaries with terminals at their desks.

Except for data processing professionals, the older users usually were hourly employees who did the same tasks every day. Today's information workers rely on their PCs to support a variety of tasks. Executives probably have networked PCs in their offices. So do professionals and so-called knowledge workers. They use these systems to retrieve information to use in executive information systems, or to plug directly into their spreadsheet programs. This is *dynamic information,* not the static reports of the past. Modern employees don't just read data. They use it.

Their jobs require greater amounts of management analysis. They make use of different types of knowledge. Often, they work at higher skill levels.

Organizations are changing along with their people. Modern firms are flatter and more flexible. It's not just the people who have changed. Their work and their organizational status have changed as well.

The high-value employee

We face a shortage of skilled employees. People are no longer interchangeable parts—they never were. People are an investment, and a very costly investment to boot. A primary goal of any information system should be to get maximum value from this investment.

It can cost an organization at least $6000 simply to fill a position. Other estimates place the cost even higher, as much as the first two years' salary. That is only the cost of recruiting, interviewing, testing, and finally filling the position. It costs even more to integrate the new employee into the organization. Training costs vary with the nature of the job. They often are substantial. There are continuing expenses such as the costs of supervision, keeping employees updated on new methods and technologies, and of course their salaries and benefits. There's another potential cost, too: the value of information departing employees could take from the organization.

The mobile worker

There is one expense that is almost certain to decline. That is the cost of gold watches and other awards for long-term employees. Few stick around any more to collect them. Few employers encourage them to do so. Statistically, an individual is likely to change jobs once every two to five years. Most individuals change careers at least two or three times in their working lives. That figure is rising; those now entering the work force may change jobs as often as seven times before they retire.

Even those who stay with the same organizations do not often stay in the same jobs. In any group of employees, it's likely that at least half have experienced some kind of job change within the last year. They may have moved to different assignments or departments. Even in the same positions, their responsibilities may have changed markedly. That means their requirements for information also have changed, often dramatically.

The second generation

Modern employees have another characteristic, too. Increasing numbers of them are second-generation computer users. They have already encountered computers, often in school. Some developed healthy interests that spur them to continually look for better and more effective ways to use them. They can make good use of ready access to data.

Another group has had a much different reaction to the early experience. The computers intimidated them at the outset, and the training experience totally turned them off. Now, they will touch computers only when they must. If these people are to reach full productivity, they need easy, nonintimidating means of access.

Serving today's workers

Today's employees are being required to do more things with more data, and more types of data. They are not the data entry clerks and specialists of the past. This has meant substantial changes in the data they need, and in what they do with it.

One visible result of these trends is the need for IS professionals to become more aware of their organizations' other functions. They must learn more about the enterprise so they can apply their professional talents more precisely to meeting the company's needs.

The enterprise network provides a new and better way to give employees the kinds of information access they need. For the people in charge of providing this information, it means:

- Devising new means of access to existing information
- Recognizing that these means must adapt to new demands from changed jobs

- Providing for multiple applications
- Establishing a universal point of access to corporate information

The Problems with People

An enterprise networking project can run right into a running feud between champions of the two types of systems. Often, these people are strong advocates who don't just disagree with the other side. They are openly resentful. One big source of conflict: standards and procedures that are the mainstays of most MIS departments. Yet if PC users feel confined to particular working methods, they may become very frustrated when more attractive options present themselves. Thus, mainframe people are known for their belief that "micro" people have too little respect for proper controls and standards.

Meanwhile, those on the PC side (who rarely use "micro" any more) see the large-system people as stubborn barriers to change and flexibility. They see IS professionals as people who interfere with their ability to do their jobs.

Neither stereotype is correct. Most large-system people accept the need for change; the holdouts are more noisy than numerous. Most PC people recognize a need for reasonable order and control. Still, there are some people who do fit these stereotypes. There are just enough of them to cause some trouble when you try to get them together on a single enterprise network. Resisters on both sides are often trying to protect their investments in skill and experience.

For IS professionals, this attitude may be the result of a lifetime of professional conditioning. They have been taught that computing activity should revolve around the large, central computer. Modern knowledge and practice, including enterprise networking, have challenged that belief. The network, and even the individual user, is becoming the central focus. This requires that many of these pros reject a lifetime of teaching and conditioning. It's not easy, either for the subject or for the organization that's trying to create the change.

Other sources of conflict

This is just one source of human conflict in enterprise networking. The people who populate the enterprise network will also give you problems like these:

- There are too few of them.
- They don't have the right skills.
- They're afraid of change.

- They don't like to work with other people.
- They play political games.

Thomas Jefferson once described democracy as organized anarchy. Enterprise networking brings with it a kind of corporate democracy. Put these two ideas together, and you may have a good picture of what you're up against.

Too Few Good People

It seems incongruous that, even in the worst of financial conditions, there has been a shortage of skilled people to fill critical positions in networked systems.

The labor force as a whole has simultaneously experienced large-scale layoffs while employers fear a shortage of employees with the right kinds of skills for an evolving business climate. IS is no exception. It's not so much that the profession lacks people; it lacks the right kinds of people. There has been a shortage of the kinds of employees who must make things happen in a new environment.

Being unprepared

A complicating problem is that companies haven't built up the necessary human infrastructure to support their networks correctly. Professionals often have failed to see PCs as serious business machines. That

One view of networking

- Downsizing as democracy
- Democracy as organized anarchy

Moral: learn how to live in a less orderly environment

Figure 2.2 Networked systems give employees more freedom and flexibility at the loss of structure and control.

Too few people

- Qualified employees in demand
- Networks often increase their workloads
- Solutions:
  - Divide tasks
  - Assign specialists

Figure 2.3   It's not that there are too few people in the workforce. There are too few qualified, well-trained people.

attitude is fast disappearing, but it has already had a serious impact—among other places, on the careers of employees who misjudged the PCs' role in modern business.

There is another unfortunate legacy, too. Only a few years ago, few companies had developed adequate PC support departments. At many places, the entire LAN support responsibility rested on a couple of self-selected in-house gurus. They became jacks-of-all-trades and ended up doing nothing well. They found themselves spending most of their time responding to emergencies. Long-range planning stopped the instant the phone rang. In-house PC experts were so busy fighting fires they never had the chance to practice fire prevention. There were no adequate procedures for capacity controls, backups, off-site storage, disaster recovery, or security administration.

Again, this situation is slipping into the past, but there are places where it still exists. More seriously, past neglect has forced present-day organizations to play catch-up.

Fearing layoffs

Many people fear enterprise networking and its companion, system downsizing. They believe it is a prelude to a personnel downsizing that will eliminate a lot of systems jobs. This is not usually the way it happens. According to a 1990 *PC Week* survey of more than 200 companies, central MIS staffs were cut at 16 percent of the sites that had downsized their systems. Sixty-nine percent said central MIS staffs remained the same, while 14 percent said IS staff had increased at their firms.

Those results may be skewed toward the rosy side. Follow-up interviews reached several MIS directors who anonymously suggested that staff cuts were still possible. Perhaps more important, many employees were worried about their jobs, enough to cut morale sharply. When layoffs do happen, PC technicians and support people are just as vulnerable as large-system staff members.

Heavier workload?

Enterprise networking can also mean that the workload for the IS organization will increase. The department will have a broader diversity of systems to support. There will be multiple links to maintain, and more places for something to fail.

Wrong Skills

One conclusion of the 1991 Downsizing/Rightsizing Corporate Computing Conference was that IS personnel require tools for creating distributed and client/server applications. These same employees must also have the skills necessary to use these tools. If they do not have these skills now, you must help create them. Mainframe programmers can need up to one year of retraining before they can work competently in object-oriented computing environments.

New needs for technical skills

- Yesterday
  - Cobol
  - Conventional databases
  - Computer degree
- Today
  - C, CASE, OOP
  - SQL, client/server
  - Business and technical degrees

Figure 2.4 Yesterday's skills were highly specialized. Today, an employee needs more wide-ranging knowledge.

Employees—including both IS professionals and users—need a completely different set of skills than they did as recently as 10 years ago. In the past, employers looked for knowledge of Common Business Oriented Language (COBOL) mainframe security and, in general, a strong technical background. Now, an IS professional must be more diversified. C and Structured Query Language (SQL) are the languages of choice, and a business degree is a sought-after complement to a technical education.

The so-called people skills have also become more important. In the past, a computer professional was expected to work independently on specific technical tasks. Today's IS employee must be as prepared to work with other people as with technology.

Lag control

As companies standardize on PC and workstation technology, the primary workforce skill requirements are shifting to graphic user interface (GUI) environments like Windows, OS/2, or X Windows. The dominant need for programming experience is in C or the C++ object-oriented development language. But many large companies that are downsizing from mainframe environments have hundreds or thousands of COBOL programmers. Correcting this lag can be a major challenge. It means you must wait out a long learning period before key people are ready to take their new roles.

"People skills" are more important

- Yesterday
  - Independence
  - Technical skills
  - Ability to follow
- Today
  - Teamwork
  - Communication skills
  - Ability to lead

Figure 2.5 Technical skills are still important, but employees must learn human relations techniques as well.

The learning curve can be slippery for the employees, too. There are new tools and new terminologies. These often are completely unlike tools and terminals they have used on the mainframe side. Now, these experienced hands must make their way back to the top. Some of them might have a rough time. They're being thrust into an environment of new systems in which they have no background.

Resistance to Change

"Change is an unnatural act, particularly in successful companies; powerful forces are at work to avoid it at all costs." So said Michael Porter in a *Harvard Business Review* article.

Resistance to change is an old management bugaboo. Every manager has had to confront it sometime. Resistance to change has itself proven highly resistant to change. Certainly, that has been true of the great changes that accompany enterprise networking.

Some of this resistance comes from employees who feel comfortable with their old systems and don't want to change, particularly if that change threatens their jobs. Among the employees who are likely to feel most threatened—and consequently are likely to resist change— are IS professionals. Most have accepted the idea that the future involves networks and PCs. Some still resist the idea of turning their applications over to users. Sometimes this resistance takes the form of outright sabotage.

Closing the skills gap

- Build your own work force
  - Recruiting
  - Training
- Ease the transition
  - Form user groups
  - Encourage self-education

Figure 2.6 There are several ways to build a skilled workforce. The most effective, though not the quickest, is with a long-term strategic plan.

Skills checklist

1. What new skills will the enterprise network need?
   - Graphical user interfaces
   - Programming languages
   - Object orientation
   - People skills
2. How will you obtain people with these needed skills?
   - Available on current staff
   - Retraining
   - Hiring

More typically, the IS staff is willing to accept change, but has not been trained and prepared to cope with it. This problem can feed on itself, since veteran programmers understandably dislike the idea of becoming novices again. This is particularly true when the PC experts assigned to train them tend to be younger. The threat of staff reductions can also be a morale-buster.

Resistance isn't limited to habit-bound IS staff members. The employees you're trying to serve can be just as stubborn. Cheryl Currid, the consultant and columnist, points to "users who still lurk in the hallways of corporate America. They are technology-resistant, clutching yellow writing tablets, calculators, and calendars. Their old, tried-and-true methods still work, and they don't want anyone fixing them."

The challenge for a LAN administrator is to manage the human factor among other employees as well. Not only do they resist change, but they also seem to have a host of inventive, though unwitting, ways to make things go wrong.

To cope with resistance

- Tap employees' self-interest
  - "What's in it for me?"
- Build involvement
  - Form teams
  - Encourage participation

Figure 2.7   To overcome resistance, give employees a stake in the change.

PC operators constantly frustrate security professionals with their less-than-careful habits. These are people, for example, who use stick-on notes to post their passwords in plain sight. In particular, those who have come to regard PCs as personal tools may not understand that in a networked environment they may become responsible for corporate data that needs more protection.

Many security experts and PC managers say education is a critical part of their security policies. Training is a high priority, concentrating on such subjects as how to recognize hazards and observing security procedures. One bank's security training program includes sessions in such subjects as managing change.

The idea behind this: installing a new network is a major change in the way an organization does business. A system is most vulnerable at times of change. It's a time when errors are frequent; a new program disk may contain a virus; access controls may not yet be in place or may not work properly. The training is intended to help managers monitor and educate their employees more closely during this period.

Says one PC manager, "Users need to understand that even transferring a file from a floppy disk to their hard drive is a significant change in their system." That means there is a potential hazard they should learn to recognize.

This is one area where IS professionals can continue to use their talents in a networked environment. They can do what they do well: maintaining the security, validity, and integrity of the data. This lets the users go about their own jobs. It also frees them to find new ways to retrieve and use the organization's data.

When users resist

When a Chicago area hospital installed a network a few years ago, it observed conventional wisdom and tried a simple application first: a system used to reserve conference rooms. The process had previously been done manually.

The conversion turned out not to be simple at all. Instead of making room reservations from the PCs on their desks, users would continue to walk out to the reception desk to make their reservations in the log book traditionally used for this purpose. A commonly expressed attitude: "If I did it that way before, why can't I keep on doing it that way?" The hospital found itself having to maintain a dual system, and that brought new problems. Rooms reserved through the log book were not always recorded in the computerized system.

People were actively trying to avoid the system, its manager said. Apparently, the technology outstripped the employees' ability to use it. In any event, conference rooms are now again reserved via the paper record.

Changing work habits

New systems change work habits. Sometimes it is for the better; sometimes it is not. The big difference: whether the employees perceive the change to be an improvement in their working lives. For example, a Boston-based bakery and restaurant chain improved its ability to monitor store operations, giving management the ability to spot excessive costs almost as soon as they happened. Managers also spotted some procedures store managers had not been scrupulously observing.

The employees, however, named the system "Big Brother." They complained that they were being excessively monitored. That complaint may have masked another difficulty: there was little in this system to suggest that it would help employees improve the way they do their own jobs. The dominant emphasis was on monitoring to punish transgression. Employees felt they were being held to higher standards, but the system gave them no help in meeting them.

Success story

Meanwhile, a New York consulting firm set up a networked communication and scheduling program that helped unify the organization and make it more cohesive. Users found they could share documents created by their word processors, and the system was much more efficient than its predecessor at scheduling appointments and meetings. Many users found new ways to capitalize on the system.

One of the main keys to success: users, who formerly had to request information from the MIS staff, found they could get it themselves, and get it immediately. They also liked the ability to schedule meetings without repeated exercises in telephone tag.

Trouble at the top

Change can also be threatening at the management level. Technical change can send out tidal waves of political infighting, fueled by fears of losing jobs or losing power and importance. Technology doesn't happen by itself. It always has its human and organizational consequences. When you change a system, you often also change things like budgets and organizational charts.

Why people resist

Most often, resistance stems from fear. When IS professionals resist the conversion to smaller systems, there's a good chance it's because they are afraid of what might happen to them.

Other employees are paralyzed by procedure. They match up lists by hand, rekey information from hard copy reports, and keep documentation that no one ever reads. It's the "we've always done it this way" syndrome.

You can turn resistance in a more constructive direction. Try to replace "What's going to happen to me?" with "What's in it for me?" Show reluctant employees how they can benefit from the changes in their way of working life. Most employees want to be able to do their jobs better; only a cynical few do not. Show them how the new technology can improve their value to the organization. This is an opportunity for them to become more productive and better-appreciated employees.

Working with Others

Another problem with people is that they have to work with each other. They don't always do it very well.

This is a particular problem with those IS professionals who tend to be loners. The profession has many who relate better to the technology they use than they do to other people. For them, the appeal of their jobs is that they can work in relative isolation. They interacted mainly with others in their own profession. That's changing as the IS department is increasingly required to address business goals as well as technical ones.

Many of those who have moved from mainframe to network environments describe the hardest part of the change this way: "I had no idea I was going to be directly involved with so many people." People who had become accustomed to dealing with other technical people now have to interact with users and business managers—people they might once have thought of as the "great unwashed."

Not only that, but a networked environment presents a greater variety of tasks and challenges. There may be an increased support load, simply because there are more PC applications available, and more systems running them. This increases the need for good interpersonal and communication skills. Not everyone has these. You often must develop these skills through training.

Office Politics

People play political games. They do so in any corporate enterprise. The larger the enterprise, the more they do it. There are many who feel that the way to the top is not by doing your own job well, but by making someone else look bad.

It's not unusual for proponents of change to feel the subtle revenge of their corporate colleagues. As Currid put it in an *Infoworld* column, "Our society doesn't place IS professionals in jail for exposing new computing theories, but it does have ways of dealing with people who defy conventional wisdom." Some advocates of change receive less-than-subtle warnings to keep quiet and go along with the system. Others find themselves shunted out of the mainstream, doing only minor projects. Performance appraisals slip, and the fear begins to develop that should times become worse, the boat-rocker would be among the first to go.

Meeting Your Staff Needs

One way to meet your staffing needs is to recruit qualified people from outside. There's one problem. Qualified people are in as short supply outside your organization as within. The best people are in demand and can be hard to find.

Even if you can hire someone with top credentials, that is still no guarantee of success. Sometimes you can be your own enemy. There's the tale of a company that landed a skilled C programmer to join a new workstation project team. Instead of putting him on the job where his skills were badly needed, someone immediately shipped him off to learn COBOL. That's what the company had always done.

Comb the campuses

Hiring recent graduates lets you start building a staff with the type of people you expect to need. The drawback is that many recent graduates have not been trained, either, in modern programming skills. University courses are not always geared to many kinds of work you expect from their graduates. The schools do lag behind the times, but it's not entirely their fault. They cannot possibly teach every specialty in a fast-changing world. You have to participate in the training.

A strategic approach

One approach that can help: develop a strategic staff development plan. Take inventory of the needs you expect to have, both now and in the future. For each need, develop one or more specific strategies to meet it.

This can be a time-consuming process, and the outcome can be frustratingly long-range. It requires the cooperation of IS, user departments, and the recruiting staff. But it can be worth both the investment and the wait.

Old Employees, New Skills

Giving people the opportunity to learn can be a worthwhile investment. Start early, so you can take some time and do a thorough job. It makes little sense to throw away your employees' talents and experience unless they are simply unable or unwilling to adapt.

There are many ways to ease this transition. Consider an in-house user group. In the past, these groups have been something like hobbyist clubs, but they can become valuable sources of knowledge and morale-building.

Plan round tables and workshops to help employees learn and get their questions answered. Bring in expert speakers to deliver talks. Make sure the experts address the individuals who have the most direct responsibilities for the subject at hand.

Independent learning can help many employees. Some companies have begun loaner programs, where they keep systems on hand for employees to take home with them at nights and on weekends. An alternative is to provide financial aid for professionals who want to buy their own systems.

Retraining, however, is not entirely the answer. The trainees must be willing and able to take on a tough challenge. Some will not learn readily enough; others may not want to abandon lifetimes of well-honed skills to go back to beginner status again.

Meeting the training challenge

The average Fortune 1000 firm spends $1.7 million for its first high-end client/server application. That same average company spends $800,000 to retrain its employees.

Getting people together

- Train in interpersonal skills
- Form self-directing work teams
- Try matrix management
  - One technical supervisor
  - Another representing users

Figure 2.8   Training and flexible management techniques can help build teamwork.

Those figures are from a survey published late in 1992 by Forrester Research Inc., a market research firm in Cambridge, Massachusetts. The survey considered networks that served at least 100 users, spanned multiple sites, and had direct effects on the companies' finances.

Typically, the initial retraining costs $12,000 to $15,000 per person. Continuing education to keep up with advancing technology cost between $1,500 and $2,500 per employee every year.

"The main obstacle isn't technology," said one IS manager. "Training, personnel, and politics are a much larger challenge."

Trainees aren't alike

Your training challenges will be nearly as diverse as your network. There is not one class of trainees, but three:

- Professionals responsible for network installation and management
- Application developers
- The employees who use the system

Learning the network

Information professionals may once have resisted the inroads of PCs and networks, but now they have strong incentives to go beyond mainframe-only skills. Demand for their traditional abilities is diminishing. There are fewer mainframe-only shops, and the survivors have become ripe candidates for outsourcing to outside contractors. Some pros released in this process can find jobs with the contractors, but there aren't enough positions for everyone.

Trainees aren't all alike

- Network managers
- Application developers
- Employees who use the system

Figure 2.9   Each group requires a different training approach.

To someone from a strictly mainframe tradition, enterprise networking can look like an intricate way to do things backwards. The lack of organization, control, and security can be absolutely frightening to someone accustomed to a more well-ordered environment.

As many IS pros are learning, though, that can be an opportunity. They can learn the new technology. Networking is probably easier for them than for someone whose experience is solely with stand-alone PCs. The newest networks are easier to install and manage than their predecessors. In addition, these professionals can render valuable services by bringing their sense of discipline to the enterprise network. If security and standardization are missing from many current networks, there are few people better qualified to correct these omissions than the current crop of large-system graduates.

Learning to build new applications

Application developers face a longer and more gradual learning process. Many of their new tools are radically different. So are the methods. The transition from COBOL to object orientation requires that they adopt a whole different way of thinking.

If the learning curve is longer, that doesn't mean it is steeper. In an early episode of *The Paper Chase,* a character points out that "None of us is a zero." Everyone in the incoming law school class had ranked near the top as an undergraduate. Experienced programmers are much the same way. They didn't get where they are by being stupid. Intelligent people can learn new methods. Intelligent people who have chosen careers in high technology should count on it. What it really takes to succeed in an enterprise network environment is an open mind. If you're willing to learn the new methods, you shouldn't find it all that hard.

Development tools

Automated software development tools can help speed up both the learning and the application development process. In particular, the Graphic User Interface (GUI) applications that are so much easier for users also make themselves much easier for developers. A GUI application-building tool can sharply reduce the training time and effort.

Reduced effort is not the same as no effort. Training an experienced professional on an easy-to-use package might seem like one of the least of your migration challenges. Things are not always what they seem.

Many organizations pay too little attention to the critical task of converting programmers to new methods. They don't recognize how great a change it can be. Usually, the trainees are grounded in mainframe COBOL or other text-oriented, procedural environments. The migration to enterprise networking requires that you change their entire way of thinking to GUI, client/server lines. Some employers give their professionals too much credit. They give their programmers a tool, a manual, and an afternoon. With these, they must get ready for a new way of thinking. Some professionals can handle that. Others can't. The difference usually is not in their intelligence, but in their motivation. It takes a highly motivated employee to complete an unguided self-study course. Some employees are more highly motivated than others.

Learning while doing

Not all programmers need formal classroom training, either. One on-the-job alternative is to use a pilot application as a training exercise. Pick a team to be the pioneer on the new application. Team members should represent the rest of the programming staff. They should relate well to the others and serve as role models.

While developing the pilot application, the team should carefully record its learning process. Record what members did to get up to speed on GUI development. Note the challenges and errors the team encountered, and describe how members successfully dealt with them. As the pilot gives way to large-scale production applications, the team will have the right information to conduct small, specialized workshops for the rest of the staff. This approach yields a curriculum tailored to the company. Also, the teachers are coworkers the programmers respect and understand.

In the classroom

Classroom training, particularly off-site, has the advantage of exposing the staff to other organizations and ideas. Nearly all GUI development tool vendors offer on-site or off-site programmer training. These typically take the form of two- to five-day workshops that combine classroom work and hands-on experimentation. Major consulting firms like Andersen Consulting (Chicago) and CAP Gemini America (New York City) also offer programmer training on the more popular tools, usually as part of a larger systems integration project. Microsoft University (Redmond, WA) offers training in Visual Basic, SQL Server, and Windows programming in its 10 regional training centers.

Phase it in

Whatever the training format, don't rush the process. A good training program proceeds through three phases:

- Get programmers acquainted with the new personality of GUI applications. Even experienced programmers need to gain an understanding of this new way of working.

- Train them to work with a specific application-building tool.
- Show the trainees the design alternatives that are available for legacy mainframe applications.

Don't rush it

The second phase can be critical. Ease the programmers into the new environment. Make it a migration, not a sudden conversion.

The first step in this phase is to make the trainees comfortable with the PC environment. Recreate a mainframe application with an ordinary text interface on a PC. This preserves the mainframe look and feel, foregoing the strange appearances of a GUI. You also can hide the network by treating the server as a virtual drive.

Try to avoid the culture shock of absorbing too many changes at once. Don't try to reprogram the students, forcing them to adapt to PCs, and on top of that present them with the GUI and the client/server environment. Trainers recommend a PC-based COBOL implementation, such as Micro Focus COBOL, as a good tool for this phase.

The next step is to acquaint programmers with well-designed, off-the-shelf GUI applications like Microsoft's Excel spreadsheet. Let the students play with the application and learn how it works. Well-built commercial products often provide the best models of how a GUI application should look and act.

Don't rush training

- Ease people into their new surroundings
- Avoid culture shock

Figure 2.10 Training should be a migration, not a crash course.

Once programmers are familiar with the PC environment and with the flavor of a GUI application, they are ready for phase three: taking the mainframe application that was ported to the PC and rebuilding it for the GUI.

Don't rush this process. You must give the trainees as much time to get comfortable with the environment as you would give an executive. The most technically competent person in the world can easily get lost in new surroundings.

Dealing with Reluctant Users

Most professionals are motivated to change. It could mean their jobs. That consequence isn't always as clear to the line employees who will use the enterprise network. They can resist change for any number of reasons, including:

- A feeling that the computer interferes with the ways they do their jobs. Some users in this group don't want to give up old methods. Others may be in parts of the organization that look down on the computer-proficient.

- Lack of basic training. Some employees doubt the value of their computers because no one has ever taught them more than the rudiments.

- Cost-conscious department heads. They see training as a scheduling problem, or as a cost that will be charged to their operations. They pull strings to keep employees at their desks and out of training courses.

- Inadequate long-term training. Typically, employees will remember the training they use. A Word Perfect training graduate may be completely competent producing routine reports and correspondence. Several months later, when the time comes to produce a merged mailing, the employee will have forgotten how to do it.

For every reaction, an action

These are common user responses. Because they are common, there are also established ways to deal with each of them:

- Create a *shining star*. Work with a few sharp, willing students to create a model of success. Use it to show reluctant trainees how much more they can accomplish by accepting the new system.

- Require basic proficiency. One survey says that most people who learn PC applications do so without taking formal training courses. Often, this self-acquired education is valuable, but sometimes it can be inadequate. You needn't require basic training for everyone, but you should require that everyone demonstrate at least a minimum level of ability.

Create a shining star

- Build a model of success
- Use it as an example
  - Show reluctant employees what it can do for them

Figure 2.11   Work with a few good volunteers to create a good example.

- Identify managers' objections. As any salesperson knows, that's the first step toward overcoming them. Show reluctant department heads how the training can improve their overall performance. If cost charge-backs are an issue, offer "scholarships" to a few promising employees. Let these employees serve as shining stars to demonstrate the results.

- Recognize that training is a process. It is not a one-time project that comes to a definite end. Employees will continue to need refresher training in old methods and update training to learn new ones.

Meeting Resistance to Change

New systems and methods are supposed to produce happy results. Nope. Too often, people react with fear, denial, and anger. An enterprise network is a major change in people's lives. They won't accept that change just because it looks good to you. It must also look good to them. Training is one area of frequent resistance. It is only one of many.

The key: Reach people in their WIIFMs. Answer the burning question, "What's in it for me?"

The best way to do that is to show them. Use the shining star approach to show reluctant employees exactly what is in it for them when they accept the coming changes.

Some are faster than others

People accept change at varying rates. Based on these rates, you can classify them into several groups:

- The *experimenters*. You'll have a few of these, but probably only a few. These are the people who are willing to try anything new, just because it's new. They tend to be fickle, though, dropping yesterday's trend as soon as tomorrow's appears.

- The *early adopters*. They also are willing to try new ideas. They aren't interested in newness just for its own sake. They want to see if the new methods can help them do something better.

- The *practical-minded*. This is usually your largest group. Its members are willing to accept new ideas, but first they must be convinced the new ideas are really good ideas. They will accept new technology only when the early adopters have demonstrated that it truly is an improvement.

- The *late adopters*. They don't really want to change, but they'll grudgingly accept it if they must.

- The *resisters*. These are the people who actively dig in to fight off the new way of doing things. Sometimes, they disguise their opposition with rational-sounding, highly intellectual arguments.

Early adopters are the key

The key to a shining star method is to identify the early adopters. The experimenters will identify themselves. If you aren't careful, they'll trample you in the rush to see what's new. The early adopters don't always make themselves obvious, and that can be the source of a serious mistake.

People learn at different rates

- Experimenters
- Early adopters
- Practical minds
- Late adopters
- Stubborn resisters

Figure 2.12 Work with each group in turn to bring about change.

Consider this scenario: you announce that you are linking up a department's LAN to give employees direct access to a customer database. The experimenters will quickly take up the cause. Their enthusiasm makes them look like prime candidates to become shining stars. You need go no further, you might think, than to use these bright, eager people to lead the way. You don't even bother to discuss your plans with anyone else in the department. The enthusiasm, the shine, and the light will soon burn out. Your supposed champions will soon be off to play with some other new toy.

In contrast, once a few early adopters get their teeth into the project, they will become its most substantial long-term boosters. They will put the new technology to work, test it, and suggest worthwhile improvements.

The trick is to find them. There's no sure-fire method, but there is one technique that can be a big help. It comes from the example of a newspaper which upgraded its editorial computer system. Management needed someone to teach and sell the new system; the choice was a bright, eager young staff member who had expressed a strong, early interest in the new system.

This champion proved to be an experimenter, and soon his active imagination turned to something else. Meanwhile, a couple of other staff members got together one evening to express their mutual disappointment. They were both interested in computers, eager to learn the new system, and anxious to put it to use. Both agreed they would enjoy helping other staff members get comfortable with it. But no one had come around even to talk about the new technology, much less to solicit their involvement.

These two were unseen early adopters. Both were quiet people, not prone to great bursts of enthusiasm. They could have been great assets to their organization, but no one else knew it.

The key to finding people like this is to keep on talking. Don't stop when you think you've found your shining star. You could be disappointed. Discuss the change with everyone in the department. You easily could find a couple of serious-minded early adopters in the group. As a bonus, you can help reduce resistance in another way: by helping everyone to feel actively involved.

Step by step

With a few early adopters on your side, you can create a shining star that will keep its luster. Then, you can approach your large group of cautious, but practical-minded, employees. Let the early adopters demonstrate the WIIFMs. Once it's clear that there really is something in it for them, your pragmatists will come on board. So, perhaps, will some of the late adopters who, even reluctantly, conclude that the change is a good idea.

At this stage, three of your four major groups are ready to accept the change and put it to work. That leaves only one other group: your most troublesome. These are the active resisters who have vowed not to change, regardless of the consequences.

You might have to resort to those consequences. Discipline and discharge are not pleasant subjects, but neither is active resistance to the organization's chosen course of action. Those who refuse to adapt may have to go elsewhere.

Dealing with Internal Politics

The trouble is, those who refuse to adapt do not go quietly. The dirty subject of office politics comes into play as the forces of change and the forces of resistance come into head-to-head conflict. The negative campaigners of public politics have nothing on the skilled practitioners of office politics. Internal politics is all about power: how to gain it, how to keep it, or how to be free of it.

The political issues in enterprise networking stem from the unprecedented growth of PCs and LANs. The PC boom all but ambushed traditional IS departments. They were accustomed to taking their time. They carefully built uniform policies, procedures, and standards. But before they could even sit down and start thinking about managing PCs and LANs, these systems were already in place.

The result: LANs and WANs grew up without any central plan or sense of organization. Traditional IS people looked on the PC uses as undisciplined upstarts. To PC people, "discipline" meant repression. The year 1984 failed to produce George Orwell's Big Brother, but it was about that time PC users began to look at traditional computing managers in that light. While MIS sought to establish control, the PC users fought to keep the freedom their desktop systems had brought them. The PC revolution was initially a contest between similar but competing forms of technology. It quickly became a contest between different kinds of people.

Battles of the revolution

LANs are the offspring of departmental necessity. PCs and early forms of office automation had created new opportunities and needs. IS could not meet all these, and it certainly was not geared to respond as immediately as the departments would like. So, the departments decided to make expanded use of the PCs already on their desks. They set out to meet their own needs. LANs not only could do that, but they could do it at much less cost than traditional systems and methods.

At first, interoperability was not an issue. LANs were built to be self-contained, working within single offices and departments. Soon, though, employees came to recognize that if they could profitably share information within their workgroups, they could share it even more profitably with other workgroups. It is a valid idea—the very basis of enterprise networking—but it had a far-reaching effect. It created problems and issues the employees could not resolve within their own departments. Human factors began to arise, too. To communicate with other groups, department heads had to relinquish some of the control they had held over their local networks.

The center fails to hold

Someone else had to establish a degree of uniformity. Again, the traditional IS shops responded slowly. The information center became a short-lived expedient. Usually, the IC was a low-level branch of the IS department, responsible for so-called end-user computing. In that position it was caught between the demands of employees and the requirements of its superiors. It might have a mediating force, but it simply became a battleground instead.

Meanwhile, employees' demands for access to the outside world continued to escalate. No sooner could they exchange information with the next office or the next floor than they saw needs for similar contact in another building, another state, or another country. They had the advantage of maturing technology. They could network LANs to other LANs, to WANs, and to mainframe hosts. IS was never happy with the unplanned spread of network kudzu. Now, its homeland was under attack.

Easy to love

Access was not the PC users' only need. They had also learned what it was like to operate flexible, responsive desktop computers. PC technology is not always easy to learn, but it usually is more accessible than large systems. Individuals could make their PCs work for them. They didn't have to defer to, as they saw it, the high priests of an information bureaucracy.

Ironically, many of these users were busy building their own bureaucracies. Their computing power was expanding. So was their knowledge of how to use it. They built powerful alliances with other departments. At the heart of these coalitions was the ability to respond more quickly and easily than the established IS channels.

As the expanding networks tapped into mainframe territory, people also began to notice that the large-system applications were crude and unresponsive. Why, users asked, can't these applications be made as accessible and pleasant to use as their PC counterparts? It was a good question that went to the heart of PC-IS warfare. The short answer is that the two groups simply don't think alike.

Not harder, just different

Large-system people usually value such qualities as control, focus, and adherence to standards. The cost of their technology, and the need for its utter reliability, encourage this type of thinking. To someone who has spent a career in this professionally tended landscape, LANs are like weeds grown wildly out of control.

The problem is not that PC and LAN technology is inherently hard to learn. After all, most of its experts are self-taught. The problem is simply that it's different. It lacks the central control mechanisms to which mainframe experts are accustomed. That makes them wary of the new technology.

When forced to manage PC technology, large-system people have usually tried to apply mainframe methods and procedures. They have succeeded mainly in curtailing the networks' potential and alienating their users. PC networks are built to be flexible and inexpensive. They do not have—and often do not need—the exhaustive control and regimentation that's built into the typical mainframe platform. LANs are also usually multivendor environments, not the single-source system to which IS people are accustomed.

Just as the two types of systems are technically different, they attract different types of people. Where the mainframe world has placed a premium on orderly thinking, PCs and LANs are the products of inventors and entrepreneurs. Like their systems, LAN/WAN personnel have come a long way from the garages where they started, but their attitudes still go back to their origins. They are strong on flexibility and new ideas, but weak in maintaining the mission-critical applications that require a mainframe sense of order.

Mutual fear

To make things worse, each side seems intimidated by the other. PC users feel IS managers do not understand their technology or their methods. Mainframe workers feel threatened by the rapid switch to PC LAN technology. A third group feels left out. These are the telecommunication engineers who see data networks bypassing their technological bailiwick.

The long-standing groups feel under attack from brash newcomers, but they hold more power than they may realize. Most ranking IS managers walked career paths that started in the mainframe ranks. When traditionalists and their familiar technology compete with the new people and methods, these managers naturally tend to favor their own kind.

This isn't prejudice, but it can seem so to the PC LAN people. They often find themselves with this uncomfortable compromise: they're allowed to expand their networks, but are subject to policies and procedures that keep them from making full use of their available assets. They feel unfairly blamed when these oil-water mixtures don't work out.

Facing the challenge

All this means that the greatest challenge in building an enterprise network may not be to integrate diverse systems, but to get the people who run them to work together.

To some extent, this problem is correcting itself. Compared with even a couple of years ago, people on both sides have stepped away from their hardened positions. PC management is becoming more professional, and large systems people are learning how to adapt their skills and experience to a changing world.

Still, there is enough potential conflict to present a serious challenge. There still are some large-system holdouts who fight, and even try to sabotage, the new technology. You must also persuade the last holdouts for total PC freedom that they can serve their best interests by adapting at least some degree of uniformity and control.

Serve the organization

The most important point to get across to both groups is that they exist to serve the organization. Stubborn insistence on a single point of view will not do that. The IS professional who actively opposes LANs and WANs is working to deny the organization the full ability to compete in today's business world. The PC manager who takes a purely departmental view of the world is denying the organization the big-picture benefits networking can bring.

Your incentive system should reward cooperation. Set goals and appraise performance on how well an employee contributes to the organization's success. Make it clear that intransigence in either direction will be a negative factor when you make personnel decisions.

Training is an important factor, too. Teach not only the methods and technology of the new systems, but help people from both sides understand why their counterparts think the way they do. For holdout warring factors, understanding is the first step toward peace. And if it's your job to bring about that peace, understanding can help you, too.

Build Involvement

Dealing with human factors requires a comprehensive strategy. Your problems won't respond permanently to a single action. Nevertheless, there is one response that can play an important role in any personnel strategy. That is to build a sense of involvement and ownership among employees.

Get involved

People particularly resist change when they feel it is being imposed from the top. That's a natural reaction. They mistrust the change, and the management that is trying to bring it about. They fear the change will benefit the organization, but not them.

Overcome that fear by building a sense of involvement. Within the context of achieving your overall goal, give the affected employees material roles in determining how the change is to take place. Listen to their suggestions, and implement those that are worthwhile. Set up work teams and planning coalitions. Of course, employees given this kind of opening will act at least partly in self-interest. That's the point. They can make material contributions to their own well-being. When they are able to do that, they begin to claim ownership of the project— to think of it as "ours" instead of "theirs." They trust their own judgment. The plan they have helped create is no longer mysterious and threatening.

Get it together

While building participation and ownership, let key employees from all the involved departments work together on the plan. Get mainframe and PC people together. Get them together with leaders of the user departments. Involving all these people, and getting them together, can do a couple of things:

- It can help each side overcome its unrealistic expectations of the other.
- The collective wisdom of all these highly involved people can't help but produce a better system.

When planning an enterprise network, involve as many people as possible, as soon as possible. Their active participation helps them feel that the project can be a vehicle for success and relieve fears that it will become someone else's launching pad instead.

When Financial Guaranty Insurance Co. (FGIC) prepared for this type of change, it became the site of serious internal battles. Conflicting demands from different departments created political friction. Users complained that they had to painstakingly check data from the old system before they could enter it in the new system. The firm overcame many conflicts with the help of well-educated programmers. They understood the bond insurance business and recognized how the different parts of the LAN-based system would fit together. Even so, there were times when executive force was necessary. The data was cleaned up only under orders from top management.

Try matrix management

Another response many organizations have used is to farm out IS professionals to the user departments. They use a matrix management approach in which a professional has two supervisors: the traditional IS manager and the manager of a user department.

Clive Finkelstein, originator of information engineering—the linking of information systems with business strategy—says he believes the optimum form of corporate organization, at least through the twentieth century, will be a matrix structure.

Typically, he says, a growing company evolves through these organizational forms:

- *Entrepreneurial.* This is the typical start-up organization. It is informal, and everyone reports to the chief executive officer.

- *Bureaucratic.* As the organization grows, the lines of authority become more hardened and formal, with controls designed to promote greater efficiency. All lines of authority still lead to the CEO.

- *Divisional.* Some managers become more knowledgeable about their specialties than does top management. They become division and department heads, with considerable autonomy within their own areas.

- *Coordinated.* The divisions become semi-independent business units or product groups. Contacts between the heads of these groups and the rest of the organization consists mainly of coordinating activities.

- *Matrix.* This is Finkelstein's ultimate organization for the 1990s. It is a highly participatory structure which appears to violate the Biblical injunction about trying to serve two masters.

Matrix management and IS

The organizational chart of a typical matrix alignment might look like a spreadsheet. Rows could represent IS teams; columns could represent user departments. An IS professional could be assigned to work in any of the open blocks. That person would report both to one of the team leaders listed on the left and to the head of one of the operating departments listed across the top.

For example, an IS professional working in a marketing department still reports to IS. This department continues to be a source of standards, planning, and implementation. The professional may be assigned by IS to work on a particular project. That individual's specific assignment will be to work directly with the marketing staff on any way in which the project involves marketing.

The IS professional remains a professional. At the same time, he or she gains a first-hand picture of what the department needs to better conduct its work. The delegated professional could report, for example, that "engineering isn't happy with the project we've designed for them. They'd like to make these changes . . ." This approach provides an opportunity for better communication between the two departments, and better understanding of what each can expect of the other.

Building Teams the New Way

Enterprise networking has evolved to meet the needs of people and their organizations. Network administration must evolve in the same way. Enterprise networking as a source of information is a tool of modern, information-driven management. The technology is of little value unless it can work in tandem with today's organizations.

Build a team that can balance the technical and human sides of enterprise networking. Instead of a vertical organizational chart with boxes and lines of authority, the enterprise network needs a broad-based team approach. Matching the technical challenge of building the network is the organizational challenge of building the team.

Down the line

You cannot get the most from a network if you manage it like a traditional data processing shop. These departments originally existed mainly as report generation resources that needed expert management. In line with this purpose, MIS shops usually have formal, pyramid-shaped organizations. The typical department head rose through the ranks from programmer to systems analyst to manager. Subordinate

Org charts are out

- Replace the boxes and lines
- Make everyone a team member

Figure 2.13   Lines of authority can just get in the way of teamwork.

managers usually view their responsibilities as maintaining and operating a technical resource.

This vertical structure has helped MIS gain an image as a specialized bureaucracy, isolated from its internal customers and their needs. Its members view their main responsibilities as solving technical problems, not business problems.

This approach doesn't work under an enterprise network. Just as the network supports flatter, more flexible workgroups, it requires a similar form of organization for its own success. The network is a management tool, not just a technical challenge. Everyone who works on the network should expect to analyze and help solve any problems that come up, whether they involve the technology, the people, or the organization.

Ignore this at your peril

When a major financial institution downsized from mainframes to LANs, it appointed an executive to head the reorganized MIS department. This manager had come up the traditional mainframe career path.

Soon there were complaints within the network staff. The new manager didn't understand networks, his employees complained. He didn't know much about communication, either. User support employees felt left out and isolated. Even people in traditional IS positions felt the manager was not effectively taking charge.

All these problems had a single root: the manager didn't understand the network. He thought it was just a different kind of mainframe network. He did nothing to change his approach or adapt to the new system.

Computers aren't supposed to communicate

Computers have no inherent power to communicate. Networks make them do that. You'll often encounter the same problem in human relations. Technicians as a group aren't great communicators, either, yet modern management styles put a premium on communication.

To date, few organizations have human management policies to accompany their technical policies. Surveys have found these organizations overpopulated with talented, but frustrated, specialists. Their employers neither encourage nor reward exceptional effort. You can gain a competitive edge by making yourself the exception.

Acronym soup

Tennis is an elegantly simple game until you encounter its scoring system. Computers can also appear much simpler than industry terminology would make them seem. Networking in particular is rife with odd abbreviations. Most don't even qualify as acronyms, which are supposed to be initials that form pronounceable words. These can be useful shorthand for communication between professionals, but they also can keep outsiders out.

Not only do technical people speak a strange-sounding language, but many have what are called "poor communication skills." Often, they don't communicate well with outsiders because they don't know how. Sometimes they feel that even their superiors don't understand them.

What we have here, in the famous movie line, is a failure to communicate. The failure stymies effective communication among members of diverse groups. Yet that is exactly the kind of communication modern organizations require.

Workshops can help. Encourage people from different parts of the organization to join discussions and present their ideas, both in formal and informal settings. Train current and prospective managers in listening skills, too. Make it clear to team members that selling ideas and solving problems are among their main job functions.

Getting oriented

Because communication is so important to your success, start dealing with it early in the planning process. Schedule an orientation session for everyone who will be involved with the project. That includes all the people who will design, install, manage, and use the system.

As in the fable of the blind men and the elephant, you'll find that members of each group—programmers, communication technicians, LAN administrators, and so on—have their own narrow views of the enterprise network. The orientation should teach each group the com-

Training creates communication

- Build presentation skills
  - Help people sell their ideas
- Build listening skills
  - Help people become astute customers

Figure 2.14 Concentrate on the communication process—both ends.

plete functions and business purposes of the networking project. Include topics like these:

- The network as a system
- How the network is configured
- The operating systems, standards, media, management systems, and other software
- A profile of the intended users
- The network's business goals, and how it is intended to meet them

Revise the orientation program as needed to account for changes to the network.

Define your goals

The plan must state your strategic goals for the network. Define how the network will meet the organization's objectives. Define the services the network will offer. Describe how to make use of them.

Include a plan to manage the people in charge of the technology. Cover everyone, including:

- LAN managers
- Communication specialists
- Systems analysts
- Programmers
- Operations workers
- Database managers
- Support technicians
- Trainers

For each of these specialties, describe the normal career path and the training and cross-functional needs. Define the criteria for appraising performance and making decisions on promotions and training.

Tie the technical issues to the human management issues as much as you can. This presents a picture to upper management of a single effort that includes both technical and human components.

Group rewards

The new form of organization is based on independent work teams. There are fewer layers of management, and an employee has fewer superiors. People form teams, and it is the team's accomplishment that contributes most to the company's success.

Your appraisal and reward system should reflect this. It is traditional to appraise each employee privately and to use this appraisal as the basis of a confidential salary action. Team members must work together and be open with each other. You must generate the kind of atmosphere in which people feel free to do that. You can do it by appraising the team's performance and attributing it to all the members.

An employee may be reluctant to participate in a discussion or express an idea that might be rejected. The employee is afraid it will become a black mark in the personnel file. That's a danger when each employee is appraised individually. When it's the team's reputation at stake, this employee may be more willing to speak up. Rejection may not be comfortable, but it no longer carries a heavy penalty at appraisal time.

Teamwork counts

A diverse group does not function well in a highly structured environment. Vertical organizations tend to make decisions at the top, then expect people at lower levels to execute them. A team orientation involves everyone in the decision-making process. The supervisor's job is to support and encourage the process, not to give orders.

Top-down management is particularly troublesome when people from diverse disciplines must work together. Almost inevitably, the orders passed down from the top will reflect a narrow perspective. People from other fields, who might have something to contribute, will be ignored.

One company replaced its top-down organizational chart with a system of teams. One team was responsible for each network segment. Members represent all the involved interests such as LAN management, MIS, and the users.

Normally, when a problem arises within the network, the affected group is responsible for taking care of it. This arrangement is not perfect, but it has solved many routine network management problems.

Intergroup cooperation

The groups work together to solve any problems with bridges, routers, or other shared devices. This is an example of the cross-functional communication you must promote. Encourage the groups to view problems and issues as interrelated. When something goes wrong, don't try to blame someone else. Look for ways to work with someone else to solve them.

Where Enterprise Networking Fits

*The basic rule of networking: don't mix
apples and oranges. The basic reality of networking: they've already stirred up a batch of
fruit salad.*

No network exists in a vacuum. Enterprise networking coexists with
several other related trends, both technical and organizational:

- *Downsizing.* When better networks are built, they can handle more
  of the jobs formerly done at much greater expense on large systems.
  Increasingly, these jobs are being moved to LANs with high-powered
  servers, or to networks based on Unix servers. Downsizing usually
  relies heavily on the extended use of networking. That makes it a
  natural—even necessary—companion to enterprise networking.

- *Client/server computing.* This is the service-oriented alternative to
  the traditional large-system host. Its focus on the desktop instead of
  the central system is also a natural companion to enterprise networking.

- *Distributed computing.* Here is yet another natural pairing. Distributed computing is associated, though not inevitably, with
  database management. It is the theory that people should have
  access to all the data they need to do their jobs, wherever that data
  might be. This access should be *transparent*. The employee should
  not have to know or care where the data is physically stored.

Why Bother?

Is all this necessary? Increasingly, the answer is yes. In today's business world, there is a thin line between success and failure. Just look

at the computer trade press: it's full of stories of companies that a few years ago were the most innovative and successful in the business, but since have headed toward bankruptcy court.

Many factors go into an enterprise's success or failure, of course, but one of the most important is employees' access to information. Information, or the lack of it, can tip the delicate balance between Rodeo Drive and Court Street. Information plays such a critical role because it is one way to get an edge on your competition—or for a competitor to get the edge on you.

Gaining the edge

Consider just a few of the more notable success stories of recent years: Federal Express in transportation, Word Perfect in PC software, and Nordstrom's in retailing. Notably, none of the three offer products or services that differ greatly from their competitors'. There are plenty of overnight delivery services. PC word processors routinely emulate each other's features. Even after several years of mergers and notable failures, there is no shortage of department stores. Yet each of these three firms has staked out positions of competitive advantage.

The answer, of course, is information. Each of these three firms has used information to give itself an edge:

- Federal Express pioneered the use of computerized tracking systems that can pinpoint the movement of thousands of packages, resolve delays, and keep customers informed.

- Word Perfect uses information as the backbone of its vaunted customer support system.

- Nordstrom's has used its information to identify those things that serve its customers best. The store then applies this knowledge to create a tradition of personalized service. Its use of that knowledge has gained it both a strong repeat business and a recurring role in Tom Peters' management best sellers.

That's not all

It's not just that these firms have used information. The key is *how* they have used it. In each case, the successful organization has used its information for the specific purpose of improving customer service.

There's another common element, too. For each of these companies, the competitive edge could be fleeting. Other carriers have established their own package tracking systems. Other software firms can hone their own customer service departments. Other department stores can find

Information isn't enough

- You have to use it
- The best use:
  - Customer service

Figure 3.1   Information has no value until you use it.

new ways to make their customers feel important and well served. In another price range entirely, consider how well Wal Mart has done that.

There are also plenty of examples to demonstrate another fact of business life: today's success could become tomorrow's failure. That's why it's important that you keep finding new ways to share information and put it to use. A sound enterprise network cannot only help you gain a competitive edge. It can help you keep it.

Networks and information

Information is available in many forms: mailing lists, marketing research statistics, tips on planned new products. In the highly competitive banking industry, one of the most valuable marketing tools is a computer application that analyzes customer records to pick up trends and buying habits that could become the basis of new marketing campaigns. The data might show, for example, that people who respond to a savings account promotion often will later open checking accounts. That suggests a marketing campaign promoting checking accounts to recent new savings account customers.

The obvious first need is to have the information. The customer service rep in Philadelphia should have full access to the price list and specifications kept on the system in Seattle. A farm implement manufacturer should be concerned that information available at headquarters in Chicago is just as readily available to a field service office in Yeehaw Junction, Florida.

A typical employee these days is more likely to work with information than with things. Information is a tool. The employee needs information in the same way that a mechanic needs a wrench. The enterprise network meets that need.

Meeting other needs

Enterprise networks can meet other needs, too, including these:

- *Improving communication.*   Networks let employees exchange information through electronic mail, file transfers, and shared applications. The wider the network, the wider the communication. It can even extend outside the organization, such as the electronic data interchange (EDI) networks that link industrial customers and suppliers.

- *Reducing barriers.*   Time and distance have always hampered business operations. An enterprise network can effectively reduce both to nearly zero. Furthermore, a network can give business units, and even individual employees, the freedom to pick their own locations.

Information is a tool

- Most employees now work with information
  - Fewer work with things

Figure 3.2   Knowledge workers use information as the tools of their trade.

- *Reducing cost.*   Networks give workers ready access to information so they can make better decisions more quickly. They also reduce your need to use other costly communication methods like the telephone and overnight delivery services.

How the network meets the need

The enterprise network does all these things by providing better access to information. The network isn't the only possible information source, but it is an increasingly important one. Networks can multiply the power of information in ways like these:

- *Quick communication.*   Not only can computer networks move information almost instantly, they can handle a growing variety, including numbers, text, and graphics.

- *Providing a single access point.*   An enterprise network can provide a single source for all kinds of information—or at least what seems like a single source.

- *Access to marketing data.*   This also means access to markets. A company with an enterprise network has more information available, and can do more with it.

Multiplying the power of information

- Quick communication
- One-stop access
- Central management
- Market information

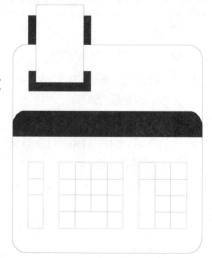

Figure 3.3   Once you have information, you can make it valuable in many ways.

It's not just the technology

Network planners sometimes seem to take their cues from the old television series, "The Six Million Dollar Man." The title character was created, it was said, because "we have the technology." It may have made for an entertaining adventure series, but an enterprise network should have a much more solid foundation than the simple ability to create it. The network should respond to a business need, not just to technical considerations.

In 1988, a long time ago when the computer industry is concerned, J. Mark Sterling of IDC Canada predicted these three developments:

- *The emergence of enterprise-wide systems.* In conventional terms, Sterling said, this usually meant a merger of data and communication. A computer network does exactly that, but Sterling believed correctly that the trend would go much further. "What really is involved," he said, "is a new concept of systems that says a network must become the system."

- *A closer coupling between people and information systems.* The growing uses of sound and graphics are expressions of that trend. This is just one example of how enterprise networking is adapting itself to the needs of its clients; they no longer have to adapt to the needs of the system.

- *The integration of the information system into the corporate mainstream.* This also has happened much as Sterling predicted. Until

Behind enterprise networking

- Systems go enterprise-wide
- People get more involved with information
- The system joins the mainstream

Figure 3.4   Some of the developments behind enterprise networking.

the arrival of desktop systems, the standard computing model had been that of a separate data processing system. The new model is that of a computer on nearly every desk. Technology represents only one of these three trends. The other two represent people and the organization. In a modern enterprise, networking is inevitably linked to the organization. And the organization is made up of its people.

Serving Today's Organizations

By serving your employees, an enterprise network also serves your organization. People are the organization. They are not possessions or separate entities. An organization that fails its people fails itself.

That's why enterprise networking is much more than a technological issue. The purpose of a network is to serve the organization by serving its members. While it's important to select the right technological features when planning an enterprise network, it's important not to become too caught up in the features themselves. What's really important is how these features—and the network that offers them—provide actual, on-the-job benefits to the people who are trying to do their jobs.

Enterprise networking and downsizing

Enterprise networking exists with, and is related to, several other contemporary movements. Among most important is downsizing to PC

People are the organization

- Fail them . . .
- Fail yourself

Figure 3.5 An organization and its people are the same.

networks. In many organizations, downsizing and enterprise networking are parts of the same pattern of development.

Though the two movements are closely related, they are not precisely the same. Downsizing programs are generally driven, at least at first, by the desire to cut costs. High-end PC servers often have enough power to handle applications that used to require mainframes. The servers cost a whole lot less. Successful downsizers report savings from 30 to 50 percent.

Others have learned that the cost savings aren't as great as the difference in hardware and software prices would suggest. The costs of transition and training can eat up the initial savings. Downsizers also often discover that the benefits of better communication and information exchange ultimately become more important than the reduced costs.

Even so, cost is the incentive that drives the typical downsizing project. Better use of information is a serendipitous byproduct. Enterprise networking reverses these two incentives. Here, the main objective is to improve your efficiency and your competitive position. That you can tie much lower-cost technology into the network is a happy coincidence.

There's another difference, too. Though it doesn't have to be this way, downsizing usually envisions a switch primarily to PC LANs, perhaps with a larger system or two in a server role. The heart of enterprise networking is to tie all kinds of systems into a single entity. Instead of the PC servers of a downsized environment, Unix-based open systems are taking on the central roles in enterprise networks.

There is another difference yet, and it may prove to be the most important. The heart of enterprise networking is sharing information, not using some particular type of system. More specifically, enterprise networking leads to distributed processing, placing data wherever in the system it makes the most sense to place it, then

Enterprise networks vs. downsizing

- Downsizing
  - Driven mainly by cost
  - Uses least expensive equipment

- Enterprise networks
  - Incentive is to share information
  - Goal is transparent, universal access
  - System choices are based on results

Figure 3.6 Downsizing and enterprise networking have a lot in common, but not everything.

granting access to all authorized seekers. Ideally, they will have transparent access. They shouldn't even be aware of where the data they are retrieving is stored.

To acknowledge the differences between downsizing and enterprise networking is not to ignore their great similarities. The two often coexist in environments where it's hard to tell one from the other. And there has been this documented effect: once an enterprise network starts to take shape, the emphasis begins to shift away from larger systems toward PCs, even when there is no conscious downsizing program in place. There is a comparable shift on the human side. The people who design, install, and maintain enterprise networks are more likely to have PC backgrounds than large-system IS experience. It is the PC people who have the most experience in both the theory and execution of mixed, nonproprietary networks. For traditional IS professionals, learning these new skills has become a matter of professional survival.

The system and the organization

The human and organizational effects of enterprise networking extend beyond PC and IS professionals to functions like product development and shipping. Take the case of Dakin Inc. of Brisbane, CA. Dakin makes stuffed animal toys, a line of business unusually sensitive to both recession and competition. Dakin has seen plenty of both. Success in this atmosphere depends on responding quickly to fast-changing market trends. No wonder, then, that the executive in charge of credit and customer service began to think of the firm's mainframes in this light: "They just took up space and slowed us down."

The mainframes and their terminals went out. So, sadly, did large numbers of IS staff members. In their place, the firm installed a single midrange system and networked it to employees' PCs.

One result was that the company vastly improved its ability to keep in step with its industry's rapid changes and seasonal product cycles. Another effect was that it ended what one executive called a "culture of dependency" in which employees had to wait for service from the IS department. The new system lets them download data from the midsized server and incorporate it in their documents and spreadsheets. Instead of reacting, they can take the initiative.

Sara Lee's networking recipe

Few firms have done more to take advantage of advanced networking methods than the Sara Lee Corp. Most of the firm's divisions have learned to capitalize on the benefits of another enterprise networking feature: distributed processing. The firm has found several ways to

Benefits of change

- Quicker response from leaner systems
- Ending "culture of dependency"
- Taking initiative instead of reacting

Figure 3.7   You don't have to wait for results.

retrieve information from any networked location, and to take advantage of that capacity. Its systems range from LAN-based decision support technology to cross-platform databases.

Distributed processing lets the company place applications and information on systems that are physically near the departments and individuals who use them. The distributed environment is dedicated to giving people access to the data they need. It gives employees ready access to all the information within the networked environment, no matter where the data is or what technology is needed to retrieve it.

Technical variety

An enterprise network can cover a variety of technologies. It can take in distributed processing, client/server architecture, portable network operating systems, graphic user interfaces (GUIs), computer-aided software engineering (CASE), and both local and wide area networks (LANs and WANs).

Sara Lee relies heavily on client/server systems in which the client component is responsible for presenting and manipulating data at the workstation, and where the server portion is on mainframes, minis, or LAN-based systems. This approach has allowed the company to take advantage of each platform's strengths.

For example, one division has been working on a network of six customer service systems on various hardware platforms. Part of the program can run on the server, while another part is on the client workstation. These systems make use of protocols such as LU6.2, Novell's transport protocols, or transport tools supplied by database vendors. These allow interprocess communication across the network between the client workstation and the server, be it a mainframe, midrange system, or PC server.

Market orientation

Techniques like these have let Sara Lee and its divisions make transitions from production-oriented large systems to those that emphasize quick response, market information, and customer service. Customer-oriented systems do a better job of reflecting the world in which vendors serve customers. This means you can pay more attention to meeting your business objectives. You know the system will be flexible enough to respond to changes in market needs.

That is only one of several advantages. Others include:

- *Greater ability to adapt to changes.*   Management has a strong interest in more cost-effective technology. At the same time it expects accurate, complete, and timely information. Many employees have grown accustomed to the freedom and flexibility of per-

Customer-oriented systems

- Quick response
- Easier access
- Up-to-date market information
- Adaptability
- Cost-effectiveness
- Efficiency

Figure 3.8   Customer-oriented systems reflect the real world better than older production-oriented systems.

sonal computers and have developed growing appetites for access to greater amounts of information. They want the flexibility to retrieve corporate data using the desktop platform with which they are most familiar.

■ *Easier access to more data.* The client/server architecture has improved access to data. At the same, it has allowed the company to select the most cost-effective hardware platform available for a particular use.

■ *The ability to use more cost-effective systems.* To assess cost-effectiveness, Sara Lee has developed a method that balances employee needs with the demands of the project. The client/server architecture lets the system components be placed close to the individuals who use them. This decentralization promotes efficient application processing and has reduced network traffic. Distributed processing, combined with the client/server architecture, allows each platform, from mainframes to PCs, to work in unison. Often, the existing mainframe and minis, with their high-speed I/O buses and large disk drives, have become effective, networked, on-line data depositories.

■ *More flexible choices of methods and tools.* Distributed, client/server platforms make departmental employees more efficient by giving them the flexibility to choose the method and tools by which they will retrieve and use the corporation's information resources. These systems move the responsibility for gathering and manipulating information away from the MIS staff and into the hands of those who use the information to do their jobs.

■ *More efficient application development.* Sara Lee was no exception from the long-standing tradition of an equally long-standing development backlog. The networked environment provides a platform for faster and more efficient development. One reason for this increased efficiency is the wide range of object-oriented and graphic development tools now available for PCs. These offer a friendly and intuitive programming environment that simplifies the development process. This sharply reduces the time—and thus the cost—of getting new applications on-line. Another benefit has been to speed up the traditionally tedious process of application development. For example, host-platform emulation products, such as Micro Focus COBOL and California Software's Baby/400, allow programmers to develop COBOL and RPG applications on a LAN. Once completed, these can be moved to a host platform for execution, or run on the network as a LAN-based application.

But there are some drawbacks

Along with the multiple benefits, there is this continuing problem: networking hardware and software are available from a multitude of vendors. The greatest technical challenge of enterprise networking is to integrate diverse systems. These systems are complex and require a high level of expertise, perhaps in the person of outside consultants. It is wise to consider outside help if you have these needs:

- Specialized industry knowledge and skill
- Strategic or competitive positioning
- Action within a limited time
- Transfer of knowledge from outside experts to the existing systems staff
- A third-party perspective
- Someone to act as a catalyst in carrying out change

Into the Future—Slowly

Some converts to enterprise networking report quick paybacks. United Parcel Service (UPS) now has about 1000 PC networks that link a total of 35,000 PCs throughout the organization. Since 1988, these PC networks have been gradually taking on selected mainframe applications. Some of these networking projects have logged a 40 percent return on the investment. In one case, a new network installation paid for itself within six months.

Despite this record of success, UPS has not gotten rid of its large systems. They are still in service, as resources to store large volumes of data. The difference now is that the large systems play the role of servers, not hosts. Much of the processing takes place on the PC networks. Then the data goes to the data center for permanent storage. The mainframe still has an advantage in this role. Not only can it store large volumes, but the data is also better protected.

Mixed media

Few organizations are downsizing all the way to sole reliance on their PC networks. Those who have made the heavy investment in large systems naturally want to keep those systems in service. Most of the mainframes they are replacing are older units which are near the ends of their useful lives and would soon be retired in any event.

Many IS professionals also still believe that a large system does a better job of maintaining data integrity. However, the best reason for

New roles for large systems

- Large-volume storage
- Server, not host
  - Workstations do most of the processing
- Security when needed

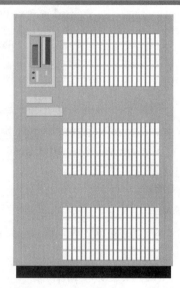

Figure 3.9   Use of larger systems will decline, but existing units can find new roles.

maintaining a large system is sheer capacity. Even the most powerful PC servers sometimes lack the memory capacity and channel bandwidth to handle duties like high-volume transaction processing.

For most organizations, the direct switch from a mainframe all the way to a pure PC LAN is still something for the future. Instead, the typical enterprise network is likely to be a hybrid of mainframe, Unix, and PC hardware. In particular, the Unix-based open systems are establishing themselves as intermediate stops on the downsizing path. They offer most of the power of larger systems, but the accessibility and ease of use of desktop units.

Taking it slow

Organizations are also displaying caution in the speed at which they adopt new systems. Some are increasingly using desktop systems for mission-critical applications that formerly ran on larger systems. Few are prepared mentally or technologically to run their entire companies from the desktop.

One reason: although desktop systems are approaching the functionality of their larger counterparts, they aren't there yet. Accordingly, a general pattern has developed of installing pilot applications on the desktop, with the goal of giving these applications the security, reliability, and integrity of mainframe applications. These protective features are not built into PC networks as they are into larger systems. That only means you must be careful to install your own protection to replace that which is not inherent in the system.

There is little inclination to completely replace mainframes. The trend instead is to reserve the big iron for applications that demand its extra features and capacity.

The role of Unix

In what might seem like a reversal of the usual form, one information systems company has been moving its database applications from PC networks to Unix systems.

The company took advantage of a wise early choice: the Progress database management system (DMBS) that runs on any of several platforms. These include DOS, Unix, and VMS. The first Progress application was purchased from an outside developer. It was a DOS-based system for manufacturing control. Later, the firm developed its own financial system using Progress, but this time chose the Unix version.

The reason: the performance of the PC network had been only marginal for the original application. Employees would suddenly find their workstations disconnected from the system, with lost data, time, and tempers. The Unix environment offered so much better performance and reliability that the company has been porting other applications to that environment.

The change has affected people as well as systems. The company has found its employees are not only more productive, but also more enthusiastic and creative about their work. Without the reliability problems to worry about, they keep finding new ways to make use of the system.

Tossing the Salad

A major challenge in enterprise networking is to mix and match the hardware and software from a diverse variety of sources. Enterprise networking usually requires interoperability among individual workgroup systems. There are three main ways to achieve it:

- Get everything from a single vendor.

- Use multivendor front-end tools to query a database.

- Develop your own applications.

The single-vendor solution

If you buy everything from one source, you get a certain degree of inter-operability. For example, Oracle databases operate on a variety of servers including PCs, Unix servers, and large systems. Likewise, the firm offers front-end products for nearly any type of client. Gupta offers database products for a variety of servers, but it concentrates on Windows for client workstations.

Yes, there's a catch. If you rely on a single vendor for both client and server applications, you must control the hardware and software configuration of every computer in your organization. In other words, you must be a small business.

Multiple front ends

The next step up is to use a uniform client application to gain access to databases from multiple vendors. Gupta's SQL Windows is designed to do this and is one of the few to support a full range of server systems. Forest and Trees takes another approach. It is primarily a read-only application with an emphasis on analyzing the data you retrieve.

SQL Windows is also an example of the third level: a mature client application that offers a full range of application-building and database access features. This range includes IBM's DB2, the Sybase/Microsoft SQL Server, OS/2 Extended Edition, and Gupta's own SQL Base servers.

Some products, particularly those that are new to the market, support this wide range. More often, a new client product supports only one or two of the most popular SQL databases. In particular, few PC-based front ends yet connect with high-end mainframe databases.

Your range may be controlled by your hardware and software choices. For example, a PC running Windows can operate a multitude of front-end choices for SQL Server. A Macintosh, on the other hand, is limited to a few generic products.

What You Can Do

The typical organization's approach to enterprise networking is to make haste slowly. That's also the prevailing approach to companion developments like downsizing and client/server computing. Few companies are trying to save money by throwing away modern, functional equipment.

Critical missions

Another trend is a steady upward movement in the type and importance of the applications being incorporated in enterprise networks.

Early converts don't seem quite ready to run their entire companies from their desktops. Some are developing enough confidence in network technology, however, to start converting mission-critical applications.

Several firms are installing core business applications on their networks. Their goal is to install mainframe-style reliability as well. They are building in functions that provide for integrity and security. Once available only on top-end hardware, they have become widely available for networked desktop systems.

Also being transferred: mainframe work habits and procedures. For example, one health care company has set up a claim processing system using networked PCs running OS/2. The system uses a database management system running on an existing mainframe, plus new network servers. "These servers have been installed much like larger systems, with uninterruptible power supplies, backup provisions, and controlled physical access," system planners said.

High-return applications

Some types of applications have proven to have higher potential than others in an enterprise network. They make good use of existing resources, provide good training grounds, and can form the basis of further expansion. That makes them ideal candidates for early development. Three stand out:

- *Decision support.*   This includes all forms of direct access to corporate data. Uncounted thousands of employees spend their workdays

High-return applications

- Consider these first:
  - Decision support
  - Document imaging
  - Improved contact between system and user

Figure 3.10   Start with applications like these.

retyping information from one application, say a mainframe report, into another application, such as a spreadsheet. One of the most productive early applications you could choose is one that lets these employees directly import corporate data into their desktop applications. You'll not only save time, but you'll eliminate a leading source of errors.

- *Document management.*   Computers have not created the paperless office. It's been just the opposite. Nevertheless, you can profitably use an enterprise network to reduce the cost and workload of creating, editing, routing, and generally shuffling documents. An enterprise network uses products that let you standardize formats, build compound documents, and make sense of routing and filing. This again can save time and expense. It also provides the foundation of an integrated communication system.

- *Simplified downsizing.*   Often, the only thing wrong with a mainframe application is its user-hostile interface. In that case, it's unproductive to rewrite the entire program to port it to a different platform. Simply put a fresh face on the existing foundation.

No big scrap iron

Particularly in its early stages, the downsizing movement was seen as a way to transfer large-system applications all the way to PC-based networks. In an enterprise networking environment, PCs and LANs become increasingly important, but larger systems often still find their places.

For other firms, downsizing to a PC LAN has been an interim step. What they would really like to do is to supplement existing mainframes with Unix servers running relational databases. Advanced Unix servers boast parallel processors that can handle many heavy-duty on-line transaction processing (OLTP) applications. The catch: the parallel processors were not available as early as many would-be customers hoped. Accordingly, the LAN servers filled in until the more advanced systems were available.

Initial networking projects often avoid the direct transfer of applications from mainframes to enterprise networks. The risk is high, but there's no real advantage there, experts say. Instead, the big payoff from enterprise networking is using it to improve old applications. You can provide updated features like distributed processing, better access, and greater ease of use.

The more typical role for a mainframe in an enterprise networking environment is as a secure, high-capacity database server. For example, the Merrill Lynch systems development group in Somerset, New

Jersey, has designed and set up an accounting system that is based on DB2, IBM's mainframe-class database management system.

Here, the application development has moved to the network. The networked developers use a network-based SQL system, XDB systems' XDB-SQL, that is compatible with DB2. This system runs on a 486-class server running under OS/2. This arrangement lets the developers take advantage of the network's flexibility. They can then move the completed application to the mainframe DB2 system. Meanwhile, the database management system remains on the mainframe.

Keys to Success

Enterprise networking clearly offers great potential. But as consultants are often asked, what does it take to get these results *right now?* Peter S. Kastner, of the Boston-based Aberdeen Group, says he advises his clients to look for these factors:

- *Existing PC networks.*   That translates into experience with PC networks. Enterprises that have networked their PCs have an advantage over those that carry out enterprise networking one desktop at a time. Once the networks are in place, the added cost of adding new applications and servers is small.

- *A relational database management system.*   The RDBMS has many strong points that make it ideal for enterprise networking:

  Strong ad hoc query capabilities

  Transaction management support

  Integrated development tool sets for building client applications

  The ability to serve diverse networks

  The ability to split processing duties between client and server

- *A gradual approach.*   Nearly all successful enterprise networking programs begin with small pilot projects, with quick payoffs, built around the client/server model. Later projects incorporate the organization's most mission-critical applications.

- *Keeping the mainframe.*   Few organizations plan to discard their mainframes or the so-called legacy applications that run on them. There are two good reasons:

  There are few tools available that can readily translate the older applications to an enterprise networking environment.

  Even if it was possible, the typical IS organization lacks the staff resources to do the job.

A suggested approach

Kastner suggests this approach:

- Start with a few pilot applications to gain experience and gain a quick picture of the possible payoffs.
- Re-engineer mission-critical applications that can benefit from conversion to enterprise networking and the client/server architecture.
- Stabilize those mainframe applications that are not due to be upgraded soon. Enhance them with client/server front ends.
- On the strength of this experience and its results, plan a full migration.

In Kastner's experience, most clients see these results:

- They *exceed their expectations* for cost reduction, completion time, and economic payoff.
- They *met their expectations* for productivity improvement and the ability of the IS staff to adapt to the new environment.
- They often *fell short of their expectations* of available development tools, though these are being improved.

Solving Networking Problems

The advantages of enterprise networking don't come without offsetting dangers. Don't let potential problems discourage you, but don't ignore them, either.

Enterprise networking has plenty of success stories, but it has also had its share of disappointments. Success is not easy or automatic. In some ways, enterprise networking is a controversial area. Even its strongest proponents acknowledge that you must face and resolve several issues. Each issue represents a potential pitfall.

That's the bad news. The good news is that for every potential problem there is a proven solution. If you are aware of the dangers and know what to do about them, they should not discourage you from an enterprise networking project.

Among the most serious issues you must face:

- *Unexpected costs.*   The downsized, client/server systems that make up an enterprise network often cost much less than their large-system counterparts. The careless look at these figures alone and get trapped by unexpected costs. The solution: make sure you account for the new expenses as well as the new savings.
- *Stick-shift security.*   Modern networks lack the build-in security and reliability of older host-based systems. Once-secure corporate

Warning signs

- Hidden costs
- Do-it-yourself security
- System changes mean organizational changes
- Few network management tools

Figure 3.11   Like all good things, enterprise networking has some problems.

data can be increasingly exposed to theft and error. The solution: don't expect a security system to work by itself, like an automatic transmission. It's more like a stick shift that you must operate yourself.

- *Human problems.*   Taking full advantage of an enterprise network will often mean that you must re-engineer the organization as well as the system. This has its natural human toll and often brings corporate politics into play. The solution: recognize the human as well as the technical side of enterprise networking.

- *Tool shortage.*   Particularly during the early going, you'll find a shortage of tools to manage the network. The solution: make full use of the assets you do have on hand.

It May Not Cost Less

A prominent assumption about enterprise networking is that it should cost a great deal less than traditional large-system computing. Many converts not only meet but exceed their cost-saving goals. It is vital, though, that you set realistic goals.

Particularly when enterprise networking includes downsizing to smaller systems, you can sharply cut hardware and software costs. You also can decrease application development times, reduce maintenance costs, create more intelligent applications, and achieve greater flexibility.

Financial balance

- Possible savings
  - Equipment
  - Application development
  - Flexibility
- Possible expenses
  - Personnel costs
  - Unexpected results

Figure 3.12   The costs and benefits may not be quite what you expect.

The pitfall here is to focus on the savings and to overlook some significant costs. You'll incur many of these in the human part of the conversion.

Dramatically lower costs of both hardware and software do not readily translate into direct savings of the same amounts. There are many hidden costs, particularly the expense of training both IS professionals and client employees in how to use and capitalize on the new system. A Gartner Group report suggests that the cost to put a client/server application into reliable, everyday service may be just about the same in a traditional large-system mode.

Even if this proves to be the case, your network can help you come out ahead. The benefits you get may not be the benefits you expected. You will gain the most not by up-front cost savings, but by making employees more useful and productive. According to Gartner's figures, enterprise networking can boost employee productivity by 30 to 50 percent. That's because enterprise networking makes much better use of the corporate data.

Unexpected benefits

At Hyatt Hotels, a networked reservation system produced more than a 20 percent cost saving in leasing fees and maintenance. Even so, the greatest benefit of the new system is the ability to respond quickly to changes in a highly competitive marketplace. One example is an express reservation and check-in service through a toll-free telephone number. Hyatt had earlier tried and failed to establish such a customer-service feature on the mainframe-based wide area network that supports its reservation system. Now, phone operators at Hyatt's Omaha location field each call, then log onto a specific hotel's computer over the company's Transmission Control Protocol/Internet Protocol (TCP/IP) network. Once connected with the hotel, the operator can confirm a reservation, down to the room number.

Cost isn't everything

Sara Lee has enjoyed the expected benefits of reduced maintenance costs and other expenses. That still is not the primary benefit the firm says it has gained from its system. Distributed, client/server platforms give employees the flexibility to choose the method and tools by which they will retrieve and use the corporation's information resources. The goal has been to empower employees by giving them better use of use corporate data. To meet that goal, designers created a variety of reports and standard data inquiries. They also made it easier to get answers to decision support questions using familiar tools. These include such PC-based tools as spreadsheets, databases, word processors, accounting applications, executive information systems, and decision support software. These systems move the responsibility for gathering and manipulating information away from the MIS staff and into the hands of those who use the information to do their jobs.

Getting a handle on the cost

The original impetus of the downsizing movement was the idea that low-cost, PC-based hardware could take on much of the work previously handled by larger systems. Even the most powerful PC network servers came at only a fraction of the price of a mainframe of similar capacity. The earliest converts looked at the vast savings and placed their orders. Then they learned that there were many hidden costs they hadn't anticipated.

Much the same learning experience has carried over into client/server and enterprise networking. It's still true that moving from central mainframes to distributed smaller systems can save vast amounts of hardware cost. It is also still true that many, though not all, of these savings are offset by hidden expenses.

People cost more

Many of these are personnel costs. The system may cost less, but the people will cost more. You can't necessarily avoid these costs. You can anticipate them and make realistic financial projections. Among the human costs that can catch the unwary are:

■ *Training.* You will need a new mix of skills, in both user and IS departments. Many current staff members will have to be retrained or, in the extreme, replaced. A common transition expense is retraining COBOL programmers in client/server languages and techniques. Some others are less obvious: training the IS staff for new roles that emphasize support instead of control, and training users to work with the new system.

■ *Management and support.* At least for the present, this is a labor-intensive activity. There are not yet many centralized management tools available for the multivendor networks of a typical enterprise network. Until they are available, user support, network support, and trouble shooting will require large amounts of human effort.

Software costs more

Another source of unexpected costs is the software basis of a client/server system. The hardware may be inexpensive, but the software is not. Steve Roti, consultant and *DBMS Magazine* columnist, offers these financial rules of thumb:

■ The server operating system can cost several thousand dollars.

■ Figure at least $1000 per workstation for front-end and network software.

Sources of unexpected costs

- Training
- Management and support
- Communication
- Planning
- Upgrading

Figure 3.13   It's easy to underestimate the people-related expenses.

One reason for unexpected costs

- Hardware is inexpensive
- Software isn't

Figure 3.14 Don't be fooled by lower hardware costs.

- Depending on the system, the database server itself can cost from $1000 to multiples of $10,000.

Roti was speaking strictly about the system. He did not include the considerable cost of training and other personnel costs.

Watch out for these

Other costs that can catch the unwary include:

- *Telecommunication.*   The object of client/server computing is to make all the information on the network, no matter where, available to any authorized user, no matter where. As the organization makes increasing use of this capacity, not only will network costs be much higher, but they will also be harder to predict.

- *Capacity planning.*   Another area where tools still are hard to find is the ability to anticipate the traffic volume on client/server networks and to design them accordingly. Existing analysis methods tend to emphasize transaction processing. They don't allow for interactive file sharing and ad hoc queries.

- *Upgrading.*   Many client/server applications now available were originally developed for PCs and LANs. They aren't always adapted or adaptable to larger networks. You may find yourself facing major costs to upgrade to more robust software or to multiple servers.

What you can do

It makes sense: if you are not aware of a potential cost, you are equally in the dark about ways you might avoid it. Investigation and awareness are the first and best cost control measures. They can help you identify cost-saving measures like these:

- *Make best use of existing resources.*   Many employees are familiar with basic PC software like spreadsheets and word processors. You can capitalize on that body of existing knowledge. For example, many available report writing tools use a spreadsheet model to let users generate reports or queries. Not only can they start from familiar ground, but there is also no need to rewrite applications. This can help give users a feeling that this application is "theirs," not "yours." That can lead to remarkable increases in both their productivity and their job satisfaction.

- *Recycle software.*   One advantage of object-oriented programming is that it produces modules you can use again in other applications. Even short of an object-oriented environment, the client/server environment lends itself to recycling. Your object should be flexibility, not detailed planning of every module. Use standard interfaces and tools that are designed for use and reuse.

Are Networks Less Reliable?

A serious issue in enterprise networking is the fear that networks will prove to be less reliable than the host systems they are to replace. Conventional wisdom holds that a PC network is not as reliable as a mainframe or minicomputer. The large system acts as a central point of contact for dumb terminals. It achieves hardwired levels of reliability, backup, and fault tolerance a LAN cannot approach. An internetworked system of diverse networks offers even greater potential for trouble.

That's true—and not true. An application of Murphy's Law suggests that a LAN offers many new places for things to go wrong. That doesn't mean something necessarily will go wrong, even at the proverbial worst moment. It does mean you must create some protection inherent in a large-system environment when you switch to smaller systems. You can't just sit back and assume they'll be there—or worse, that you don't really need them.

Here are some points to remember:

■ *A large system is not exempt from trouble.* Computers were going down, and data was being lost and corrupted, long before the first PC reached a corporate desktop.

■ *There are ways to enhance the reliability of a networked system.* Take a hint from NASA's emphasis on redundancy. If one part of the system fails, a well-planned backup can still let people get their work done.

■ *A network can add valuable new functions.* There are capabilities that older systems can't provide.

Smaller systems often work better

Many MIS managers who have investigated networked systems have come away convinced that a LAN can be more secure and reliable than a larger system. Generally, available networking technology should not be a problem, says consultant Cheryl Currid. "Desktop computers, client/server databases, and the networks that connect them are powerful and cost-effective alternatives to mainframes. Some of the technology might not be rock-solid yet, but the risk/reward relationship is too compelling to ignore."

The Keystone Group, a Boston-based mutual fund company, has used a downsized system to provide for longer lasting backup of its data. Under a mainframe system, the backup files were stored on magnetic tapes. Tapes can degrade over time. The PC-based system stores the backups on optical disks. These don't last forever, either, but they do have much longer life spans than the tapes.

The rules are different here

"In many ways," says Currid, "the challenge is to recreate some safeguards of the mainframe world. Unfortunately, it isn't as easy as porting things down intact. LANs speak a different language, and some things defy precise translation. The technology is different, the tool set is different, and the expertise needed is different. Both people and procedures will require reprogramming, and that takes a little time."

"Unfortunately, nobody has come up with an easy-to-install, shrink-wrapped pack," she continues. "Since all corporate shops are a little different, nobody has figured out how to develop a one-size-fits-all model. That makes it as much a creative process as a technical one. Meanwhile, pioneers will have to contend with less than a well-marked path."

These things can help

The basic problem is not that smaller systems lack security and reliability. It is that these things do not exist automatically as they do on
larger systems. You must create them yourself.

The solutions to problems of LAN reliability are generally simple.
Among them:

- *Maintain a central help desk.*   Provide full-time access, too.

- *Obtain and use the best network management tools.*   Use them to
  diagnose network problems, often before they become severe.

- *Make sure all connections remain in good condition.*

- *Back up data frequently.*   Do so particularly on file servers. Keep at
  least one copy of the backup data off-site.

- *Back up the system as well as the software.*   Provide alternate facilities and routes.

- *Install uninterruptible power supplies.*   Do so particularly for network servers.

- *Install fault-tolerant features.*   For example, mirrored servers or
  disk drives. Some network operating systems can detect the failure
  of one drive and automatically switch to its duplicate. Future systems may do the same for entire servers.

- *Make use of available reliability and security features.*   These are
  generally available in network-oriented hardware and software. For
  example, on the software side, DOS and OS/2 database management systems are taking on tasks that once required a minicomputer or mainframe. LAN-based database servers offer many of
  standard features of large-system DBMSs, such as rollback and
  two-stage commit.

Redesigning the Enterprise

Because people and technology are becoming so closely entwined, it is
only natural that this further truth has emerged: when you re-engineer
your computer system, you also re-engineer your organization.

Enterprise networking envisions new ways of doing business.
Employees not only have access to all kinds of new information
resources, but they are also expected to use them. The company has
installed the system to improve its competitive position. The installation will do no good unless the employees use the new system in the
expected new ways.

One company that learned this lesson is a Dallas computer retailer.
Caught up in the intense competition of its field, the dealership found

itself forced to re-engineer its business to make better use of network technology. The strategy worked: the company survived while many of its competitors went out of business. But a company official likened the experience to suffering two to three times the force of gravity in a fast-moving airplane.

Maybe We Don't Have the Technology

Among the most frequent complaints of enterprise networking converts is that available application development tools for the new environment are still lacking.

New styles of application development are making traditional line-by-line programming obsolete. Graphical displays and similar features can make developers just as productive as they make the employees who use the completed applications. That's the ideal. In practice, many developers feel the available tools still fall short of the potential.

Alternatives to in-house development are also scarce. Managers cite a lack of packaged applications for the client/server environment. For example, one technology manager went looking for a basic general ledger application. He says he could find many written for mainframes, but not one satisfactory package for client/server.

One possible reason: the major software developers in the PC arena have their origins in single-user products and methods. Many network products are simply these traditional PC applications with networking features grafted on. They do not take advantage of a multiuser network.

A shortage of tools

- Application development
- Network management
- Client/server applications

Figure 3.15 You won't always find everything you need to work with.

For example, these network-adapted PC products do not generally reflect the basic client/server division of duty, in which the client system serves the individual and the server holds a bank of common-use data.

There is also a problem familiar to single-use PC owners: these products are not designed to work well with each other. An enterprise network requires that differing systems and applications work together; even under Windows, standard PC applications seldom do that well.

Other Problems

The three big problems of money, security, and people generally rank as the most serious obstacles to a successful enterprise network. There are others. You can't quickly exhaust the list of problems that threaten your enterprise networking success. You can expect to encounter many smaller problems that could prove as troublesome as the larger ones.

Application migration

If many people are unwilling to accept change, so are many applications. For example, a Boston life insurance company decided to move its database of about 180,000 policies to a PC network. One of the first things the company discovered was that the network file server wasn't large enough to handle the workload. A more powerful file server solved the problem, but it was an unexpected difficulty and expense. Company officials also describe it as a learning experience.

Other organizations are surprised to learn that they can't migrate every function of their old technology to a new system. One company wanted to move its mainframe-based applications to PCs running Windows. The firm found it would have to do a lot more recoding than it thought, and it still wasn't totally pleased with the results.

Help wanted

Some migrating applications represent technology that may be as much as a quarter-century old. PCs have been around for a little more than a decade, and PC networks are still in their infancy. That creates a staffing problem as well as a technical challenge. You may well find yourself with a staff well schooled in mainframe techniques, but too few people who know their way around modern networks.

Knowledge of LAN techniques doesn't necessarily qualify an employee to manage an enterprise network, either. It's one thing to set up a small LAN running one or two familiar PC applications. These rudimentary networks are in no way ready to handle client/server databases or mission-critical applications.

Software shortage

Another possibility also presents itself: you can invest time and money in PCs, workstations, LANs, and servers, then have nothing to run on them. There are still few specific client/server products available on the market. This should change as vendors naturally respond to the market. Until then, though, you may have to count on modifying large-system applications, or stretching the limits of popular PC programs.

Getting things together

There once was a time when you could buy entire network systems from a single vendor. The various hardware and software pieces were designed to work together. It was something like buying a suite of complementary designs to furnish a room.

The decor of enterprise networking can be described as "early garage sale." You drive around town, picking up a system here, a piece of software there and networking tools somewhere else. Then when you get home, you have to get them all to work together.

Don't underestimate the difficulty of doing this. Even consultants and system integrators have saddled their clients with poor hardware installations. Even after a good network is in place, count on having to fiddle with it every month or so. You have to make sure the servers have adequate memory and disk drive capacity, and that important work is not being jammed up in network traffic bottlenecks.

Early converts are now discovering a related problem. They properly design their enterprise networks to work in tandem with the organization, matching the firm's structure and supporting its objectives.

Then, business conditions change, and the enterprise has to change to meet them. That means the system is now out of sync with the organization. For example, if you have divided a database among operating units, it can be hard to put it back together again when the units are realigned. You also could find yourself in a situation where employees need access to resources they did not need before.

What Can You Do?

Those who have been through the process offer these tips for successful conversion to enterprise networking:

- Learn how the network will relate to the organization's goals and operations. Decide in the planning stages how you will react when those goals and operations change.

Guidelines for success

- Match the network to the organization
- Map it out in advance
- Pay attention to people
- Don't quit too soon
- Don't rush the process

Figure 3.16 Suggestions from voices of experience.

- Before you commit yourself to any particular hardware or system, work out the technical and logistical details of installing and using it. If you spread the system over multiple platforms, make sure each has the capacity to handle its share of the work—now and in the future.

- Pay attention to the people. Take the time to train them. Go further and try to make them feel comfortable with the change. Don't ignore their concerns or assume they will disappear automatically. One of the best ways to overcome resistance is simply to show that you understand.

- Make the commitment. The transition could easily take five years. Make sure everyone is prepared to go the distance. That includes you.

- Don't rush. Some companies feel they have to unload their entire mainframes onto networks immediately. The time-tested advice is to do just the opposite: start with easy, noncritical applications. Use the experience you gain there to plan the migration of your more important assets.

Exactly What Is Client/Server, Anyway?

The client is not a computer. It is a person.

Levi Strauss & Co. may be most famous for its rugged clothing, but it is also a client/server pioneer. Starting in 1991, the firm embarked on a pilot project of replacing its mainframes and minicomputers with a client/server system. The objective: to show that client/server features like object-oriented programming, workstations, a relational database, and Unix servers can do the job in production systems.

During the project, code named Orion, eight programmers and analysts learned new ways to create applications using object-oriented techniques. The firm developed a pilot Unix application that it tested in several of its business units before the full client/server system was set up.

Levi's is not scrapping its mainframe. The company plans to continue to develop applications on the mainframes or the Unix platforms. It will use the platform that seems best for the purpose. The mainframes are also taking on new roles as database servers, maintaining a central data depository for the worldwide corporation.

The pilot application is a shipment tracking system that lets managers and customer service representatives track materials and finished products as they move among suppliers, factories, and warehouses. It connects to an electronic data interchange (EDI) system with which suppliers feed shipment information to the Levi's system. That information initially is stored on a mainframe; individual business units then can retrieve it and store the data on their own Unix servers.

Development of the new system was only part of the changeover; Levi's also reorganized its customer service program to capitalize on the new opportunities it provided.

The tracking system's developers went through two major phases:

- Modeling and categorizing object classes
- Writing the actual program code

The first step was the low-tech phase. It was also the toughest. The most important type of hardware was the index card. The task was to define various classes of objects. The developers had to parcel out the responsibilities of each object and to decide how each class would interact with the others.

This required a major change in the programmers' way of thinking. After that they found the coding easy, although they were working in Smalltalk, a language unfamiliar to many of them.

The process created not only a productive new application, but also a useful legacy. Many objects developed in this process can be used again. The project also led to guidelines, which future developers can follow in building further client/server applications.

A Matter of Definition

Client/server is at the heart of enterprise networking. It's also among the fastest growing areas of business computing today. But exactly what is it? It can incorporate many elements, and these elements can easily be different in every organization. At Levi's, as in most installations, the client/server installation centered on a database management system. It also involved more, including EDI, object-oriented programs, and a localized re-engineering of customer service. In your organization, the practical applications could be something else entirely.

Technical elements of a definition

One way to describe client/server is as a business opportunity for consultants. Thanks to client/server, their business volume should increase 34 percent annually, and they should maintain that rate for a full five years. "We have virtually no systems-integration project currently under proposal that doesn't contain some aspect of client/server architecture," says one.

One reason the consultants are so busy is that client/server is a mix-and-match approach to systems design. It uses products and technology from a wide range of vendors. It involves the organization as well as its technology. Many corporate managers find it intimidating to deal with such a nonstandard package.

One working and workable definition of client/server computing is this:

> Client/server is a technology that increases productivity by logically dividing data processing between back-end servers and front-end clients.

Notably, that definition does not mention databases. Though database management is by far the most common and best known use of client/server technology, it is not the only use. Any system in which a client receives the favors of a server is, properly, a client/server system.

At your service

That still is not a full definition. The technology exists for a purpose. You can express the basic purpose of client/server systems this way:

> To give developers and management the power to serve their users by giving them easier, more thorough, and more meaningful access to information.

This part of the definition includes two important elements:

- *Serving the user.* Client/server is not just a technological phenomenon. The client is served so the individual can be served. That individual is a customer, whether inside or outside the organization. In other words, the system does not just serve another part of the system. It serves people.

The two faces of client/server

- Front-end client
  - Provides the workstation interface
- Back-end server
  - Manages the database
  - Processes queries
  - Returns results

Figure 4.1   Client/server doesn't have to be a database, but it usually is.

Defined by what it does

- Serves the user
  - The user is central
  - The computer is not
- Provides useful information
  - Not just data

Figure 4.2   Client/server is a service, not a system.

- *Information, not data.*   The object of a client/server system is not just to "access" raw data, but to retrieve it in a useful form that helps people do their jobs more efficiently.

Other definitions

Client/server database management is only one type of client/server system. Others include:

- File sharing
- Computing engine sharing
- The X Window display system, typically found on Unix workstations

Each of these applications uses a client and a server, the matched pair of applications that make up any client/server system. Each has an established process to talk with the other. Through this process, the client makes requests for services, and the server fulfills them.

It's common to think of the client as residing on the user's workstation. In a typical database system, a central server responds to requests from workstation clients. That's the most common arrangement, but it isn't necessarily the case. Take the case of X Windows. It's been accused of working backwards. By this definition, the workstation half of the tandem is a server. This server applies a graphical interface in response to requests from a client application that may be running elsewhere on the network. There are also those who say this distinction is just talk, and that X Windows operates like any other kind of client/server system.

The human definition

Then there are those who say client/server is not really a technical creation, but a state of mind. Client/server emphasizes people, not technology. It sets priorities, starting with the basic relationship between a client and a server. Client/server systems have grown up in the same atmosphere, and respond to much the same kind of thinking, specifically modern organizations' strong interest in customer service.

Client/server is above all a human technology. It helps people do their jobs. The ultimate client is always a person. Client/server works with modern styles of management that seek to empower front-line employees by giving them more authority to make more decisions. Client/server technology supports that process by providing the information with which to make those decisions.

That's why this book comes down so hard on the horrid term *end user.* That term envisions the human client as sitting out at some remote point, removed from things that are really important. *End user* has

Client/server is a state of mind

- A changed business philosophy
  - People come first
  - The system's job is to serve them

Figure 4.3   Client/server emphasizes people, not things.

almost become synonymous with *necessary evil*. In a client/server setting, the individual is at the center of things, not out at arm's length.

Client/server and other forms of networking have been criticized as a return to the past. Critics lament losing the freedom formerly associated with purely personal computers. That may be happening, but not to a great degree. A properly conceived client/server system enhances the power of individual employees. Instead of restricting them, it provides openings to resources that could not possibly have been available on a stand-alone system.

The key phrase is *properly conceived*. It isn't enough just to meet the technical definition of a client/server system. If you focus only on the technology, you run the risk of replacing a rigid old system with a rigid new system. A client/server system must meet technical standards, of course, but the technology gains value only when you use it to expand human potential.

Best Performance in a Supporting Role

Though client/server is more than database management, the database usually is the server portion of the client/server pair. It's not normally a highly visible role. Front-end products with their windows, graphics, and colors have the glamorous part of the job. Database management is a server occupation, attracting little notice until something goes wrong.

The typical database server is a faceless product that has no direct or visible contact with human clients. That makes it a little harder to describe and understand a server than it highly visible front ends. One thing is certain, though. Database servers, many running on PC-based front ends, have been developed to a point that they offer the performance and reliability of larger systems, at personal computer prices.

Taking advantage of the network

The secret to this high performance is that today's database servers aren't limited by the computing power of the individual systems on which they run. They have the advantage of all the computing power the network has to offer. The network establishes the division of labor between client and server.

The computing power to do this has been available for quite a while. Like all else in networks and client/service computing, the key to success has been teamwork. It took client/server databases to maximize the network's power and put it to useful, productive work. The earliest networks were either host-based, dumb-terminal systems or LANs put together to share files and printers. The client/server database "exploded the box" and made the network a system in its own right.

Client/server is based on software, not hardware. It is the software that took the local area network beyond file and printer serving and turned it into an enterprise-wide computing asset.

Reasons to convert

A common reason to install a client/server database is to downsize from mainframes and minis. Other enterprises are acting for just the opposite reason: they are upsizing, from stand-alone PCs to networks, or from file-server LANs to enterprise networks. Downsizers in particular are seeking lower cost. The cost of even a top-end LAN server is a fraction of that of a larger system of the same capacity.

The anticipated savings often are less than expected. One reason is the software basis of a client/server system. The hardware may be inexpensive, but the software is not. Then there is the considerable cost of training and other personnel expenses.

Client/Server Is a Relationship

Though a client/server system usually includes computers, networks, and dedicated hardware, strictly speaking, it doesn't need any of these things. Client/server is a software architecture that exists whenever two programs talk with each other in a client/server relationship.

A client/server database

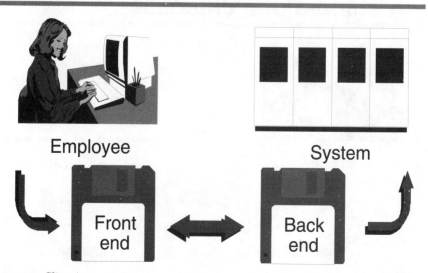

Figure 4.4   Client/server splits the workload.

This is a *peer-to-peer* relationship. The server responds to the client, but neither is truly superior to the other. Peer-to-peer is another term whose definition depends on the circumstances. For example, a peer-to-peer LAN gets its name because it does not absolutely rely on a server. In mainframe practice, peer-to-peer refers to ready communication with a host system. When discussing client/server architecture, peer-to-peer describes the cooperative relationship between the two major components.

You don't own me

In the enterprise network, the peer-to-peer definition distinguishes client/server from two other leading architectural styles:

- The *hierarchical* architecture, in which one process is said to *own* a subsidiary or *child* process.

- The stand-alone or *monolithic* architecture in which a single program controls all database processes from keyboard input through query processing and final output.

The hierarchical form of architecture is usually mainframe-centered. The parent and child processes might have some resemblance to modern client/server architecture, but they do not operate as equals. The child depends so greatly on the parent that if the parent

A stand-alone database

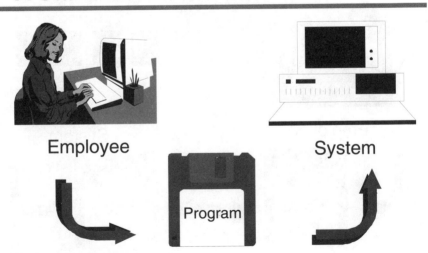

Employee   System

Program

Figure 4.5 One person, one database.

dies, the children usually perish automatically. Though users of these systems are in no mortal danger, there is a similar relationship. These systems have reputations as being slow, clumsy, and unresponsive to users' needs.

The monolithic architecture is the most simple and straightforward. This group includes many mainframe programs. It also takes in many personal computer standbys, including those that follow the Dbase standard.

Though this is the simplest form of database application, it can be the hardest to use effectively, particularly if performance is an issue. A stand-alone program must attend to all these functions:

- Read the data file format

- Record changes and new information

- Retrieve data, with as little delay as possible

- Know and observe its own internal processing logic

- Present a consistent, easy-to-use interface

Shipping and receiving

A client/server application must do these things, too, but it splits them up. The server system's developer should already have taken on the job of managing the database. The application developer usually needs to worry about the front-end system, at the client end. The front-end system handles the screen display, accepts input, and sends queries to the database. When the requested information comes back, the client system takes care of displaying and printing it. A modern front end also can massage the information, interpret it, and import it into a PC-application program.

The front end need not have anything to do with the server's processing logic, data format, or retrieval methods. The server should handle that, translating the client's instructions into its own internal language. The server should already have the means to do this when it is installed. Neither the application developer nor the user should have to worry about it.

While the stand-alone database program is a single application, by definition a client/server system has two. If it were not already in place, creating that second program would represent much extra work for application developers. Some application programmers might be tempted to write their own back-end programs to match their front ends. Usually, though, that is wasted and unnecessary effort (See Wheel, Reinvention of).

The front-end developer's most important task is to create a system that can link the back end with the human component. This system should have only three major tasks:

- Present an attractive and efficient interface to the user.

- Send the appropriate data queries to the back end.

- Present the results of the query and manage the data locally.

The front-end system has fewer functions than a stand-alone database manager. What's more, many front-end products come in shrink-wrapped form for installation on client PCs.

Establishing communication

There is a third element to client/server computing: getting the two major elements to talk with each other. That also is the application developer's responsibility, but it can be easy. Each server DBMS has a well-defined method of communicating with its clients. The client developer must simply choose the right method.

The usual communication method is the server's application program interface or API. (Some call it an application programmatic interface, but the extra letters seem unnecessary.) The API usually takes the form of object libraries. The client program makes calls to functions in those libraries. These object library function accordingly then contact the database. Many PC database applications now have client/server APIs built in.

Other forms of client/server

Database management is by far the most familiar form of client/server computing. Database management using Windows or another graphical display is the fastest growing client/server subspecies. Neither the database nor the interface is an essential client/server element.

There is no reason to assume, either, that client/server requires a particular division of labor between its two major components. For example, many developers assume that they are supposed to provide a user interface and other elements of the *presentation services* at the client workstation. That belief ties in with the desire for a graphical interface. There is also a natural expectation that the task of managing the database is properly assigned to the server.

The best reason to divide a client/server application in this way is that it's a good idea that suits your need. The worst reason is that you think it's required.

There is no single right way to divide the application logic. There are many variations on the standard scheme. One notable example is the Sybase approach to its SQL Server. This is a back-end DBMS, but application programmers can write stored procedures that are managed and executed on the server side. The advantage of this approach is that you can establish a uniform set of business rules, security provisions, and data integrity measures, applying to everyone who uses the database. There's no need to write them separately for every front-end application. The more widespread practice, though, is to write these procedures within the front-end application that works on the client system. This approach leaves the server completely free to process incoming commands.

Not the division

It isn't really the separation of powers that defines client/server or makes it valuable to its users. Just the opposite is true. You can identify a good client/server program by how well its elements cooperate, not by how effectively they are separated. You can exercise many elements of the application on either side, or both, and you can let process control pass between them.

Client/Server as a Growth Industry

For organizations torn between reduced budgets and increased expectations, there are many good reasons to look seriously at client/server. Cost is the big reason. A switch to client/server usually involves downsizing to less expensive hardware. The anticipated cost savings aren't always as large as expected, but any saving can be worthwhile. There are other reasons, too, for client/server's growing popularity:

- *The increasing reliability of client/server systems.* With proper planning and precautions, moving even your mission critical applications to a client/server system is no longer a high-risk enterprise. Lower-priced systems are increasingly able to do the job.

- *More ways to extend networks.* Networking is becoming increasingly sophisticated and popular. The number of network installations has been steadily increasing, and so has the rate of growth.

- *The boom in electronic mail.* Organizations are looking for ways to integrate the e-mail systems that have grown up on various types of systems. LAN-based e-mail has been responsible for much of the growth; now, companies need to connect these islands with disparate e-mail networks that have grown up on other systems.

Behind the client/server boom

- Greater reliability
- Better networks
- Electronic mail
- Growing demand
- Best use of available resources

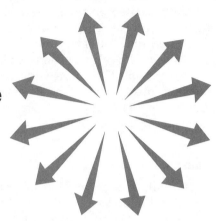

Figure 4.6   Acceptance by IS pros has helped, too.

■ *Peace talks in the turf wars.*   There still are a few IS professionals out there who think of "end users" as unworthy, if not unwashed. They still resent having to give more people access to their highly protected data. For the most part, though, the profession is growing into its new role as a source of advice and expertise, bringing new levels of service to their internal customers.

■ *Facing reality.*   A great infrastructure of PCs and LANs is now in place. In an era of tight budgets, it only makes sense to take advantage of existing resources.

■ *Growing demand.*   It's safe to predict that non-MIS employees will continue to need and expect greater access to information. Their need continues to grow, and so does their access to reporting and analysis tools.

Few organizations expect anymore that they can hermetically seal their data to protect it from theft and corruption. Those who recognize the need for broad-scale access can take steps to deal with that need. They can use their experience and expertise to provide the necessary levels of protection in a changing environment.

Client/Server Issues

There are really two views of client/server. One sees client/server as it might be. The other looks at client/server as it exists right now. While vendors and trade press writers tend to focus on the future, working managers have to concentrate on the present-day realities.

Some of these qualify as hard realities. In many organizations, there is still a gap between the promise and the performance of client/server systems. This is true in terms not only of system performance, but also of other key indicators like cost.

Theory vs. reality

In theory, converting to client/server should be easy. Just plug in the right hardware, hand a development team a set of application building tools, and you're there. In the ever-present real world, you'll probably run into some problems. You can solve most of these by adjusting your perspective. If you're coming from a large-system environment, you'll find that there are major differences between the applications with which you're familiar and the new breed of software. If your background is in PCs, you'll encounter the complications of widespread networks and multiple use.

Software and data are no longer solely on a single system where you can exercise tight control and management. Resources may be scattered around the building, or even around the country. Response time may be slower than users expect, as data queries scour the network looking for pieces of information here and there. The usual security measures may not be in place. Information may be vulnerable to the accidental keystroke that erases everything. No matter how much you try to persuade hesitant beginners that they can't do this, they can.

Unresolved issues

- Performance short of promise
  - Cost
  - System performance
- People problems

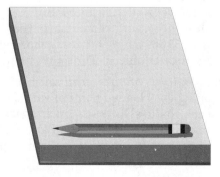

Figure 4.7

You have to establish training and procedures to guard against such hazards. All can be prevented, but you must take active steps to prevent them.

People problems

Since client/server has its human as well as its technical side, many challenges involve people, not technology. Often, the client/server system supports a new form of organization that empowers employees by granting them better access to information. Or, you'll find that the best way to make use of your expanded information resources is to re-engineer the organization.

Technical managers often find themselves dealing with a new list of people-related problems. Their co-workers are experts at marketing or finance, not IS. Many must be trained or even forcibly motivated to take simple steps like backing up their data.

What you can do:

For most organizations, these difficulties are in the future. There are some who have already had the experience, and they recommend steps like these:

- *Make sure you have a specific benefit in sight.* Don't switch to client/server because you've heard someone else's success stories. Find out, in advance, exactly how you expect to achieve your own success.

- *Train the trainers.* Often, a distributed client/server system involves employees at several locations, or at least several departments. Train one or two employees from each site who can then take responsibility for training the rest of the staff at that location. This helps involve the remote employees and makes it easier for them to learn and, more important, accept the new system.

- *Have support available.* The trainers, or employees they train for the purpose, can take most of the responsibility for supporting employees at their sites. Support the hardware as well as software. Have necessary repair parts readily available. For example U-Haul, with 1100 remote offices, keeps technicians and parts available at its 83 district offices. That puts help within a day's drive of any office.

- *Introduce changes gradually.* A retail chain decided to replace its aging, overloaded point of sale (POS) system with a PC-based system that could also track inventories and report daily sales data. The first step was to install a PC in each store. Employees had some time to become familiar with the new computers. Only then was the new software introduced.

Keys to success

- Set a visible goal
- Don't skimp on training
- Support the employees
- Avoid sudden change
- Be consistent

Figure 4.8 You can overcome most problems. It just takes some effort.

■ *Develop consistent standards for application development.* Programmers working on individual PCs tend to go their own ways. Keep this under control by establishing standard styles and methods. Make sure, for example, that everyone uses the same naming conventions.

Limited distribution

One key problem is that full distributed database systems are hard to achieve. Ideally, data in an enterprise network should be spread around in locations that make practical good sense. In practice, most existing distributed systems are compromises with reality. The most common approach is to use one central database server as a central control point, receiving and dispatching messages from both clients and remote databases.

The next chapter will discuss this subject in more detail. The implication for a client/server system is that all the traffic on this distributed network must pass through a single point. Even in a nondistributed system, the server in a client/server system ends up doing much of the client's work. The central server can quickly become overloaded, and traffic on the network will be gridlocked.

In effect, says consultant John Girard, system designers effectively turn their database servers into "little mainframes" that look more like traditional timesharing systems than true distributed databases.

Partitioning guide

Girard, of New Science Associates (Mountain View, California) suggests that to get the most value from a client/server system, you must effectively partition the workload between clients and servers. This lets you make the most efficient use of available resources like processors, hard disks, and networks. Girard lists seven types of partitions and advises that you base your choice on the nature of the job to be done:

- *Partition 1.* This is the traditional time-sharing setup in which a dumb terminal on the desktop connects to a single central server. Though client/server is supplanting this type of arrangement, there are situations when it still is the best way to allocate resources. These include straightforward character-based applications, a need for high security, or another good reason to maintain central processing resources.

- *Partition 2.* Here, most processing remains centralized, but you want to run a more sophisticated interface on the desktop. The X Window system using X terminals is a leading example. The terminals work with the server to apply graphical interfaces, but the significant processing takes place at the server.

- *Partition 3.* In this partition, PCs or workstations emulate terminals, but apply their own interfaces. An X Window system running on a workstation, instead of a terminal, is an example of this

Models for client/server partitions

- Time-sharing model
- Improved display
- Terminal emulation
- Remote procedure calls
- Front end/database
- Interactive databases
- File server

Figure 4.9   There's no "right" way to divide client from server.

approach. It frees the server of all interface responsibilities, reducing the workload on the server and the network.

■ *Partition 4.* At this level, you can begin to divide applications and display processing between the client and server. You can use remote procedure calls (RPCs) so the separate pieces can maintain communication with each other. You can take advantage of RPCs to fine-tune the workload distribution between front and back ends.

■ *Partition 5.* This is the level most commonly associated with client/server database management. The entire application runs on the client, retrieving information from a server database such as Oracle, Ingres, or SQL Server.

■ *Partition 6.* Partitioning at this level is still mainly in the future. It will use RPCs and other data access instruments to let databases interact between themselves and with the clients. Developments on this level will improve the ability to distribute databases across multiple systems. They will have the speed and coordination they need to support intensive applications like on-line transaction processing (OLTP).

■ *Partition 7.* This partition is hardly in the future. It is the basic system of LAN data access using network file servers. The client remains responsible for all processing services. The server acts only as a place to store the data. The main advantage of this system is that it can give the client access to larger databases than it could handle alone. It does nothing inherent to improve the clients' performance; that depends on their own processors and other components. It does nothing, either, to monitor multiple access to files. The application programs must take care of this.

Shifting Access and Responsibility

A client/server system gives users more access to corporate data, and more control over how they use it. This can cause experienced IS hands to blanch. They worry, with good reason, that some users, at least, lack the knowledge and sensitivity to protect their information from theft and corruption.

If the users' roles are changing, though, so are those of the professionals. This is the key to maintaining security and integrity while giving employees the vast advantages of greater access to information.

Reengineering IS

A conversion to client/server often accompanies a reorganization of the client departments. You need the new organizational structure to make best use of the new technology, and vice versa.

The same is also true of the IS function: you can't effectively set up new systems using old methods. It has long been a standard practice to divide a project into individual elements such as hardware, software, and networking. Each was staffed by experts in that technology.

A client/server system does not lend itself to that kind of compartmentalization. It is an intricate web of functions, as interrelated as a box full of fish hooks. Just as the varied elements of the system must work together in intricate new relationships, so must the teams who produce these systems.

The Textron Financial Corp. (Providence, Rhode Island) learned this in 1991, when it set up its first client/server project. In response to its hard-knocks education on this project, Textron has developed what it calls a consultancy model of client/server development. Textron places development in the hands of a team of multitalented generalists.

There is no longer a high value on expertise in a single technology. It's more important that a staff member have at least a basic understanding of all forms of technology involved in the project. Meanwhile, skills like project management and systems integration are at a premium.

Employees get involved

IS functions are being reorganized and redirected in other ways, too, as employees become increasingly involved not only in using applications, but also in creating their own. Distributed databases and new kinds of query tools are giving users both better access and more control. So have executive information systems (EIS), report writers, and other utilities. Their use raises questions, though, about who is responsible for protecting and backing up the data these tools retrieve and manipulate.

There are two reasons not to give this responsibility to the typical employee:

- Employees are notoriously unreliable about backing up PC data. That's not true of all, of course, but it is true of enough to cause some real concern.

- The ability to write data, which you must do when backing it up, is inherently more dangerous than read-only use. It's easy to imagine the unthinking user archiving a serious mistake.

In the past, of course, IS controlled access as part of protecting the data. It's no longer practical to do this. Employees need information. Deny it to them, and you deny it to your organization. IS professionals are most concerned about safety and management. A natural division of responsibility should be obvious:

- Place the query, EIS, and reporting tools in the hands of employees who can make good use of them. Some organizations even hand over application development responsibilities to this group.

- Assign to MIS the task of continuing to monitor data integrity and to take care of technical problems.

Do-it-yourself applications

For example, the University of Texas faced a soaring demand from employees for the available applications on its mainframe computers. Meeting the demand, the school learned, would require a new mainframe and a doubling of the MIS operation every two years. The university couldn't possibly afford it.

The solution was to let employees develop and maintain their own applications, using available tools like Adabas and Natural. The MIS staff was converted from a programming role to one of training and supporting the employee-developers. The employees do make some mistakes, and the professionals sometimes must bail them out. Still, enough employees are sufficiently computer conscious to assess and answer their own needs. It's also been established that the employees make no more mistakes than the professionals. The errors are no more serious, either.

Meanwhile, the MIS staff continues to take responsibility for running the completed applications and taking charge of campus-wide data.

Other approaches

Some organizations are not willing to go that far. Instead, they take the approach of giving users free rein over the data extracts they retrieve without giving them the ability to modify the data at its source. Decision support applications often use this approach.

Typically, such an organization will maintain two copies of its corporate database. One is kept as a read-only resource that is constantly updated by authorized sources. The other is a snapshot, taken at intervals that can range from several weeks to several hours. This extract stays on line for users who want to analyze information and produce reports.

Like an Old Relation

*The relational database is like a long-lost
family member who has just put in an
appearance. Just as you're getting
acquainted, some folks are saying it's over
the hill.*

The term *database* dates back to the 1960s. It came into use to describe an organized collection of facts stored in a computer. Ideally, you could index, retrieve, and manipulate the data in organized fashion. The organization was usually hierarchical, with all the sense of ownership and control that idea always entails.

This basic data storehouse has undergone inevitable change and improvement. Among the most important of those changes was the relational model.

Heart of the Network

Wherever you find enterprise networking, the relational database is not likely to be very far away. At the heart of a client/server system you will often find a relational database. Client/server is equally central to enterprise networking. SQL is also very visible. It's the native tongue of relational database management.

The relational model incorporates several important ideas:

- *Key values.* You can take these from one set of data to look up related information in another.

- *SQL.* A special-purpose language, Structured Query Language, is the common tongue of relational database management.

- *Table format.* Relational data always appears in the form of a table.

Constant companions

- Client/server computing
- The relational database

Figure 5.1 The relational database is the standard client/server application.

Table-setting

You will always see relational data in neat rows and columns. Each row describes an item, person, or activity, something like a noun in English grammar. Each column heading is like an adjective. It reflects some standard characteristic. This makes the data easy to organize and manipulate; it also reflects the values of the mathematicians who have devised and promoted the relational model. It's no coincidence

Relational database characteristics

- Standard language
  - Structured query language (SQL)
- Standard structure
  - Data appears in table form
  - One column is the key
  - It uniquely identifies each row
- Security and integrity
  - Built in
  - Need not be added on

Figure 5.2 The relational database has several key qualities.

that another influential computing model, the spreadsheet, uses the same row-and-column structure.

Using SQL, you can extract data from any of several tables. If you have established a *relationship* between two or more tables, you can retrieve data from any of these data sources. As a simple example, an employee roster table may show that an employee works in the accounting department. You could instruct the system to look up the accounting department in another table and find out who the department manager is.

This process of extracting linked data from multiple tables is a *join*. Without the ability to link the two tables and retrieve related information, this database would offer no truly efficient way to identify the employee's manager. In a simpler flat-file system, each employee's listing might also include the name of the employee's department head. If there were 250 people in the department, you would have to enter the manager's name 250 times. If you appoint a new manager, you will have to change all 250 entries. With your luck you would find and correct only 249.

In a relational system, the manager's name appears only once: in a table of information on each department. It's something like a cross-reference for computers. You can readily look it up, and the computer can look it up a lot quicker than you can.

The lookup mechanism is called a *key*. This is a value, such as a part number, that appears in two related tables. It establishes the relationship between information in the two tables. In the employee-department-manager example, the table of employee information could contain the employee's department number. Using that number as a key, the system could look up the same number in a table of information about each department, such as its name, its office number and, of course, the manager's name.

Another major characteristic of the relational database is its use of views. You can create a view, a virtual table, of selected rows and columns of one or more tables. Ideally, you can treat a view exactly as if it were a real database table.

Relational isn't everything

It's a good system with one significant drawback. The real world is not always that neatly organized. We work with ideas and images, not just facts. These don't always align themselves neatly in rows and columns.

Graphics in particular are now often stored in databases. There are databases that can manage pictures as readily as dates, numbers, and classifications. Once there was this inside joke: the only database applications to use this technology were real estate listings and identification badges. Then someone discovered document imaging, now one of the fastest-growing database applications to be found. The combined field of database publishing has broadened both of its elements. Multimedia in its present form is also a form of database management. The relational system is also under serious challenge from database methods based on object orientation.

Don't knock the row-and-column format. It's the best way known to manage data that lends itself to formal organization. But the less structured types of databases have proven their value as well. Several styles, alone or in combination, will most likely have long-term roles to play, providing the true data base of your enterprise network.

Today's Relational Database

Credit for inventing the relational database goes to Edgar F. Codd, the IBM database guru who in 1985 issued 12 rules for evaluating a relational database. Many database products now claim to be relational. Most of these claims are valid, although no one has ever produced a product that meets all 12 of Codd's requirements.

Though the relational model has been around for a while, in the last few years it has gained acceptance as a central feature of enterprise networking. In fact, it has made a quick transition from birth to, perhaps, late middle age. Just as business users are beginning to embrace the relational database, some critics are suggesting that it has passed its prime. Perhaps it will soon be replaced by some newer idea, like object orientation, that is better suited to unstructured types of data.

The original idea behind many of Codd's rules was that a relational database must be designed as such from the outset. You cannot create a true relational database by grafting a relational front end to some other kind of server.

A more recent version of Codd's work presents 333 separate features grouped into 18 categories. Most users prefer a much simpler set of standards. From a technical and performance standpoint, relational theory has two main goals:

- *Data independence.* The data's contents and your ability to use them should not depend on the physical structure of the database.

- *Data integrity.* The system should prevent inconsistencies and anomalies while processing the data.

Two main relational goals

- Data independence
  - You shouldn't be limited by the database structure
- Data integrity
  - It should be built in, not added on

Figure 5.3 The relational definition has hundred of elements. They boil down to these.

What makes a database relational?

The relational model defines three main characteristics:

- *System architecture.* This is the way in which data elements are represented, from indivisible atomic elements to complex composite entries.

- *Data operations.* The system should use consistent operators and methods to manipulate these data objects. SQL usually performs that role.

- *System constraints.* These are the rules that govern operations, so the results will be predictable, and you can protect data integrity.

Not even IBM has ever met all original 12 requirements, much less the expanded later list. Relational database management systems today are judged against a shorter list of standards. Though the short-list standards have much in common with the original 12 rules, they have different roots. The primary purpose today is not to distinguish among products, but to judge how well a DBMS meets the needs of client/server duty in an enterprise network. The system can perform that role best if it has these qualities:

- The use of a *primary key* that can uniquely identify a row or record in its table. A person's Social Security number often serves this purpose.

- Provisions for *data integrity,* no matter where the data may be. This is clearly a vital consideration in distributed database installations.

- The ability to distinguish between *null values,* which represent missing information, and values of zero.

- Support for *distributed databases.* This reflects one of Codd's original rules: the fact its data is distributed should not affect an application. This standard is flexible enough, however, to include systems that potentially could do this, no matter whether they do so now.

- The ability to *update from a view.* If you create a view that shows parts of one or more tables, you can edit the information by way of the view. For example, you could create a view that displays the employee's name and job title, and the department manager's name from a separate table. Suppose the company appoints a new department head, and in the process gives the employee a new job title. You can make both changes while looking at a single view, although the data is in two different tables.

Relational Fundamentals

The relational model doesn't really describe the physical structure of a database. It describes how the database should perform—how it should appear to the user. Vendors are free to use whatever physical structure they choose to produce the desired results.

A relational database does have several standard elements. The most basic is that all data takes the form of a *table.* Each row of the table represents a particular element. Each column identifies a particular type of information. Each intersection of a row and column contains a single fact.

For example, the LAST column of a database table might contain the last name of an employee named Smith. In the same row, the SSNO column should contain Smith's Social Security number, and the column headed DEPTNO is the place for Smith's department number.

The table is a way of looking at data. A database file may contain several tables, or one table may be split among several files. This is a form of data transparency: you see the table no matter what the data's actual physical form. A table also has these characteristics:

- It is a two-dimensional matrix corresponding to the mathematical concept of a relation.

- Each table has a unique name.

- Each column has a label that describes some aspect of the objects represented by each row. Columns are also often known as *fields.*

- Each entry is an atomic value; you can subdivide it no further. Each value comes from within a *domain*—a list or range of values that is valid for that column.

- Each table has rows, each representing individual items. Rows correspond to the *records* of other database management systems; in mathematical terms they represent *tuples*.

- Each cell in the table represents a single fact.

- The order of the columns is not significant to the structure of the data. You can change the order of the display without changing the meaning of the information.

- The same is true of the order of the rows. A row's identity depends on its contents, not its position.

- You can uniquely identify each row. There are no duplicate rows.

- If a value for a particular item is unknown or does not exist, the table contains a null value.

Keeping the keys

A relational database is a collection of related tables. In Dbase, a single table is usually called a database. In a relational system the single collection of data is a table, and the database is a collection of tables.

Within each row of a database table, there should be at least one entry that uniquely identifies that row. It could be a part number, a Social Security number, or some other unique form of identification. There can be more than one unique value in a row, but one of them should be the *primary key*. When a query seeks a row of data identified by this key, it should be directed without exception to the proper row. A column that holds a primary key should not accept null values.

The test of a good primary key: it tells you something that differentiates one record from all the rest. After all, if you consider your information important enough to store in a database, it should have at least one distinguishing feature. Let the primary key reflect that feature.

A table can also have *foreign keys*. These are keys that reflect the primary keys of another table. In an employee records table, the Social Security number might be a primary key; the department number would be a foreign key to information in another table about the employee's department.

The data dictionary is a third major component of a relational database. This is a collection of database tables that contain information about the database itself. One table, for example, might contain a list of working database tables and their characteristics.

A place for everything

A database table must deal with a *single subject*. Violate that rule, and you can clog up your network with the shuffling of a poorly designed database. For example, a nonprofit organization, designing a system to manage its contributions, devised a table whose column headings looked something like Figure 5.4.

It seemed simple enough. Every time a contribution came in, an employee would enter the identity of the donor along with the necessary details of the contribution. It wasn't long before the employee assigned to this duty noticed the defect in this design.

Most of the organization's supporters made large contributions once a year, but there were some exceptions. One in particular was a loyal supporter who every month would send in a $25 check. He had been doing so, month after month, for as long as the staff could remember. Each time one of his checks arrived, the data entry clerk had to enter all the details of this donor's name and address. Not only did she know this information by heart, but it was already in the database hundreds of times.

This employee was in no way an expert on database management, but she had correctly identified the problem. She should not have to enter repeated data. Once should be enough. Though she didn't understand it in technical terms, this employee had correctly identified the issue of a *normalized* database. Normalization, simply put, is the art of making sure that a table deals with a single subject, and that subject only.

The donation database called for several items of information about the donor. Then it called for several more items of information about

Too many subjects

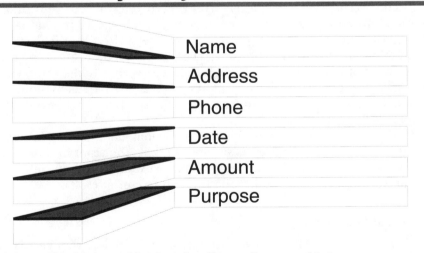

Figure 5.4   This database table tries to handle more than one subject.

the donation. That's two subjects: the donor and the donation. It would be more practical to split this table into two. One table, entitled "Donors" could contain information about the donors. Another, called "Donations," could hold information about their contributions.

Each table now deals exclusively with its own subject: people in one case, money in the other. The new field, DonorID, is common to both and serves as a key to link them. Should the organization wish to compile a mailing list of donors who have given more than a certain amount, the system could identify these key donors from the numbers in the Donation table. Then it could use the key values to pluck the full names and addresses from the Donors table.

There are two reasons to design a database system as a collection of single-subject tables. One is to make efficient use of your time and storage space. In an ideal system—one that is fully normalized—the only duplicated data would be the keys that link one table with another. This saves storage space, and the data you need will be on one convenient, well-marked place. That's the way relational databases should be used. A product usually works best when you use it as intended. A race car would be a poor choice to carry a basketball team, and a van would be unlikely to win a Formula I Grand Prix.

Relations and relationships

The relational database is based on the mathematical concept of a relation. Significantly, that's only one syllable removed from a relation-*ship*. The relational model describes the relationships between various elements of your data.

Each of these elements should be atomic—the smallest unit of data possible. For example, many databases describe certain classes of people, such as customers or employees. Short of surgery or horror movies,

A table for each subject

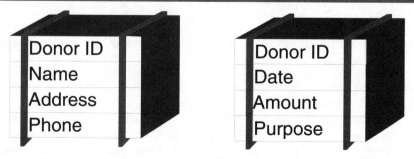

Figure 5.5 The donor identification code links the two tables.

a person is the smallest possible subdivision of this type of data. A unit of data is an *element.*

An *attribute,* also called a *property,* is one characteristic of each element. This is a single fact like the person's last name, height or Social Security number. In a database, a field or column represents an attribute. The attribute is taken from a *domain.* A domain is a list of all possible values the attribute might have. That range may be limited—the names of the 50 states for example. Or it could be as large as a major department store's inventory. You won't often find a full domain stored in a database. It would take a huge mailing list, for example, to contain an example of every existing ZIP code.

A relation brings these elements together. It represents a fixed set of attributes, within the underlying domain, for each entity in the database. In so doing, it forms relationships.

Another way of putting it: entities are the nouns of database management, properties are the adjectives, and relationships are the verbs.

A relationship can come in any of several forms:

- A *one-to-one* relationship, such as that between an employee and that person's Social Security number.

- A *one-to-many* relationship. This describes the relationship, for example, between a bank customer and each of that customer's several accounts, or between the monthly charitable contributor and each of his $25 donations.

- A *many-to-many* relationship. This would exist between your staff and your entire body of customers.

Though an entity is a single, indivisible fact, it does come in several types:

- A *kernel* is an entity that can exist independently. Joe Smith is a kernel, though he might not fully appreciate the thought.

- A *characteristic* is an entity that describes another entity. Joe's age and height are examples.

- An *association* is a many-to-many relationship and can become very complex. An inventory of items obtained from various vendors would be an example.

Because characteristics cannot be independent, it might seem that they are not proper subjects of database tables. Exactly the opposite is true. Making the wrong assumption is a good way to wander into a database design that covers more than its allotted single subject.

An entity usually has many properties. Each bank customer uses a distinctive combination of products and services. That's why it's best to maintain separate tables for the customers and the services. Otherwise, you might find yourself with something like Figure 5.6.

This structure is wasteful when a customer has only one or two accounts. It does not accommodate the customer who opens a fifth account at all. It's much better to treat each account as a characteristic of the account-holder. That way you can keep one table for account-holder information and another one like this to list the accounts. A separate table would link the customer ID numbers to the customers' names and addresses. (Figure 5.7)

The Integrity Question

Integrity in an individual is often a matter of honesty. The same is true of integrity in a database and its contents. One of the greatest challenges in designing a relational database is to ensure integrity through such means as these:

- Restricting the data values available in a column

- Limiting relationships

- Governing operations

- Validating entries

Too much or too little

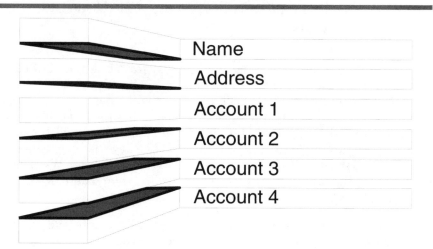

	Name
	Address
	Account 1
	Account 2
	Account 3
	Account 4

Figure 5.6   Too many accounts for some customers, too few for others.

Listings without limits

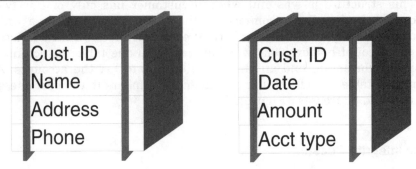

Figure 5.7   This structure lets you record unlimited numbers of accounts.

There are two main types of data integrity in a relational database:

- *Entity integrity.*   This means there can be no null values in a column used as a primary key. You can use this key to look up the contents of any row in the table.

- *Referential integrity.*   Every foreign key in a table must refer to an existing key in the related table. If not, the foreign key should be null so it does not refer to anything at all.

Usually, the best time to ensure entity integrity is when you create the database table. In the CREATE TABLE command of SQL, you have the option of declaring such a column NOT NULL. Use this power to ensure that there is a valid entry in every cell of this column.

The reference section

Ensuring referential integrity is equally important, but more difficult. It requires that you define the exact details of what the system will or will not allow, and what effect each operation will have.

Consider a table of employee records with another related tables listing members of the employee's family who are eligible for health insurance. The employee identification number is the key that connects the two tables. But what if the employee leaves the company? What will you do about the family records in the separate table? There are three possibilities:

- You can program the system to automatically delete the family records whenever you delete an employee record.

- You can have a null value inserted into the employee number column of the dependent records. The records are still there, but they are no longer connected to the ex-employee.

- You can require that all dependent records be deleted before the employee's record is deleted.

This is a simple problem. Consider what you would have to do should Human Resources decide to assign new employee numbers to everyone. There's also the possibility that the family members will legally be entitled to continued health insurance coverage for a period after the employee departs. The real world is not often a textbook case.

Data entry presents another problem. Before the system can accept the name of a new family member, it should validate the entry by checking to make sure that the appropriate employee record is on file.

Guidelines for designing databases

You won't always design the perfect database. Database designers use a process called *normalization.* In a way, normalization is like an exotic religion. As you progress stage by stage, you constantly get closer to perfection, but you never fully achieve it.

The better a database meets the standards of relational database design, the higher its *normal form.* The minimum standard for a relational database is called the first normal form, or NF1 for short. You can seek increasingly higher levels of perfection until you reach database nirvana at the fifth normal form. Above NF5 are a few higher forms named for those rare individuals who have achieved them.

For mere mortals, the main objective is NF1, a level designed to ensure a smooth-operating database under normal conditions. A database qualifies for NF1 when it achieves these qualities:

- A primary key uniquely identifies each row or record.

- The primary key should represent an identified entity type, and all additional fields should identify properties of that entity type. None should be repeated.

If a table identifies employees or customers, each would be identified by a primary key, such as the Social Security number. Each additional field would identify some property of that individual, such as the name or department assignment. It would not be proper to create several additional columns, each identifying an account for which the employee is responsible. These accounts would be repeated values, and they are not characteristics of the employee. Instead, create a separate table of account information, including a key that links each account to its responsible employee.

Are some more normal than others?

Successively higher degrees of normalization have these additional characteristics, which distinguish them from the levels below:

- *Second normal form.*   Besides meeting the requirements for NF1, all non-key attributes must be functionally dependent on the primary key. The key's attributes determine the other attributes.

- *Third normal form.*   The non-key attributes must depend on the primary key, and there must be no other possibility.

Successive levels deal with the handling of multivalued dependencies.

Practical database design

The design that works well in theory should also work well in practice. That's the theory, anyway. A theoretically correct database is necessary, but in the modern enterprise network it is no longer sufficient. It's just a starting point. The data also has to fit the organization. You're creating the database for a purpose—otherwise why would you be going through all that agony?

Good physical design is important, but good functional performance is just as vital. It makes no sense to normalize a database to a degree just short of nirvana when it fails to do the job for which it is intended. The obvious second test of a database design, then, is how well it serves its intended purposes. An extension of that test: how well does the design serve predictable future needs beyond those that exist now.

There are several yardsticks you can use, both in the planning phases and to judge your completed design. They include:

- The basic purpose the system is to serve
- The level of safety and security you want to build in
- The types of people who will use the system
- The level of performance you require

Serving the purpose

The best first step toward designing a database is to turn the computer off. Don't sit at the keyboard and try to create something for the sake of creating something. Instead, get yourself a prototype word processor—a pencil and paper—and begin to make a few notes on what you want the system to accomplish.

At this stage of development, don't worry too much about the contents of a particular table or the appearance of a screen display. Pay attention instead to the objectives you are trying to reach. Make sure you have your sights firmly fixed on that goal before you go any further.

Safety and security

Securing a database involves much more than protecting it from hackers and other highly publicized threats. You must fight crime and data corruption wherever they are likely to occur, and one of the most likely places is inside the organization you are seeking to network.

Early in the planning phase, assess the security needs of the database. Decide what you must protect, and from whom. Is there information that should remain confidential? Figure out your needs for an audit trail to record transactions that alter the database contents. What kinds of validation should you install to guard against incorrect data entries?

No security system is free of cost, including some important, but indirect, expenses. A validation process can inhibit performance. And the access controls that keep out unauthorized users also can make it difficult for authorized users to do their jobs. Many IS professionals are uncomfortable with that idea, but it's true.

Design yardsticks

- The system's purpose
- Who it's supposed to serve
- The safety and security you need
- The performance level you desire

Figure 5.8   The real test of a good design is how well it meets your objectives.

Who uses the system

Another major consideration is your employees' level of sophistication. Some people know little about database operations, and some of these would like to know even less. Computer novices require detailed guidance from their screen displays, help systems, and user manuals. To some veterans, such features merely get in the way. To complicate matters further, newcomers have a way of becoming veterans. Complicating matters further yet, even some experienced people prefer at least some handholding from their systems.

Skill is only one user characteristic. Take a close look, too, at the specific jobs employees have to do. The system should support those activities, provide information the employees need, and make their jobs easier. Too many database systems do none of the above.

How much performance?

There are two ways to measure a system's performance:

- How rapidly the system can work
- How rapidly the people who use it can work

The first standard is important only if it supports the second. A sales representative found himself in an argument with a systems professional over the performance of the sales rep's product. The IS pro pointed out that the system was a few seconds slower than competing products. The salesperson contended that this was unimportant. Those extra seconds were spent supporting features that helped people do their jobs faster by a factor of several minutes per transaction. However legitimate that claim, the pro wasn't listening. He left still muttering about reduced system response time.

That's a hard lesson IS professionals have had to learn as enterprise computing and smaller systems upset what was once a well-ordered world. The most important factor is not how well the system performs, but how well it can help people perform.

System speed is hardly inconsequential. No employee should have to spend unproductive time while the screen flashes, "Please wait." Neither should this employee be forced to do without some valuable feature because the system will not handle it.

These two needs often are contradictory. The system should offer a wide range of functions and do them quickly. The more features you include in a system, the more work the system must do, and therefore, the longer the response time. Remember, though, the only time that really counts is the time someone needs to do a job. If the system cuts minutes off a repetitive task, it can save thousands of minutes a year. A few seconds of extra response time seem small in comparison.

The real performance standard

- It's not how fast the system works
- It's how fast the people who use it can work

Figure 5.9 System performance is a factor, but not the only factor.

Capacity is another part of database performance. Consider the sheer number of records you will expect the system to handle, and the number of transactions to be made. Though small is increasingly beautiful in enterprise networking, make sure the system you choose is up to the job.

Client/Server Planning Principles

There is no free lunch, in client/server or anywhere else. Many companies have found many advantages in downsizing their databases to client/server systems. Still, the process is not risk-free, and there are pitfalls you must avoid. Richard Finkelstein, a Chicago-based consultant and writer, offers four rules to help minimize the risks of a client/server conversion:

- *Start small.* Don't risk your organization's critical applications in your first project. First, try a simple project with low risks, low costs, and low visibility.

- *Start early.* Don't wait until the last minute. Leave yourself time to evaluate alternative approaches and products.

- *Don't mix and match.* Stay as mainstream as possible and choose products that were designed to work together and have been tested together.

Planning principles

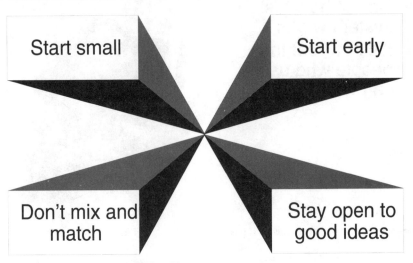

Figure 5.10   These help you avoid problems.

- *Don't rule out options.*   Be comfortable with your hardware and software choices, but don't automatically exclude any potential solution without at least checking it out.

Picking the project

Departmental decision support applications, or those that provide for ad hoc queries by users, are good candidates for the first projects. There will be a minimum amount of new technology to learn. Developers can concentrate on installing the new database server and its supporting network and application tools. They won't be distracted by the added problems of installing more complex applications like on-line transaction processing (OLTP) systems.

The database server facilities should require a small amount of tuning, Finkelstein points out. This approach allows your organization to become familiar with the issues while deploying much needed applications into the user community. You'll face lower risks and reap increased benefits—exactly the type of equation you're looking for.

Get an early start

As Finkelstein points out, an organization often will wait until the last minute to begin preparing for change. By then, the company needs the new system immediately, if not sooner. That, in turn, can lead to panic-stricken responses. These organizations will scramble for quick solutions—a sure prescription for failure.

Long before the change is necessary, you should begin evaluating your organization's strategic needs. Build a prototype of a potential application to validate the correctness of your choices and the stability of the software. Expect to spend some time learning about the new technology and introducing it to your users. Also, expect bugs.

Don't mix and match

Though a client/server system is designed to let diverse front-end systems interact with equally diverse server systems, the linkage does not come automatically. Here are some problems you can incur:

- Even if it works today, you have no guarantee it'll work tomorrow. Software and hardware are constantly changing.

- It's impossible for vendors to test their software on all possible software and hardware combinations.

- In a client/server environment, user workstations can have a potpourri of tools, memory-resident software, networking drivers, and hardware. Anything can happen in these environments—and it usually does.

Finkelstein's advice: stay as mainstream as possible and choose products that were designed to work together and have been tested together. This includes the operating system, database manager, network operating system, and application development tools.

Look for the best answer

Many organizations limit themselves because they explore too few options. For example, organizations with PC expertise often lean toward DOS or OS/2. These can work well, but they don't always offer the flexibility or power of Unix platforms. Unix and PC users will often overlook the DEC VMS system.

Also, don't limit yourself to the commonly known database servers. All database servers are different. Each database server has vastly different transaction management capabilities, performance aids, administration tools, programming and development environments, and connectivity software. Take time to understand your options and how they fit your situation.

Getting Acquainted with SQL

As information became increasingly valuable to the organization, access to it became a system requirement. Even under centralized systems, the data you need is not always in the most convenient place. If you are in St. Louis, and the sales figures for Duluth are on a system in Minneapolis, you need some way to get that information from Minnesota to your desktop. But you can't simply download all the organization's far-flung data onto your personal PC, or even a typical LAN server. Even if your system could handle it, which it can't, you need selected information, not an indiscriminate deluge.

Client/server and the relational database are responses to this need. They make widely-scattered information available to people who can profitably use it. The split-duty pattern also makes large volumes of data easier to handle; it lightens the workload on both client and server.

The nonstandard standard

In this picture, SQL is the underlying technology that makes everything else possible. If SQL didn't exist, we would have to invent it. SQL is an architecture that lets you manage the separation between client and server functions.

SQL is widely described as a standard way to retrieve data; in fact the American National Standards Institute has published such a standard.

As a language designed specifically for this purpose, SQL does an excellent job of retrieving data. That leaves one problem. Once you've retrieved the information, you probably want to do something with it. If you want to go beyond staring at the information on your screen, you must go beyond SQL and issue a separate set of instructions. For example, you might want to enter the department head's name into the proper space on a form. There's nothing in SQL that lets you do that.

That's because SQL is a highly specialized language that serves a single purpose. Unlike more exhaustive and conventional programming languages, SQL *describes* the data it seeks. Other languages, including the Dbase dialects, issue step-by-procedural-step instructions for retrieving data that meets your specifications. SQL only transmits the specifications. It's up to the database management system to figure out what it must do to meet those specifications and return the results to you.

That still doesn't do anything with the results, except to display them for your perusal. If you wish to format the results, include them in a form, or use them in a calculation, you must go beyond SQL.

One approach to this problem has been to extend the language. Standard SQL is a no-frills language. Nearly every vendor of SQL-based DBMSs has seen fit to add commands and functions of its own. Often, for example, these added commands let you add formatting to the output, such as displaying monetary amounts with the appropriate dollar signs and decimal places.

A more advanced technique is to embed SQL commands in a traditional programming language like C or COBOL. Once the calling program receives the results, you can use its commands to process and format them.

An increasingly popular approach is to issue the query and retrieve the results directly into a PC application. Many Windows front ends accept the data into their graphical displays. Increasingly, too, PC database applications retrieve and process data from SQL-based server databases. This approach has several advantages:

- It assigns the heavy-duty work to the part of the system best equipped to handle it: heavy-duty database servers which can range from high-end PCs to rededicated mainframes.

- It limits network traffic. Only the command and its response must travel over the network. Other types of systems will send the contents of an entire database across the network to a desktop station, which must then process the data itself.

- Employees can work with this data using familiar PC application programs.

Evaluating SQL

SQL has become the generic language of client/server database computing. When a client application sends a query to the server, it usually uses SQL, even when the query must be translated from the client's native language. For access to database services, SQL offers several advantages:

- Application programming is simplified. A developer need only attach the appropriate SQL statements to an application to retrieve the data the application needs.

- Network traffic is reduced. In a properly optimized system, only the query and the extracted data travel over the network.

- Different applications can use SQL to retrieve and use data from one or more central sources.

As client/server and distributed databases have risen in popularity, SQL has become almost a universal language of database access. Even products for whom SQL is not a native tongue have learned it as a second language. Nearly all database vendors offer an SQL interface for access to their products, or are now developing one. Potential clients see lack of SQL support as a serious defect. There is also a positive incentive: SQL has the potential to open up their products to wider user bases.

Appraising SQL

- ■ Advantages
  - – Simplified applications
  - – Reduced network traffic
  - – Choice of familiar applications

- ■ Drawbacks
  - – Some find it hard to learn
  - – Slow response
  - – Limited functions

Figure 5.11   Proving the point that nothing is perfect.

In particular, SQL promotes interoperability between software products. However, SQL is not without its problems and controversies. Potential users should be aware of them. They include:

- ■ SQL is often promoted as a portable language, a universal standard that can be run on any platform. It seldom works that way:
- ■ SQL is often criticized as excessively complex, for programmers as well as users.
- ■ SQL is often perceived as too slow, compared with other database systems.
- ■ SQL is often seen as too old, and unable to handle developing ideas like graphics and object orientation.

The myth of portable SQL

SQL has been described as the Esperanto of computer languages. It is supposed to be a universal language, but few people use it that way.

The ideal for many users is portable SQL, a universal query language you can use on PCs, mainframes, Unix machines, and any other database system. In practice, it simply doesn't work that way. Strictly speaking, SQL abides by a standard published by the American National Standards Institute.

The ANSI standard is universal, but it is also limited. You will hardly ever see an SQL system that adheres strictly to the ANSI specifications. Nearly every vendor extends or alters the language to add value or fit it onto a particular platform. Even commands that look identical may behave differently in different systems.

Often, this stems from a desire to make the vendor's package more versatile than standard SQL. Some vendors add unique functions or data types, most of which work well, but tempt the programmer to write programs that won't work on another vendor's platform. Other vendors add features that let programmers fine-tune the way a query is processed to get maximum performance. More differences crop up in application programming interfaces (APIs) between SQL and application programs written in languages such as COBOL.

Other differences stem from vagueness in the ANSI standard, which does a good job of specifying the language's syntax, but is less exact in describing what the commands should do.

Limited standard

Many problems with the SQL standard stem from what is also one of its strengths: its solid grounding in mathematical theory. E. F. Codd, SQL's strong-minded inventor, insists that SQL should make relational databases completely independent and invisible. Ideally, the system should not even be aware of things like file names and network drive specifications.

While that would be theoretically ideal, working programmers do have to worry about such matters. They need to optimize their systems to make the best possible use of available resources. Most SQL applications add statements to help programmers accomplish these tasks. Many SQL databases also differ in the way they handle null, or empty, fields. These are only some ways in which different versions of SQL cause programs that work on one system to fail on another.

Other differences help SQL do things it would normally do awkwardly, if at all. Consider the company that owns a fleet of automobiles, some of which are assigned to certain key employees. You cannot use a basic join to produce a list of all automobiles and their assigned drivers. It would omit those cars that do not have assigned users, and those employees who do not have assigned automobiles. There is a function called an outer join which would do that, but it is not part of standard SQL. It is an add-on, provided by certain vendors.

The complexity factor

All these variations from the standard theme contribute to a widespread belief that SQL is too complex.

Some people find SQL to be an easy, intuitive way to describe data. Others simply don't get it. Their numbers aren't limited to untrained users. Many programmers, accustomed to issuing step-by-step instructions, run into perceptual problems with SQL's descriptive approach.

A related problem is that SQL is designed to work with sets of data. One of the cardinal rules is that it returns its data as a table. The system treats it as a table, even if it has only a single row and a single column. Most procedural languages, including the Dbase variations, work with only one record at a time. Programmers who are used to this standard need to adjust their thinking to use SQL effectively. This is particularly important in transaction processing, which normally deals with only one record at a time.

Many front-end products can help both users and programmers overcome much of the complexity. A graphical front end helps users specify the information they want to retrieve, and the program constructs the proper SQL query. More advanced forms of these same products help programmers build applications that can inherently manage the difference between record and set orientation.

The performance issue

Another SQL issue is how to define performance. IS professionals are at home with ideas like benchmarks and quick response. They tend to think that the faster the database responds, the better the system performs. That's part of the picture, but not all of it. The real standard should not be how fast the system can work, but how fast the people who use it can work.

The problem is not with the system's response, but with the definition of good performance. It's important to look at response time from the user's perspective. The proper measurement is not how long it takes the system to retrieve the information, but how long it takes the user to do the job. To be sure, some SQL databases may take two or three seconds longer to react. But they will regain those seconds many times over if an improved front-end application makes it easier and quicker for the user to complete the job. It's not system-to-screen time that counts. It's the time the user needs to complete a report, update an employee roster, or complete some other task. The user who can complete a task more quickly does not think of the system as slow. Neither should its manager. The system's response time is only a tiny slice of the whole.

6

More than Basic Data

Spreading a network across the enterprise
means managing data across the enterprise.
There's more than one way to do it.

A major feature of enterprise networking is its ability to capitalize on distributed data. You can store your data nearly anywhere you choose. When someone needs it, the system can find and deliver it. Few combinations could be more natural. Distributed data often predates an enterprise network. The network simply provides expanded access to what's already there.

This is just an extension of the basic client/server layout. A basic client/server database has one database server that works for several clients, possibly on several networks. Nevertheless, one objective of a client/server database in an enterprise network is the ability to reach databases on servers all over the organization. There's nothing to say you can't have multiple servers.

Such a system uses internetworking to create a *distributed database*. Employees can retrieve information from these dispersed databases using a distributed query. A distributed query retrieves data from more than one database server, but does so transparently to the query-maker. The distributed query may not look significantly different from a query of a single database.

Ideally, the users' access to that data should also be *transparent*. An employee who needs information should not have to know the way around a network of distributed databases. The employee should only have to identify the needed information; the system should know where to find it.

Love Stories and Horror Stories

That's the simple view of distributed data. As veterans of the process can tell you, it can quickly get much more complicated than that. There are some real horror stories out there about the problems you can create for yourself by trying to set up a distributed database system. Once you let it be known that you are considering a distributed database, there will be no shortage of experts warning you against it.

Don't underestimate the challenge of building a distributed database, but don't overestimate it either. There are also plenty of success stories, which you can emulate with a little knowledge and understanding.

Getting things into perspective

To put things into perspective, here are three statements you might hear about distributed database management:

- It's the answer to my dreams.
- It's a nightmare.
- You're dreaming. There is no such thing as a true distributed database.

The frustrating thing about remarks like this is that each, in its way, can be correct. Don't let that confuse you, though. It only means there's more than one way to distribute a database. There's also more than one way to provide a distributed database with transparent access. Different people have different ideas about what these things mean. The language of technology is not nearly as precise as its users would like it to be. The people who make these varying statements could easily be talking about three different things. Consider each in turn.

About distributed database ...

- It's the answer to our problems
- It's the problem to which we need an answer
- There is no such thing
  - *And everyone's right*

Figure 6.1   It depends on your point of view.

It's great

People who have successfully installed distributed database systems will naturally feel this way about their creations. These are usually the people who have taken a careful, well-planned approach and have not tried to stretch the technology beyond their needs.

For the Public Service Company of Colorado, setting up a distributed database is part of a five-year project. Its builders began by constructing detailed models of both the organization and its data. From there, the company moved forward, toward a program of company-wide data administration. New York Life used a prototyping approach to accomplish much the same thing. Other companies have built gateways between their database management systems and users' front-end tools. All three represent the care and caution that can lead to ultimate success.

It was a nightmare

Unfortunately, not everyone succeeds. No doubt, you'll hear about the failures, in frightening detail. There is a warning in these experiences, but it may not be the warning you expect. The message is not to shy away if a distributed system would meet your needs. You are just being warned to take the careful approach of those who have succeeded.

When you hear the inevitable stories of frustration and failure, try to identify what went wrong. You'll probably learn that the surest way to fail is to rush into a project without planning. The most important part of that planning is to examine exactly what resources you have and what kind of access you need. Your database planning should go on from there.

Another important point: it is not really hard to set up a database that will retrieve information from varied locations. The problem is putting it back. Updating the information in multiple databases can be tricky, particularly in a distributed database made of systems from multiple vendors.

It doesn't exist

You can learn from others who have faced real-life problems, even when they've failed. You can't learn much at all, though, from a small group of critics who believe that no one has successfully set up a true distributed database.

These critics are selling a point of view, not useful knowledge. What the critics usually are saying is that no one has successfully set up a "true" distributed database. That's true, as far as it goes. It does not go far enough.

The opposite of a true distributed database is not a "false" distributed database. Most distributed database designs represent compromises with the ideal. Those compromises are often necessary and desirable. The purists have important roles in developing and expanding computer technology. Planning your system is not usually one of those roles.

Distribution by Degrees

There is more than one way to distribute a database. There are two main approaches:

- The *master database* approach, in which a central database manager receives all input and processes all output. When a query calls for information from another location, the master database finds and retrieves it.

- The so-called *true distributed database,* in which a query or update goes directly to the designated site, without an intermediary.

Companies that report great success generally have installed master database systems. The purists generally have in mind the second form, and they maintain—correctly—that it's not ready yet. Meanwhile, lots of companies are enjoying success with the master database approach.

The master database approach

The Oracle system is an example of the first approach. For an Oracle database to support a distributed query, it must have a valid network

Two ways to distribute

- Master database
  - Easiest to install and administer
- True distributed database
  - Purists insist on it
  - Others say it's impossible

Figure 6.2   The easier way is also the way that's available now.

link to a second Oracle database. It must also have a special database object, called a database link, which refers both to the second database and to the network link. A distributed query first goes to a database that maintains records of the links. If the query includes a reference to the database link, the first database will generate a query to the second database, asking it for the relevant data. When the second database responds with that data, the first database then does any necessary processing and sends the result to the client system.

The client doesn't even have to know that there is a second database, or how to gain access to it. The first server also acts as a client, submitting a request for data to the second server. That fits the definition of transparent access.

True distribution

A pure distributed system would send each element of the query directly to the source, without the intermediary of a database link. By formal definition, a database is truly distributed only if it lets a single SQL statement retrieve data and make simultaneous updates on multivendor databases running on different computers, no matter where they may be. They should do this without requiring that the user know what kind of database is in use, or where it is.

These administrators hold that a true distributed database system does not yet exist. Even if it were available today, they say, you would need to take extreme care in designing and justifying such a system.

Many people are afraid of true distributed databases. That's the type most critics have in mind when they speak of the dangers of distribution. "You are talking about instantaneously joining tables from, say, New York and London," one senior database administrator protested. "Can you imagine the consequences of doing something like that?" To this administrator, concerns about performance, data integrity and, most important, security, make the proposition "mind-boggling." A colleague goes further, saying you would have to be "out of your mind" even to consider it.

There is another distinction among distributed databases. Some server products cannot use SQL to communicate between servers. These server products satisfy distributed queries using remote procedure calls (RPCs), which means that they have to precode all possible queries ahead of time. Others rely on application program interfaces (APIs) to direct SQL queries to remote databases in forms these databases will accept.

Technical shortcomings

The proponents of true distribution are not just citing technicalities. In comparison, they point out, the master database approach has shortcomings like these:

The ideal distributed database

- Two-phase commit
- Excellent communication
- Low maintenance cost
- Consistency
- High performance

Figure 6.3   But do you really need all this?

- *Failing to accommodate the two-phase commit.*   Few vendors of multilocation database products have provided this form of data integrity protection.

- *Inadequate communication between databases.*   Available technology can easily fall short of holding the vast amount of data some organizations want to exchange.

- *Lack of management tools.*   Though these are being developed, the job is not yet finished.

- *High maintenance expense.*   A dozen different database servers in a dozen different states would require a dozen different administrators. Though products are available to monitor databases and networks, few if any work well in a multivendor client/server environment.

- *Lack of consistency.*   Systems from multiple vendors do not yet work smoothly together. At least for now, demand for openness and inter-operability exceeds the supply. This will be self-correcting over time, but it will take time.

- *Inadequate processing speed.*   As faster systems arrive, this will cease to be a problem, but again it has not happened yet.

The real issue

The most important point is not whether a distributed database meets a strict definition, but whether it works like a distributed database. How the system does this is an important consideration, but not the most important.

Some installations simply look and feel like distributed databases. In St. Louis, the Southwestern Bell Telephone Company has workstations tied to a fault-tolerant Tandem Nonstop computer, running Tandem's relational database system, Nonstop SQL. The Tandem computer, in turn, can connect with databases on IBM and Unisys computers in St. Louis, Oklahoma City, Dallas, and Houston.

Customer service and sales representatives can gain access to these databases without having to know which database they are using. The utility considers this a vast improvement over the previous system, which required that the employees use multiple terminals and manual techniques.

This system provides access only through the Tandem database. Operators cannot directly contact the other databases. On the other hand, there is this to be said for that system: it works.

Assessing Your Needs

The more widely you distribute your data, the more flexible you can be in providing access, but the more daunting your planning and management tasks. Assess your needs from distributed data, and plan a system to meet those needs. Start the assessment by answering these key questions:

- What kind of database systems have you inherited?
- Are there databases, either current or planned, that will need high degrees of security or reliability?
- Where is the most logical place to locate various data collections?

Dealing with the legacy

Unless you are designing a brand new system for a brand new organization, you will inherit some existing databases. These are the so-called legacy applications, left over from an earlier day of more limited networking.

When most people think of legacy applications, they think of mainframe-based applications, particularly databases, that may have to be modified or rewritten to function in a client/server world. For each, the question is whether to invest the time and expense needed to convert them.

Often, the answer is no. You can leave many older databases on their large systems, which become servers instead of hosts. You can make better use of your resources by linking networks and creating graphic front ends. The legacy application can simply stay where you found it. Concentrate on making its data more accessible to more members of the organization.

This isn't the only kind of legacy. When you incorporate several departments into an enterprise network, you are also likely to incorporate the smaller databases that run on individual PCs or LAN servers. Converting these applications usually isn't a great problem. Generally, they're in a dialect of Dbase or another familiar standard. More important, they also contain data that others in the organization might use. Also, they are scattered all over the place. These far-flung applications already make up a distributed database. You find yourself with a distributed system from the outset. This means you start with less than a clean slate. You are modifying an existing system, not starting a brand new one.

Security and integrity

Clearly, it is easier to secure a database in a single, central location than one whose elements are scattered all over the place. For a different reason, it is also easier to maintain the accuracy and integrity of your data.

Consider the employee who makes a sale and records it on a networked PC. Depending on how you record your sales data, this transaction can involve at least three major elements:

- A new transaction with the customer
- An addition of cash
- Removal of the sold item from inventory

Each element can be the subject of a different database:

- Customer records on the employee's local area network
- Financial records kept in the accounting department
- Inventory records maintained at a regional warehouse

One stormy day, the employee records the sale on the local PC. The distributed database management system sends word to the accounting and inventory databases. A stroke of lightning interrupts communication with the regional warehouse just as the system is trying to transmit the sales record. The inventory record is never updated. A few days later, another sales rep, unaware that the inventory records are inaccurate, makes a promise to a major customer that the company cannot keep.

The two-phase commit was designed for situations like this. Ideally, the system should poll the three databases and make sure each is ready to receive the transaction data. It will commit the new data to the record only if it can do so to all three databases at once.

This is hard to do when you have a distributed database from multiple vendors. A few products probably can do it, but you can do it much more easily and reliably if you maintain a single database. It might have multiple tables that also require simultaneous updates, but it's infinitely easier to do this if they all are in one place.

The Case for Distributed Databases

A centralized database may be the safest and easiest way to manage access to the enterprise's data, but it may not be the practical way. Sometimes, you should maintain database resources in different locations for very good reasons. One important reason is that a distributed database can save long-distance communication costs.

Consider the common case of a network of branch sales offices. The day-to-day work of recording and using these offices' sales data takes place at each office. Of course, from time to time, central management needs to retrieve this data to compile rollup sales reports, but this is not an everyday task. It makes sense for each office to have a local data resource. Branch office staff members can have access to their own data without running up communication charges over a wide area network. Even when headquarters needs to retrieve information, it often needs only a summary, not the entire body of raw data. You don't incur large or frequent long distance communication charges.

Another use for a distributed database is to link data that already is distributed. Perhaps those branch offices already maintain on-site databases. Distributed technology can help you gain more widespread access to this body of valuable information.

Extending client/server

A great advantage of a distributed database is that it extends the client/server principle. One element of the system can take on specialized job and do it very well. Instead of a single database server handling data from all parts of the organization, a distributed system lets a single server specialize in a single subject. More important for many users, separating database duties creates smaller bodies of data. These smaller databases require less costly server platforms. You can use these inexpensive platforms to set up databases in offices all over the country.

Even the most powerful platforms sometimes are not adequate to handle the quantity of data, or the transaction volume, of a large corporate database. This problem can arise even when the database remains on a mainframe or midrange system. When that occurs, most organizations first try a limited form of distribution. They split their databases, so it is only rarely necessary to work with more than one database.

Reasons to distribute data

- Link remote
  branches
- Use data that is
  already distributed
- Split up the server
  workload
- Coordinate activities
  at multiple sites

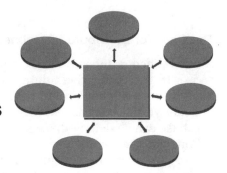

Figure 6.4   There can be some problems, but distributed data can often meet a need.

The organization's needs

Some organizations need more sophisticated distribution systems. For example, a company may ship goods from several regional warehouses. Each has a local computer with databases to manage that warehouse's inventory and operations. If large numbers of transactions involve more than one warehouse, the company could link the databases at individual sites into a distributed system. Ideally, this system should appear to the user as a single database. A query of the distributed system will retrieve the requested data wherever it might be, and will present it in standard form: as a single table that holds the results.

The Case for Playing It Safe

There is one major and enduring theory of distributing databases: it is best not to distribute them at all. Like any kind of technology, a distributed database has a mixed collection of advantages and drawbacks. Whether your database is distributed or centralized, your object is the same: to increase the availability of information to people who can make profitable use of it. One legitimate way to achieve this goal is to accumulate all the organization's database assets on a single server. There, it should be available to all authorized clients.

That's the safety-first approach. Among its adherents are consultants and columnists Martin Butler and Robin Bloor. They offer this "prime rule for distributing data:" do it only to improve performance. Usually, they say, "it is far better to have a single database that services all the applications an organization runs."

That point of view is worthy of respect, particularly in two situations:

- When you don't really need distributed data
- When your needs for security and integrity are so great you cannot afford to take a chance

Resist temptation

It's easy to become intrigued by the idea of parceling out central data to multiple sites. You can readily convince yourself you need a distributed database when you really don't. Make this important reality check: figure out whether the advantages of distribution overcome the costs and difficulties of maintaining such a system. You may have second thoughts.

You do not always need a distributed database to establish open access. You can store data as a single shared resource instead of in scattered files. Employees are still free to retrieve this data using a variety of front-end tools.

Long leap

The jump from a single server-based database to multiple databases, even on the same server, is a long one across a deep chasm. The problem that will probably appear first is that of incompatible databases. The techniques for gaining access to client/server databases vary from vendor to vendor.

Reality check

- Make this comparison:
  - The advantages you hope to gain
  - The problems you expect to encounter
- *The balance may favor a central data resource.*

Figure 6.5 Sometimes the low-tech solution works best.

Distributed database problems

- Incompatible software
- Difficult administration
- Lack of network management tools

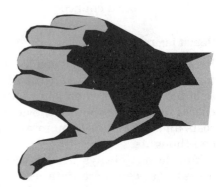

Figure 6.6   Make sure the benefits of a multivendor distributed database are worth it.

The vendors even disagree on exactly what distributed processing is. Nearly all provide ways to read and update remote databases. This facility can be limited, though; you probably can work with only one database at a time in any given transaction. This is the most basic form of client/server access. It provides for quick response from dedicated servers, and you can put the results to use in windowed environments on workstation PCs.

The process becomes more complicated when a second or third database becomes involved. For example, one database might include a table of customer data, with the customers identified by standard codes. Another, on a different server, might include a table of shipments, including the codes of the customers to whom they are sent. To retrieve a list of shipments to a particular customer, you must look up the customer code in one table. Then, you must query the second table for a list of shipments identified with that customer's code. Though most of the widely used back-end database products would perform this operation, not all will do so. Those that do may use different, incompatible methods. You may easily find yourself with three different databases on three different, incompatible systems.

A remote database operation is much, much easier when every database uses the same system. When that is impractical, at least make sure the varied systems are compatible.

Army of administrators

Another advantage of the single-database approach is that it is easier to administer. Perhaps the biggest issue in distributed computing is how to manange such an environment. If your organization has to dedicate an army of administrators to take care of the system, you could lose all the cost and productivity benefits you were trying to achieve in the first place.

There is plenty of management work to do: copying, backing up, and recovering the shared databases and client software, most likely on a multitude of servers. One solution is to automate the process, using network management software tools. Unfortunately, that solution creates a problem of its own: adequate tools for this purpose are only beginning to appear. A distributed database also may lack the performance to which you have become accustomed from your present system.

Matching Systems to Needs

Companies and industries vary, of course, but information-using organizations have one big thing in common: they need to get the right information to the right people at the right time. Few ideas could be simpler to express or harder to execute.

For example, Van den Berg Foods (Lisle, Illinois) has built an information system that lets managers take daily measurements of how effective their pricing, advertising, and distribution tactics are. They get their information from 35 separate databases running on 11 different servers, but to them it appears as a single information source on their screens.

In many ways, this is an ideal distributed database system. A manager in suburban Chicago can call for a quick update on product sales data from regional distribution centers around the country. The data may come from databases at each of the regional centers, yet it transparently appears on the manager's screen as though it were coming from a single source.

In many ways this is also less than an ideal system. The transparent access to distributed data comes at the price of flexibility, performance, functionality, and cost. Even a user on Van den Berg's level of sophistication finds that a fully functional, well-integrated distributed database is still more a future accomplishment than a present one. In their present form, distributed databases have three sources of conflict:

- You must cope with variations among vendors. A typical system might have databases from Oracle, Sybase, and IBM running on different platforms and networks in separate locations.

- Not only do the products differ, but people often use them differently. One major obstacle is variations in logical design. Different departments use different database designs. A common stumbling block is the use of different numbering schemes to identify customers or vendors.

■ Then there is the classic conflict between access and security. The more open the access, the greater the risk. Yet without access, the data can become useless.

To serve an enterprise network, a database must do many things. Among them:

■ Provide appropriate access to databases in multiple locations and environments.
■ Allow the interaction of databases from multiple vendors to sort, filter, update, and report data.
■ Grant management the power to assign types of access, such as update or read-only, to individual employees. The database design should not foreclose these choices.
■ Grant simultaneous access to multiple databases.
■ Also grant concurrent access to multiple users.
■ Support multiple APIs, network protocols, and multiple access schemes.

Customer service?

There's another source of conflict, too. The products customers need aren't necessarily the products they can get from vendors. The two basic forms of distributed data support two basic approaches to distributed access; neither is fully satisfactory to its users:

■ *Remote data access.* Here, the emphasis is on giving users easy access to information. This approach emphasizes graphical user interfaces which let users build queries using point-and-click methods. Executive information systems use this model.
■ *The distributed database.* This approach is centered on the back end: the relational database management system (RDBMS). The aim here is to establish relational databases as stable platforms from which to retrieve data from foreign databases.

Standing alone, neither is a totally satisfactory answer. Front-end data access tools are weak in navigating the unexpected twists and turns they may encounter among the back-end products. Distributed RDBMS systems are often proprietary, relying on a single vendor's product package, when you really need access to databases from diverse sources.

These two approaches are hardly exclusive. You could adopt remote data access as a front-end technique and use a distributed RDBMS for back-end management. Even a dual system might not be a fully satisfactory answer, though, because the technology easily can still fall short of the organization's demands and expectations.

Meeting the Demand

No doubt, the supply of distributed database management systems will soon increase. The demand is certainly present. The impetus for database interoperability today comes not from technicians, but from managers. These people have become accustomed to workstations and powerful PCs. They have expressed their desire—in fact their need—for greater access to information. This has put them into territory that was formerly claimed exclusively by MIS. Many MIS professionals have naturally resisted.

Meanwhile, the users are unwilling to accept MIS as a squad of rent-a-cops, barring access to the vast repository of corporate data. The organization needs that information, which means its members need that information.

Supplying the supply

Vendors' responses to this demand have come in three main forms:

- Database gateways
- Database drivers
- SQL routing software

These approaches appear in several forms:

- PC front ends with database APIs
- Relational databases using conventional gateways
- Open gateways
- Data encapsulation software

Front-end products

Since it is the most visible part of the system, the front end has naturally attracted most of the attention. Several front-end APIs have reached the market, including:

- Open Database Connectivity (ODBC)
- Call Level Interface, developed by the SQL Action Group (SAG)
- Open Database Application Programming Interface (ODAPI)
- Distributed Relational Database Architecture (DRDA)

These technologies offer ways to use a variety of back-end data sources in a consistent way. Few of them address further issues like setting up and managing communication sessions between PC users and back-end data sources. None of them include the means to coordinate the operations of multiple databases or to optimize queries, either. You will need products from other vendors to add these functions to the array. What the API does provide is a standard means of access, which lets developers working on PCs and workstations reach multiple databases.

The old way

The newer API products are replacing early technology that relied on propriety APIs and libraries. These older-generation products place a library of routines on the workstation. The user can invoke these from within an application to gain access to the back-end data. The library accepts the user's SQL statements and sends them to a driver for the target database. The driver does several things. It maps the user's terminology to that of the database. It also processes function calls and validates the input. A final task, if necessary, is to translate the SQL calls to match the server's dialect of that supposedly universal language. This translated query is sent over the network to the database. The process is reversed to deliver the returning information to the user.

Variation on the theme

The newer API technology follows a similar pattern. The main difference is that the older technology used proprietary calls to different databases; the newer method relies on a standard set of calls. The database API provides these for application developers, who can tailor their SQL statements to match.

That does leave the front end at the mercy of the back. Vendors of back-end products must set up the necessary drivers to respond to the APIs. Some may choose only to support a subset of the full API functions. That means your front-end product may try to offer features the back end is not prepared to support. Another possible limitation, which some database vendors have been working on, is interfaces that function only with their own versions of SQL.

Multiple approaches

ODBC is Microsoft's approach to the problem; it is a version of the SQL Access Group's call-level interface. A major difference: SAG uses the International Standard Organization's RDA protocol to support its APIs. Microsoft has written its own protocol, which is designed to be smaller and less demanding of processor resources.

ODAPI is a Borland effort, and it is expected to acknowledge the RDA standard. Borland and Microsoft also differ in the roles they assign to SQL. Under ODBC, SQL is the only way to retrieve information from the database. Calls that arrive in some other form are translated to SQL, even if they are intended for non-SQL databases. Under ODAPI, SQL is only one possibility. The Borland system supports both SQL calls to the client/server database and native-language calls to other databases, particularly including Borland's own PC products.

IBM, meanwhile, has gone its own way with DRDA. DRDA is not a front-end product; it is an application-level protocol for sending SQL instructions to remote databases. It is possible to implement several APIs along with DRDA.

Among relational database vendors, the strongest support has appeared to go to ODBC, a Microsoft product closely identified with the burgeoning success of Windows. It is also possible to map an ODBC API to DRDA.

New Kinds of Gateways

Front-end APIs represent a developing new technology; conventional gateways are a development of an older technology. Gateways for relational DBMSs were originally designed to help users migrate from older database systems, such as hierarchical and flat-file systems, to relational DBMSs. The early versions were strictly proprietary. Each relational DBMS vendor developed a gateway to encourage users to consolidate their data on the vendor's relational platform.

More recently, gateways have become an important platform for database interoperability. A proprietary interest is still quite visible. The new relational DBMS/gateway architecture consists of a vendor's distributed relational DBMS and an associated package of connectivity and gateway software. This is the basic form of master database architecture, in which a DBMS server plays the role of a broker. It stores information about remote databases—both its own and those stored in foreign servers—and manages the distribution of queries and updates to them. Though the broker DBMS is a single-vendor product, the distributed database operations usually take place over a layer of connectivity software that is portable over varied protocols from different vendors.

The gateway's job

The gateway's task is to translate information about the distributed database's resources into the host database's format. Its function is similar to a database driver, but it relies on the host database that runs on a server, not on a separate library installed on client systems.

This approach has many advantages you'd expect from a system that bears the label *conventional:*

- It is a stable, transparent type of platform.
- Developers who are familiar with the host database's dialect of SQL can gain access to distributed databases from other vendors, without having to learn the other systems' variations.

There are, as usual, some tradeoffs:

- Though conventional gateways offer access to diverse resources, the initial contact is over a proprietary system.
- These systems often limit themselves to conventional SQL, denying you the enhancements that might otherwise be available from the remote database systems.
- A query passes through multiple steps, and each requires a duplicate set of data. This cuts down speed and increases the demand on resources.
- Some database vendors—though a small and diminishing number—offer only limited support of other vendors' products through their host systems. All provide access to the major IBM and Digital Equipment Corp. databases, but they have been reluctant to give access to the databases of their more direct competitors.
- Gateway software is not a high-income type of merchandise for a vendor that gains most of its revenues from database management products. The features they support tend to lag behind those available from the database products themselves.

The unconventional gateway

A flexible variation on the gateway approach is the open gateway. It tries to combine the strengths of the front-end approach and the conventional gateway. Unlike many such efforts, it generally manages to avoid combining the drawbacks as well.

Its main difference from the conventional gateway: instead of being a proprietary, vendor-centered system, it takes on the role of a neutral third party. It is an independent, nonpartisan broker of transactions between diverse databases.

An open gateway consists of a central dictionary and gateway software that provides a link between front-end clients and back-end data sources. It generally offers all the functions you need to establish transparent connections between clients and multiple servers, and to route queries to the proper sources. You can set up your own interoperability software, independently of the DBMS system. This means you are free to set up a variety of database servers. You can add even more later.

Most open gateways also provide APIs with which to build applications, and even new gateways. These might give you access to new and developing types of database operations, such as document image management.

It sounds ideal. It's not, of course. This technology may grant access to multiple databases, but only to those which support it. Since this is new technology, early support was limited to only a few of the major database vendors. Also, since this is new technology, that picture has been changing.

The Software Connection

If you're looking only for basic transportation of your data, connectivity software might do the job. This is a single-purpose type of product designed to maintain connections between applications and databases. Such a product can take SQL statements from the client and deliver them to the proper database, using the proper networking protocol to get there.

Often, these products tend to focus on particular databases, or on particular networking protocols. The typical installation gives one type of client access to one type of database. If you need more functions, or more versatility, you will have to supplement the software with other products.

Database in a Nutshell

Naturally, the approach that many find most promising is just that—a promise. Database encapsulation uses object-oriented techniques not just to connect clients with multiple databases, but also to fuse them into a single entity. Remote databases are encapsulated, using special software modules that present their functions to the clients. The clients can use the remote databases simply by selecting the proper functions.

This is about as close as you can come to complete, transparent data access. You can enjoy functional literacy in a variety of database dialects. Whatever the remote database, you can read, write, update, retrieve, and do other useful things. Encapsulation effectively isolates the database structure from the client.

Object orientation

Encapsulation uses an object-oriented approach which treats the interface modules as objects. If you select a module for a particular function, that module includes the instructions necessary to retrieve the proper database resources. This built-in logic can also allow for the differences among target files.

You've got to carry that load

Encapsulation also has its drawbacks. The greatest is that it is still a new, developing technology. There are a couple of others:

- There is a heavy demand on client resources. Managing the session, interpreting queries, and assembling the result sets are all done at the client; in other systems, these are usually server functions.

- Not everyone is familiar with it. The object orientation, in particular, can be a major conceptual hurdle for developers trained in more conventional programming techniques.

Transparent Data: Clear as Mud

The distributed database and data transparency are not the same thing, but they do go together. Behind the goal of a fully distributed database is the objective of transparent access. An employee who needs to retrieve a particular piece of data should simply issue a request to the system. Wherever it might be stored, the system will look it up. The system, not the employee, is responsible for knowing where to find the requested information. Ideally, not even the application software should have to account for the data's location.

Like the distributed database, there is more than one kind of data transparency, and more than one way to achieve it. The ultimate form of transparency is full location transparency. The database can manage the routing of queries and updates. It can also recover from the failure of any node. This degree of transparency isn't always necessary, or even a good idea. There are other forms of data transparency, including the OLE/DDE combination in Windows, that may serve your needs better.

Transparent data access

- More than one kind
- More than one way to achieve it
- You may not need it

Figure 6.7 Distributed data and transparent access have much in common.

The first part is easy

It is easy to define the network structure and the physical location of databases, and to do it within the system. This does a great deal to conceal the pathfinding process from individuals and their application programs. If a system was fully transparent, it would also reorganize data when necessary, and perhaps even alter the network itself, without having to involve the client side of the system.

Standards, such as Network File System (NFS) from Sun Microsystems, the Distributed Computing Environment (DCE) from the Open Software Foundation and IBM's Systems Network Architecture Advanced-Peer-to-Peer Communications LU 6.2 are now in place. These standards let application programmers pour data from its current location to wherever it is needed. NFS, in particular, originated in Unix, but now runs in many environments. It could become the foundation on which to build transparent access.

These systems offer access to files on systems with different architectures, but that's only an entry-level requirement for data transparency on distributed databases. They fall short of meeting the rest of the requirement: that you can use data without worrying about where it is located or in what format it's stored.

Simpler forms of sharing

That isn't the only possible type of data transparency. You can exchange data on any of several levels, among applications and across networks. Included are these familiar examples:

- Data exchange among *like applications,* including similar applications running under different operating systems.

- The ability to *cut and paste,* such as the Windows clipboard.

- *Dynamic data exchange* and *object linking and embedding* (DDE and OLE), both Windows features that someday could escape the confines of single-user DOS.

All in the family

A simple kind of data transparency is the ability to exchange data between different versions of the same software. For example, someone using a DOS version of 1-2-3 can readily retrieve data produced by 1-2-3 operating under Unix or on a mainframe. This type of activity has some value, but it stops far short of the currently recognized need. The restricted scope of these cross-platform applications limits their usefulness. For instance, while you can gather information from a Dbase system on a Unix-based host while you're using Dbase on a DOS system, this capability doesn't do you much good if most of the data you need is in an Oracle database.

Local transparency under Windows

Another form of transparency—though it's not always recognized as such—is the ability to cut and paste between applications. This has become a staple of the DOS environment, particularly when supplemented with Windows. The process is crude, but it's sometimes effective.

Windows' dynamic data exchange goes further, but it too falls short of providing the easy data access needed over diverse networks. One problem with DDE is that you can use it only between true Windows applications; DOS applications cannot participate. More critically, DDE is not really about data transparency. It is simply an interprocess message protocol.

In a way, DDE is similar to the transport and session layers of the Open Systems Interconnection (OSI) networking model: it establishes connections between processes, but it does not concern itself with how the data is represented or encoded. Making sense of the data sent is the responsibility of the sending and receiving applications. Thus, while you can achieve data "transparency" with DDE, you can only do it if you program each application to recognize the other applications' data formats. DDE simply masks the complexity of moving data from one application to another. It is not a data-transparency solution itself.

The next step

Object linking and embedding goes a step further and illustrates some possibilities of full data transparency. OLE associates the data with the application that created it in the first place. More specifically, in OLE, if you took an illustration made in Corel Draw and imported it to a Ventura Publisher document, you could still modify it from Corel with all that program's graphic tools. You wouldn't have to invoke Corel. Pointers associated with the illustration notify OLE-aware applications of what you're trying to do. While you see the illustration in Ventura, physically it remains a Corel file. All you are working with in Ventura is a hot link to the illustration and its application.

Objects and containers

OLE manages data by dividing information into two parts: objects and containers. Objects are instances of a user-defined class that holds data, its structure, and the actions that programs can take using the data.

To manipulate and link objects to applications, OLE uses containers as the controls for objects. The application you are using doesn't have to worry about the exact properties of an object imported from another program. To use OLE, all the application, or its programmer, needs to know is how to use the container. If the container's simple controls aren't sufficient for the job, OLE calls the object's original application to do the work. This is a preview of the full capacity of transparent data systems, and it shows how they can be made to work.

OLE has a few problems. It relies on the precarious structure of DDE to support data communications. Of more immediate concern, it's not easy to transport documents made from OLE objects. In the previous example, if you move the Ventura document to a system without Corel Draw, the illustration would vanish.

Distributed object management

On another level—one that directly involves enterprise networks—Sun and Hewlett Packard have been working on a Distributed Object Management Facility (DOMF) that builds on established networking standards. DOMF is designed to serve as an object request broker (ORB) on a network. Whenever an application manipulates an object, DOMF will not only locate the object, but also ensure that the requested operations take place while maintaining the object's original format. For instance, if you wanted to modify an object, say an Excel spreadsheet under OS/2, from an Ingres database manager under Unix, you would simply make the change. DOMF would take care of the details.

Digital Equipment's Application Control Architecture (ACA) represents a competing approach. Instead of DOMF's object-handling approach, ACA manages data by converting it all to DEC's Digital Data Interchange Format. Like DOMF, ACA provides an object-oriented command, control, and communications solution to the problem of data transparency.

In other respects, though, the two approaches are much different. You can think of DOMF as an object manager of object systems. You add applications and objects to one of its networks with a class-definition language similar to C++. ACA, on the other hand, provides dynamic real-time binding for objects with its runtime API.

This isn't clearly better than the more static Sun/HP approach that requires you to explicitly label every object. DEC's approach requires a preprocessor for each particular architecture on a network that connects new objects to the API. By providing hooks for new object models and managers, the Sun/HP ORB makes it easier to maintain object-data integrity while still allowing inter-application operation. ACA can achieve the same result, but it requires more effort.

Beware of Hiding Too Much

Most forms of data transparency have a single objective: the user need not worry about all the messy details. There's a little-recognized danger, though, that in trying to protect the user from an application's nitty-gritty details, you will protect the user too much.

There are two good ways to use transparent data access:

- To find resources, without requiring that the user know exactly where to look for them.

- To exchange data, without requiring that the user understand all the details of how the exchange is made.

These make the employee's job easier. Stop there. It does not follow that more you hide the easier the application is to use. It's possible to hide too much.

Total transparency inadvertently perpetuates the mistaken image of the user as a mindless drone. Today's users are sophisticated knowledge workers. You must do more than just feed them information on demand. They manipulate and evaluate information. They even need information about their information. Often, knowing the source of information plays a big part in assessing its value and credibility.

Suppose the figures on a manager's EIS display a sharp dip in customer service ratings in the Southeast. The figures in question were rolled up from branch-office databases in Atlanta, Tampa, and New Orleans. But from which office did they come? A programmer who goes overboard on data transparency could readily hide this vital information.

The important distinction is this:

- Conceal *pathfinder* information with which the system finds and processes information. Normally, the user does not need to be a direct witness to this process.

- Make available *source* information with which a user can identify the information's origins.

People and technology

This is another example of how the organization's use of technology is closely linked with its people and the way they work. In a distributed environment, the employee initiates a transaction on one node of the network. The transaction then flows to other nodes scattered around the network.

The system must closely regulate this traffic. When one node executes its part of the application, the request will travel automatically to the next node. If this process takes more than a few seconds, the system should send regular progress reports back to the employee. These are necessary for two reasons:

- They help keep the employee up to date on the progress of the transaction. A good employee can use this information to serve customers better and to spot problems, so they can be solved early.

What's wrong with this picture?

- The data is available
  - And the display is gorgeous
- But the employee is kept in the dark

Figure 6.8 Truly transparent data may actually be a disservice to employees.

- They help network managers to debug applications and find the sources of problems. The more information the system provides to troubleshooters, the easier it is to shoot the trouble.

Picking a Platform

In theory, SQL is supposed to provide a universal language that allows any client to talk to any database server. In practice, it hardly ever works that way. Hardly any vendor limits itself to the standard version of SQL. The recognized standard is a limited one, and virtually every vendor has added enhancements to expand the feature list of its product.

SQL has brought a large measure of standardization to database management, but it has not become a universal tongue. This means that when you choose software, you must make sure that the front end and the back end will talk with each other. If some day you decide to install a new client or server, you will again have to make sure that everything matches up. It often means you must buy all your products from the same vendor. It's a basic law of economics that when a customer's options are limited, the price goes up.

Even less-than-expected savings are still savings. That's why PC LANs have been so popular as client/server platforms. For some users, though, the LAN is a way station en route to an upsized system, most likely a Unix server. Database servers are now available on a variety of platforms, three of which are the most important:

- *Novell Netware.* This option gains its importance, of course, for its wide use in local area networks. Several database servers now can run as Netware Loadable Modules (NLMs).

- *OS/2.*   As a back-end operating system for a database server, OS/2 offers low cost and reliability for small networks.
- *Unix.*   This system offers symmetric multiprocessing and other features that make it a sound choice for larger networks.

What to look for

The anticipated size of your network is one clear basis for a choice. Still, deciding among options is not a single-factor decision. There are several other considerations. What's more, these interact with each other and with the operating system and hardware platform. Among the most important questions are:

- *Performance.*   Most client/server databases handle two types of operations: on-line transaction processing (OLTP) and decision support. OLTP generates intensive levels of activity, recording sales, checking prices, and adjusting inventory records. Decision support is a more deliberative type of activity, involving perhaps one or two queries of the database. Good OLTP performance is the ability to handle multiple transactions with dispatch; good decision support performance is a timely response to a query. Check the system's performance in the areas that represent your present and anticipated activities.

Selection factors

- Performance
  - Transaction processing
  - Decision support
- Connectivity
- Protection
- Scalability

Figure 6.9   Making a choice is more than a one-factor decision.

- *Connectivity.*   This is the ability to work with a variety of users and systems. This usually requires standardizing on a single protocol. Options include Novell's IPX/SPX, TCP/IP, generally associated with Unix, and the Named Pipes of OS/2. The Novell Requester gives Netware the ability to use Named Pipes.

- *Integrity protection.*   The operating system can greatly affect how well the database management system can keep your data safe and accurate. For example, an operating system that prevents unwanted writes to code or data memory areas adds a strong measure of data protection.

- *Scalability.*   This is the ability to grow as your network expands. Netware and Unix will accommodate large amounts of memory. OS/2 and Unix adapt to virtual memory through disk swapping. Some versions of Unix can deal with multiple processors. All these are ways to provide additional resources for your database as it grows and demand increases.

Choosing your master

In nearly all currently implemented forms of distributed database management, a query goes first to a single master database. That database then acts as a client. It passes queries to the other database and retrieves the results. This question then arises: how do you choose this master database? The answer could mean the difference between peak performance and perpetual logjams.

Some SQL systems include routines to optimize this choice. If the query is to retrieve a customer's name from one database and a list of 500 shipments from another, it makes sense to send the query first to the customer record database. They then can send a single item, the customer's identification code, to the secondary database, from which it retrieves the 500 shipment records. The system then forwards the package of information to the client.

The key here is that those 500 shipment records make only one transit of the network. Should the query retrieve the shipment data first, it would then have to collect those 500 records, send them to the customer-record file, then forward the results to the client. In either case, one set of data will have to cross the network twice, from the secondary database to the primary, and then to the client. In the first instance, only the single customer record must make the trip twice; in the second, it would be all the shipment records.

Disaster preparedness

Updating can present even more serious problems. A distributed query that fails at least will leave the database intact. An update operation that fails can corrupt the data.

The two-phase commit is intended for purposes like these. It's not intended for every case, though. This is a difficult feature to create and maintain. That makes it a feature you should consider only if you have a real need.

Avoiding the embrace

There is also the increased danger of a global deadlock. A deadlock occurs when two users fall into unwitting competition for the same resources. An operator in San Francisco tries to record a sale from the Atlanta warehouse to a California customer. When this system issues the update command, it locks the San Francisco customer record for its exclusive use. Then it tries to do the same with the shipment records in Atlanta. Meanwhile, an operator in Atlanta is similarly trying to record a sale from that site's inventory to another California customer. The Atlanta system locks its inventory record, then tries to do the same with the California customer file. The result: each user has placed an exclusive claim on data the other needs to complete the transactions. The result is a deadlock; early database programmers called it a deadly embrace. This can be a serious problem when all the contested data is on the same server. When it reaches across the nation, it can paralyze the entire network. Most systems have the means to detect a deadlock and to get the competing parties to back off and try again. Even so, it can keep anything else from happening until the situation is cleared up.

Coping with mixed media

You may be in a position where the issue of pure and impure databases takes second place to this fact: your staff wants universal access to the systems and databases of various departments within the organization. Like your counterparts in many other companies, you want to respond to this demand, although all the pieces to build a fully distributed system might not be available.

The IS staff at Amoco Production Co., Tulsa, Oklahoma, has taken a do-it-yourself approach. Since no software suppliers offered products that met their needs for a distributed system, Amoco developed its own. These are stopgap applications, until vendors supply commercial products that meet the need. That supply has been slow to develop.

When organizations like Amoco move to a client/server environment, they immediately confront the issue of how to share diverse resources. They must address the traditional problems of sharing data over distributed databases. PC networks often enter the picture. When they do, there are additional problems, such as dealing with network operating systems, LAN protocols and conflicting applications. While client/server application designers still have to wrestle with traditional problems of heterogeneous data access, they also have a whole set of new problems to tackle.

The staff members who must deal with these problems find themselves developing a new specialty: learning new technology and finding out what it can and cannot do. These grass-roots specialists need to know more than the operating details of individual software packages. They also need to understand how various technologies work together. Can you use one software package when some users are running Windows and others are using OS/2? Can Unix users tap into a database stored on a server running OS/2? What if users on a Token Ring network using Netware want to use data that is stored on an Ethernet network using LAN Manager? The answers to these questions vary depending on the software mix.

What it takes to clear the barrier

There are three main technical features that go into a fully distributed database:

- *Optimization.*   This is the art of processing a query the most quickly and efficiently possible. Optimization shortcomings can cut the performance of even the most powerful system. Optimization reflects the degree to which the system can identify and use the most efficient way of doing things.

    Consider the earlier example of a query which looks up the name of a customer in one database, then looks up all that customer's recent transactions from a database in another city. If there is only one customer, but several hundred transactions, you could send one record across the network, or you could send hundreds. The system should process this query in a way that creates the least amount of traffic. It needs help, too. If you set up databases without regard to the amounts of traffic they generate, even the best query optimization system may not help you.

- *Data replication.*   This really refers to the management of duplicate data. Well-managed data replication can help avoid optimization problems. Unplanned replication can lead to integrity problems, particularly if all the duplicate copies are not regularly updated. Sometimes, though, maintaining some duplicate data on a local system can significantly reduce network traffic. The data you maintain locally, of course, should be information that is in high demand. It is also vital that when you establish such a replicated database, you also create a reliable way to keep it up to date. Designate one database as the central repository. Regularly update the satellite databases from the central file, according to an established schedule. Strictly control any updates that might travel in the opposite direction. Limit the updates to changed information, so you are not periodically sending an entire database across the network.

- *Distributed updates.*   This includes use of the two-phase commit to ensure data integrity. A leading threat to data integrity is the update that involves multiple databases, but is cut off before it can complete the job. That could leave serious mismatches between the affected files, and it's exactly what the two-stage commit is intended to prevent. Several database products now have that capacity, but these present another danger: that you'll rely on them too much and assume all your distributed database problems have been solved. Systems that cover multiple nodes are still vulnerable to the failure of any one node, and distributed transactions are usually slower than those which involve only local data.

The best way to avoid the perils of distributed databases is to avoid distributed databases. That isn't always practical, though, as modern organizations increasingly depend on widespread access to information. Furthermore, the people who make up these organizations simply want to look up their information and get on with their jobs. What they need, in short, is transparency.

Another definition problem

Again, there is a problem of definition. The idea of sharing data in a client/server environment means different things to different people. To some, it simply means that data contained in a PC database like Dbase, originally used by one person or application, is now being shared by several users or applications. To others, sharing data in a client/server environment means that one client process can share or manipulate data from several different server databases.

The major PC databases, originally built for single users, can now reside on servers and can serve multiple users. It's still rare to see one application sharing data from two different servers. Going from one database to another is not easy.

Is Unix any easier?

Unix was written to support multiple users, so it presents fewer of these problems than do PC networks. Many server databases like SQL Server, Oracle, Informix, and Ingres operate under Unix. Unix provides a uniform environment, because protocols like TCP/IP and remote procedure calls (RPCs) are so widespread under Unix. The widespread use of TCP/IP and common RPC mechanisms in the Unix world means programmers do not have to be too concerned with how a request is going to get the server.

What's being done?

Vendors aren't ignoring the problem. A major thrust of distributed database development work is to provide easier access to remote databases. Each vendor usually does so, however, in a different way. For example, there are varied versions of SQL, particularly in the DOS-Windows-OS/2 world. This requires that the SQL statements for each database be incorporated in the program in different way. There are two main approaches:

- *Embedded SQL.* The SQL code is incorporated into that of the programming language. The program must be processed with a precompiler that compiles the SQL code separately.
- *Application Programming Interface calls.* This type of system makes calls to a library of APIs. Instead of mixing the actual SQL statements in with COBOL or C code, there would be a CALL to an SQL routine. An END SQL statement would stop the SQL activity.

The two approaches are radically different, and they are not compatible in any way.

Other coordination issues

Enterprise networking is characterized by diversity, not uniformity. More problems lurk, and all have something to do with getting multiple resources to work together.

A typical environment has a mix of operating systems installed on desktop, server, and host machines. There are also different database systems and network operating systems, all from different vendors. It's an understatement that these present complexities. Each competing network operating system—LAN Manager, LAN Server, and Netware—has completely different transport mechanisms and completely different transaction protocols.

The same thing is true of database products from different vendors. One database responds to SPX transactions, another responds to Named Pipes calls, while others respond to NetBios or APPC calls. If a program were written to directly communicate with each database, it would have to use three APIs just to establish a link with those servers over the LAN.

Decision-Making Guide

Consultants favor varying approaches to evaluating your need for distributed management and what components to select. A good first step, though, is to decide what kind of system comes nearest to meeting your needs.

Unless you are very fortunate, no system will do everything you want. In the present-day market, you will not find a perfect fit. You will also find that some important features are still destined for future release; they are not available today.

Key features

Whether now or later, a distributed DBMS should include these key features:

- *A distributed data dictionary.*   This is a directory that keeps track of what data is stored in what location, and how to gain access to it.

- *Transparent two-phase commit.*   This is necessary to ensure that when data is updated, all the pertinent changes are made. Unfortunately, this is also found most often on the list of future features.

- *Multiple-site views.*   An employee can retrieve data from multiple sites and have it appear as a single table.

- *Optimized queries.*   With this feature, the system figures out the best way to join distributed database tables, minimizing network traffic and staying within the processing capacity limits of individual nodes.

- *Integrity protection.*   The system must maintain referential integrity among multiple sites. If a table at one location depends on a master database record, that table should be updated whenever the master record is changed.

- *Continuous operation.*   Other activity at the site should not interfere with remote access to its resources.

- *Location independence.*   You could move data from one location to another without affecting application processing. This is important, should you have to realign the system to support new objectives and forms of organization.

- *Concurrent use management.*   The ability to lock records and prevent deadlocks must span the entire distributed system.

Other points to consider

Among the other issues you must resolve in considering a distributed database are:

- Synchronizing data between servers
- Achieving transparent access

- Backing up data
- Implementing stored procedures, triggers, and codified business rules
- Ensuring that the staff is qualified to create client/server applications
- Scheduling application development
- Providing database administration
- Implementing mixed systems such as:

  LAN servers
  Mixed network protocols
  Mixed database products

E-Mail: The Natural Network Application

More than just a way to avoid busy signals,
E-mail can redirect your entire focus, from
managing transactions to managing human
relationships.

Few things are more natural on a network than electronic mail. E-mail is doing for data communication what the telephone did for the human voice. You can talk with anyone else on the same network, without the irritation of busy signals, voice mail, and endless rounds of telephone tag.

The key phrase is *on the same network*. Electronic mail can reach only those with whom you have connections. A big opportunity, and a big challenge, of enterprise networking is to multiply the number of connections. You can extend your e-mail links to far-flung sites across diverse systems.

E-Mail Grows Up

Originally, e-mail was a way to send electronic memos by computer, usually over a limited-range network. Many companies now have several e-mail systems, each running on a single system. Often, each local area network has its own e-mail system. A big problem in linking the enterprise by e-mail is that these multiple local-use systems are still in service.

Today, e-mail does much more than just provide personal communication in a limited area. It is becoming the basis of a host of enhanced communication services. These will greatly affect how you and other organizations do business, both internally and with each other. Companies have integrated fax and voice mail with their e-mail systems. E-mail has also become the foundation of an entirely new class of applications called groupware or mail-enabled. Innovative users are also using e-mail to support management activities, like total quality management.

In short, e-mail can justify an enterprise network all by itself. Before it can do that, though, it must overcome several barriers. Many systems still have user-hostile interfaces; most of these are character-based systems that predate modern ideas about the relationship between computers and people. The need to serve those multiple clients is another major challenge, and it has led to yet another: the difficulty of integrating e-mail with other applications.

Thus, e-mail's potential is still mostly unexplored. Consider Lotus Notes, a highly lauded groupware package that suffers from one big limitation: few people really seem to know what it's good for.

No doubt, these problems will be overcome. As they are, electronic mail will play an increasingly important role in your enterprise. In the words of the International Data Corporation, e-mail can even change the organization's entire focus. You go from managing transactions to managing relationships among the people who make up your organization.

What e-mail can do

- Exchange messages
- Integrate with voice, fax
- Provide a basis for application development

Figure 7.1   Exchanging messages is just the beginning.

Delayed in the e-mail

- Modern interfaces
- Ability to serve multiple clients
- Integration with other applications

Figure 7.2   These barriers still must be overcome.

E-mail evolution

E-mail has its roots in the office automation (OA) systems that preceded the widespread use of personal computers. OA systems were usually based on midrange computers, and the early e-mail systems reflect that. They were included in major vendors' packages, such as Digital's All-in-one, IBM's Profs and Personal Services and the Wang Office.

The arrival of PC LANs in the late 1980s held a promise of lowcost electronic communication. LANs were slow to catch on, though, and the early installations were mainly devoted to sharing laser printers and other costly peripherals. Then, falling hardware prices helped give networks a growth spurt. New electronic mail systems became the first type of application specifically intended for a LAN. E-mail even became a primary reason for installing more LANs. There were approximately 6 million e-mail boxes in 1987; within three years the total had reached 17 million. As this growth continued, users learned that e-mail is not just a simple medium of communication. It can multiply the value of a network, and it can grow as the network grows.

Technical developments have also contributed to e-mail's growth. There is now a set of protocols called X.400 to help standardize the development of e-mail systems. A companion X.500 standard soon will provide for directory services. Both vendors and users have begun to accept these standards, making e-mail a day-to-day business tool, instead of an optional accessory to a single vendor's OA system.

E-mail can change your focus

- From managing transactions ...
- To managing people

Figure 7.3   This makes e-mail a natural component of enterprise networking.

Those single-vendor systems still present problems to present-day e-mail installers. If these proprietary systems are to give way to enterprise network e-mail, you have two options: replace them or find a way to connect them with the network.

There are two main incentives. One is cost. Just as with any other kind of downsizing, a PC-based system costs only a fraction of the same capacity on a mainframe. The other is the business need. E-mail has grown because it fills a need for better interpersonal communications, among co-workers and among members of diverse business groups.

Enabling mail

The term "mail-enabled" may seem like something from the lexicon of political correctness. In truth, it describes electronic mail's most recent evolutionary form. This is a process through which e-mail could someday replace many single-purpose applications now used on personal computers.

In this respect, e-mail is true to its roots in office automation. The old OA systems gradually gained new functions to meet the needs of their users. The new e-mail systems are doing the same thing. Electronic mail is evolving into new forms that support networked and group applications like workflow, routing, scheduling, and electronic conferences.

Strictly speaking, these are not e-mail functions. They are a step beyond: mail-enabled applications or groupware. A quick way to get a reaction from a Lotus official is to suggest that Notes, the firm's groupware product, is just a form of electronic mail.

The evolutionary process continues, and it's not certain exactly what forms future groupware applications might take. E-mail itself is adapting to a role within this process. As the terminology suggests, this is an enabling role. People who work with a mail-enabled application might use e-mail services, such as address lists and transporting, to enhance both their applications and their work.

Architectural change

Accompanying e-mail's new role is a change in its basic architecture. E-mail is shifting toward a modular, client/server type of design, and PC networks are replacing the older host-based systems.

On the client side, newer systems can support the variety of desktop devices you'll find in the typical office. They also let users customize their desktop systems to suit their personal needs. Meanwhile, the server component provides three important services:

- *The directory.*   Also called an address book, this function naturally holds information on users' addresses. Expanded versions include more personalized information. For example, a listing might list the word processor on each person's system. The system could use that information to translate a transmission into an appropriate format.

- *The message store.*   This is the repository for the actual messages.

- *The transport mechanism.*   This is the service that routes the message to its recipient.

Client/server e-mail

- Client function
  - Desktop interface
- Server functions
  - Directory
  - Message store
  - Forwarding

Figure 7.4   E-mail is shifting from a local network service to a client/server format.

Servers may soon also have a filtering mechanism that can rank messages by their importance. That way, you can choose to read only the memo from the boss; less critical items can wait until later.

Arrested development

Few e-mail products have yet reached the level of sophistication and multivendor interaction needed to stand up in an enterprise network. Lotus Development has identified four levels of e-mail management:

Level 1: *Monitor* network traffic and service

- Keep track of the status of e-mail network components, like gateways, directories, servers, and post offices.
- Chart delivery times.
- Track network use for chargebacks to the using departments.

Level 2: *Control* to prevent and correct problems

- Clean up obsolete messages.
- Add, change, or delete directory entries.
- Control traffic flow during peak hours.
- Conduct remote restarts.

Level 3: *Automate* support and maintenance activities

- Record directory changes.
- Reroute around failed links.
- Synchronize deliveries.
- Manage after-hours delivery of large mail attachments.

Level 4: *Access* for management and control.

- Let administrators monitor, control, and automate e-mail management from local or remote workstations.

Few e-mail products have yet made it past level 1, Lotus says. Most e-mail vendors are only beginning to provide tools to monitor their own e-mail systems, never mind those from other vendors. Some vendors, including Lotus, Retix, Hewlett-Packard, and Soft-Switch, are beginning to incorporate control and automation features from the second and third levels.

E-Mail and the Organization

There is one major reason for e-mail's soaring popularity. Few applications have done a better job of serving the organization by serving its people. Modern business styles demand better forms of personal communications. E-mail meets that need. It supports the kinds of personal relationships the modern business environment requires. This environment includes:

- Flatter, team-oriented structures
- An emphasis on customer service
- Re-engineering

Quality circling the wagons

The Apache raiding parties that terrorized the Southwest about a century ago were all-volunteer armies. Warriors would choose to fight only under the leaders who had earned their respect and confidence. The sole test of leadership on the warpath was the ability to command a following. Geronimo was such a leader, though contrary to legend he was never a chief.

The chiefs, who held civil authority, were also selected by merit. They ruled by consensus, not by edict. One of their main functions was what we would now call conflict resolution.

It was a fluid, responsive organization that met the needs of nomadic people. Their strongest loyalties were to their families, their communities, and ad hoc alliances, formed only if the group needed them. To try to draw an Apache org chart is a frustrating experience. The idea that the Apaches were a single tribe was an idea that came as a surprise to the Indians.

Some advanced corporate organizational forms are equally flexible. The self-directed work team has much in common with the Apache war

What e-mail supports

- Workgroup teams
- Customer service
- More responsive organizations

Figure 7.5   A big value of e-mail is that it supports modern organizational forms.

party; an ad hoc group, formed to meet the needs of the moment. The group leader was the best-qualified person, or often just group consensus.

Also, corporations have become flatter, with fewer chiefs and more indians. Managers have learned to become mentors and facilitators, not authority figures.

Corporations have typically carried out these new organizational reforms in response to the quest for quality. They establish quality circles and total quality management. Whatever their name or purpose, these structures rely on information and quick communication. E-mail fills that need. Mail-enabled applications should contribute to an even greater role.

Serving the customer

Customer service is another major objective of the 1990s' corporation. It is part of a movement that also includes total quality and flatter organizations. Good service often requires that you empower employees to make decisions and take responsibility. Employee participation requires knowledge. That, in turn, requires good communication— another role for expanded forms of e-mail.

Customer service is internal as well as external. As the common slogan says, "If you aren't serving the customer, you should be serving someone who is." This has had serious implications for IS professionals, whose functions increasingly require that they directly serve the internal customers they used to call end users.

Re-engineering

No one engineered the corporation in the first place, but a process called re-engineering overlays these other changes. Re-engineering is a methodical process of streamlining the enterprise. It implies that the organization and its data will be reshaped in tandem. E-mail can have a key role in enabling this process. It helps break down organizational barriers and supports the kind of communication and teamwork modern organizations must have.

The E-Mail Application

To fulfill its function in the flatter, more flexible organization, e-mail must be fully accessible. That means it must be more than a separate function, and even more than an application that has been specifically mail-enabled. It should bring information to an employee, no matter what kind of application that employee is using. In other words, every

Customer-oriented systems

- Quick response
- Easier access
- Up-to-date market information
- Adaptability
- Cost-effectiveness
- Efficiency

Figure 7.6   E-mail helps start the chain.

application should be mail-enabled. This is a PC type of process that should extend to host and workstation applications as well.

From the employee's point of view, an application should include mail as a utility, much as a word processor incorporates a spell checker. E-mail should also be transparent. Just as with a distributed database, neither the individual nor the application should have to know the details of how a message is routed, whether it's to an adjoining LAN node or over a WAN. In appearance, it should be as simple as a pull-down menu.

The E-mail system of the future should also have these qualities:

- It should be integrated with fax, voice transmission, and other forms of messaging.

- It should be seamless, letting you transmit files from their native applications. For example, you could transmit a spreadsheet that includes all its formulas, not just the text format that is most generally available now.

E-mail is getting these qualities, and it is constantly growing in ability and sophistication. Many applications come with e-mail APIs built in.

Each environment will support more customized messaging capacities. These will let developers describe and tag the message content in detail. These new messaging abilities will go far beyond most people's present idea of electronic mail. Systems to come will develop the idea of messaging to include groups, routing, and filtered selection. That means electronic mail soon will be much different from simple person-to-person messaging.

Future applications may well use electronic mail as their foundations, building on such present-day functions as calendar and scheduling utilities. These are being expanded into broader functions like conferences, filters, agent facilities, and workflow applications.

Going with the workflow

To develop these applications, and to make best use of them, advanced forms of e-mail must:

- Adapt to changing organization structures. Host-based systems are seriously weak here.

- Build on e-mail's many strong points while making up for its weaknesses.

Workflow automation may do just these things. In particular, it promises to overcome some of e-mail's current weaknesses while capitalizing on its strengths. The International Data Corporation has published this definition of workflow software:

> Workflow empowers individuals and groups of individuals in both structured and unstructured work environments to automatically manage a series of events to achieve the business objectives of the company. At the same time, workflow software should provide information to management, which can extend or modify business processes as conditions change.

Electronic mail obviously will play a basic role in developing these types of applications. It can provide the infrastructure that serves as a foundation for further development. Simply adding workflow abilities to an existing electronic mail system can vastly expand the system's powers. It can route forms and messages. It can provide consistent interfaces to mixed environments. It can help applications work together and can give them the inherent ability to exchange data.

The expanded electronic conference

Many mail-enabled applications to come will not be new applications, but expansions of existing ones. For example, electronic conferences have been available at least since the mid 1980s. With e-mail as a foundation, though, it becomes the corporate equivalent of the electronic bulletin board. You can select the topic of a conference and post it on the e-mail system. Other employees can add their comments and reply to others in a freewheeling e-mail discussion.

You can conduct an entire meeting on the e-mail system. You don't have to coordinate schedules, and you don't have to spend inordinate amounts of time that everyone knows are unproductive. There's no requirement that everyone be there at the same time, or even at the same place.

Another advantage: the e-mail system maintains a record of the entire exchange—electronic "minutes" of the meeting. There should never be any serious question of who said what.

Electronic communications will never replace face-to-face human interaction, but it can streamline the communications process.

Welcome back

E-mail is not without its drawbacks. One is the familiar experience of coming back from vacation to find several hundred unread messages in your electronic mailbox. Even the normal daily message flow in some systems can make you wish for some way to set priorities, distinguishing between important communications and electronic junk mail.

An advanced e-mail system can include a filter to answer that feel-like-crying need. You can set up the filter to monitor your incoming mail and sort it into categories you have established. Along with the categories, include instructions for handling that kind of mail. You can ask the system to delete mail automatically in one group, forward another class of message, or send a standard response to another group.

You could use this power to:

- Forward immediate-action messages to your vacation replacement.

- Reply to routine messages with a notice that you're away and expect to be back next week.

- Automatically delete all messages generated from internal mailing lists.

You can even filter mail before it reaches the desktop. A server-based filter can manage the complete mail system by setting up system-wide standards. For example, you could set up the system to delete all messages over a certain age, or to notify an employee that his or her mailbox has accumulated a large backlog.

Getting There from Here

E-mail's promise is not all in the future. A well-integrated e-mail system will pay off in enhanced productivity and lower cost of ownership.

This is particularly true in the long run. The promise is there. The challenge is to achieve it.

The basic question: How do you pass messages among systems that have different formats, different message transport protocols, and different addressing schemes? There are several choices for designing an integrated e-mail system. Each has advantages and disadvantages. These choices include:

- Setting up point-to-point gateways between each system

- Using a public e-mail service such as a message switch

- Setting up an e-mail backbone that uses existing protocols, the developing X.400 standard, or a proprietary approach such as Soft-Switch

- Message switching, in which you maintain an in-house message switch by developing your own or using technology from vendors such as Novell

The gateway approach

Gateways translate messages and addresses from one type of mail system to another. A point-to-point gateway is a portal that lets each type of system communicate directly with every other type. E-mail vendors and third parties supply gateways that can connect just about every popular e-mail system to any other, including LAN-based, host-based, minicomputer, or public e-mail services.

You'll need one gateway for each possible pair of system types. Each system must have a gateway to connect with every system except itself, which means the number of required gateways can quickly multiply in a diverse network. If you must connect seven systems, for example, you'll need twenty-one gateways.

For smaller, less diverse networks, point-to-points can be economical and (relatively) easy to install and maintain. They're a good choice for up to three e-mail systems, which would require only three gateways.

In more complex environments, though, you will quickly experience just the opposite of economies of scale. Say, for example, you have cc:Mail on a PC LAN, IBM Profs at corporate headquarters, Digital All-in-one at the division level, and a Novell MHS system on another LAN. The four mail systems would need six gateways for all to communicate. Integration, equipment, communication, and administrative costs will quickly grow as the system becomes more complex.

Management, installation, support, and administrative staffing add extra costs as well. In a system with six gateways, you will need administrators with experience integrating six different pairs of e-mail environments. You'll rarely find such a combination of talent in a single employee. Someone will also have to be familiar with all the individual e-mail systems themselves. Other problems with gateways: they can be performance bottlenecks, and there is some risk to the integrity of the messages that pass through them.

Going public

For many companies, it might be more practical to use a public e-mail service. Services like AT&T Mail, MCI Mail, GEIS QuickComm, and GTE Sprintmail provide switching services. These services route messages among dissimilar e-mail transports using gateways between the services and your messaging environments. They also provide X.400 services.

These commercial gateways are available to most e-mail environments. These include host systems such as IBM Profs, midrange systems such as All-in-one, and PC LAN e-mail systems including Novell MHS, Lotus cc:Mail, Microsoft Mail, and CE Software Quickmail.

For example, GTE Sprintmail provides a PC LAN e-mail gateway function at the service. With the Sprint Message Xchange (SMX) service, the company provides the interface between cc:Mail and Sprintmail. To the cc:Mail system, Sprintmail looks just like any other cc:Mail post office. SMX service also provides expanded X.400 service to LANs; it gives cc:Mail users transparent access to X.400.

This is typical of a public e-mail service in which the provider owns and maintains the gateways. You don't have to buy, install, maintain, or administer them yourself. A cc:Mail user can maintain cc:Mail addresses for all correspondents, whatever their systems. The provider maintains the gateways and makes the necessary translations. You need no gateways at either the sending or receiving sites.

There is a price, of course. For high-volume use, public services can be very expensive options, even with the volume discounts that usually are available. Count on paying a $500 registration fee, plus standard rates for all your transmitted messages. If you are using an X.25 packet-switched network, you also pay for the X.25 service and an additional registration fee. You also pay destination charges, typically around 40 cents per message. International messages are usually higher. In addition, you usually must purchase and maintain gateways between your e-mail systems and the service.

On the other side of the balance sheet, public networks save administration, maintenance, and support costs, and the start-up costs are low compared with installing your own gateways. And they are available from anywhere in the world. They also provide a secure, low cost way to talk with trading partners.

Get some backbone

A backbone is a central system that uses a single e-mail protocol, such as X.400 or Soft-Switch, to distribute messages between individual networks. The backbone translates the messages from the networks' formats into its own, then retranslates them into the format of the receiving station.

A backbone makes it much easier to maintain e-mail systems on diverse networks. Adding a new e-mail network is almost as simple as plugging it in. For example, if you want to add Microsoft Mail for PC Networks to an existing X.400 backbone, you would buy an X.400 gateway. You could then send messages to All-in-one, Profs, cc:Mail, and Da Vinci e-mail users. Their systems are also connected by gateways to the X.400 backbone.

Backbone architectures can be easier to manage and administer and can save equipment and resource costs. Administrators, mail managers, and support personnel need only learn their local e-mail system. Then you can provide central management for the backbone. A backbone system also simplifies planning and makes it easy to manage setup, growth, and administration.

Using a common backbone also simplifies communication with trading partners and with other business units that may have diverse e-mail systems. X.400 is emerging as the primary backbone for international and intercompany e-mail. Most public e-mail services provide X.400 services, and many large companies are setting up X.400 backbones. As the market grows, X.400 gateways are becoming increasingly stable and widely available. Vendors are investing more in research and development to improve performance and interoperability. This is helping to make their products more stable and easier to manage. Growing volume is also decreasing the cost of setting up an X.400 system.

No technology is without its problems, and X.400 is no exception. Setting up a backbone requires central planning and software development; in turn, these tasks are demanding of staff resources. Unresolved problems include directory integration, management tools, and e-mail APIs for mail-enabled applications.

The message switch

A new approach to e-mail integration is to build a message switch on a single computing platform. This switch accepts incoming messages from a variety of transport protocols and delivers them without going through an external gateway. The message switch's primary benefit is that it eliminates the need for gateways.

Novell is taking this approach with its NetWare Global Messaging architecture. According to Novell, NetWare Global Messaging will support multiple messaging protocols, including SMTP, SNADS, X.400, and Novell MHS through Netware Loadable Modules. Alisa Systems (Pasadena, California) has taken a similar approach, but this system keeps the directory database in its native format.

Dealing with Directories

However you choose to link your e-mail systems, you must keep directories current and available. An integrated e-mail system must have a way to manage and coordinate internal and external categories. Like other kinds of data on an enterprise network, these should operate transparently. They should provide a single, comprehensive directory, even if it contains listings from diverse and incompatible systems.

A major limitation of current e-mail directory systems is that most systems come with an unfortunate built-in assumption: that the local directory is the only directory. Often there is no provision at all for exchanging information outside the local network. There are some utilities that will import and convert the information from remote directories, but this usually is not enough to manage the directories effectively.

What you need

Effective management requires much more, including ways to:

- Map names and addresses between e-mail systems
- Record changes, deletions, and additions
- Provide access to remote directory information through native interfaces
- Allow administrative control over directory sharing, security, and scheduling
- Provide status and reporting information for network management
- Provide integration with non-e-mail directories, such as corporate directories
- Integrate external e-mail directories from suppliers, customers, and business partners

What's available?

Several vendors are making or have announced directory integration products. These include Digital, Novell, and Soft-Switch. There are also several new approaches, such as Alisa Systems' Information Switch.

Soft-Switch provides directory integration for All-in-one, Profs, X.400, cc:Mail, and other hosts on VM or MVS platforms. Like Novell and Digital, Soft-Switch converts directory information into a proprietary format, which is based on a uniform naming convention.

Novell's directory synchronization product provides directory replication and reconciliation among Novell directories and with SNADS and SMTP. The initial version did not provide integration with other popular LAN-based directories such as cc:Mail or Microsoft Mail, or with X.500, Profs, or Digital Distributed Directory Services.

Information Switch transfers messages among disparate e-mail systems such as cc:Mail, Microsoft Mail, Novell MHS, CE Software, and Digital. It also synchronizes directories, and provides for directory search and retrieval. The product is an SQL database application running on a VAX. Unlike other directory integrators, it stores addresses in their native format and only converts them when you transmit them to an incompatible directory. This approach eliminates the need for multiple gateways, since it converts the directory information only when necessary.

Offsetting the potential of this new technology was the first release, which offered no integration with X.500, Profs, or SMTP. The release was also limited because it ran only on a single platform.

X.500 is coming

The developing X.500 standard will provide a uniform protocol for integrating directories. This is mainly future technology, though, and few products are yet available.

What You Can Do Now

The number of available products for integrating e-mail systems continues to grow. With careful planning, you can put together a sound system now that also will accommodate future growth and technical development.

Nina Burns, a Menlo Park, California messaging consultant, offers these suggestions to help:

- Identify your users' needs and expectations before you design the system.

- Try to minimize the number of disparate systems you must support.

- Make sure employees don't lose any of the functions they are now accustomed to using.

- Make the integration as transparent as possible.

Steps to success

- Identify users' needs
- Minimize variety
- Preserve existing functions
- Strive for transparency
- Allow for growth
- Provide expandable directories
- Expect delays

Figure 7.7 Keys to a good system now and a better system later.

- Assess the state of your in-house expertise, and the costs of supplementing your internal knowledge from outside sources.
- Be realistic about where you are today and where you want to be in the future.
- Design a system that can grow and change with the organization.
- Include a plan to integrate directories from all e-mail systems and corporate directories.
- Plan to do much development on your own, in order to fill gaps in current technology.
- Minimize the number of suppliers with whom you deal.
- Make realistic plans and budgets for system administration and management.
- Add 12 to 18 months to any vendor promises.

Enabling Groupware

E-mail used to be a convenience. Now, it is maturing into a technology that could become the core of enterprise networking. One reason for this is the mail-enabled application, also called groupware.

Mail enabling makes users more productive by letting them work from their favorite applications; they don't have to drop out into separate communication or e-mail programs. The employee who is finishing a report or a financial analysis can forward the finished product to its recipients with the click of a mouse button. Early mail-enabled applications have been concentrated in the Windows environment for PCs, but soon this feature is almost certain to become part of many products.

What is groupware?

Groupware is another of those enterprise network products whose definition involves a state of mind, instead of technical specifications. There's no single technology at which you can point and say, "That's it." Authorities are divided on a formal definition. Some say groupware and mail-enabled applications are the same thing; others classify groupware as a type of mail-enabled software.

Much of the current interest in groupware is based on supporting interaction among people. These people may be members of single departments, members of work teams, or even people from far-flung parts of organizations who work on related parts of a project. They can even be members of different organizations, such as an auto manufacturer that has learned to control quality by working in close partnership with its parts' suppliers.

Groupware has particularly strong implications for the people who make up the enterprise. Terry Winograd, Stanford professor and director at Action Technologies, predicts that "groupware is going to make people more directly conscious of the interactions among people—the responsibilities, the commitments, the communications—and personalize something people usually think of as depersonalizing."

New uses

The expansion of e-mail has been a kind of self-fulfilling fantasy. Office automation software originally became popular because it provided a straightforward way to move documents from one place to another. Once people had e-mail systems to use, they began to think up ways to use them. A system was in place to move information. People began to use that system for other purposes, such as to schedule meetings or monitor the progress of a joint project. The systems became part of the way in which people worked.

Some things people have wanted to do are beyond the scope of the original e-mail systems. In response, electronic mail is fast becoming the foundation for mission-critical applications using mail-enabled software. As only one example, PC electronic mail vendors have begun to add features like calendars and scheduling to their systems. Until only recently, these were features found only on midrange and mainframe office automation systems.

New kinds of applications

New kinds of software are also appearing. One group of particular interest offers application development tools so you can customize the software to support almost any kind of business opportunity. Lotus Notes is the best-known product in this group. Users can expand on Notes' e-mail abilities by building custom applications that share database resources.

Client/server foundation

Vendors have also found ways to transform e-mail into a foundation for client/server applications. To carry out these features transparently, the applications have to be tailored to an API. One of these is Lotus' Open Messaging Interface (OMI). Microsoft has been working on a competing product called Messaging API (MAPI). An industry group that includes Lotus, Borland, Novell, IBM, WordPerfect, and Apple has also been working on yet another API called Vendor-independent messaging or VIM.

These APIs should mean that applications no longer would have to be tailored to specific network protocols. What it will mean is another question. Three separate standards hardly qualify as a common-use API.

The special role of Notes

Lotus Notes holds a special role in the development of groupware. It's been by far the best-noticed and most successful example of its type.

The key to that success is that Notes relies on open platforms and the client/server model. This makes it easier for both users and third-party developers to build links with other applications. Significantly, the impetus behind Notes extends outward from users, by way of their PCs, instead of downward, by way of large-system hosts.

On the client side, Notes provides access to many client/server applications, including those for Windows, OS/2, and the Macintosh. Notes includes an interprocess communication (IPC) feature that provides at least some degree of integration and interoperability among applications. For the largest number of users, those who run Windows, Notes provides an IPC in the form of Object Linking and Embedding (OLE). OLE is itself a set of APIs that initially work only among Windows applications, but can include other features, including data exchange by network.

As a server application, Notes can tap the expanding power of platforms like Netware. In this role, Notes is being set up as a set of Netware Loadable Modules (NLMs) to run on a server. This will give Notes access to the Netware Global Messaging system for links with external mail systems.

From Workgroup to Workflow

Beyond the idea of mail-enabled and workgroup applications is workflow management. This is a new term, but it is really just an extension of earlier e-mail developments.

Workflow systems automate business procedures, taking advantage of computers, networks, databases, and messaging systems. With workflow software, employees can create and move data among individuals, departments, and even organizations. They can do it transparently, of course, without regard to geographic location or the respective computer systems.

Workflow management is a logical extension of groupware. Basic e-mail systems provide a way to transmit messages. Groupware uses this ability to do an ever-growing range of useful tasks. Workflow software manages the process.

Types of systems

Workflow software comes in several varieties. The most common include applications that manage document flow or automate tasks and processes.

Some do both. Image processing systems, for example, support document flow by automating paper-based systems and procedures. Vendors such as Filenet Corp, (Costa Mesa, California), Viewstar (Santa Ana, California) and Intergraph (Huntsville, Alabama), include workflow components in their image management systems.

Usually these systems rely on proprietary hardware and software. Other workflow products are more general-purpose, using existing technology. They tend to be more versatile and less expensive.

Available products

Befitting an embryo technology, available workflow management products vary in their features and approaches. Reach Software Corp. (Sunnyvale, California) and Action Technologies Inc. (Alameda, California) offer systems designed to work with existing PC LANs. Larger vendors, including NCR, DEC, and AT&T lean toward complete, proprietary packages.

ATI's workflow application breaks activities into small units that the network can carry and track. Its model defines 12 different actions between two parties, based on personal understandings and commitments. It manages the process by managing those activities.

Other systems approach the problem from exactly the opposite direction. They let individuals chart their own workflows, and a document's content can decide its routing.

Workflow from groupware

Notes and Beyond Inc.'s Beyond Mail include some workflow functions. Beyond users can write macros to build their own workflow applications using the program's E-mail platform. They can create forms such as purchase orders. They can also write business rules to route the forms around the organization.

Notes relies on databases that are replicated across a network. It can compile related documents from different sources in the distributed environment. Notes users can build data views, set up procedures to move work from one mailbox to another, or build process-oriented applications in a shared database.

Making the choice

Existing products, and those yet to come, differ greatly even in their basic approaches. The newness of workflow management means there is no clear consensus on what it is supposed to do, much less how.

Newsletter publisher Esther Dyson places workflow products in three groups:

- *User-centered* systems are designed around user needs. Notes and Beyond are examples.

- *Process-centered* systems rely on data, files, and applications. Sometimes called top-down systems, they monitor the work cycle and the state of transactions in progress. ATI's system, with its 12 monitored actions, is an example.

- *Work-centered* systems fall midway between the two. They tend to evolve from the center out. In some systems, a document's content can determine its routing. These systems fit into this category.

No matter what type of system you favor, it is important that you study this developing market. It is even more important that you make a choice that fits your particular way of doing business.

Be sure you understand what you're trying to accomplish. Include employees and management in design decisions. Most important, don't let workflow obstruct the flow of work.

The tool should never become more important than the job it's supposed to do.

Understanding X.400

If X.400 is the emerging backbone of enterprise-wide e-mail, what is X.400? The simple answer: it is a message handling system (MHS) whose protocols have been adopted by the International Standards Organization (ISO). The X.400 protocols define a standard for store-and-forward messaging, including message creation, routing, and delivery services. It runs over an X.25 packet-switched network or asynchronous dial-up lines.

In practice, X.400 lets you build e-mail systems that can span a variety of systems. You might have IBM's Profs and SNADS on an IBM mainframe, All-in-one on VAX/VMS systems, Wang Office on Wang VS machines, HP Office on Hewlett-Packard minis, and Unix on TCP/IP systems. On PC networks, you might find a mixture of Lotus' cc:Mail, Da Vinci's Email, and Microsoft Mail. CE Software's Quickmail often appears on Mac LANs.

X.400 is the most likely choice to link these diverse systems in an enterprise network. X.400 is vendor-independent, it can run on a variety of computer systems, and it is used and accepted around the world. X.400 software is available for a variety of computers, either as native applications or as gateways.

Like nearly any standard, X.400 is less than rigid. It comes in two basic versions, identified by the year each was issued: 1984 and 1988. Most existing X.400 mail systems use the older specification. The newer version has one key advantage: it lets you use asynchronous lines, a useful tool for PC or laptop users who are not now connected to X.400 networks.

What is X.400 made of?

X.400 works on client/server principles. The client side is a *user agent* (UA). The server is the *message transfer agent* (MTA).

The user agent works like a mailbox. It is the main point of contact with the user. The UA prepares, submits, and receives messages. Other services include text editing, presentation services, security, message priority, and delivery notification. The user agent observes no standards except the message format. The product developer is responsible for providing a user interface.

The message transfer agent routes and relays the messages. Its responsibilities include establishing the store-and-forward path, maintaining security, and routing the message. The user agent sends its message to the local message transfer agent. The MTA checks the message for errors. If all is well, it sends the message on its way. If the message is intended for a local destination, it goes to the appropriate local user agent. If the message is not local, it goes to the next MTA. The MTA repeats the process until the message reaches its destination.

A collection of MTAs makes up a *message transfer system* (MTS). Other X.400 components include:

- *Distribution lists* (DLs), which are like electronic routing slips.

- A *message store* service that, naturally enough, stores messages until recipients retrieve them. It complements the user agent for PCs and other systems that are not always on line.

- *Access units,* which provide connections to other kinds of communication services like telex and the postal service.

For e-mail system managers, X.400 provides for a *management domain,* a group of MTAs and their associated UAs managed by a single organization. An administrative management domain (ADMD) is run by the telephone company or another outside communication service. Its private equivalent, a PDMD, can be run by any other type of organization; normally that would be the user.

Wait, mister postman

In operation, X.400 mimics the postal service. It handles a message much like a letter, complete with an electronic envelope. The address portion of the envelope includes the information necessary to deliver the message. X.400 can deliver messages to other X.400 users via a message transfer service. It can also reach other communication facilities such as Telex, via an interpersonal messaging service.

As with the postal service, you must identify each recipient by a unique address. That can be either a primitive name, which identifies a unique entity such as an employee number, or a descriptive name, which identifies a specific destination.

Normally, an X.400 service will look up the name in its directory to find the address. X.400 addresses consist of attributes that describe a user or distribution list, or which locate the user distribution list within the mail system. Attributes are personal (such as the recipient's name), geographical (street address, town, or country), organizational (business unit), or architectural (X.121 address, user agent identifier, or management domain). In practice, X.400 names are long and complex. Give users a break by offering them aliases.

The message transfer system also handles two other kinds of traffic: probes and reports. A probe is like an empty envelope. Use it to find out if you can deliver a message as expected. You might send out a probe to test a path, asking the receiving MTS if it can accept a particular message type. If you test first with a probe, you reduce the chance that the recipient system will reject an important message.

A report does much the same thing, but after the message is transmitted. It is a status indicator that relates the progress or outcome of a transmission.

Directories and security

The 1988 version of X.400 suggests that you use the coming X.500 directory service to record names, store distribution lists, maintain profiles of user agents, and identify authorized users. X.500 lets users create names that make sense to them; they need not use those that are best understood only by the system.

There's one slight problem: X.500 isn't finished yet. Some pilot projects are under way, but there have been few, if any, commercial applications.

The 1988 specification also has new security facilities. These authenticate the originators of a message, verify those who originated a delivery or nondelivery notice, check that the message or its contents are unaltered, and verify that all recipients received copies. It also provides return receipt and registered mail services.

This is not a complete e-mail security system. X.400 provides nothing, for example, to find out whether someone is impersonating an authorized user. There is nothing, either, to make sure that no one delays, reorders, or improperly duplicates a message.

The Promise of Open Systems

Open systems make ideal enterprise network backbones. Potentially, they can solve many problems when integrating diverse systems. The key word is potentially.

Charles Schwab & Co., the San Francisco-based discount brokerage house, had a problem. Its mainframes were too slow.

An older system based on mainframes simply wasn't keeping up with the pace of Schwab's rapidly expanding business. To make things worse, it was costly to run and maintain. In effect, Schwab was paying a high price for inadequate performance.

Accordingly, the brokerage became one of the first businesses anywhere to commit itself to a distributed client/server system based on protocols devised by the Open Software Foundation (OSF). It was a risky move because, when the project was begun early in 1992, the OSF standards were still largely unfinished products.

High Risk, High Return

Even so, Schwab was prepared to spend four years and risk an estimated $25 million in personnel costs alone to make the change. The high risk also promised a high return. The new system offers much more power at much less cost. Even more important, it is a distributed system that can offer solid support to Schwab's expansion-minded business objectives.

The system is based on OSF/1, a Unix-based operating system designed for client/server platforms. It also was designed to make use of two further OSF standards that, at the project's outset, were still under development. These are the Distributed Computing Environment (DCE), which was to tie applications together across the distributed network, and a Distributed Management Environment (DME).

Supporting expansion

The system would support a rapidly expanding business. At the time Schwab launched the project, revenues were up 74 percent from the previous year. The company also was busy expanding its network of offices. It had added 48 new offices in the previous two years, and the expansion was continuing. The distributed system was to play an important role in supporting this growing domain. It was to be a key component of a business re-engineering program.

One of the first planning tasks was to develop data models and to examine work processes, and to reshape them into more logical, efficient forms. For example, the company had previously handled mutual fund business at central headquarters; with the help of the distributed system it could move this activity to branch offices.

Elements of the plan

Programs such as Schwab's generally are a form of downsizing. Downsizing often means a transition from mainframes to PC networks. For many organizations and many types of data, that can be a very big jump. This kind of downsizing also requires that you get diverse systems to work smoothly together.

Open systems represent another option. As a downsizing option, they have much of the flexibility of PCs, including graphical interfaces. They also are based on more powerful workstations and servers. Open system are usually based in Unix, a stronger networking system than PC-based systems.

An even more important role for open systems is as the centerpieces of enterprise networks. Open systems are based on accepted, industry-wide standards. They reduce the need to manage diversity by reducing the diversity. The leading open system standards also include links to other existing systems, both larger and smaller.

Schwab's complete plan includes these elements:

- A client/server platform based on OSF/1, using systems from IBM, Hewlett-Packard, or Digital Equipment.

- A DEC-based transaction processing system that uses remote procedure calls (RPCs) to tie applications across disparate systems.

- A Fiber Distributed Data Interface (FDDI) backbone to link three buildings at the San Francisco headquarters.

- Routers that interconnect two kinds of local area networks: those using Transmission Control Protocol/Internet Protocol (TCP/IP), associated with Unix, and Novell's IPX protocols for PC networks.

- A platform to manage distributed computing and enterprise networks, based on OSF's forthcoming DME standards.

Open Systems and the Enterprise Network

A big reason for the growing interest in open systems is their ability to support distributed computing. Distributed computing is at the heart of enterprise networking and client/server computing.

Look at the way you use computers now. Compare that with the way you expect to use them in the future. If yours is a typical organization still considering enterprise networking, the current picture is probably something like this: You have a mix of hardware and software from different manufacturers. Separate work groups, many in different geographic regions, operate their own computing resources. These groups share little information and few resources. Because most of the systems are proprietary, it is hard to exchange information among them without major programming efforts.

The smiling crystal ball

No doubt your view of the future sees all these problems solved. You want to share processing and data across heterogeneous environments. You want to be able to use resources available on different computers all around the company. Sometimes even simple needs can be important: to gain access to data on another department's computer or to have the use of a remote printer. On a larger scale, you recognize that the desktop computing revolution has ironically replaced one form of centralized computing with another. Instead of central control at the mainframe, you have dispersed control at the departmental and LAN levels. You'd like a system that is easier to manage. Still, you don't want to revert to the mainframe days, when data was so carefully man-

What you may have now

- Mixed hardware
- Mixed software
- Workgroups using differing standards
- Little information sharing

Figure 8.1   Most enterprise networks start from situations like this.

What you'd like to have

- Access to distributed resources
- Shared processing across diverse environments
- Easy management

Figure 8.2   These are typical enterprise network goals.

aged it could hardly ever be used. You want a system that uses information to truly empower your employees.

Such an integrated future would be a vast improvement over the situations most organizations now face. The vision naturally makes you anxious to get from here to there. You want to get rid of the unplanned melange most organizations have inherited and move to a system where everything works together, no matter what or where it is.

Open and distributed

That's why the movement to enterprise networking is also often a movement to open systems. The logic is simple: if a system is truly open, it knows no limits of geography. Ideally, access to a computer in the next state should be no more difficult than access to a computer on the next desk.

In short, the open system can easily be a distributed open system, one that shares information and resources throughout the enterprise.

Beyond client/server

A distributed open system is a step beyond client/server computing. In a basic client/server system, one server meets the needs of several clients. In a distributed environment, there are several servers, perhaps one in each department. Each serves a group of clients within its group. Each also is available to members of other workgroups.

Whoa, there

There is one big problem. Many organizations that have rushed to embrace open systems have charged into brick walls of resistance. Businesses need distributed open systems now, to capitalize on business opportunities and to keep from being left behind. A continuing lack of tools and applications often restrain them.

The reason: open systems depend on standards, uniform specifications that all elements can meet so they can work together. From a business standpoint, the people who develop these standards have worked at a frustrating, mule-like pace. The standards' bodies are properly interested in making sure they get it right, but they sometimes seem oblivious to the immediate needs of their ultimate customers. Within a few years, these bodies may complete the groundwork for products their business clients need immediately, if not sooner.

Frustrated by the delays, many business organizations have taken matters into their own hands. Their responses follow two main patterns:

- Forming their own business-sponsored standards' groups, and setting their own specifications without waiting on the more conventional process.

- Patronizing vendors who can meet their needs now, though they do so with proprietary systems.

Either response can be a necessary compromise or a dangerous pitfall. The difference lies in the attitude with which you act. Is this a well-planned step with an identified migration path toward your ultimate goals? Or do you blindly hope things will work out? The key question:

Getting past roadblocks

- Impatient users have:
  - Formed their own standards' organizations
  - Patronized vendors who have products ready now

Figure 8.3 Be sure this is a well-planned move, not just a reaction.

Once I have completed this step, what do I plan to do then?

Before you go on, make sure you have a good answer.

Defining Open Systems

In one sense, open systems simply seem to create more confusion. The choice between PC networks and larger systems can be difficult enough. Now, these powerful, Unix-based workstations and servers add yet another category to worry about. You can't just ignore them, either. They are more powerful than comparable PCs—which in turn often are more powerful than some larger systems. Though more costly than PCs, they still are much less expensive than larger systems.

More important, they extend the benefits of Unix to the entire enterprise. These benefits include better network communication, increased interoperability, enhanced security, and much greater processing power. Open systems also promise to support distributed applications that will significantly enhance productivity throughout the organization.

Unix made simpler

Unix has been around for a long time, of course. It's often been criticized as excessively complex and demanding, particularly in the hands of business users. In the last few years, though, new products have made Unix more accessible and have displayed its advantages.

RISC-based systems running Unix have adapted an old idea, scalable architecture such as the IBM S/360 or the Digital VAX. They have applied it in systems nearly as inexpensive as PCs at the low end and as powerful as mainframes at the top. RISC-based servers provide the file and database services that formerly were the domain of mainframes and minis. Meanwhile, RISC-based workstations are ideal for a new generation of applications, like imaging and animation, that require massive computing and graphics processing ability.

Improving output

Open systems can improve productivity in two significant ways. Compared with competing systems, they are more powerful, more responsive, or both. They also offer the benefits of multitasking. Faster desktop systems demand more from the servers that support them; Unix servers can help meet that demand. In short, open systems offer too many benefits to ignore.

On the other hand, few organizations are ready to make the financial and organizational commitment that Schwab has made, converting wholesale to a Unix-based client/server system. For most companies,

What open systems offer

- Power and responsiveness
- Multitasking ability

Figure 8.4 They put heavy demands on servers, though.

the cost is prohibitive, and the payoff is uncertain. Sometimes, a wholesale conversion could actually reduce productivity. The more practical scenario is that open systems will increasingly coexist within your enterprise network, sharing their assets with both PCs and larger systems. Today's mix is likely to include Intel 80×86-based systems running MS DOS (with or without Windows) or OS/2; RISC systems from Sun, HP, IBM, Digital, and others running varieties of Unix; and various proprietary computers with operating systems like MVS and VM. The challenge, then, is to integrate these open systems with your other network resources.

Dual definition

Like many ideas in enterprise networking, the definition of open systems is a bit fluid and subject to interpretation. It has both technical and operational elements. The technical part of the definition includes network protocols and application program interfaces (APIs). On the business side, open systems mean unimpeded access to applications and information.

Departmental users look at open systems in relation to the work they must do and the information they need to do it—the business perspective. Vendors think of open systems in technical terms—in terms of the types of technology they are trying to sell. It's important that you keep both elements in mind. Judge the technology by how well it can meet the organization's needs.

Not just Unix

You cannot identify open systems by Unix alone. Though Unix is the usual operating system of open systems computing, open systems are more than Unix applications. They must meet other needs and standards as well, including these:

- *Allowing for innovation.* The purpose of open systems is not to achieve a technology where everything looks the same, but to establish an atmosphere where all kinds of information technology can work in unison.

- *A management role.*   The business view of open systems must receive at least as much respect and attention as the technical definition. The main purpose of the technology is to serve the business client.

Hire yourself a system

Don't think about buying a computer system. Think in terms of hiring it. When an individual applies for a job, you judge that person's qualifications to do the job in question. You probably also consider the candidate's adaptability and potential. Can this person respond to changing situations?

Evaluate your system the same way. Base your decisions on how well the system can do the job, and how well it can adapt to your future needs. The real advantage of open systems is that they often can meet exactly those requirements. The International Data Corporation (IDC) has identified three major components a true open system should include:

- Products and technology based on established standards

- An open development infrastructure

- A solid management directive

The Role of Standards

Standards are probably the most familiar component of open systems. The standards are important, of course. They form the basis of such useful working features as portability and interoperability. They do not by themselves establish open systems.

One source of confusion is that people tend to think of open systems and proprietary systems as direct opposites. By that logic, the use of generally published standards distinguishes the two.

The real opposite of an open system is, naturally enough, a closed system. A closed system involves the risk that you someday can't adapt or expand it as you would like.

A proprietary system is not necessarily either open or closed. Even the most open system has some elements that are proprietary to individual vendors. A proprietary system does have some of the same risks as a closed system, but you can control and balance that risk. Often, proprietary systems offer higher degrees of service and innovation than those that hew tightly to the accepted standards. A fully open system reduces the risk of being left at a dead end, but it also denies you access to individual vendors' innovations.

What's more, existing standards don't define everything. In some areas there is more than one standard; in others, there is none at all.

Open development

You don't just need an open system. You also need an open environment that ensures that your technology will be useful and long-lived. If you are to keep your system open, you must set it up it in the most effective possible way for the largest possible body of users, now and in the future.

A true open system uses a building process. Your newly developed technology can take advantage of existing technology. You should design the new elements so they take advantage of existing components. You should also design the new elements so future developments can take advantage of them. Standards help assure you that you can maintain this process, and that you can continue to build on your previous work.

Application development in an open system also requires discipline. It's easy to take an open system and slam it shut by using closed applications. For example, you could buy an SQL database, whose query language observes an established standard. Most versions of SQL include proprietary extensions. If you rely on these extensions, you have effectively closed the system.

There is another common hazard in the incompatible networks that tend to spring up throughout an organization. Often, these develop because their users have felt left out and ill-served by the corporate development process. These networks do often serve short-term needs, but they will be in place for years, standing in the way of more permanent solutions.

Manage the process

Technology must serve the organization. It should never be the other way around—though it often is. Without directions from management, you will continue to have isolated islands throughout the organization. People will use information as a weapon, trying to overregulate its use when your real objective is to expand it.

You must make sure your technology choices reflect the needs of the entire organization. Use the available management tools to control this process:

- Establish requirements.
- Include them in requests for proposals.
- Ensure that the final purchase decisions reflect the results of this process.

Make sure, too, that management directives reflect the needs and views of all involved groups. This consensus-gathering process becomes increasingly important as organizations decentralize their decision-making processes.

Enjoying the Advantages

Beware of anything that sounds too good to be true. It probably is. That age-old advice applies to open systems as much as to anything else. Still, open systems potentially offer advantages to all three main classes of users: IS professionals, management, and employees.

Productivity and control

IS professionals will enjoy some of the most tangible benefits. They will find these benefits in three general areas:

- Increased productivity and faster user response
- Better control of the information technology environment
- Cost control

Open systems can vastly improve programmers' productivity, because it makes their skills more portable. Common development environments and management schemes will give MIS a single set of skills the entire staff can gain and use.

Staff members will not have to recreate existing applications from the bottom up. This will free them for other tasks such as developing new applications and responding to users' requests for changes. IS can handle these much more swiftly, reducing the lag time that is a traditional source of complaints.

Something for everyone

- System professionals
  - Better productivity
  - Technical control
- Management
  - Emphasis on business objectives
  - Better ability to plan
  - Responsiveness to business conditions
- Employees
  - Ease of use
  - New opportunities

Figure 8.5 Sound too good to be true?

Open systems will bring a greater sense of control to MIS, from both technology and management perspectives. Because open environments are more predictable, IS management will be more readily able to allocate resources and manage change.

Benefits to management

Management can also enjoy three major advantages:

- Less emphasis on technology and more on business
- Better ability to plan and manage technology investments
- Better response to changing needs and objectives

Management's job is to run the business. Ideally, an open system will let managers do exactly that. The best thing technology can to for a manager is to make itself invisible. Then, management can concern itself with now to use the technology to improve the business. There will be less need to worry about how to make the technology work.

Systems, software, training, and development expenditures within open systems will come in manageable chunks. That means your planning can be more accurate. Management can plan investments smoothly and in natural increments, taking a longer term approach to the return on these investments.

Open systems also help create a flexible, transportable environment. As organizations change roles, or as they create new divisions to tap market opportunities, their applications, data, and systems can move with them. They will also be readily able to add new resources to serve their new goals.

Serving the internal customer

The object of an enterprise network is to give employees easier access to more information. Open systems can play a major role in meeting that goal.

In the past, many employees resisted the proliferation of computer technology in the workplace. Sometimes, the employees had emotional reasons to resist. More often, they found the computers simply too hard to learn and use. This suggests a failure to seamlessly integrate the technology with the job requirements.

Technology should make an employee's work easier, not harder. With open systems, employees can gain new opportunities on which they can capitalize without having to understand the technology.

Today, the best-rewarded employee is often one who understands how to navigate the network, reach the mainframe, and use a complex report writer. The employee who can do these things is better prepared to distribute information from corporate databases. Open systems can help make information more readily available to all employees, so they can put it to productive use. Employees who learn how to retrieve this information, and to link it with business objectives, will reward themselves while rewarding their organizations.

There Are Some Problems

All this describes an ideal application of open systems. As anyone knows who has looked into the subject, most open systems applications are far from ideal. One big area of conflict has been between two competing ideas of proper timing. Businesses want useful systems and applications—yesterday. The bodies that set standards have taken a careful, even leisurely, pace. Vendors have been caught between their customers' demands and a lack of standard specifications for their products.

The result has been that customers and vendors have tried to fill the voids, adopting standards of their own where none exist now. If the idea is to maintain open systems, that is a step in exactly the wrong direction. A second major complaint is that vendors have not yet come forth with all the applications and utilities their customers need to use and maintain an open environment.

Product scorecard

Still, the field is maturing. A year-end 1992 report showed this picture:

Problem areas

- Timing lag between:
  - Business needs
  - Technical development
- Homegrown solutions
  - Vary from standards

Figure 8.6 Vendors are beginning to meet business needs.

- Available now

  Transaction processing monitors

  Transparent file access and management services

  Distributed transaction processing

- Due later

  OSF's Distributed Computing Environment (DCE) including directory and naming services

  Transaction processing over DCE

  Application management functions

  Systems and network management

- Due much later

  Distributed security, and time and object management services

  Access to non-SQL databases

  Distributed backup and restoration ability

  Ability to manage multiple data types

  Global data dictionaries

Significantly, there is a strong link between standards development and vendor interest. In the first category, standards are well established and vendors have developed firm plans to issue products. In the second group, standards and product plans were both still under development. In the final group there has been little movement, by either vendors or standards bodies.

Barriers to success

The User Alliance for Open Systems, an arm of the Corporation for Open Systems (COS), has identified nine barriers to success. To carry out an integrated business information systems environment, you must overcome these:

- The user community lacks a process to identify common requirements for open systems.

- The user community has no way to exert collective leverage on vendors to implement common requirements.

- Resources invested in systems and applications, and the attitude and culture of the work force, make it hard to evolve to an integrated business information environment.

- There are not enough open systems.

- Current business practices encourage a short-term approach to solving business problems, while ignoring long-term integration issues.

- There is no visible linkage between the use of open systems and accomplishing business missions and objectives.

- There is a fear of being unable to compete using open systems, causing an unwillingness to change.

- There is no documented, coherent vision of broad-based enterprise integration, or of the role open systems play in achieving that vision.

- There is no shared vision for developing an open systems process.

Take careful note: most of these are management issues, not technical problems. The only one that is purely technical is the lack of available open systems.

There are some technical problems that do exist. Among them is a particularly stubborn one: how to update legacy systems and applications to function in an open environment. It's not often practical just to give up on these systems. They represent considerable investments in hardware, system software, application software, and networks. There are also less tangible investments like expertise and training.

One reason it's hard to migrate to more cost-effective systems is that these legacy applications often serve critical day-to-day functions. You must keep them up and running. Making matters worse, this software often does not work well in an open, client/server environment for which it was never designed. As a further complication, the original source code often is either lost or too poorly documented.

Three Levels of Standardization

The standardization that creates an open system can take place at each of three levels:

- *Standard hardware and software platforms.*   PCs are an example here: most use Intel chips and the DOS operating system, often overlaid with Windows.

- *Standard applications.*   Standardization here does not always contribute to an open environment. When an organization standardizes on particular systems or software packages, it locks its employees into the chosen systems. They are unable to take advantage of competing applications.

- *Middleware.*   This is the layer of software that often lies between an application and the operating system or platform. Middleware is not part of either the application or the platform. Examples include databases, graphical interfaces, electronic mail, management tools, and application development tools.

Three levels of standardization

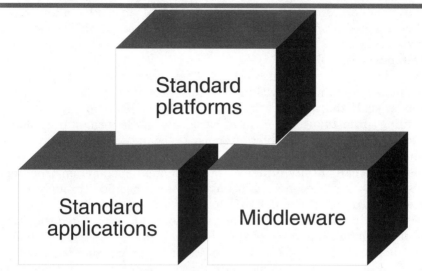

Figure 8.7   Middleware is becoming an increasingly important link.

Middleware's critical role

With the recent emphasis on open, standards-based technology, middleware is drawing more attention. It is becoming more independent of specific platforms. It uses standard protocols and interfaces when they are available and mature.

There are also many examples of middleware that are not based on standards. It often is appropriate to use this non-standardized technology. If proprietary technology solves a business problem, and if there is no standards-based solution available, you would be foolish to overlook the proprietary solution.

Standard middleware is the model adopted by users who decide to standardize on a particular component or set of components. Users who want to find standardized middleware, such as a specific vendor's database, should make sure they are not trading off software portability for hardware portability. They could find themselves locked into a software architecture instead of their desired hardware line.

There are alternatives in the standardized middleware model that can minimize this potential pitfall. Standardization at the middleware level represents the most flexible open systems' model. It offers more choice and, if implemented in a disciplined way, does the best job of avoiding proprietary products.

Maintaining a profile

To guard against being locked into a particular form of middleware, many businesses and standard setting organizations have adopted a process called *profiling*. A profile is a suite of standards. These standards specify the functions you need to meet the requirements for a given purpose.

Profiles can pay off in many ways. They give you a way to capitalize on the use of standards within your own organization and on a much broader scale than would otherwise be possible. In a business setting, profiling often takes the form of corporate guidelines, standards, or specifications. The companies often use these in the standards requirements sections of RFPs.

A profile can specify either a complete open systems environment (OSE) or an application-specific environment specified through Application Environment Profiles (AEP).

An AEP identifies the needs of the application area, cites the standards available that meet those needs, and notes any gaps that may exist between the needs and the standards. There may be nonstandardized technology available to fill these gaps. Application areas that could have their own profiles include Computer Aided Design (CAD), PC software and supercomputing.

Making MUSIC

Since there are many standards and technology choices in the middleware area, there is a multitude of ways to organize them within profiles. The Central Computer and Telecommunications Agency (CCTA) of the United Kingdom has developed a model to use in developing profiles. The model is known as the Management, User Service interface for programs, Information and data formats, and Communication interfaces. All that boils down to the acronym MUSIC. You can find elements of the MUSIC model in middleware. Using the MUSIC model, you can compare the various approaches taken by open systems and standards organizations.

The standard-setters

A model can also represent an OSE profile. Varying marketing conditions and customer needs can often produce differences among various organizations' profiles. Several standards organizations have produced OSE profiles, including these:

- *X/Open's Common Application Environment (CAE).* X/Open's model is based on its XPG (X/Open Portability Guide). Version 3 of this profile (XPG3) is a widely accepted profile in the industry today.

- *The Open Software Foundation (OSF) Application Environment Specification (AES).* The AES originally specified many formal standards. Examples of items that have been added to the AES include the Motif Graphical User Interface, Distributed Computing Environment (DCE), and Distributed Management Environment (DME).

- *Unix International's (UI's) Atlas for Open Systems.* Atlas is a framework for procurement similar to IBM's Systems Application Architecture. Atlas specifies Unix System V Release 4, Open Systems Interconnect networking standards, and the popular Motif and Open Look GUIs. It also specifies such distributed computing technologies as OSF's DCE and Sun Microsystems' Open Network Computing (ONC).

- *The National Institute of Standards and Technology's Application Portability Profile (APP).* APP is heavily based on formal standards from the Institute for Electrical and Electronic Engineers (IEEE).

Impatience with the process

One of the most frustrating characteristics of these organizations is that they have been exceedingly slow in publishing their standards. That delays the products business customers would like to have right now. This frustration has spawned many new kinds of standards coming from new kinds of standard setters—often user-driven. Examples include the User Alliance for Open Systems and Standards for Open Systems (SOS).

Both organizations are trying to ease the move to cost-effective open systems by putting forth their members' requirements. They seek improved productivity, quality, and customer satisfaction.

SOS consists of executives from 10 large customers: American Airlines, Du Pont, General Motors, Kodak, McDonnell Douglas, Merck, Motorola, 3M, Northrop, and Unilever. These executives have met several times as an informal group to exchange views about how to speed up the commercial availability of open systems based on vendor-neutral standards.

SOS focuses on establishing requirements for profiling. It is looking for quick results by taking advantage of existing processes, instead of defining and carrying out a new set of processes for information exchange.

The Corporation for Open Systems (COS) is an international non-profit organization made up of users, vendors, and government agencies. Its goal is speedier introduction of standards-based open-systems products and services. COS also helps organizations achieve practical interoperability. COS is also the umbrella organization for the North American MAP/TOP Users Group, the OSINET Corporation, the ISDN Executive Council, and the User Alliance for Open Systems.

Two Open-Systems Choices

Open systems are supposed to be uniform. In fact, they may be a little less uniform now than they were a few years ago.

In the past, distributed systems have been proprietary. Each major computer manufacturer designed its hardware and software to provide interoperability among that company's systems. If you stayed within your chosen vendor's system, things could hardly be more uniform.

Modern desktop-centered computing can make uniformity seem like an impossible dream. Two industry-sponsored organizations, though, offer competing systems that could easily reduce the available choices to no more than two. One of those choices comes from the Open Software Foundation, the other from Unix International. Both aim to provide distributed platforms that span multiple architectures, protocols, and operating systems.

OSF's product is the Distributed Computing Environment (DCE). UI calls its effort the Atlas distributed processing architecture. DCE and Atlas both address distributed computing problems, but they do not compete directly. DCE provides basic distributed computing services. Atlas extends those basic services.

DCE and Atlas both seem destined to become recognized standards for distributed computing. DCE responds in particular to the needs of customers who are trying to create distributed environments on their own. Between them, they represent most major vendors in the computer industry—more than 200 organizations.

Independence from Unix

Both UI and OSF are best known for their competing versions of Unix, but neither distributed environment depends on any particular operating system. DCE works as well on Macs as it does on Unix. Atlas also provides interoperability with non-Unix operating environments. UI and OSF are open-systems organizations in which Unix is only part of the broader open-systems philosophy. Like distributed computing, this philosophy is based on interoperability, scalability, portability, and compatibility among different architectures.

Either lets other systems communicate and share information. Sun Microsystems SunOS, for instance, can work in harmony with IBM's AIX and Systems Application Architecture (SAA). DEC's Ultrix, VMS, and Network Application Support (NAS), along with multiple architectures from Bull, Hewlett-Packard, and Siemens-Nixdorf, are among the first to incorporate DCE.

The two systems can work together as well. UI has incorporated OSF's DCE into Atlas' basic structure. This means UI will take advantage of the OSF's interoperability features.

How do they work?

Both systems rest on client/server foundations. A distributed computing environment includes two or more client/server combinations in a potentially huge network. With more than one server, you can split, modularize, and spread the applications, services, and data across the servers. Servers can then pass information among themselves; a server thus can be a client to another server.

A distributed environment consists of several important elements:

- *Communication.* This is the backbone of distributed computing. Both DCE and Atlas support OSI networking protocols. They also support others, including TCP/IP and X.25.

- *Remote procedure calls.* RPCs manage communication among applications distributed across heterogeneous networks. Distributed systems also need name or directory services. These manage and control location changes of resources, applications, and even users. They also need time services to synchronize the activities of the various computers in the distributed environment.

- *A distributed file system.* This component provides global file access. Examples include Sun's Network File System (NFS) and OSF's DFS.

- *Security.* As with any kind of network, you need authentication and authorization mechanisms to deter unauthorized users.

- *Transparency.* Human clients can use all these features without having to worry about them, or even to know that they exist.

The LAN factor

Open systems also have important foundations in local area networks. LAN technology includes several methods including RPCs, transport protocols, and network authorization systems to help provide interoperability at the local network level.

These developments alone are not enough to support an enterprise network. In combination, they also are often insufficient. What's more, they don't work readily together. It can be a disheartening challenge to try to figure out which platforms, protocols, naming services, authorization systems, and other features work with which other elements of the network. Expanding the scope from a LAN to an enterprise network multiplies the complications. What's more, you won't soon be rid of the varied LANs and other disparate systems that probably have sprung up around your organization. As a practical matter, you'll probably find yourself integrating them into the system, not replacing them.

DCE and Atlas can overcome many of these problems. DCE incorporates various forms of technology into an integrated product. Atlas adds additional functions.

Distributing applications

Distributed environments provide the platforms for distributed applications. The first distributed applications have generally been simple ones like e-mail and distributed file systems. The most common early use of distributed systems was to share resources like database information and printer services. As the technology evolves, distributed computing software developers should provide more sophisticated applications written to capitalize on the distributed environment.

A distributed application's most important feature is transparent access to all the data it needs. For example, your organization's marketing department may use one server, the sales department another, and inventory control a third. You can create a single database application with data distributed across all three servers, even though the individual workgroup data resides on the individual servers. When you want to incorporate marketing information, sales figures, and inventory levels into one report, your application sends requests to all three servers and consolidates it on your desktop system.

What Is DCE?

The Open Software Foundation's Distributed Computing Environment (DCE) is designed as a comprehensive enterprise-wide networking scheme. It's gained attention from many vendors, including some non-OSF members. Unix Systems Laboratories (USL), owner of Unix System V and co-developer with Novell of Unixware, says it will integrate DCE into its future products.

One big advantage of DCE is a true distributed file system. This system is based on the Andrew File System (AFS) developed at Carnegie-Mellon University. AFS provides a common environment for any workstation on the network.

DCE also is strong in Remote Procedure Calls (RPCs). The DCE RPC lets a program on one system call a subroutine on another, even if the second system has a different processor and operating system. If the target system is different, it can translate the information to its own format.

Network security is also a major DCE feature. It lets the target system authenticate each procedure call setup. This keeps hostile users—or just ham-handed ones—from writing programs that might cross a network, make unauthorized access, or damage files. The authentication can have multiple levels with associated privileges. For example, an individual may be allowed to read data, but not to change it.

Several vendors have been working on DCE products on both Unix and proprietary systems. They include HP, Digital, and IBM.

Inside DCE

More than 100 vendors now support DCE. They include IBM, DEC, Bull, HP, Siemens-Nixdorf, and Hitachi. Their customers include the European Commission, American Express, Nippon Telegraph and Telephone, and Boeing.

A key to that level of interest is OSF's multi-vendor, multi-technology approach. It is the result of OSF's Request for Technology process, which solicits technology from the computer industry at large. Interested companies submitted their products; from those submissions, OSF chose those it judged to be the best in the industry. It included these in DCE. Sources of the chosen technology include start-ups such as Transarc, OSF members DEC and HP, and even UI member Sun. Specifically, DCE's technology includes:

- Enhanced Network Computing System/RPC from HP and DEC

- DECdns name service from DEC

- DIR-X X.500 directory service from Siemens AG

- Kerberos security service from MIT with HP extensions

- PC-NFS from Sun

- AFS 4.0 distributed file system from Transarc

- LM/X PC integration technology from Microsoft

- Concert Multi-Threads Architecture from DEC

- DECdts time service from DEC

Basic services

DCE's services fall into two categories: fundamental distributed services and data sharing services.

The fundamental services group includes tools with which software developers can build user services and applications. These services include:

- *Remote procedure calls.* An RPC lets you build applications that use individual procedures running on computers across a heterogeneous network. It includes two components that help in building client/server applications:

  An RPC facility that provides simplicity, performance, portability, and network independence.

A compiler that converts client and server interface descriptions into C source code. This lets RPCs behave in the same way as local procedure calls.

- *Directory service.* The directory service provides a single naming model for resources such as servers, files, and disks across the distributed environment.

- *Time service.* DCE maintains a distributed time reference to synchronize activity and events among the computers on a network.

- *Threads service.* Threads control program flow. They let an application process many commands simultaneously. Programmers can use this feature within local or distributed environments. Thread service is also useful in client/server control, because a server can initiate many threads to clients.

- *Security service.* This service authorizes, authenticates, and manages user access to individual hosts on the distributed network. It includes a secure RPC to protect the integrity of communication, Kerberos authentication to validate the identity of a user or service, authorization tools that control user access to resources, and a user registry to manage user account information.

Data sharing

The data sharing services are based on the Fundamental Distributed Services standard. These provide extra functions without the need for extra programming. In DCE, these services include:

- *A distributed file system.* DFS is the key information-sharing component. It joins the files and directories of individual workstations and provides a consistent application interface.

- *Diskless support.* The distributed file system supports diskless workstations and provides protocols for diskless support.

- *Personal Computer Integration.* PCI lets Unix, MS-DOS, and OS/2 users share files, peripherals, and applications.

The Anatomy of Atlas

Atlas focuses on features DCE does not initially handle. It incorporates DCE in some of its base-level services. Then it maps these DCE services to other services so applications can be portable and interoperable. Beyond the DCE functions, Atlas supports distributed transaction processing and fault-tolerant support services.

Since Atlas incorporates DCE, applications should be portable and interoperable between them. Atlas uses DCE's application program interfaces (APIs). An Atlas application that uses that system's extended features will not have these available if ported to DCE.

Atlas is based on Unix System V. It groups common functions together in layers. These functions are visible to other layers through APIs. Atlas is based on UI functional specifications that include:

- *Operating System and Network Communication Services Layers.* System V release 4.0 is Atlas's basic operating system. The Open Systems Interconnection (OSI) protocol stacks and tools from the ISO extend SVR4 to provide standardized communication among heterogeneous systems. It supports X/Open APIs and offers service and provider interfaces defined by UI and Unix System Laboratories. It also supports stacks that conform to the Government Open Systems Interconnect Profile, tools to manipulate stacks and data, and tools to help migrate from TCP/IP to OSI.

- *System Services Layer.*   UI defines this layer as the core of the distributed computing environment and the foundation on which the components that support distributed applications and tools are built. It includes:

  Directory file system and data storage services.   These provide transparent access to distributed file systems.

  Client/server computing.   Client/server is the basis for providing Atlas services. The most important part of this framework is RPC, which provides the mechanism for distributing applications that are split across multiple systems.

  Naming services.   These services manage a system of references to systems and network resources. Atlas follows the federated naming model established by ANSI and the European Computer Manufacturers Association. This model provides for composite names, consisting of components from multiple naming models, not just a single syntax. This makes it easier to port applications written under different naming schemes.

  Time services.   These services synchronize system clocks for proper communication among disparate systems.

  Object management services.   Object technology provides transparency and incorporates this fast-developing technology into the framework.

- *Applications Services Layer.*   This layer includes the user interface, a transaction monitor, and network management. These services support the top Atlas layer, Application Tools. The user interface service supports X Window GUIs, including Open Look and Motif. It also supports transaction processing services from both large systems and local workstations.

- *Security Services Layer.*   Two mechanisms address security authentication and access control.

- *Interoperability Layer.*   This layer includes network services to allow interoperability among disparate systems. It includes OSF's DCE, IBM's SAA, DEC's NAS, and PC LANs.

Elements of a Mixed Strategy

An effective heterogeneous networking strategy has these main elements:

- It adapts to multiple architectures as part of a single, standardized solution.

- It is a well-supported standard that scales well and is manageable. Today, that means TCP/IP; in a few years, OSI may be a practical alternative.

- It offers a suite of standard services, such as file sharing, network printing, and remote access.

Because some users still require traditional PC network protocol support within individual LANs, it will be necessary to support these protocols on LAN servers. If PC memory is adequate, add TCP/IP to each client PC to provide a common standard of service. TCP/IP is standard in all Unix systems.

For standard services, there are two choices based on the predominant networking service in use. You can introduce Unix systems into a PC LAN, or you can add PCs to a Unix LAN. In the first case, the file sharing and printing solutions are likely to follow PC LAN practice, either Netware or LAN Manager. You can ensure PC LAN continuity by running the appropriate service (Portable Netware or LAN Manager for Unix) on the Unix system.

In the second case, the Unix systems will usually be using Network File System (NFS) and related protocols. PCs can use DOS versions of the same networking service, such as that provided by Sun Microsystems' PC-NFS. This initial decision will affect which lower-level architecture you use. If you decide to migrate to TCP/IP on all systems, NFS becomes the obvious choice for file sharing, because it uses a widely available, scalable network architecture.

Local Networks: Exploding the Box

Once upon a time, a local area network let a small group of people share resources. Now, a LAN is one link in a network that lets large groups of people share resources.

If necessity is the mother of invention, the local area network is the offspring. When traditional MIS shops were slow to respond to employees' needs, these internal customers became internal entrepreneurs. They brought in personal computers. They hooked these computers into LANs. These local networks let department members share the information and facilities that became available through network servers. They also let departments spread the costs of laser printers and other expensive gear among multiple users.

LANs have an effect called "exploding the box." From laptops to the buildings that house mainframes, computers originally had single housings. That's true no longer. As a common phrase goes, "the network is the computer." A computer system can consist of several computers, the network that connects them, and a variety of special-purpose servers.

Degrees of Integration

Enterprise networking also explodes the box, but it uses a bigger charge. Now, the system is not just a local network, but a large, enterprise-wide network. Enterprise networking forces you to adjust your perspective. If you believe file and printer sharing is all you need, you still are thinking in terms of a departmental LAN, not an enterprise network. Organizations are learning that often isn't enough.

The LAN represents only the first of four networking levels:

- *Local networks.* At this level, employees need to share data files from time to time, but the traffic is not heavy. There's little need to translate data to another format.

- *Formal software sharing.* At this level, the organization has decided to begin a formal program of data and software sharing. You may also need access to midrange and mainframe computers. The differences in data formats among these dissimilar systems can be a significant challenge.

- *Interoperation.* It's important that systems at this level work together. Client/server applications are in operation. Disparate data formats have become a serious consideration.

- *Full data transparency.* Employees can log onto any PC or workstation and, if they are authorized, retrieve data from any other part of the network. The network appears to them as a single entity, not as a collection of individual components. If you have achieved this level, disparate data formats are no longer a problem. The system takes care of them automatically.

Most organizations are still at the early stages. Many would like to get to the later stages. A few pioneering firms have reached the top levels. For most, though, true integration remains a long-term goal.

Four levels of networking

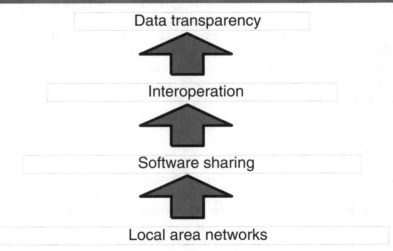

Figure 9.1 A LAN is the starting point for higher-level networking.

Building block

Not everyone needs to go all the way. It's obvious that the basic resource sharing of a local area network is a major asset to many users. Not everyone needs a unified enterprise network. Unless you do, it makes little sense to invest the time, money, and anguish it would require to progress further up the scale.

Don't knock the LAN. There's a reason for its popularity. Furthermore, LANs are essential components of enterprise networks. In most organizations, enterprise networks will be made up mainly of linked LANs. LANs also have something in common with mainframes: since they're probably already in place, you might as well make use of them. One of your main tasks, then, will be to locate and understand the LANs in your organization and to get them ready for wider-area service.

LAN Fundamentals

LANs carry data in much the same way the telephone system carries voice signals; many LANs use telephone wire. The biggest difference is in the way the two systems transmit their signals.

A voice signal coming over a telephone line is continuous. When you speak into a phone, the other party hears you almost instantly. Before a LAN transmits information, it assembles the data into *packets*. A packet serves much the same function as an envelope. The information is slipped inside; on the outside, the network operating system adds the origin and destination addresses and other data that will help the network get the packet to its destination.

Each type of LAN has its own type of *network operating system* (NOS) software to translate the electronic addressing and route the packet properly. Each NOS uses its particular kind of *protocol*. Like the rules of diplomacy, a network protocol establishes the rules for translating and dispatching the messages. The protocol establishes such things as how to identify each computer, how to verify the information they transmit, what to do in case of an error, and how to tell when the transmission is finished. Usually, a single LAN will use a single protocol, but that isn't always the case. You may have a PC running Novell Netware and a mainframe running its proprietary operating system. In that case, there must be a gateway between the two. The gateway serves the diplomatic function of an interpreter, translating the protocol of one machine into a form the other can understand.

Many kinds of networks

Networks come in a confusing variety of sizes, types, hardware, and software. They range from the simple to the complex. To begin to simplify the discussion, available LAN types can be placed in four major categories. Significantly, they roughly correspond to the levels of networking discussed earlier. The progression also illustrates how a basic LAN might grow into a full enterprise network:

- *Print and file sharing.* Simple switching mechanisms let small groups of users share resources. They range from manual switches to *zero-slot LANs,* which permit file transfers via a cable between two computers. The network might have a single laser printer, for example, letting several users share this resource. Or, representatives coming in from the field may plug in their portables to move information to the office system.

- *Peer-to-peer networks.* This is a fast-growing form of local area networking designed for small businesses and departments. The main characteristic of a peer-to-peer LAN is that it does not need a designated file server—though it can have one. All workstations and other nodes are created equal. All users might have direct access to a word processing file stored on one system's hard disk. They could work with this file directly; they need not transfer it to their own systems. Network members can also share printers and other resources. Computers in this type of system are usually PCs running under DOS. These are simple systems that have become popular for good reason in local area networking. They are limited, though, in their ability to work with other networks.

- *Client/server LANs.* Here, higher-powered units provide major resources for a network that typically serves a single office or department. A file server is usually the minimum requirement. A client/server LAN can also have any number of specialized servers, such as those which manage communication or carry database files.

- *Enterprise-wide internetworks.* These are groups of LANs linked together, perhaps with wide area networks (WANs) in the picture as well. They give users in one office or department access to corporate-wide data, perhaps from a database server in another location entirely.

The Client/Server LAN

The most common LAN pattern is client/server. Individual workstations are the clients. The network gives them the assets of one or more computers designated as network servers. These come in many forms and functions:

- *File servers.*   These are the central points of access to the network. Most network operating systems are designed to support these servers for DOS workstations. All access passes through a server. This is also where the system applies any necessary security screening. Originally, servers were also the central points for network access, though this function is gradually gravitating to workstations, particularly in Macintosh and Unix systems.

- *Database servers.*   These are central, of course, in larger-scale client/server systems. In truth, they are a special kind of file server. They store and manage database files. That's often a large enough job alone for a dedicated server. This pattern spares the file server the workload of database management.

- *Communication servers.*   These let users share modems and expensive outside access lines such as connections to wide area networks.

- *Electronic mail gateways.*   These are communication servers that provide access to e-mail and similar services. They run communication programs like CC:Mail, DaVinci, and PROFS. They also can provide fax services, though fax produces large graphic-image files whose transmission can clog up a network.

- *Print servers.*   Printer sharing is a basic LAN function. Dedicated printing gives larger networks higher-capacity printer sharing facilities without taking resources from other network operations.

A variety of servers

- Database servers
  - Important, but not the only kind
- File servers
- Print servers
- Communication servers
  - E-mail
  - Fax
  - Voice mail

Figure 9.2   Servers can provide many kinds of services, some familiar, some not.

Specialized servers

Some newer kinds of servers are also being developed. They include:

- *Fax servers* use internal fax cards to transmit network users' outgoing faxes and manage the incoming messages. There still is one remaining problem: how to distribute the incoming faxes.

- *Voice servers* are an extension of conventional voice mail systems. They also can incorporate existing e-mail systems. The day may come when an employee can call in to pick up his or her electronic mail, though there is a human limit to this potential: it's hard to comprehend a message that plays for more than a few minutes. These systems may take advantage of a developing technology, the Integrated Services Digital Network. ISDN is designed to carry both voice and data messages over the same lines.

- *Video servers* could become important as document imaging spreads. Imaging systems store graphic representations of documents. Their storage and processing will demand a high-powered server.

- *Library servers* manage volumes of archival data stored on CD ROM disks.

Most LANs now are based at least on file servers. Other specialized servers may handle communication, printing, and other functions. Though it's common to think of a server as a high-powered PC, this isn't always necessary. Smaller units often can do the lighter, specialized work. Normally, each server is a separate computer. It is possible, though, for more than one server to share the same enclosure. Each, however, should have its own dedicated bus structure.

Planning principles

This separation of powers carries out one of the three major principles of planning a LAN, or any other kind of network for that matter:

- The network should be *modular.* You can add the special services you need simply by installing servers which provide those services.

- The system should have an *open architecture.* Proprietary formats limit the ability to add modular units for the specialized purposes you might need.

- The network should have a *sound, well-planned architecture.* Think of the network as a unit. Don't make unplanned, piece-by-piece additions.

LAN design principles

- Modular design
  - To add services as needed
- Open system
  - To broaden your options
- Planned architecture
  - To work as a unit

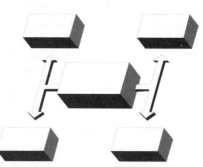

Figure 9.3 Multiple pieces from multiple sources should all work together.

When planning or evaluating a LAN, start with the file server. Then, build out from there. Avoid the problems that plague many unplanned networks. They are like the orphan Topsy of *Uncle Tom's Cabin*: "I 'spect I growed. Don't think nobody ever made me."

One reason networks spring up like Topsy is that system managers look for products instead of planning a system. A *solution* is something you plan and develop, not just something you buy.

What Are LANs Made Of?

Clients and servers are the most visible and hardest-working parts of a local area network. These are, after all, the computers the network is intended to link. Connecting them, however, requires a confusing conglomeration of bits and pieces. Some are hardware, some are software, and some combine elements of both.

Nearly any kind of computer can function as a server when its task is specialized and light-duty. At the other extreme, heavy-duty database service can require a high-powered superserver with its fast processors, multiple disk drives, and other features that equip it for this demanding type of duty.

Short of that, the most effective PC-based servers have these two main characteristics:

- An 80386 processor, or higher. Many network operating systems, and some network applications, take advantage of the capabilities of the 386 and later chips, versus the earlier 80286.

- A large, fast hard disk. Nothing affects the server's performance more.

Network adapters

Every networked computer needs one of these interface cards. They translate the signals that travel along the network cables into messages the computer can understand and use. They also amplify outgoing signals and convert them between parallel and serial formats.

Generally, a card will incorporate one of three prevailing networking standards: Ethernet, Arcnet, or token ring.

An adapter card has one other major function: media access control or MAC. This is a control system that keeps signals from different computers, or *nodes,* from interfering with each other. The process usually takes one of three forms:

- *Carrier sense multiple access (CSMA).*   This is something like carrying on a conversation over the telephone: you wait for the other party to finish talking, then it's your turn. A CSMA board listens for traffic on the network; if it finds none, it is free to transmit its own signals. A CSMA board also, out of necessity, includes a tiebreaker system for those times when two stations detect an opportunity and begin transmitting simultaneously. Ethernet systems use a method called CSMA/CD, or carrier sense multiple access with collision detection.

- *Sequential station numbers.*   This method, used in Arcnet, assigns a number to each node. Access is like waiting in line at a deli. Each number is called in turn, and each station waits for its number to come up.

- *Token passing.*   An electrical signal called a *token* is passed from station to station. When the token arrives at each station, that station is free to transmit. As its name suggests, a token ring network uses this system.

Network cabling

To have a network, there usually must be wires. That's no longer a universal requirement. No-cable networks use infrared flashes to transmit messages among nodes. For the most part, though, the circulatory system of a network is its cabling.

Like nearly everything else in networking, cable comes in multiple varieties:

- *Twisted pair.*   This may sound like a rock group or something in an X-rated movie. Actually, it is the ordinary lightweight wiring commonly used in telephone systems. You probably can run your network over telephone wiring that is already in place, though in practice you'll probably find your needs exceed the available wiring. The best twisted pair wiring for data transmission meets the specifications for a version of the Ethernet protocol called *10BaseT.*

- *Shielded twisted pair.*   Also called data-grade twisted pair, this type of wiring has an external shield to insulate it from electrical interference. It is common in token ring installations, where it adds insurance against damage and interference. The drawbacks: it is expensive and hard to handle.

- *Coaxial cable.*   This is the cable in cable television. It consists of a single central wire surrounded by a shield. It shares the advantages and disadvantages of shielded twisted pair. Some varieties are stiff and hard to install.

- *Fiber optic cable.*   If money is no object, this is the type to use. Since it uses light instead of electrical signals, this type is immune to electrical interference. It can also travel long distances without the need for amplification. It is particularly useful in areas where machinery is in use, or where there is a great distance among nodes.

The topic of topology

Topology refers to the physical layout of the network cables. There are three basic varieties:

- In a *bus* network, the network begins with a single strand of cable. At each station, a T-connector holds a wire that branches off to the station's adapter card. This format uses less cable than the others and is the least expensive, but it is also the least reliable. A cable break can shut down the entire network, and each of the many connectors is a possible failure point.

- A *star* network consists of a single cable from each node, leading to a central wiring hub. It is easier and neater to install, and a break in one cable doesn't affect the remainder of the network. This system uses more cable, however, and the hub itself can be a costly, complex installation.

- In its simplest form, the *ring* topology is simply a bus whose ends are connected to form a loop. It rarely exists in this form, but it often is emulated. Here's how:

  A token ring network suggests that a token used for media access control passes from a station around a ring topology. That's a logical conclusion, and it's almost correct. Most token ring networks connect their cables in a star topology. As the token is passed, however, it emulates a ring, passing from node to node as though they were wired in a circle.

A typical bus network

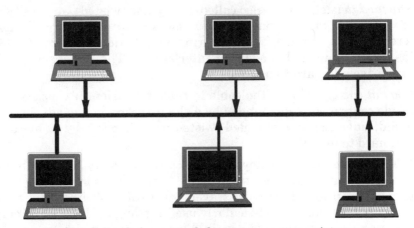

Figure 9.4   The simplicity of a bus network does not mean easy maintenance.

A typical star network

Figure 9.5   A token ring network also uses a star configuration, but passes a token to each node in turn.

Network Protocols

As mentioned earlier, network adapter cards usually support one of three networking protocols: Ethernet, Arcnet, or token ring. The choice of standards dictates other elements of the system such as topology, media access control, and the type of cabling.

These protocols are also sometimes known as standards, which is natural enough. Their official designation is *standard protocols*. They are the creation of committees established by the Institute of Electrical and Electronics Engineers (IEEE) and representatives of the electronics and communication industries.

Ethernet and 10BaseT

Ethernet, named after a poetic term for electromagnetic waves, has been on the market almost since there have been personal computers. It has the appeal of low cost and simplicity. It will provide high-speed transmission at a reasonable price, and a host of vendors and products support it. Among its more important specifications:

- A data transmission rate of 10 megabits per second

- Use of a bus topology

- Maximum distance between stations of 2.8 kilometers, or about 1¾ miles

- The use of shielded coaxial cable, or twisted-pair wiring in the 10BaseT version

- Media access control by CSMA/CD.

In its long life, Ethernet has spun off several variations. The original cabling scheme was used primarily to connect large computers with smaller terminals and workstations. The coaxial cable used as the back-

---

LAN configuration checklist

1. What types of LANs are operating in your organization now?
2. What configuration options do you have for future installations?
3. What is your preferred network operating system?
4. What are your preferred specifications for a file server?
5. What disk storage demand should you anticipate:
   - On servers?
   - On workstations?
6. What are the possible internetworking consequences of your LAN decisions?
7. What kinds of cabling offer:
   - Best use of existing resources?
   - Best long-term performance?

bone of these installations is thick, stiff, and hard to handle. Lighter cables run from connectors on this backbone to the individual stations.

A variation called *thin Ethernet* uses lighter weight cable, which makes installation easier at the expense of transmission distance. More recent variations make use of fiber optics or twisted pair wiring.

The 10BaseT variation

Earlier, 10BaseT was mentioned as a specification for twisted-pair wiring. That's part of the story. The IEEE published this specification in 1990, as a standard for bringing this inexpensive form of wiring to Ethernet networks.

The purpose of this standard was to promote easier installation; technicians need not contend with the frozen-rope characteristics of coaxial cable. Network managers have found other advantages that probably are more important.

The greatest of these is the ability to use a star topology, instead of the traditional Ethernet bus. This helps make a more reliable system; a fault in one line affects only the node to which it is attached. In addition, 10BaseT has become so widely supported it is almost generic. You can select adapters and wiring hubs from a variety of sources and mix them as you wish. For all this convenience, there is no significant performance penalty.

The token ring

This is the protocol that has IBM behind it. It is at the center of IBM's system of both local and wide area network architecture. With the right connections, all supplied by IBM, you can make a mainframe and a PC look like peers on the same network.

This is not strictly an IBM standard, though. Other manufacturers make token ring products, and the protocol is compatible with all the major network operating systems.

A token ring system operates something like a parking lot shuttle at Walt Disney World. It uses a signal packet called, naturally enough, a token. This token makes the rounds, checking at each stop for messages ready to be transmitted. If the token finds something, it packages the data into a *frame* and attaches it to the token. The token becomes *busy,* and no other station can transmit until it has delivered the frame full of data. The message travels to the receiving station, which copies the data from the frame. The station acknowledges receipt, and the token drags the message back to the point of origin. The receiving station notes that the message was received and absorbs the busy token. It then generates another token to pick up a new message from some other point on the system.

Though a token ring network uses a physical star topology, an error that blocks the token's circulation can effectively keep the entire network from operating. For that reason, most token ring networks use shielded twisted-pair cable to block out any possible contamination by outside electrical impulses.

Other key specifications include:

- Data transfer rates of 4 or 16 megabits per second.
- Maximum cable lengths of about 45 meters, or 150 feet.

Note: A system's maximum data transfer rates are like the top speed of an automobile: rarely achieved and even more rarely done safely. Only in the largest networks will differences in these specifications affect performance.

Arcnet

Arcnet, originated by Datapoint, is less well known than the others. It represents a lowcost form of networking. Arcnet usually operates in a multiple star pattern: small hubs of two to four cables each, linked to other hubs of similar size. Arcnet hubs can use either coaxial cable or unshielded twisted-pair.

Arcnet networks can cover a lot of ground. Maximum cable lengths can be up to 2000 feet; under the right conditions, the network can extend as far as 20,000 feet. Access control is by a polling system which contacts numbered stations in order. The normal operating speed is 2.5 megabits per second.

That speed is slower than some superservers deliver data. There are ways to divide the network and use multiple channels to overcome that limitation. Users have found that performance is best when you keep consecutively numbered stations close to each other and assign the lowest numbers to the most powerful units.

Network Operating Systems

Just as a computer needs an operating system, so does a network. PC operating systems used in networking applications include DOS, OS/2, and Unix. The leading network operating systems (NOSs) include:

- The Novell Netware family
- Banyan Vines
- LAN Manager
- Unix, which is both a computer and a network operating system

Top of the Netware line

Novell has by far the largest share of the NOS market. Netware comes in several versions for installations of different sizes, from large enterprise-wide networks to a handful of small-business PCs. The two most likely to be considered for an enterprise network are version 3.x and higher.

Particularly at the top of the line, Netware is a sophisticated NOS that can integrate diverse computing resources, including PCs, Unix workstations, Apple Macintoshes, and mainframes, into a single enterprise-wide system.

These versions of Netware are designed with enterprise networking in mind. They take full advantage of the 32-bit environment of the 80386 and 80486 microprocessors, providing the performance and capacity needed to build networks that span entire organizations. Netware lets you standardize on a single network operating system for a central office and remote sites.

These are powerful systems. Before you reach their capacity limits, you'll probably exceed the limits of other elements of the system.

Security is also an important element. A network administrator can control who logs in to the network, who has access to specific files and directories, and how much disk space a user can claim. There are built-in reliability features such as read-after-write verification, disk mirroring, disk duplexing, resource tracking, a Transaction Tracking System (TTS), and power supply monitoring. These increase dependability by safeguarding data against failure in critical parts of the network.

Other security enhancements include security auditing and encrypted backups. The auditing function maintains an audit trail of all security changes that take place on the server. As Netware backups files over the network, it transmits the data in encrypted form.

Remote management facilities let the administrator manage remote servers from any workstation on the network. Netware interfaces directly with IBM's Netview management application, so network alerts can go to a central administration console.

Higher versions of Netware also accommodate Netware Loadable Modules (NLMs). These are software modules, some provided by Novell, some by outside suppliers. They link dynamically to the operating system and let you add server-based applications to the server while it is running. These applications include drivers for network cards, electronic mail gateways, and products that provide additional security, work group activity, and network management functions.

Netware also lets you add needed services like communication, database access, and network management. Novell provides some of these add-on services, including Netware for SAA, Netware for Macintosh, Netware NFS, and Netware SQL 386.

Netware version 2

This is basic Netware—the NOS that's been mainly responsible for Novell's leading position in the network marketplace. This version lacks some advanced features like the add-on modules and features that take advantage of the 386 and 486 chips. It is designed for medium-sized networks with up to 100 users.

Security is a strong point with this Netware version. It assigns users to groups; each group has certain access rights. If someone changes job assignments, the network administrator can simply transfer that person to a new group. There's no need to go through all the specific access authorizations for that person. The system also lets the administrator restrict access to certain days and times and to require periodic password changes.

An add-on module adds disk mirroring and duplexing for added reliability.

The main rap against version 2: it is a consultant's make-work tool. Installation is not as easy as later-generation systems.

On the Vines

Netware clearly shows its PC roots. Banyan Systems' Vines takes its cues from standard minicomputer software. Vines is a high-end system, most directly competitive with Netware 3.11, in both price and features. Vines is based on Unix and handles all the common server functions, including communication.

A Vines server can use just about any hardware platform you want. Banyan sells its own line of server PCs, but nearly any PC from the 286 class up can be a Vines server. Like Netware, Vines is available in separate versions for 80286 and for higher systems; there are also versions for Micro channel computers and systems with multiple processors, like the Compaq Systempro.

One advantage over competing systems is a Vines feature that lets users find network resources faster by replicating directory information on servers throughout the network. This is particularly useful when the system has several servers. Another unique feature is the access to gateways, mail systems, print queues, fax gateways, and host gateways.

LAN Manager

This generic NOS is sold under the labels of several vendors, including IBM, Microsoft, and 3Com. Though the systems are identical, each vendor presents its version in a different way.

There is this requirement: all LAN Manager servers must run OS/2. Client workstations can use either DOS or OS/2. Since OS/2 is inherently a multitasking system, a LAN Manager server conceivably can run OS/2 applications while also functioning as a file server. That would make it a leading candidate to become involved in distributed processing. This is a system that lets application programs take advantage of CPU processors wherever they may be on the network.

One major drawback: except for database server products, there have been few OS/2 applications to capitalize on this opportunity.

Networking with Unix

The Unix operating system, originally developed by and for AT&T programmers, is often associated with high-powered graphic workstations. These stations usually feature reduced instruction set computing (RISC) designs, and graphic displays that use the X Window system and produce a visual effect similar to Microsoft Windows. Another popular use is to run Unix on a 386-class PC as a lowcost application or database server.

Unlike DOS, Unix was designed from scratch to serve multiple users, applications, and systems. One thing Unix does well is mix with DOS operating systems on PCs. Unix can run on a variety of hosts, including minicomputers as well as PCs. In that role, it can act as the host to a network of DOS-based PCs. For example, you can create a database on a minicomputer running Unix; operators stationed at PCs can gain access to that database through a system that makes the same files look like Unix files to the minicomputer and DOS files to the PCs.

One popular way of linking PC and Unix systems is the Network File System (NFS) developed by Sun Microsystems. A DOS version of NFS running on each PC gives the PC users simultaneous access to the server's Unix files.

An alternative offered by both Digital and AT&T is a version of LAN Manager designed to run under Unix. Client PCs use the same software to connect with a Unix/LAN Manager server they would use if the server were running OS/2. You can map drives on client PCs to both types of servers simultaneously.

Since LAN Manager is available in both Unix and OS/2 versions, it provides the ability to mix and match computer systems. This can be valuable if a large database demands a minicomputer server, or if writers and editors are using PCs, sending their output to a Unix-based publishing system.

There is this possible drawback: any translation of files between two operating systems is going to take some time. Testers have found that the response is not as quick as you would get using DOS workstations and a Netware file server, but in most applications the lag should not be critical.

Preparing the LAN to Share

LANs tend to be closed societies. The main components—protocols, operating systems, and hardware—are designed to work in small-group unison. LAN users might express doubt about how well they do that, but they're supposed to.

The components of enterprise networks aren't intended to work together. Different departments in your organization might be using Macintoshes, Unix systems, and PC networks under several different network operating systems. Never mind how you got into this situation. The question now is how you are going to make these disparate LANs work together.

Stacking protocols

NOS internetworking is based on a process of *protocol stacking*. That means loading more than one protocol into the same machine.

To complicate matters, you need two different kinds of protocols:

- A *transport protocol* handles the postal service part of the transaction. It encloses messages in an electronic envelope and forwards them to another network node. In a PC LAN, that might be a communication server.

- A *service protocol* takes care of the secretarial duties. It defines the format and meaning of the messages before they are placed in the envelope. It also helps clients make requests of the servers—and even to get responses.

Each NOS has its preferred protocols. Netware uses IPX, while LAN Manager uses something called Netbeui. Appleshare uses Appletalk. The usual Unix protocol is the IP of TCP/IP. A DOS system usually manages stacks of transport protocols as terminate-and-stay-resident (TSR) modules. At the file server, the transport stack is part of the NOS software.

If you want to link a Netware client with a Unix server, you have three choices at the transport level:

- Load IPX at the Unix server.
- Load IP at the Netware client.
- Set up a gateway between the IPX and IP systems.

Each of these options requires a dual stack that contains IP and IPX. The main difference among the three is where you put the stack. With the first choice, the dual stack will be in the Unix system. The second places it at the Netware client. The third puts the combined stack in a gateway between the two.

Transport is only one type of protocol. You also need service protocols so clients can request useful services from the servers. Again, each NOS has its favorites. Novell uses the Netware Core Protocol (NCP). LAN Manager uses the Service Message Block (SMB) protocol. The standard service protocol for Unix systems is the Network File System (NFS). Appleshare uses the Appletalk Filing Protocol (AFP).

Where to stack

Your choice of a location for the stacks involves some tradeoffs. A stack on the client side presents three big problems:

- The multiple TSRs can require more memory than you want to sacrifice at the client station.

- Most client-based stacks require difficult dual logins.

- Server-based stacks are easier to administer.

On the other hand, there is one potential drawback to stacking at the server. A server with a limited stack of protocols may also be limited in the applications it can run and in functions like network management. If you want to connect networks with different operating systems and topologies, you may have to sacrifice features like application compatibility, peripheral access, or e-mail. Dual stacking at the client eliminates the need to convert from one service protocol to another. That means you can preserve all the functions of the NOS.

Clients and servers

You'll find these protocols already at work in the standard client and server software from the NOS vendors. The software for DOS clients is usually a TSR. The server has matching software, usually installed by the system vendor. Gateway stacks also come preinstalled.

The client side is your responsibility. It should be easy: just load a pair of transport protocol TSRs and another pair of service protocols. Anyone who's tried to work with four TSRs at a time knows it's not easy at all. TSRs are partly successful adaptations to DOS' lack of multitasking power. They often conflict with each other. In transport protocols, the conflicts often become turf wars over control of the network adapter board.

Two of the industry's major figures have stepped in as peacemakers. Microsoft's Network Device Interface Specification (NDIS) and Novell's Open Data-Link Interface (ODI) are two specifications for creating drivers that can share network cards. Two NDIS-compatible drivers can share the same card. So can two ODI-compatible drivers. Most driver-stacking software requires that the drivers be of the same type, for example, all NDIS or all ODI. Another approach, advanced by card maker Syskonnect (Saratoga, California, lets you run different stacks simultaneously, without either trying to take over the adapter.

Other interoperability issues

Resolving the questions of protocol stacks is only one issue you must face. There are plenty of others, including:

- File access
- File naming
- Network management
- Wide area connections

Interoperability problems often first appear when users on dissimilar LANs need access to the same files. Before you connect these LANs, you must make sure applications running on both networks can retrieve and use the files in question. If they can't, you have two alternatives, neither of them pleasant. You can install new applications. Or, you can forget about connecting the LANs.

Even if you have applications that can use the files you want to share, file naming can still be a problem. It can arise any time dissimilar clients need access to the same files. If you are joining opposing formats, there must be a set of rules to handle the conversion.

Network management is another problem. With LANs expanding around the world, management becomes increasingly complex. You must deal with backup, different time zones, and even quirks in routine maintenance.

Serving remote users

If you plan to serve remote offices, the choice of transport and service protocols will affect your plans. Sometimes, an apparent solution to your problems is only an invitation to different kinds of trouble.

For example, Novell's NCP can have disadvantages in wide area networking. Normally, NCP requires that it receive a response to each request before it makes another request. Suppose you want to copy a 32KB file across a WAN which supports a maximum frame size of 512 bytes. It will take 63 frames to do the job, and NCP must acknowledge each frame before the next is sent. If each acknowledgement takes one second, that would add more than a minute to the transfer time.

One solution is to use Novell's SPX instead of IPX, since SPX allows multiple outstanding requests. Most applications, however, don't use

SPX. Another possibility, under Netware 3.x, is to use burst mode IPX, which lets clients and servers send multiple frames without waiting for individual acknowledgements. Burst mode will only help when a large block of data is broken into smaller blocks. Small blocks sent individually still must be acknowledged individually.

Selecting Netbios as a transport for interoperability also opens up some difficulties. Netbios servers typically use broadcasts to locate devices on a network. If a server has 40 devices in its domain, it will send out 40 broadcast frames to try to find out which LAN each device is on. If a device doesn't answer, the server continues to broadcast every few minutes until it gets a response. Those broadcasts eat up wide area network bandwidth.

You can use the Netbios Remote Name Directory service to address this problem. The service turns the broadcast frames into specific route frames. The Remote Name Directory takes up memory, though, so you would want to list only a few devices this way.

Unlike IPX, NCP, and Netbios, IP was designed with wide area networking in mind. It is the most mature interoperable WAN protocol in common use today. That means the types of problems you can encounter with IPX, NCP, and Netbios are rare under IP.

Another advantage to IP is that it supports TCP/IP, the Unix-based protocol of which it is a part. Some organizations have chosen IP because it will allow them later to convert to OSI.

Given a rare opportunity to start a network from scratch, one such company installed an HP 9000 series mini as a server. This system supports Netware and LAN Manager simultaneously. It has an IPX stack for Netware and an IP stack for LAN Manager. This lets clients with different operating systems gain same-time access to the same files on the network server. The company is particularly interested in LAN Manager because unlike Netware it supports TCP/IP. This will make the future conversion easier.

Opening the gateway

A gateway offers another path to network interoperability. A gateway is typically a PC with two network cards, two transport protocol stacks, and the ability to translate service protocols. To each network, the gateway PC looks like a client, and to each workstation it looks like a network drive.

With a gateway, neither clients nor servers give up valuable memory. On the other hand, gateway performance usually is slower than with other interoperability options. Protocol conversion takes place in the gateway, and that can cause network requests to back up. This means gateways are best suited for systems in which only a few clients need access to different types of LANs.

You usually can install a gateway quickly and easily. It is a two-step process:

- Install the gateway.

- Create a new virtual drive at each client using standard network operating system commands.

None of the above

There's another possibility that might be right for you. Don't try to link diverse LANs. Take the opposite course and standardize all your LANs on a single NOS. That may not be the most glamorous solution, but it does promise the best performance with the fewest technical problems.

Human problems may be something else. Employees who have become accustomed to their own systems might have to adapt to change. There are always some people who won't do that readily. Still, facing this problem might be easier than facing the long-term task of linking diverse networks, then keeping them running. Not only do you avoid technical problems, you save money on support, administration, training, and equipment.

Linking LANs and Unix

Communication between PC networks and other systems has been slow to develop. We know how to do it, but it's such a complex process many organizations decided not to attempt it. Then came demands from internal customers, looking for better access to corporate data resources. These employees were also generating large amounts of new data on their own.

To meet these needs, IS departments often have agreed to live more diversly than they would otherwise accept. In all but the most forward-thinking, diversity is a necessary evil—evil because of the difficulties necessary to meet internal demand. Open systems have solved some of these problems by offering more uniformity and portability, but they have also served to increase the diversity and complexity of existing installations.

Technical questions

The technical issues of integrating PC LANs and Unix can be over-whelming, particularly to those whose previous experience was mainly in departmental networks. Despite the growing interest in open systems, integration often is still a complex task with a quagmire of confusing options and details.

```
┌─────────────────────────────────────────────────────────────┐
│                    LAN integration checklist                  │
│                                                               │
│  1. What is your need for file access or transfer between:    │
│     ■ Workstation and LAN?                                    │
│     ■ LAN and LAN?                                            │
│     ■ LAN, WAN, and mainframe?                                │
│  2. What types of internetworked applications do you expect to use? │
│     ■ Groupware                                               │
│     ■ Imaging                                                 │
│     ■ E-mail                                                  │
│     ■ Database                                                │
│     ■ Other                                                   │
│  3. Can you use existing cables?                              │
│  4. What types of specialized servers do you need?            │
│     ■ Database                                                │
│     ■ Print                                                   │
│     ■ Communication                                          │
│     ■ Other                                                   │
└─────────────────────────────────────────────────────────────┘
```

The typical installation has a mix of PC and Unix networks. Connecting these is different from matching different types of personal computers. PC and Macintosh networks use de facto standards like Netware, or purely proprietary solutions like Appletalk. These systems let you share files and peripherals, and they are beginning to acquire client/server abilities as well.

Different types of PCs do not necessarily work well together. That often is the case with Macs and Intel PCs. Most vendors try to support multiple standards, but some focus a single solution, such as carrying out Novell's IPX protocol. If you have a different networking scheme, those application packages will be out of reach.

Workstations networks adhere more closely, though not precisely, to accepted industry standards. That means they will interoperate well. A typical Unix workstation network consists of file servers with diskless clients booting off the servers. Some clients may have local disks as well. The underlying protocols are usually TCP/IP running on Ethernet. Most of these networks also use a version of Sun's Network File System (NFS). The user sees a single directory structure will and can easily gain access to files from multiple servers. NFS can be a system administrator's nightmare, but if you install it properly, it is transparent to most users.

Three approaches, two that work

If you have both PC LANs and Unix, you can choose from three basic strategies, each with several variations:

■ Install PC emulation software on the workstations.

- Use the workstation servers as they are and install Unix networking on the PCs.

- Set up the PC NOS on the workstation network.

The first approach wastes resources. It uses workstations to do the many jobs a modern PC can readily handle. The PC will do a better job at less cost.

What's more, you deny yourself the workstations' high performance. The vendors who develop the PC emulation software always lag behind PC technology. Workstations were stuck with EGA emulation long after VGA became commonplace. Now that Super VGA is proliferating, the emulators finally can use 16-color VGA. This limited approach may be right in some circumstances. For most purposes, though, one of the other two is probably a better choice.

Unix on PCs

The next approach lets PCs talk with Unix systems in their native networking formats. This approach can have differing levels of complexity:

- If all you need is access to a Unix application, a simple terminal emulator might be enough.

- A more elaborate method is to hook the PC up to the LAN and load TCP/IP drivers. You then can use the terminal access and transfer files using standard Telnet or FTP utilities.

- If PC users need access to a GUI application on the Unix system, this usually means loading X Window software on the PC. X servers can be standalone applications, or they can run under Microsoft Windows 3.x or later.

- If you need full access to the distributed file system you can also load NFS drivers. Depending on the NFS software, the file system can appear to the user as an extended DOS directory. This is a good approach if the PC users in the organization are at least somewhat familiar with Unix.

The Unix-on-PC approach can be a good choice if the organization leans toward Unix rather than PC-based networking. It's important, though, that you take care of users who spend most of their time using PCs.

Most major networking vendors support the NFS driver approach, at least to some degree. Sun Microsystems is the chief proponent of this approach. Novell also supports this approach. The company has added TCP/IP and Netware NFS to Netware 3.11. Unix users can reach Novell file systems as if they were NFS file systems. This provides access to all files and resources on the Netware system. Netware NFS also lets PC users employ Unix systems for print output.

Sunconnect, the Sun subsidiary that focuses on connectivity products, offers this approach with its PC-NFS product. PC-NFS lets PCs connect with Unix networks and provides complete NFS and TCP/IP facilities on the PC. Users can still share PC software by putting it on an F: drive, which is really an NFS file system. Employees also can browse for file and print servers, then use the best server for their needs. A built-in SNMP management agent runs on the PCs, so any SNMP-compliant network manager can manage them.

Other PC networking vendors offer products that give PC users access to native Unix systems. For example FTP Software markets a line of TCP/IP-based software for a variety of computers. Besides standard Unix look-alike utilities like FTP and Telnet, FTP also lets PC users use Unix systems as electronic mail servers, and gives them access to NFS file systems.

Unix networking on PCs does have some drawbacks. One is that heavy demands via a PC network can impair a small server's performance. Therefore, some experts believe Unix networking on PCs in the Sun model (PCs running NFS and using Unix NFS servers) is not viable.

PC NOS on Unix

The most-used approach is the opposite: install a PC NOS on a Unix network. Both Novell and Microsoft supply versions of their network operating systems that run directly on Unix platforms. Novell's product is Netware for Unix, while Microsoft offers LAN Manager for Unix (LM/X). Banyan's Vines, already built on a core of proprietary Unix, is moving to SCO Unix.

The Novell version is probably more comprehensive. Unlike some competing products, the version of Netware in Netware for Unix is not far behind the current Intel version. It's also available on more Unix platforms, many of which Novell has ported directly. Versions are available or forthcoming for AT&T/NCR, Prime, Sun, AS/400, RS/6000, Stratus, and others.

Microsoft's approach is a little different. Although it originally developed LM/X, Microsoft placed primary responsibility for future versions in an OEM's hands. The first OEM was Hewlett-Packard; after version 1.1 was released, AT&T became responsible. LM/X runs on fewer systems than Netware for Unix, but it does run on many common Unix platforms, including Sun, AT&T/ NCR, IBM, SCO, and Hewlett-Packard.

Either approach is suitable where PC users require only limited access, usually file sharing, to Unix resources. Both products also offer greater access. You can have LM/X running on an SCO Unix server that also has NFS file systems mounted. A LAN Manager user can work with NFS-mounted file systems as if they were just another shared drive.

Most hardware vendors also support both NOSs. Hewlett-Packard takes what it calls a NOS-neutral approach, leaving the final choice to the customer.

Sunconnect provides NOS access through its Netware Sunlink product, which allows users to run Netware code on the Sun server. This approach is aimed at heavy Netware users. They usually find the PC interface is easier to understand and use than the Unix command line.

Using what you get

Once you've gained access to resources, the next challenge is to make good use of them. Useability is a key issue that should figure prominently in your decisions.

Graphical user interfaces make the system easier to use. They also require another choice: Microsoft Windows from the PC world, or the X Window system of Unix. The recently developed Unixware is a third choice.

Microsoft's approach is to try to keep the user in the familiar Windows environment. You can install an NFS system on a server that's also running LM/X. The user simply sees the Unix files as another directory structure in the Windows File Manager.

Novell offers LAN Workplace, which gives users easy and consistent access to Unix systems. It also has the advantage of running under DOS, Windows, and the Macintosh.

The Unix user has it a little easier. When the user mounts a Novell file system which is running Netware NFS, it seems to be just another set of Unix directories with Unix file semantics. You can do normal Unix operations on files in the Netware system.

The DOS memory limit

DOS users have another problem: the familiar 640K limit on main memory. Network drivers can claim 160K or more. There's been some help. Beginning with version 5.0, DOS lets you load their drivers into so-called high main memory. You can also take advantage of extended memory managers. Also, the vendors of network systems are responding with drivers that automatically load themselves into high or expanded memory.

Networking Networks:
The Software Side

If you connect two or more personal computers, you have a network. If you connect two or more networks, you have begun to create an enterprise network.

An individual LAN can be only so big. Considerations like distance, location, reliability, and performance effectively limit the number of computers you can connect to a LAN, usually long before you reach the network's rated capacity. In most installations, 20 to 50 nodes is tops. That's not many for an organization that has several thousand users. Chances are, you have more than one LAN in your organization—probably many more than one. Chances are, too, you want to link these individual networks. That's the process of *internetworking,* and it works on principles grouped under the related term *interoperability.*

Companies are discovering that they can multiply the benefits of enterprise networking by extending local data access to the entire organization. They connect LANs, and tie these linked LANs to networks at other sites. The result is an enterprise-wide network that can tap into the computing resources of the entire organization. It shouldn't matter whether these are in Portland, Oregon or Portland, Maine or anywhere else in the world.

Magic Act

The object of enterprise networking is to create an illusion. You want to weave diverse network technologies into a web that looks like a single network. You want to hide the details of the hardware and software; at

The first step

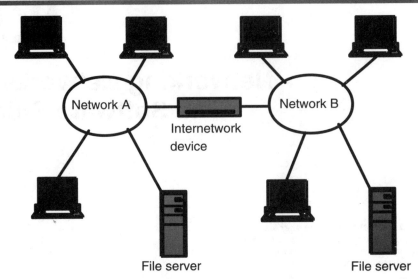

Figure 10.1   Two LANs makes an internetwork. The internetwork device, usually a bridge or router, controls traffic between the LANs.

the same time, you want your networks and applications to work well together.

You probably have several types of computers and networks already installed. Perhaps there are IBM mainframes that talk to other hosts using System Network Architecture (SNA). DEC VAX minis might talk to each other with DECnet over Ethernet hardware. Unix machines and workstations usually are commonly connected through Ethernet and TCP/IP. Macs may speak an Appletalk dialect. DOS PCs may use Netware, LANtastic, 3Com, LAN Manager, Banyan Vines, or some other PC network dialect. These diverse systems might be joined by Ethernet, Token Ring, and perhaps FDDI.

The essence of internetworking is this: from your PC or workstation, you can retrieve resources from each of these systems as easily as files from your local disk drive.

Several network software and hardware options can provide *some* of this transparency *if* you assemble the right pieces. There are some problem areas, though, including these:

- Network hardware
- Network software protocols
- Differences in operating systems
- Variation in application programs

The potential solutions to these needs involve both hardware and software, and they are not necessarily over-the-counter products. The hardware and software work together, and you cannot realistically separate the two. With that in mind, this chapter concentrates on the software components; the next deals mainly with hardware.

Keep it simple

One internetworking trend is to support multiple computer platforms under a single network operating system. Current and coming NOS systems support DOS, the Macintosh, OS/2, Windows, and several Unix desktop clients.

These developments help, but they can make administration harder than necessary. Among the best things you can do for easier administration is to establish a one-to-one relationship between network administrators and Netware binders. Each binder, or its equivalent file under another NOS, should include every user on the system. It should provide such information as user identification, passwords, and other security features.

Maintaining protocol

An important internetworking question is whether your applications and network devices support the right protocols to maintain communication across the system.

Protocols are the languages of networking. They establish the rules for packaging information for transmission. Major internetworking protocols include:

- *TCP/IP.* Transmission Control Protocol/Internet Protocol. This was originally developed for the Department of Defense. Since DOD is a major computer equipment customer, this protocol has become almost universal, particularly under open systems. TCP and IP are two different protocols that do different functions, but work together.

- *NetBIOS.* Network Basic Input/Output System. This is an IBM-developed protocol developed for networks that use Microsoft products. It has become virtually a generic protocol for PC LANs, and most network operating systems offer NetBIOS compatibility.

- *IPX/SPX.* Internet Packet exchange/sequenced Packet Exchange. This is a protocol developed by Novell. Since Novell is dominant in PC networking, this system—again a combination of two protocols—has come into widespread use.

- *SNA.* Systems Network Architecture. This is the protocol IBM has long used to communicate among within its mainframe host-based networks.

■ *DECnet.*   Digital Equipment Corporation Network. A set of protocols developed by the Digital Equipment Corporation (DEC) for use within that firm's operating environment.

Stacking them up

Networking software usually reflects a stacking system. Internetwork communication takes place on several levels. The software places these in protocol stacks. The most common are:

■ The seven-layer OSI standard

■ The four-level TCP/IP standard

■ Proprietary protocol stacks, including Appletalk, DECnet, and Netware's XNS

The OSI model carries the seals of approval of most international organizations. TCP/IP is the one most business organizations use. In addition, some proprietary network protocols have become de facto standards. These include the Netware and Appletalk protocols. Other proprietary protocols include NetBIOS, DECnet, Vines, and LAN Manager.

OSI: piled higher and deeper

The Open Systems Interconnection (OSI) model separates network communication activities into seven layers:

1. *Physical.*   Transmits the bit streams of data across the physical transmission medium.

2. *Data link.*   Packages the data for transmission and defines the addressing scheme.

3. *Network.*   Addresses and delivers the packets from one node to another, including routing among multiple networks.

4. *Transport.*   Sends and receives data, and notifies the user of any errors.

5. *Session.*   Establishes, maintains, and concludes the communication session.

6. *Presentation.*   Provides translation services for communication among diverse systems. This layer converts data to and from a machine's native internal format.

7. *Application.*   This is the layer that makes direct contact with the application program.

OSI and the seven layers

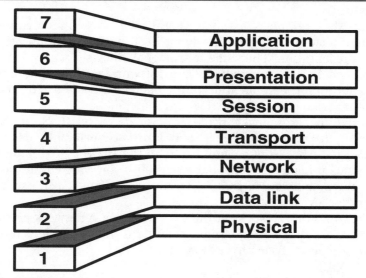

Figure 10.2   The OSI model is often used to explain types of network activity. The lower three layers generally deal with network functions, the top four with applications.

You can divide these seven layers into two groups: the application level and the network level. Application level communication takes place at the top four layers. These govern activities inside a file server when it receives a Netware request, when a database server receives an SQL query, or when a print file reaches a print server.

Network level activity takes place below the application level, mainly at the physical, media access, and network layers. The physical layer administers the rules of sending signals over a given medium, such as twisted pair, coax, or fiber optic. Media access includes the protocols for using each medium, such as Ethernet or token ring.

The transport and network layers are where data streams from application layers are organized in packets and placed in electronic envelopes. Address instructions guide bridges and routers in high-speed delivery decisions.

Framework for discussion

Even when it's not actively in use, the OSI model and its seven layers provide a model for describing the elements of a network.

Not every network conforms exactly with this model. For example, a peer-to-peer LAN makes little use of layer three, the network layer. The model does not attempt to describe how various sources have designed their protocols. Sometimes, though, even the departures from the pattern can help you understand a networking system's structure.

Take the example of a simple DOS-based LAN. DOS occupies parts of the top two OSI layers, involving itself with both applications and their presentation. The same is true of Windows if it's in use. Also at these two layers is a *redirector*, a software module that intercepts requests from the application to the operating system. The redirector routes these requests to the network instead.

Sprawling across levels three through six is NetBIOS, the Network basic Input/Output System. This is a protocol originally designed for IBM's PC LAN and is a counterpart to the BIOS of a single PC. Net-BIOS has a home of sorts at the session layer, controlling the flow of data among networked PCs. Different uses, though, will use it at several other levels as well.

A network driver works at the network layer. A network protocol like Ethernet or Token Ring occupies the data link layer, and the wiring makes up most of the physical layer.

TCP/IP: the common tongue

If any standard has become the Esperanto of enterprise networking, it is TCP/IP. It may not be the most advanced kind of networking protocol. It operates in only four layers, compared with the seven of the rival OSI standard. Generally connected with Unix, it requires some adaptation to work with PC networks. Those who have worked with it say it takes some getting used to.

In spite of all that, TCP/IP does have one thing going for it: it's available technology that works. That puts it ahead of whatever's in second place. TCP/IP also incorporates the Simple Network Management Protocol (SNMP) that's become a staple in enterprise network management.

It doesn't do everything

TCP/IP does an excellent job of connecting disparate computer systems, but it doesn't do everything equally well. For example, it probably would not be wise to use TCP/IP to connect two Netware systems. In that case, it's easier and more effective to use Novell's own IPX. In addition, you can't expect to take care of complex enterprise networking with TCP/IP alone.

TCP/IP has also been criticized as primitive. Each TCP/IP package may handle print services differently. You may lack the full ability to manage access to network assets.

Strata of TCP/IP

TCP/IP uses four layers. The lowest layer, working just above the network hardware interface, is the Internet Protocol (IP) layer. This layer handles internetworking and corresponds approximately to the OSI model's network layer. IP can also split packets for transit and reassemble them in the proper order at the destination.

Above the Internet Protocol are four protocols, including Transmission Control Protocol (TCP) and User Datagram Protocol (UDP). The OSI counterpart is the transport layer. TCP provides reliable stream service to ensure delivery. UDP provides a less reliable datagram delivery service. Application programs may use either protocol. TCP uses the connection as its fundamental abstraction. A pair of endpoints identifies the connections.

At the next layer up are several protocols common to Unix network programs:

- A File Transfer Protocol (FTP), which a Unix FTP program uses to transfer files.

TCP/IP vs. OSI

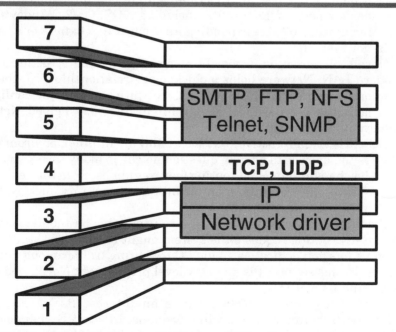

Figure 10.3 The TCP/IP functions overlap the seven OSI layers.

- The Simple Mail Transport Protocol (SMTP) serves e-mail programs. It has many, though not all, of the functions of the X.400 e-mail protocol.

- The Simple Network Management Protocol collects and reports network information.

- The Network File System.

Network File System

Sun Microsystems has developed an important Unix network application, the Network File System (NFS). It provides on-line shared file access that is transparent and integrated. Many vendors of Unix products hold licenses to use it.

NFS is almost transparent to ordinary users. The file names appearing in a directory could be either local or remote; the system does not distinguish between them. NFS is built from two independent pieces: a general purpose Remote Procedure Call (RPC) mechanism and a general purpose External Data Representation (XDR).

How Novell Does It

Novell has approached interoperability from two directions. Netware provides support for PC clients, including DOS, OS/2, Windows, and the Macintosh. Novell is expanding its product line to take in a variety of larger systems.

Novell, of course, is primarily responsible for the structure of the modern LAN. Netware holds a chicken/egg relationship with the conventional client/server LAN pattern. Netware supports the configuration, and the popularity of that configuration has helped Netware achieve its leading sales record.

Novell is equally active, but less familiar, in other environments. Here is the answer to a trivia question no one is likely to ask you: Netware has had bridging and routing features almost from the beginning. These have only recently spun off into a separate product, Netware Multiprotocol Router (MPR).

Traditionally, Netware has kept a routing table on the file server to direct any routing requests the system might receive. The stand-alone product lets you dedicate a single PC to routing traffic among multiple LANs. In this service it is an entry level product, but Novell has plans to expand its features.

In its Unix version, Netware uses an Internet Packet Exchange (IPX) for datagram delivery, while Sequenced Packet Exchange (SPX) rides atop IPX and guarantees delivery. At the application layer, the Netware Core Protocol manages file and printer services and other resource sharing. More recent versions of the Netware protocols provide add-on modules to support networking connections to the Mac, OS/2, and Unix. A version of Netware is also available for DEC VAX systems.

Netware and the OSI stack

Viewed in relation to the OSI stack, the Netware approach includes:

- Network core protocols (NCPs) are distributed naming services used at the presentation level.

- A NetBIOS emulator operates at the session level.

- A sequenced packet exchange (SPX) occupies the transport level. It works on top of IPX to manage data delivery.

- IPX is the internet package exchange at the network level. This is Netware's protocol for transmitting information among applications. IPX also exchanges data with the Netware shell and the NetBIOS emulator.

- An open data link interface (ODI) is Novell's standard device driver. It operates at the data link layer.

Netware and the OSI stack

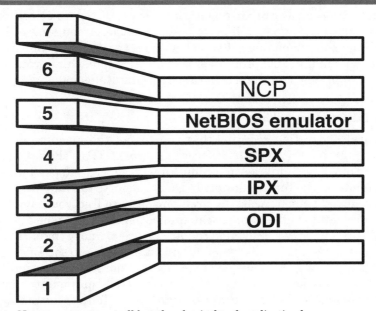

Figure 10.4 Netware operates at all but the physical and application layers.

Conflict Resolution

The good news is that you can resolve most internetworking conflicts. The bad news is that you cannot resolve them easily.

Say you want to connect DOS and Unix LANs. One way is add software on the PC. If you want to talk with Netware file servers, you can install a Netware protocol stack. To talk with the Unix LAN, install a TCP/IP stack at the DOS machine, along with software to support standard Unix applications like FTP, Telnet, mail, and possibly NFS. Nothing changes on the network file servers. All the action is at the PC.

There are several problems with this approach. Among them:

- Two protocol stacks may have to share the same network hardware.

- The dual protocols can strain the limits of DOS memory.

- Much of the configuration and administration is decentralized on widely scattered PCs.

- Higher network software costs a lot.

Low cost, high memory

The least expensive node approach is to have both Netware and TCP/IP share the same hardware device. If you use the same Ethernet cabling for your DOS and Unix network hardware, it should be simple to make the physical connections. If the DOS machines use Arcnet, Token Ring hardware, or nonoriginal forms of Ethernet cabling, you face further incompatibilities you must resolve. Among these Ethernet variations is the popular 10BaseT with its twisted pair cables.

If you run multiple protocol stacks on a DOS machine, you have two further options: run them separately or simultaneously.

The DOS memory ceiling

Separate operation requires that you reboot the machine every time you want to switch to a different network. That should make the choice obvious, but it doesn't. Simultaneous operation can make heavy demands on the limited supply of DOS memory. You may find that you have solved your networking problems only to find you have too little memory left to run any practical applications. This can be a particular problem under TCP/IP, which requires more memory than its Netware counterparts. There have been many adaptations to the DOS memory limit, but few real solutions. Several vendors offer versions of the TCP/IP stack for use under DOS. As standard equipment, all support file transfer (FTP) and terminal emulation (Telnet) for a Unix host. Some also support NFS and electronic mail as extra cost options.

The National Center for Super Computing (NCSA) has developed a public domain version of TCP/IP for DOS and Macintosh computers. NCSA Telnet supports file transfer, terminal emulation, and e-mail. It is popular with universities and government agencies where several thousand copies of a vendor-supplied TCP/IP stack represent a major expense. A public domain client version of NFS is not yet available.

FTP provides for file transfer between DOS PCs and nearby Unix machines, but this scheme is not transparent to DOS users. Most commonly, a user must invoke FTP as a separate program to copy files between networks. A better arrangement would let NFS transparently attach itself to Unix LANs. You then could copy files between more distant networks. NFS lets a DOS user mount a remote Unix drive as a file server, just like you could mount a Netware or Appletalk volume.

The server alternative

An alternate scheme for sharing between Netware and Unix LANs is to do the work at the file servers. There are two basic approaches: Carry out Unix TCP/IP protocols under Netware, or use Netware's IPX/SPX protocols under Unix.

Novell offers an enhancement, to Netware 3.11 and up, that uses the TCP/IP protocols, including Unix-style FTP and Telnet applications, as a Netware Loadable Module (NLM). Novell's NFS provides only for a server. This product lets you mount parts of a Netware file server as an NFS drive from a Unix network. The Novell product does not let you mount Unix volumes on the Netware LAN for DOS access.

Netware NFS is only available for Netware 3.11 and up. On smaller or older Netware LANs that run version 2.x, Netware NFS is not an option unless you completely upgrade your Novell software.

For larger networks, Netware NFS can quickly be a costly approach. You must buy a copy of the NLM for each Netware file server you wish to use.

A second approach is to run Netware protocols on Unix. An advantage of this scheme is that PCs running DOS or OS/2 can treat the Unix LAN as a transparently as a Netware server could do. Until recently, this Netware under Unix option was only available for a few Unix machines. More recently, Netware protocols have become available for Sun SPARCstations.

Operating system conflicts

The operating system is where most compatibility problems lie. If you consider simply the most popular desktop systems, DOS, OS/2, MacOS, and Unix, there are differences just in the way they name files. Then there are further differences in these files' formats. The files also reflect formats and other peculiarities of the applications that created them.

Speed Up with FDDI

Fiber Distributed Data Interface has been called the next plateau in high-speed networking. With an operating speed of 100 megabits per second, FDDI is finding employment at the departmental level and above. One of FDDI's great assets is in backbone networks, which it can turn into the interstate equivalent of local highways like Ethernet and Token Ring.

Most major vendors, including IBM, HP, and DEC, offer complete FDDI systems. Hub and router sources like Synoptics Systems Corp., Cisco Systems Inc., and Fibronics Inc. also offer FDDI modules and components. Their customers include Euro Disney in France and the Florida state government.

High speed, high cost

FDDI's speed doesn't come cheaply. Though prices have been dropping as sales increase, products like adapters, concentrators, and hubs are more expensive than their less speedy brethren. That doesn't include the cost of fiber optic cable, which is expensive to buy, install, and maintain. It's no wonder several vendors have been working on ways to run an FDDI system over more prosaic copper wire.

Token Ring spinoff

FDDI uses a dual, counter-rotating token ring topology. Since tokens can travel either of two rings and use either of two station connections, the system is highly reliable. Should there be a break in the system, the circuit can simply reverse course. A Station Management (SMT) feature manages this process as well as all aspects of ring operation at the physical layer.

Still under development are standards for operating FDDI over copper wire. These Copper Distributed Data Interface (CDDI) standards use twisted pair cable like that used in Token Ring and in the 10BaseT variation of Ethernet.

What it's good for

FDDI is a strong candidate for the high-volume network applications like imaging and multimedia. The most common current use is in backbones that connect departmental LANs, wide area networks, large systems, and LAN servers.

Cost Control

A PC network interface card costs about $1000. That could prove to be the lowest-cost item in an FDDI installation. An FDDI interface for a Unix file service can run up to $12,000. Plan to invest $400 each in patch panels for wiring closets, plus $20 for every cable end.

The cable itself costs 41 cents per foot and up—with emphasis on the up. Labor runs $45 to $60 per hour. Though cable installation costs are comparable to copper wire, installing the cable-end terminals is time-consuming and costly.

There is one way to keep costs under control: when installing any kind of cable, include fiber optic cable for future use. The cost of installing multiple types of cable is usually lower than installing them individually. You can defer any further cost until you make use of the cable.

In a campus network environment, consider fiber optic repeaters for Ethernet and Token Ring LANs. You can also install these along with other work, making sure that they will adapt to FDDI in the future. Another advantage of deferring costs: they're likely to be lower later.

FDDI and OSI

FDDI is geared to the physical medium of fiber optic cable. That means it falls toward the lower levels of the OSI stack.

FDDI includes two Physical Layer Medium Dependent standards (PMDs). Together, they define the physical link parameters, connectors, and cables for both single-mode and multi-mode fiber. Similar standards are being developed for copper wiring.

A physical layer protocol specifies transmission details such as line states, clocking requirements, and rules for encoding and decoding data.

A media access control standard defines the FDDI token rules, packet frame formats, and addressing conventions. SMT deals with monitoring, management, and configuration of the ring and connections.

IBM's APPN

IBM's entry in the internetworking race is its Advanced Peer-to-Peer Network (APPN). Peer-to-peer in this case is not a low end LAN; it is IBM's effort to integrate its larger systems into the world of enterprise networking. In this version of peer-to-peer, anything from a mainframe to a DOS workstation can work together as equals.

IBM introduced APPN in 1986 for its AS/400 midrange line. It has since been adapted to other platforms including OS/2 and is envisioned as a long-range successor to systems like TCP/IP.

FDDI's structured star

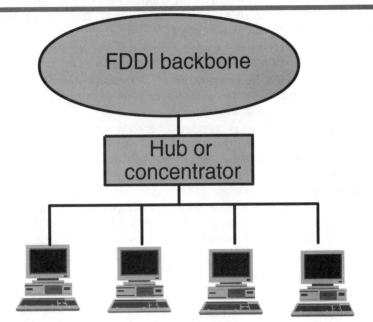

Figure 10.5 FDDI uses a form of star topology, connected to a collapsed backbone.

APPN spans the network and transport layers of the OSI stack. It sets up client/server sessions and dynamically routes data through the network. APPN has three basic components:

- *End nodes.*   These are the places where applications live. These can be either clients or servers and are responsible for initiating sessions.
- *Network nodes.*   These locate resources and route data.
- *Central directory servers.*   Recent additions to the package, these are special hosts that can locate resources more quickly than other network nodes.

Working together

Either a terminal or a PC running OS/2 can serve as an end node. OS/2 servers, 3174 controllers, and AS/400 servers can be network nodes.

The network nodes dynamically set up session paths and route data. They make up the key to APPN. They have recently been extended to mainframes, eliminating the static, host-based forms that were previously required.

Network nodes maintain tables of all resources, including applications and physical nodes, to which they are connected. The network nodes also keep maps of the network topology. They create these maps with information gathered from neighboring network nodes.

When an end node needs to locate a network resource, it contacts the nearest network node, which checks its resource database. If the network node doesn't know the location, it will broadcast a location request. The network node that does handle the requested resource sends a reply that the calling network node inserts in its database. Once it has that information, the originating network node checks its topology database, chooses a route and transmits the message.

The central directory server shortcuts this process. Before it issues a broadcast, a network node can seek a location directly from a host system configured as a central directory server. This server stores information on all available resources in a central database.

Making Connections with Middleware

It's hard enough to get diverse systems and applications to work together. If this chapter so far has shown nothing else, it should be that the means of getting them together are equally diverse. There are many gaps to bridge. A new class of software, *middleware,* has been invented to help build those bridges.

Middleware is specifically directed at the problems of linking the pieces of client/server systems. It is a layer of software that provides a common interface and translation between an application and the operating system. In that sense, middleware acts like an API. Middleware goes farther, though, adding a level of intelligence that helps an application find the information it needs.

New, existing products

Both new and older products have found homes under the middleware umbrella. The class ranges from IBM's Systems Application Architecture (SAA) and Digital's Network Application Services (NAS) to simple messaging programs. Their common element is the ability to hide complexities and disparities of different network protocols and operating systems. Ideally, the application has a single interface into the middleware environment. If so, you could move the application from one environment to another without change. One user has compared good middleware to an electrical outlet. The power is there. You don't have to worry about the system that generated it.

Middleware categories

Middleware is an idea that is still under development, and it includes several types of products.

Message delivery systems are a fast-growing category. These use APIs to connect various e-mail front-end applications to server-based message processing systems. Other forms of middleware include systems that use remote procedure calls (RPCs) and structured query language (SQL). In systems that use multiple platforms and protocols, these let applications retrieve, exchange, and store data without regard to their underlying networks. They also let you mix different front-end applications and back-end database managers.

In each case, middleware earns its name by fitting in between the network and the application. It shields users from complex network addresses by providing a software bridge between the application and the operating system. It is equally kind to application developers. They can spend more time writing good applications and less time worrying about network mechanics. Middleware also lets you take advantage of varied products; you are less likely to lock yourself into a short list of proprietary products.

Network in disguise

Middleware products disguise system resources through a process of *encapsulation*. Encapsulation hides the details of individual system elements behind an interface that is common to all those elements. In application development, it gives programmers a generic interface they can use effectively to reach all the networks in the system. When the system changes—as it will—you need only adapt the encapsulating software. The applications' relation with this software will remain the same.

Middleware and the database

Middleware has become particularly important in managing client/server databases. Among the reasons:

- Despite the trend toward downsizing, many key databases are on large systems, and will continue to be. The mainframes offer processing power, security, and management control. They also represent very large investments. Since there are mainframe databases, it will be necessary to provide transparent, high-performance access from PCs and LAN servers.

- Middleware helps solve the problems of transparent access to distributed databases. It provides an intervening database manager that serves as a gateway to varied files and systems in other locations.

Making up middleware

Middleware generally has four basic components:

- A client API, which the application uses to contact the middleware program.
- A network gateway that manages the network linkage.
- An SQL translator that converts SQL commands from a client into the data management language of the server.
- Host server software that provides access to data sources on large systems.

Not all these systems have all four components. The API, for example, is generally limited to database management. Nevertheless, these do form a common pattern.

The middleware API

Each middleware product has its own API, consisting of procedural calls that let the application program communicate with a DBMS. Using these API calls, a program can connect to a DBMS, retrieve data, and end the connection.

Beyond these basic functions, each API has a unique set of features. As in so many other components of enterprise networking, no two database managers have identical APIs. Each API also has its singular syntax. That means middleware itself—supposedly a solution to the problem of network diversity—can become part of the problem. Even front-end products that support middleware APIs probably will support only the most popular.

The network gateway

The network gateway component serves as a protocol converter and gateway concentrator. It transmits API messages over a network,

Middleware components

- Client API
- Network gateway
- SQL translator
- Server software

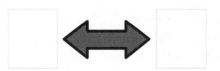

Figure 10.6   A middleware application will have some or all of these features.

using a designated LAN protocol. When you need to use a WAN protocol, the gateway function will handle the conversion. Here, too, a particular middleware product may handle only a popular selection of
network protocols.

You can load the gateway on a client workstation or a server. On the
server, it acts as a concentrator that supports application connections
from multiple workstations.

Translating SQL

SQL is supposed to be a uniform language of database management. It
isn't. Every SQL vendor has its own additions and enhancements,
using commands other SQL versions do not understand—or worse, do
not understand correctly. A middleware gateway can translate calls
from, say, a PC-based SQL Server installation to a mainframe-
mounted DB2 database.

A typical product will:

- Convert the SQL syntax and semantics.
- Convert data types.
- Map the server's database catalog so it looks like the client's catalog.
- Adjust collating sequences.
- Translate error messages.

The network gateway component does this translation. Depending
on which version of SQL generates the client system's calls, the gateway might choose one of three methods of translation:

- No translation, because none is necessary
- Simple changes, such as adjusting punctuation
- A complete rewrite of the SQL command

Different gateway products use variations on this scheme. Some
change data formats to match the incoming command, instead of
translating the command. Others make no translations, requiring that
you use compatible versions of SQL. Some of these do give you the ability to write your own translation mechanisms.

The host server

The host server retrieves data from a remote database and returns it
along with any messages to the client applications.

Host servers differ in the number and types of data resources with
which they can connect. Vendors of this type of product usually try to

achieve fast performance and to minimize the competition for resources. They also try to emulate features that are available on the local database server. Some features available from various vendors include:

- The option to run short or long transactions. A short transaction releases locks on database resources as soon as possible. A long transaction holds those resources until it is sure the transaction is complete.

- Support for remote procedure calls. RPCs are valuable for gaining access to nonrelational databases on mainframes. They are standard mainframe transactions you can call from a gateway's API. Once an RPC retrieves or updates data, it returns the result to the client using function calls in the middleware program's mainframe API.

- The ability to reverse the client and server roles. A mainframe acting as a client can let a mainframe program initiate a process on a workstation. The mainframe can poll remote workstations and servers and can automatically transfer data.

What to look for

Middleware is no panacea. Though it helps make connections across diverse networks, it is not an automatic, one-size-fits-all resource. Some pointers for making successful decisions:

- Evaluate available products to make sure they offer the features and performance you need.

- Verify vendors' claims. Some advertised features may be available only in future, not current, products.

- Ask for references, concentrating on those whose work and systems are similar to yours.

- Test candidate products to make sure they meet your performance objectives.

Networking Wider Areas

LANs were designed small, and they're destined to remain small. A main reason is that a LAN is really just a computerized party line. Everyone on the same LAN must feed his or her work into the same circuit. If someone else is using that circuit—if the line is busy—you simply must wait your turn. This works moderately well if the LAN serves a small group, but it's not at all acceptable for an enterprise network. No matter how big or how fast your LAN, it's still a party line.

Things to check

- Performance and features
- Feature availability
- Vendor references
- Test results in your applications

Figure 10.7   Make sure a middleware package will do the job you expect.

TCP/IP and Netware, alone or in combination, have captured much of the short-distance network integration market. They make a natural combination for integrating DOS LANs and Unix servers and workstations.

If you are to truly network the entire enterprise, you often must extend beyond individual offices and buildings into the domain of the wide area network (WAN). Particularly in large and midsized organizations, a LAN is just a stepping stone to the enterprise network.

There are two main obstacles to LAN-WAN integration:

- WANs are not just larger LANs. They operate in much different ways and at much slower speeds.

- WANs are most efficient at handling steady streams of data. LANs send their signals in short bursts.

WANs grow in importance

The distinction between LANs and WANs is narrowing, as WAN technology is adopted and adapted to form links between LANs. A major example is ATM, which is both a WAN and internetworking system.

There is one long-accepted protocol, designated X.25, for connecting computers and terminals over long distances. X.25 is a packet switching system that operates by assembling messages into electronic envelopes. If you use a commercial data communication service like Tymnet or Sprintnet, your messages have been packaged to X.25 standards.

X.25 handles that kind of service well, but at a maximum speed of about 64 Kbps. It was designed for the needs of a simpler era, when the challenge was to reduce a high error rate in long-distance data transmissions. The transmitted packets include extra messages to help detect and prevent errors.

As internetworked LANs gain an increasing role in enterprise networking, X.25's low speed and high overhead have made it inadequate for the job. Not only are modern transmission systems much faster, but they have their own error correcting mechanisms, independent of the packet switching mechanism. X.25 predates most existing LAN protocols. These now have their own error-correcting mechanisms. In an enterprise network in particular, then, an X.25 transmission now carries a lot of excess baggage.

Long-distance protocols

The main challenge in choosing WAN products and services is that there may be too many choices available. Public carriers and product vendors are upgrading their services and systems to adapt to expanding LAN users. They are using or considering several types of services, both new and old, to help ease the transition between local and wide areas. These include:

- *Frame relay.* When communication software creates electronic envelopes, it assembles the address and contents into packets. Frame relay uses similar structures called frames, and introduces these into such internetworking facilities as bridges and routers. Many public carriers offer frame relay services; so do most makers of bridges and routers. Some organizations now employ it directly in enterprise networks. Frame relay runs at higher speeds than most competing technology. Combined with its ability to package messages, it can greatly reduce long-distance transmission costs.

- *ATM.* Neither an automated teller nor a type manager, Asynchronous Transfer Mode represents the state of the future art. ATM is a high-speed advancement on SMDS technology, which can reach high speeds now and even higher rates later. Not only can it handle multiple data streams, but its high capacity lends itself to graphics, voice, and other forms of multimedia. Most of this high performance is still in the future. The main question about ATM right now is whether to wait for it, or to use what's available now.

- *SMDS.* This telephone carrier service uses a standards-based technology that's been around for a long time, but has yet to see widespread commercial use. Bridge and router manufacturers are adding this facility to their products, but the public carriers are still experimenting. SMDS is intended as a universal service available to anyone; frame relay may be available only at designated central offices.

- *SONET.* The Synchronous Optical Network was developed to take advantage of fiber optics. It has a potential future role in high-speed communication. It can also serve as a backbone carrier for ATM.

"Look at the overall"

In one of the garage scenes of *All the President's Men,* Deep Throat cautions Bob Woodward that he's concentrating too much on small details. "Look at the overall," says the mysterious source. That's good advice, too, when you are trying to make sense of wide-area transmission options.

If you are considering these options, you probably have one or more LANs at multiple sites. You need some way to move data among these sites, preferably at high speed. One option—viable if you have only a few sites—is to install dedicated lines between each pair of sites. The number of lines you need multiplies with the number of sites; a seemingly simple solution can quickly become very complicated.

For most organizations, the better choice is to emulate the telephone company. Set up a switched network in which all sites have connections to an enterprise-wide WAN. This can be a private system with dedicated switches you control yourself, or you can use a public network. One advantage of the public network approach is that you can connect with other organizations as well as your own.

In a typical installation, each site has a gateway router attached to one or more LANs. This router is the point of contact between these LANs and the WAN. The WAN then meets the often-sought objective of transparency. Anyone on the system can set up a connection with anyone else, without worrying about that colleague's location. The WAN becomes just another element in the enterprise network.

The big problem with this picture was that until recently, X.25 helped make the WAN a very lethargic part of the system. Think of the newer forms of technology as ways to speed up the process.

Moving Up to Frame Relay

In many ways, frame relay is next-generation X.25. It is a step forward from packet switching. Frame relay uses frames much as X.25 uses packets, but it takes advantage of the higher speeds and lower error rates of present-day networks. Frame relay can operate at up to 2Mbps, and it lacks most of the extra bits X.25 adds to its packets. As a result, frame relay carries your messages both more quickly and more efficiently.

Frame relay also takes advantage of an ability to send multiple data streams over a single circuit. That means carriers can transmit more data over their circuits; sharing these circuits should help keep costs low.

Frame relay appears in many kinds of internetworking equipment. Most bridge and router manufacturers have incorporated frame relay interfaces into their products. It is also available from public carriers including most long distance telephone services. Some organizations have incorporated frame relay in their own enterprise networks.

How frame relay works

Frame relay has three main elements:

- An interface to the carriers' networks
- A protocol
- Routing abilities

Frame relay corresponds to layers one and two of the OSI stack. The use of existing protocols at the basic layers makes it easy to provide for frame relay in bridges and routers.

X.25 uses the data link layer for hop-by-hop error and flow control. Each hop generates a sequence number, and acknowledgements flow backward as the message moves forward. Frame relay bypasses much of this process. Each frame includes a number used for routing, but there is no flow control, and no acknowledgements are returned. Compared with X.25, frame relay is a low-fat, highly streamlined process.

Other systems, at higher levels of the OSI stack, manage the end-to-end functions. Each network node keeps track of how to forward frames to a particular connection number. As each frame comes into a node, that node looks up the next destination in an internal table and moves the frame on to that destination.

Frame relay reality

Probably the best thing to remember about frame relay: don't expect too much. It has the capacity to cut through the delays of X.25, but it may not be as speedy in actual service as its performance statistics suggest. You might not even need it.

Disposing of X.25's error correction and verification features helps make frame relay transmissions much faster, but there is an obvious tradeoff. If frame relay doesn't manage errors, some other part of the system should. No matter where you do it, this process will take some time. Modern transmission systems have fewer errors than before, but there is no such thing as an error-free system.

Another problem presented itself in tests of early frame relay applications. The system would sustain a high transmission rate for a while, but it would throttle back when asked to handle long transmissions.

One likely reason for this is not within frame relay itself, but in the conservative design of some transmission systems. Features designed to minimize errors with repeated checks and return acknowledgments also can increase network traffic, delay transmissions, and build backlogs.

These can be fixed. It's still important, though, not to think of frame relay as a miracle technology that will accept large dumps of data as fast as you can ditch them. If expectations of all-out speed are disappointed, frame relay does have two other key advantages:

- Compared with older products, it is simpler. That makes it easier to install and manage.
- It might provide a pathway to the further advantages of ATM.

Some frame relay users say they have adopted the system with two objectives in mind: to cut current transmission costs and to be prepared for coming applications of ATM.

Waiting for ATM

Asynchronous Transfer Mode, also called *cell relay* or *cell switching,* represents yet one more step in the evolution of packet and frame switching. That makes it the next step beyond frame relay. The frames of frame relay are variable-length packets. ATM's cells have fixed lengths.

Those cells give ATM a unique ability that's been likened to a food processor; you can put any kind or size of data in, and it all comes out in uniform cells. The conversion from variety to uniformity means you can efficiently transmit even complex and diverse data. That capacity promises to give ATM a key role in multimedia.

ATM can reduce all kinds of information, including graphics, voice transmissions, and video signals to its quick, efficient package of uniform cells. It then can send these at speeds of up to 600Mbps—probably higher in the future.

ATM offers another advantage if you're in this common situation: you don't have many wide-area transmissions, but those you do send are large—say 100 Gbytes and up, maybe two or three times a week. Transmissions of this size over public data networks can quickly run up costs. At the same time, your long idle periods make it hard to justify the cost of a dedicated line. ATM's quickness would reduce the transmission time and materially cut your costs.

Basic ATM layout

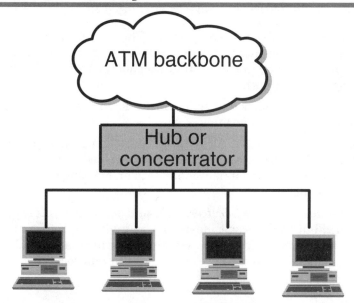

Figure 10.8 ATM uses much the same star configuration as FDDI.

Linking LANs with ATM

For most users, multimedia transmission might be nice someday, but what about getting a few figures from the database in another department? This is where ATM might have its most immediate and important impact.

Unlike some other methods, ATM avoids the party line problem. A LAN uses a single shared transmission medium that depends on users taking their turns. It transmits variable-length packets. ATM is a switch technology that uses fixed-length cells. The fixed length makes traffic much easier to predict and manage. This means ATM is scalable. The only thing you need to do to increase the network's capacity is to add more switches.

Virtual circuits

Instead of relying on the network party line, ATM creates its own virtual channels or circuits. The system sets up one of these virtual channels between a message's origin and destination. You then can send a managed flow of fixed size cells to the recipient and receive a similar flow in return. ATM also uses virtual circuits for signaling and network management.

ATM can combine a group of virtual circuits into a virtual path. This is a bundle of virtual channels that all serve the same destinations. These virtual paths offer several advantages:

- *Simplified network architecture.*   The system can separate network transportation into items that relate to a particular virtual channel and those that can travel simultaneously to all the destinations on a single virtual path.

- *Better performance and reliability.*   The network needs to deal with fewer aggregated entities.

- *Quicker service.*   ATM reduces both setup and processing time. Much of this work need be done only once, when it sets up the virtual paths. You can add a new channel to an existing path with very little processing.

- *Enhanced network services.*   Virtual paths are internal to the network, but that doesn't mean they're invisible. You can use a virtual path to serve an identified workgroup or to create an ad hoc network of people who work together, but at different locations.

Using ATM

ATM may someday appear in several parts of your network: hubs, routers, the desktop, and public network services.

The desktop will become an increasingly important site. The makers of future workstations may equip their products with ATM interfaces the way some build in Ethernet or FDDI today. The multimedia capacity and high performance will probably be important to architects, engineers, financial analysts, medical imagers, and publishers.

Initially, at least, most organizations that adopt ATM will be pioneers, clearing away old technology and building new structures from whatever is available. In the next few years, product vendors and communication services will incorporate ATM in their wares.

So what's wrong with it?

ATM sounds too good to be true, and you know what they tell you about that. Yes, there are some drawbacks. There are three in particular:

- *New technology.*   ATM is still a young technology. Products and services that support it are only slowly arriving on the market. You may lay out an ambitious plan based on ATM only to find out that, for now anyway, you can't get there from here.

- *High cost.*   Most forms of technology go down in cost as they become more widely available. Expect this from ATM, but for now figure on at least $9000 per network node.

Evaluating ATM

If you consider an ATM installation, ask these questions—and be sure you get good answers:

- Will you have to change your network management procedure? If so, how?

- What interoperability problems will you encounter between ATM and your existing installations? Take careful note: that question does not ask *if* you will run into problems.

- What yet-to-be-developed standards might create interoperability problems in the future?

- Are the products and services you need available now?

- What training and support will your staff need?

SMDS and SONET

Two other forms of wide area connection are likely to be affected by ATM's arrival. SMDS is being leapfrogged by it; SONET could become an important partner.

Skipping over SMDS

Switched Megabit Data Service (SMDS) is a high-speed switched data service developed for the regional Bell operating companies. All seven RBOCS plan to offer SMDS service.

Things to check about ATM

- Network procedures
- Interoperability
- Future changes
- Available features
- Training needs

Figure 10.9   Many of ATM's considerable advantages are not ready yet.

SMDS offers higher operating speeds than frame relay. To do this, it combines the techniques of packet and cell switching. Like ATM, SMDS uses fixed-length cells, so it can switch traffic at much higher speeds. It doesn't have to pause to adapt to variations. SMDS is also intended to be a service available to all, from the regional telephone companies.

Frame relay and SMDS have enough in common that they can work together. One possible scenario is a network similar to airline hubs. The carriers will use SMDS on their trunk lines, feeding into central offices. These collection points will use frame relay to route the messages to distant destinations.

You may have noticed something, though; this discussion has dealt exclusively with SMDS as used by the telephone companies. SMDS is their product, but it is a new technology that has yet to gain widespread acceptance by other elements of the networking industry. That particularly includes the makers of products you might incorporate in an enterprise network. Here, frame relay has attracted most of the current interest, and ATM is becoming the technology of the future.

Seeing SONET

The Synchronous Optical Network also originated in the telephone industry as a specification that could take advantage of fiber optic transmission. Its most important role could turn out to be something else: a foundation for ATM.

Objectives of SONET's developers include:

- Provide higher speed transmission, taking advantage of optical networks.

- Establish compatibility with European standards. SONET includes a system of multiplexed digital transmission rates that adapt to both North American and European rates.

- Provide for economical transmission of small amounts of traffic, within the bulk payload of an optical signal.

- Form a basis for future developments in service and network management.

SONET makes an ideal ATM backbone carrier. It can carry a stream of ATM cells as a payload inside one of its own frames.

Another advantage is that SONET can carry synchronous payloads. That makes it a logical successor to existing wide area telecommunication services.

Making choices

As usual, there are no ideal choices. You must balance options, considering such factors as cost, availability, and service.

Another difficulty is the knowledge that today's best choice might be rendered obsolete by tomorrow's developments. That might be an argument for waiting for something like ATM to be more fully developed. By that time, though, there easily could be some further development that seems well worth the wait.

Consultant William Stallings suggests that you approach the decision by working backward. Decide what your requirements are likely to be five or ten years from now. These may include:

- Greater use of applications that involve high volumes of data, including high-resolution graphics and image processing.

- Extended enterprise networking using the client/server model.

- Increasing reliance on multiple LANs at multiple sites.

For many, the best solutions may be the ATM and SONET, individually or in combination. SONET is well suited to customers who have high-capacity demands, but only a few sites. If you are in that situation, you could set up an efficient system that uses dedicated point-to-point SONET lines.

Otherwise, ATM by itself may be your best choice, particularly in the long run. ATM can carry many types of traffic, and you can easily scale it to match your own traffic volume.

Meanwhile, frame relay is a less expensive option that is available now. It is an attractive choice if you feel it will be adequate for your short-term traffic needs. Both frame relay and SMDS offer migration paths to ATM.

Chapter

11

Networking Networks:
The Hardware Side

*Managing diversity has become a major chal-
lenge in human resource management. Managing network diversity can be just as
important to the organization's success.*

Someone once figured out that the average LAN had 6.3 users. No
doubt at least seven people immediately needed to talk to each other.
That's why networks composed of other networks are becoming the
rule, not the exception, in most computer-using organizations.

That raises another problem. A LAN can be hard enough to design,
install, and maintain. Working with mixed networks makes LAN management seem easy. You may find yourself with several network segments that differ in topology, protocol, and operating systems. They
may contain PCs attached to Ethernet or Token Ring networks, Unix
workstations running under TCP/IP, and mainframes running SNA or
any of the other protocols unique to large systems. Most of these components were originally designed to talk only with others just like them.

Your mission, if you decide to accept it, is to tie these segments into
a single working system.

Finding Common Ground

To create a serviceable mixed network, you must meet two requirements:

- You need a way to transfer information between disparate forms of
  communication.

- You must interconnect varying network topologies.

On the software side, that means at some point you must establish a common protocol to move information between common layers of the OSI or TCP/IP stacks. On the hardware side, internetworking tools like gateways, bridges, and routers take advantage of that information-transfer ability.

This chapter concentrates on the latter group, under the banner of internetworking hardware. Hardware is a flag of convenience, used for the sake of this discussion. In an operating internetwork, hardware and software work so closely they are inseparable. Most of the elements work at, near, or with the physical level of the OSI model, but that also is not exclusive. Some work at the highest OSI levels.

Traffic control

In its simplest form, an internetwork uses an intelligent device to connect two LANs. This device might be a bridge, a router, or some combination of the two. The internetworking device does much the same job as an air traffic controller. It monitors all the packets of information that circulate on each LAN. When it detects a packet on the first LAN that is addressed to a station on the second, it forwards it to the other network.

Linking one building's LANs

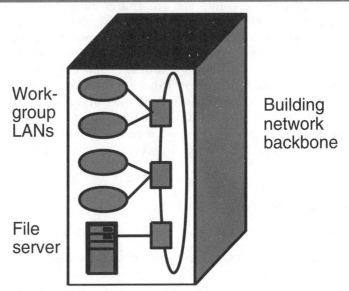

Figure 11.1   You can link LANs in individual departments and workgroups with a backbone system.

Of course, if air traffic control was really that simple, it would not be such a high-stress occupation. The same is true of networking. Even in a simple internetwork, things can get complicated. For example, the two networks might be using different operating systems or protocols. Then the internetwork device will need the help of a gateway to translate the signals between the incompatible protocols.

Multiple networks

In a typical installation, you can link several work group networks into departmental networks. These, in turn, can have ties to an enterprise-wide backbone. This is the basic approach, but it can have many variations. For example, if you have a large building or a corporate campus, you will probably want to install a network to connect all the departmental LANs into a site network that is then tied to the corporate backbone.

This backbone can itself be a LAN: a Token Ring network that has several internetwork devices connected to it. Each internetwork device, in turn, links one or more office or department-level LANs. In this installation, they function as subnetworks. More recently, fiber optics have become a popular choice for backbone service.

An internetworking device directs data packets destined for other subnetworks onto the backbone. Just as an airplane bound from Atlanta to Dallas is directed to a designated air traffic corridor, the backbone serves as a direct route to the destination. There, another internetworking device—like another air traffic control center—assumes control.

Some internetworking devices can direct messages among their connected subnetworks as well as with the backbone network. The direct routing minimizes traffic on the backbone, and the system usually works better. On the other hand, you also can maximize performance by connecting widely used resources, like file servers and gateways, to the backbone network. Users from all over the system will want access to these devices. Placing them on the central network minimizes the amount of traffic and switching that is necessary to reach them.

Wider areas

When an organization wants to connect widely separated resources, another level of networking comes into play: the wide area network or WAN. Like other networks, the WAN usually carries its messages in packets. Because of the distances they must cover, however, WANs generally use different types of protocols.

Linking the enterprise

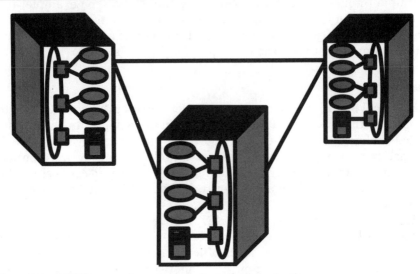

Figure 11.2   A WAN connects separate units in the organization.

Managing the connections

The interconnecting devices are, naturally enough, key elements in any internetworking system. Whether they are bridges, routers, or something else, they serve one vital function: moving information packets from one network to another.

These devices come in a confusing variety, and making the right selections is a challenging task. It's less important what technology you choose, however, than how well the chosen device does its assigned job. Questions to consider in making a selection include:

- Reliability
- Efficiency
- Ability to select the best communication path between networks
- Ability to control who may talk with whom
- Ability to identify network problems and faulty components
- Sensitivity to LAN protocols, and the ability to mix protocols
- Ease of use
- Ability to monitor network use
- Expansion capacity

The larger the network, the most important these functions are. It's important that you choose components that will fulfill these functions; the technology they use to do so is secondary.

Building blocks

You can view an enterprise network as a collection of building blocks. Existing self-contained networks are the basic structural components. The servers, workstations, and other key components work with each other, using common operating systems and protocols.

To connect these independent segments, you must cross the boundaries between them. These boundaries are the sand traps on the golf course of enterprise networking. Somehow, you must get over, around, or through them.

Instead of woods and irons, your tools consist of things like bridges, routers, hubs, and gateways. Their purpose is to get you past the trap. They do not alter the network on either side. They just transport packets of data from one network to the other. To do that, they must satisfy the physical requirements of both networks. They also must transport the data from one network to the other and deliver it in a form the receiving network can understand.

If you need wide area connections, your tools must hit long shots over deep rough. Here, you will need matching pairs of tools: one to transfer the data from the originating network to the WAN, the other to make a connection from the WAN to the receiving network.

Inspecting the tool kit

Among the most important internetworking tools are these:

- *Bridges* connect network segments that use either similar media or different physical media, such as fiber optic and coaxial cable. They can also adapt to different protocols and different OSI levels.

- *Routers* connect networks that may use different topologies, but share a common protocol.

- *Gateways* connect LANs to larger systems. Gateways operate at the top OSI levels. They give you a sophisticated way to connect systems built on totally different architectures. They can also link two LANs that run different communication protocols.

- *Hubs* were originally simple connection points, but *smart hubs* now can exercise internetworking logic of their own.

As these products mature, they are taking on each other's characteristics, and the boundaries between these types of products are growing dimmer. A case in point is the *brouter,* a hybrid of the bridge and router. Because so many internetworking tools now share the characteristics of other types, the brouter has all but lost its unique identity.

Network Organization Schemes

Managing diversity has become a key idea in human resources management; it is just as important in managing interlinked networks. Corporate managers increasingly recognize the strategic importance of interconnecting diverse networks and computing platforms.

There are plenty of "solutions" you can buy. Any number of interconnection products are available, including varied types of bridges, routers, and gateways. With these, you can build a flexible, cost-effective backbone for enterprise-wide computing. Such an internetwork will connect LANs not only with each other, but with diverse networking environments throughout the organization.

Internetworked systems usually have elements on all or most of these levels:

- Workgroup subnetworks. Typically, these are interconnected groups of PC LANs.

- Departmental subnetworks. Several workgroup networks may be grouped into an interlined departmental system. This system will use one or more routers to provide the contact points between the workgroup nets.

- Site networks, connecting the departmental subnetworks at a particular location.

- The enterprise-wide backbone. This is an interconnection of the departmental subnetworks throughout the organization.

The working group

At the workgroup level, you can interconnect several LANs that will let group members share data, information, and applications. Most network operating systems provide server-based routing plus requester services to let a workstation that uses one NOS contact a server that uses a different system. At this level, the servers can use a Routing Information Protocol (RIP) to exchange routing information. In a larger network, RIP is inefficient enough to bring another meaning to mind, but at this level it is usually a cost-effective solution.

The departmental level

Internetworking at the departmental level can begin to involve subnetworks at remotely-located sites like those in neighboring buildings.

You may need more intelligent bridges and routers, particularly if you must connect diverse types of networks.

Showing some backbone

The backbone must be the sturdiest element of a corporate internetwork. It requires high-performance routers, including those that connect LANs to WANs. Your need here is for both high performance and the ability to link dissimilar networks.

The normal course in building an enterprise-wide system is to start at the department level. Link a few small LANs, then move up to increasingly larger networked systems. Only after you have installed several of these smaller networks should you consider enterprise-wide access.

Many network elements already in place may reflect unplanned, haphazard installation. An odd mixture of PCs, workstations, LANs, WANs, minicomputers, and mainframes may already be in place, representing many different vendors and operating software of equally diverse background.

An evolutionary approach can gradually bring uniformity to what the orderly mind can easily see as chaos. The system plan should adapt as technology changes. It must cover such issues as cable planning and maintenance, growth and capacity planning, and choices of standards.

Building Bridges

A bridge is a good choice when you need to link LANs, either locally or remotely, and you worry about loading LAN segments with unnecessary traffic. Bridges identify the packets and frames they pass and pass on only those addressed to nodes on the other side. Bridges cannot distinguish between packets created under different protocols at the network layer.

Bridges can move packets or frames between different kinds of media. The client PCs do not need any special software or hardware to benefit from the actions of repeaters and bridges.

There is a special type of bridge called a *learning bridge*. This type of bridge has software that broadcasts a message. All network nodes respond. The bridge software reads the source address of each packet or frame and associates source addresses with LAN segments in an internal table. The bridge software uses this table to limit the traffic crossing between LAN segments and to prevent problem packets or adapters on one LAN segment from affecting connected segments.

Modern bridges monitor the traffic so closely, special software in the bridges can furnish information on both traffic volume and network errors. Bridges are busy devices, though. They must evaluate packets on-the-fly.

Low bridge

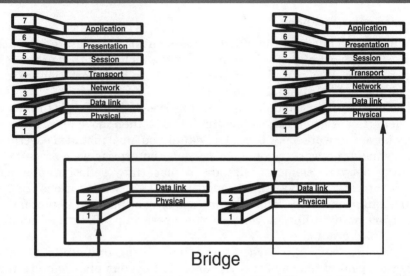

Bridge

Figure 11.3 Bridges work only at the lowest levels of the OSI model. They can't distinguish among different protocols.

Two OSI levels

A bridge operates at the physical and data link layers of the OSI model. The bridge connects two compatible addressing schemes, identified at the data link layer. The bridge operates by forwarding packets between the data link layers of the connected networks.

Since a bridge works no higher than the data link layer, it can't recognize the difference between packets sent under different protocols. This happens at the network layer. The bridge simply forwards a packet regardless of its protocol. Devices on the LANs must make the identifications.

To function as a bridge, a PC must have two network cards, one for each of the two networks the bridge is to link. It also needs software that will enable it to bridge the two networks.

Three kinds of bridges

Just as there are metal covered bridges and wooden covered bridges, network bridges come in several types. They include:

- Transparent bridges
- Source routing bridges
- Source routing transparent bridges

You can use a transparent bridge with any protocol. You cannot use it in a mesh network that offers more than one path between any two points. A transparent bridge will choose one path and disable all the others.

Source routing bridges are just the opposite. They cannot distinguish between different protocols, but they do support mesh networks in a rudimentary way. The bridge does not disable extra paths, but once committed to a path, it cannot readily switch to another.

Source routing bridges appear often in Token Ring networks. IBM's Token Ring adapters have source routing drivers and expect all stations which communicate with them to offer source routing as well.

As you might expect, source routing transparent bridges combine the characteristics of the other types. They act as source routing bridges for those protocols that support it, and as transparent bridges for protocols that require this service. You can't use these advantages simultaneously, but you can use this type of bridge to accommodate different needs in the same enterprise network.

The future of bridging

Since bridges work at the lower OSI levels, they are less complicated than routers and other devices that work at higher levels. Because they are simple, bridges often have been the technology of choice for straightforward, internetwork connections. That picture is changing, though, for several reasons:

- Users are beginning to understand routers better, and their complications are less daunting.

- Bridges are gaining some routing functions, and routers are gaining some bridging functions. The distinction between the two is geting dim.

- Bridges no longer have a large price advantage over more flexible technology.

The merging of bridges and routers is likely to continue. The simplicity of a bridge will always be an asset in systems that do not demand higher levels of technology. Nevertheless, many future systems will demand those levels. While some bridge-only products probably will remain on the market, the distinction between bridges and routers could become so dim it will effectively disappear.

Routers Do More

Like bridges, routers connect separate LANs, but they do it in a more sophisticated way. Routers work at three layers of the OSI model, including the network layer where packets can be addressed and directed to designated destinations.

Routers connect LANs that use the same protocol. Common types of routers include:

- An IP router that handles TCP/IP packets.

- An IPX router that handles IPX/SPX packets.

- A DECnet router that handles, naturally enough, DECnet packets.

A router can be either a PC or workstation with network boards and appropriate software installed. It also can be a single-purpose device made strictly for this duty.

Smarter than smart

Routers are more discriminating than bridges. Router software reads address information and decides how to route the data across multiple internetwork links. Routers don't examine every packet or frame, only those specifically addressed to them.

The programs in *static routers* expect you to pick the shortest path between the two points. You must enter the routing information manually, so every change in the network system will require a corresponding change in the router's information bank. More sophisticated products, *dynamic routers,* make packet-by-packet decisions based on the information they glean from other routers and network devices. With this

Routers work at a higher level

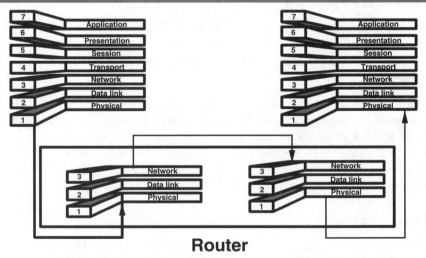

Router

Figure 11.4 Routers work at the network level and can identify packets that use different protocols.

information they assess the efficiency and reliability of different routes between the source and destination, and choose a route accordingly.

Because routers don't read every network packet or frame, they don't work as hard as bridges. That means they smaller loads on their host CPUs. Because they allow only specially addressed packets and frames to pass between LAN segments, they put the lowest stress on the internetwork links.

Routing strategy

When a router finds the best path to a destination, it relies on a routing strategy. The best strategy depends on a combination of two factors:

- The route with the fewest connections
- The route with the fastest line speed

These are not necessarily the same.

Just as airlines direct most of their routes through hub airports, routers sometimes do much the same. For example, there might be a direct route from Point A to the familiar Point B, but it is an inefficient, low-speed connection. The router might decide to send the message by way of Point C, a central location served by high-speed connections with the other locations.

Three types of routers

Routers come in three basic types. All three do the same job, but there are differences in their physical installations:

- *Box routers.* These are usually high-end installations. They take their name from the large rack-mounted structures that usually enclose them. These routers can transfer packets at high speeds. They usually require expensive, vendor-supplied router cards.

- *Hub routers.* Also called *concentrator routers,* these usually take the form of add-on cards for a hub computer. These usually are proprietary systems, but most come from one of two sources, so matching usually is not difficult.

- *PC software routers.* This software turns a PC, preferably a fast machine with plenty of memory, into a router. For the most part, maintaining this router is as simple as maintaining the PC.

Look for features

Physical characteristics aren't the only basis for considering a router. The more important consideration is whether the router has the features you need and supports the protocols in your networks.

Performance figures are easily overrated. Except on the largest networks, you probably can't tell the difference between top-of-the-line products and those that are much less expensive. The best purchasing advice is to pick the lowest-cost system that provides the functions and features you need.

Those functions are becoming more sophisticated. Among the features some router vendors now offer are:

- *Crash containment.* This feature ensures that a fault on one network will not drag down other connected networks.

- *Detour.* This is the ability to reroute network traffic around a failed link. This is a particularly good function for a router, since routers are generally more reliable than communication lines.

- *Instant failure reports.* Even if the router effectively compensates for a network failure, it should report any problems instantly. You can't solve a problem unless you know about it.

Router development

Early routers supported only one local interface, one or two remote interfaces, and a single protocol, usually TCP/IP. Today, most routers can handle multiple interfaces and multiple protocols with ease.

Routers can also support concurrent communication among several different LAN systems such as Ethernet, Token Ring, and FDDI. Even so, they can do this only if each node uses the same protocol.

Picking the best path

Routers use address information available at the OSI network layer. This gives them the ability to find the best internetwork path between two nodes. They can also consider several different definitions of the best path: shortest, fastest, fewest hops, least congestion, fewest errors, or some combination of these.

There are three standard protocols for making this evaluation:

- *Routing information protocol (RIP).* This is a simple protocol that uses vectors and counts hops to choose a route. It does not consider other factors like speed, cost, quality, or congestion.

- *Open shortest path first (OSPF).* This protocol lets a router monitor the status of each link and react at once to changes.

- *Interior gateway routing protocol (IGRP).* This is Cisco Systems' enhanced, proprietary, routing protocol.

Managing the Gateway

Gateways are the most intelligent forms of internetwork connection. That's why you'll often find gateways between LANs and large systems. That's also why they are the most sophisticated way to link the networks in your enterprise.

Gateways translate data formats. They also and open and close sessions between application programs. They operate at every layer of the OSI model. Sometimes, a modem and PC form the hardware element of the gateway. The classic IRMA card is another type of LAN gateway hardware. A common type of gateway links the PC-based LAN to a device which uses a completely different data alphabet and signaling system, such as IBM's SNA communication system for mainframe computers.

Gateways provide two similar functions:

- They give LAN users access to other host computers.

- They connect network operating systems of different types.

Gateways do it all

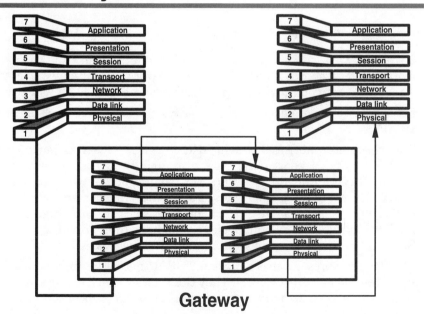

Figure 11.5   Gateways work at all seven OSI layers and can maintain contact with all kinds of systems.

Two major purposes

The traditional and most common use for a gateway is to give LAN users access to the data on a minicomputer or mainframe. The system usually lets the user establish terminal and printer sessions with the host computer. Other services may include file transfers and remote job entry (RJE).

Gateways also make several networks with dissimilar operating systems appear to users on the other side of the gateway as a single, uniform network. For example, a TCP/IP gateway can give users on a PC network access to a minicomputer on the other side of the gateway. At the same time, users of Unix workstations on the network with the minicomputer can gain access to a file server on the PC network.

The gateway PC

Personal computers often serve as gateways. A PC-based gateway uses both network and communication boards to connect two LANs, or to connect a LAN to a host computer. As with PC-based bridges and routers, the PC must also have communication software to link the two systems. Users on the LAN will also need communication software to gain access to the host computer via the gateway.

Types of gateways

Gateways come in several basic types:

- 3270 gateways connect LANs with IBM mainframe hosts on networks that use that firm's Systems Network Architecture (SNA). They make network devices appear to the mainframe as SNA devices.

- 5250 gateways connect LANs to minicomputer hosts, such as the IBM AS/400 series.

- Asynchronous gateways provide the services of serial ports and modems to LAN users. They are also sometimes known as asynchronous communication servers (ACSs). These gateways can provide LAN users with such services as file transfer and terminal emulation. A popular use is to let LAN users share high-speed modems by way of a modem pool. The modems then provide access to bulletin boards, electronic mail, and database services.

- TCP/IP gateways let users on non-TCP/IP networks gain access to hosts that do use this protocol. They then can use such services as terminal emulation, file transfer, electronic mail, and process-to-process communication.

- X.25 gateways provide access to packet-switched networks, including public dial-up services and private networks.

Hub of the Universe

Bostonians used to call their city "the hub of the universe," a claim most of the rest of the universe ignored. A less pretentious form of hub could become the center of your enterprise network.

In its basic form, the wiring hub, or *repeater*, is a very simple device. You put it in a central location, plug in cables from your network nodes, and all the proper connections are made inside the hub.

The simple hub displays further advantages. Placing the hub within a locked wiring closet helps boost security. If you need to reconfigure the network, just unplug the old elements and plug in the new. Is your wiring twisted pair, cable, or fiber optic? The hub takes them all. Just plug them in. You don't have a lot of excess wiring strung around the place, either. The incentive for the first hub was undoubtedly neater wiring.

What's more, basic hubs aren't just inexpensive—they're cheap. You can connect a network at a central hub for less than $100 a port. You'll find plenty of these basic hubs in service, and you'll probably find more this time next year. More sophisticated hubs naturally cost more.

The next generations

With all these advantages, it should be no surprise that vendors have added features to these simple connectors. There once was a difference between hubs and relatives called *concentrators*. Hubs were originally central connection points for LANs with star topologies. Concentrators were more intelligent and had added features designed

Three types of hubs

- Repeater
  - Makes basic wiring connections
- Smart hub
  - Includes network management
- Enterprise hub
  - Has extra bandwidth

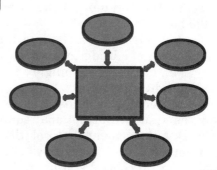

Figure 11.6   Once simple wiring connections, hubs now incorporate network management schemes.

for high-end networks. The evolution of the hub has all but wiped out that distinction.

Today's best seller is a second-generation hub called the *smart hub*. It's particularly popular for its network management features and its ability to adapt to multiple networks. A third-generation hub, *enterprise hub,* has added bandwidth and other features targeted directly at enterprise networks.

This is another area of blurred distinctions. Furthermore, vendors keep adding new features that improve their products, but frustrate classification schemes. This book will distinguish between smart hubs, which have added features, and enterprise hubs, whose features are particularly important for enterprise networks.

The smarter hub

Second-generation smart hubs cost as much as 40 percent more than standard hubs. For this price, you get added flexibility, easier management, and the ability to make use of wiring that's already in place. A smart hub is also nice to have when you want to upgrade your wiring.

There's no standard list of what features a smart hub should offer. Most fall under the heading of adaptability.

Nearly every network is subject to a constant flow of moves, additions, and changes. A central hub with modular connections can cut the time you need to attach and detach the affected nodes.

The hub can be even more flexible and open to expansion if it will accept varied types of media. For example, if you install fiber optic cable with an eye to future expansion, the only thing you need do later is to add the right connectors and a fiber module to the hub. You can also use fiber optics to interconnect hubs in a backbone arrangement.

You can also use repeater features to extend network wiring beyond its rated maximum length. For example, the popular 10BaseT wiring should have no more than 100 meters between connections. Routing the signal through multiple hubs, you can stretch the line to as much as 400 meters.

An intelligent hub can also interlink several networks, incorporating the functions of a bridge or router. It can split existing networks, combine them, or totally reconfigure them, plugging the right connectors into the right sockets.

Second generation hubs also include network management software, as standard or optional equipment. Most support the Simple Network Management Protocol (SNMP), which is becoming the most-used network management system. It lets you manage the network from a central control station, monitoring traffic, use levels, and hub failures.

Hubs for the Enterprise Network

Though second-generation hubs can link multiple networks, a large enterprise network will usually need third generation products that include features like these:

- Built-in management and monitoring features
- Bridging and routing
- Fault tolerance and redundancy
- Software-controlled port switching
- High operating speeds
- Internal routing
- Built-in security

High-end hubs offer most of these features now and will probably soon have them all—and more.

The enterprise hub integrates all these technologies into a single box. That may make it seem like a complicated piece of equipment, but it can simplify things for network administrators and troubleshooters. When something goes wrong, you'll know where to look first.

Since these features are built as an integrated whole, enterprise hubs also have good reliability records. They definitely are more dependable than unstructured networks. They're easier to manage, too. That's important in an enterprise network. You now must provide reliability, management, control, and flexibility over an ever-larger area.

Boosting performance

Enterprise hubs cope with their heavy traffic by moving it at high speeds. The speed comes from hot-rodded backplanes that include logic to reduce blocking and prevent bottlenecks. This high performance is becoming more important as faster WAN technologies like frame relay and ATM enter the enterprise network.

A feature still being developed lets the hub handle network routing, which adds speed and efficiency to the process.

Network management

Anything that helps you manage an enterprise network will be a valuable asset. Enterprise hubs offer several kinds of management aids, including monitoring, protocol analysis, and troubleshooting.

Most present this information through graphical interfaces that help operators quickly identify problem areas. For example, an on-screen signal might change from green to red when the system senses a problem. The operator can click on the colored area, and the display will locate the card that has the problem. Once the card has been replaced, the system can verify that the problem has been cured. The hub might also transmit the proper software to set up the new card.

Tolerance for faults

Enterprise networks must be more fault tolerant than smaller networks. Accordingly, most network hubs include redundant circuits to take over in case a critical component fails. The hub can back up all critical components, including power supplies and management modules. There also are often backup links for Ethernet and Token Ring networks.

Another important feature is modular construction. This lets you add and swap components to solve problems without shutting down the network. You can't afford to shut down an entire enterprise network to take care of every minor repair.

Many enterprise hubs include ways to oversee local network resources, particularly those whose users maintain or have designed them. You can do this locally, through a terminal, or remotely, using SNMP or an inbound terminal session. These features can give you a statistical picture of network use, errors, conflicts, and other problems.

Yes, there are drawbacks

Enterprise hubs do have some weaknesses. One is purely physical: some modules have been identified as likely failure points. Most vendors compensate by building in redundant versions of known weak spots.

A more critical problem is the difference between central and local network management. Network hubs naturally lend themselves to central management. Where departments and work groups manage their own networks, they want to retain local control. Physically, the difference is whether you install the hub in a local wiring closet or in a central location. But this is also a political, not a technical, decision. Enterprise networking can increase the level of central control, but department managers will not easily yield the flexibility they won through PCs and LANs. The lesson for IS management is that you might gain control, but you must be much more responsive to department needs and concerns than in the past.

The selection process

Enterprise hubs offer so many features, and in a multitude of combinations. That makes selecting a hub a lot more complicated than using one. You must understand, for example, how many networks using how many topologies and protocols you must link. You must find a hub that will adapt to both your present systems and your future migrations.

Another key point: whether the vendor builds bridging and routing into the product or whether you must supply these separately.

Since everyone's networks are different, so are everyone's needs in enterprise hubs. Look for a product whose features best match your present system and future plans. Find out, too, whether the features you need now are available now.

One important feature for nearly everyone is a network management system, preferably one based on SNMP. This is a nearly universal system that can help you get the monitoring and management information you need.

Of course, it hard to foresee everything you might need in the future. You will have to make an educated guess. The possibilities include:

- Flexibility in network configuration, separating the physical from the logical network
- User applications like fax and directory services
- Greater ability to link mixed networks, including LANs, remote offices, and FDDI
- Interchangeable modules to fit different types of networks
- The ability to handle multimedia applications
- Integration of advanced technology such as ATM

Extending the Network to Remote Users

Employees don't always spend full working days in a central office. Some work in branch offices. A corps of telecommuters may work at home. There are traveling sales and service employees who carry portable computers. You may also want to establish network links with key customers, suppliers, or both.

By one estimate, 1.5 million workers leave the office at least several times a month, either to travel or to work at home. A full 25 million have jobs that keep them away. Then there are four million who work in remote offices. Unless your network can reach them, they do not have the access to information homebound employees can easily obtain from the enterprise network. These remote employees are effectively disenfranchised, left at a disadvantage to their co-workers. This isn't fair to them, and if you don't think so, just wait until the employment lawyers get their hands on it. It isn't fair to you, either. You're depriving yourself of the better work remote employees could do if they had full access to the network and its information.

You can give them access at any of four levels. The higher the level, the more information available to remote employees. Also, the higher the level, the more you are likely to need extra hardware and software to meet their needs. The levels are:

- Electronic mail
- File transfer
- Remote control
- Remote network nodes

Access to e-mail

In many organizations, e-mail is the most important medium of information exchange. It is also among the most popular, most versatile, and easiest to install.

Many e-mail packages have features that let remote users dial a central mail hub attached to the network. The employees can use this link to exchange messages. A mail server with one or more phone lines is attached to the network, and the portables can run a remote access version of the software.

As an alternative, you can use public e-mail services like MCI Mail and the internet as gateways to the corporate e-mail system. This gets quick results with little initial outlay. Several e-mail programs including cc:Mail and DaVinci can exchange messages with commercial services.

There are some drawbacks. Since they must serve users on all kinds of systems, the public services have coarse, primitive interfaces. It can

Types of remote access

- E-mail
- File transfer
- Remote control
- Remote network nodes

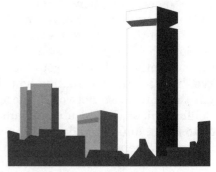

Figure 11.7 You don't always need high levels of access.

be tricky to send a message accurately and to the right destination. If you send large numbers of long messages, the communication charges can quickly add up. Though the commercial services offer basic security features, it is risky to use them for confidential information.

Moving data

File transfers are one step up from e-mail. Besides transmitting text messages, you can transfer data files. Most e-mail software includes file transfer options. There are other choices as well:

- File transfer utilities designed to transfer files between portable and desktop computers
- Standard asynchronous software programs, which also have file transfer modes

This level of access can be easy and inexpensive. You probably already have the means. Some employees will still find file transfer programs hard to use, however.

Remote control

Often used by PC support technicians, remote control programs let someone on one computer take control of another system on the network by telephone and modem. You can also use them to connect with the network while you're on the road. Once you have made the connection, the program lets you operate the remote computer from your keyboard, just as if you were sitting in front of it.

This is another lowcost option. It is also an option with drawbacks. Only one person at a time can dial into the network. Even then, remote access is only available when the host computer has been set up in advance to receive remote calls. Then, there are security risks. Dial-in access is risky in any event. Leaving this path open to a running computer attached to your network is about as safe as leaving your car unlocked with the engine running.

Remote nodes

The most thorough approach, and naturally the most expensive one, is to give remote users their own network nodes. Each remote node duplicates the local node at its user's desk, so it gives mobile employees full access to any asset they would have at the home office. You can also maintain the same security and access controls.

Within those restrictions, you have access to your home office computer from anywhere that has a telephone. You can map drives and printers, exchange files and e-mail, and even run network applications.

The drawbacks: applications often run more slowly, particularly if they use graphics. Phone charges can be high, particularly if there are many users. On the other hand, remote node access is the remote employee's nearest thing to home-office computing. The applications all work alike, and there's little need for fresh training.

The leading LAN operating systems have extra-cost utilities you can use to create remote access nodes. Install them on a server, and you can create nodes for dial-in employees.

These utilities usually do other jobs, too. They may let in-house users reach external hosts, networks, or commercial information sources.

Carriers: Public vs. Private

Once an enterprise network grows into the realm of wide area networking, you have an important decision to make. Should you set up a private network, or should you rely on public carriers?

Private networks have enjoyed a long period of popularity, starting with the deregulation and breakup of the telephone system. Particularly in large organizations, communication managers felt they could cut costs by establishing private networks that carried both their voice and data transmissions.

Now, public networks have developed and diversified so they can offer the same services as a private network, but at less cost. For voice signals, you can set up a carrier-based virtual private network that can handle voice traffic more efficiently than any private network. Accordingly, many companies have moved their voice traffic back to the public network.

Now, the same thing is happening in data traffic, particularly as the data traffic is generated by LAN applications. This LAN traffic usually travels in small, intense bursts. Maintaining a full-time network to handle these occasional spurts of traffic can be a waste of resources.

In addition, public carriers are tailoring their services to this need. Most offer, or plan to offer, services like frame relay and SMDS. These are not only faster than older systems, but they match the bursty nature of today's network traffic.

Making a choice

The choice is not automatic. It depends on your particular needs. In general, though, you can follow these guidelines:

- Public carriers have a big edge in voice communication. Usually, private-network voice transmission is practical only when you already have the unused network capacity.

- The carriers don't have a similar advantage in data communication. Arriving technologies like frame relay, SMDS, and ATM could soon change that situation.

- Public networks are engineered to provide high degrees of reliability. Few private networks can match them.

- Private networks are more economical for high-volume traffic. Public carrier charges are highly variable costs; the expenses of private networks are more firmly fixed.

- Private networks offer greater security and reliability for mission-critical transmissions.

- A private network gives you a higher degree of management over your network traffic. The carriers offer some management functions, but they seldom compare with what you could install yourself on a private line.

- Public carriers don't always offer all the services you may require.

Planning a Network Strategy

Somehow, you must combine all these bits and pieces of semi-compatible technology into a network that serves your entire enterprise. It naturally makes sense to make maximum use of existing resources. From

Public vs. private

- Public networks
  - Better for voice
  - Very reliable
- Private networks
  - Better for data
  - More secure
  - Less costly for high volumes
  - More versatile

Figure 11.8   A private network also gives you more management flexibility.

this basis, you can take an organized, inside-out approach, making the right choices from a multitude of options. The steps are:

- Identify your goals.
- Connect your small workgroups.
- Identify and meet special needs.
- Connect campuses and nearby locations.
- Link wide areas.

Goal-setting

What's a business organization without goals? Sometimes for better and sometimes for worse, modern management relies strongly on setting and meeting objectives.

An enterprise network is no exception. The most important step is the first one: deciding exactly what your network should do. That includes:

- The ways you wish to use information to advance your business. This is the basic purpose of a network. Don't go a step further until you are sure you know exactly what it is.
- Which parts of the organization should be networked to achieve this goal and which should have the highest priority.
- What kind of information these groups should exchange.

Planning nuts and bolts

- Identify your goals
- Start with small workgroups
- Meet special needs
- Connect wider areas

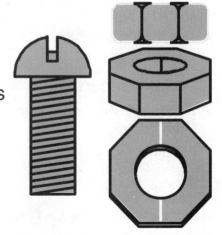

Figure 11.9 Take an inside-out approach, working with what you already have in place.

- What assets are already in place to help meet these needs and what you must add to your existing resources.

Start small

There are several reasons to start by linking small workgroups. It gives you some experience at a level where your inevitable mistakes won't have enterprise-wide consequences. It also lets you focus on the needs of the individual employees who make up the organization. If you don't serve these needs, you don't serve the enterprise.

You may have a grand design of linking multiple business units in several locations. To reach that goal, you must start from the inside out. Take an up close and personal look at a single small group of people. Identify its needs and opportunities. Do the same for other groups of similar size.

Once you learn these small groups' needs, look to see what they have in common. These common elements represent information that can profitably be exchanged.

This is also the time to take inventory of existing networks. Look for ways to incorporate them into the enterprise network. Don't hang on to obsolete technology that doesn't work, particularly if it fails to meet all your objectives. On the other hand, don't throw out existing assets you can profitably use with a little work and ingenuity.

Picking technology

Particularly in enterprise networking, your technology choices depend strongly on the needs they are to help you meet. Though you'll no doubt be thinking technology from the outset, don't make any firm choices until you have identified the small-group needs and the types of information they can usefully exchange. Then, evaluate the technology for its ability to exchange that particular kind of information and meet those particular needs.

Use the common threads you have discovered to identify the best ways to connect the individual workgroups into compact network segments. Then, you can follow the same process to combine these segments into a single network for one location.

Exceptions noted

You will undoubtedly run into exceptions and special cases. For example, you may find you must integrate Unix workstations into a network composed mainly of PC LANs. This may require technology choices that you would not use on other segments of the network. For example, you might have to network the Unix machines by way of a bridge and a high-level protocol like TCP/IP.

Expanding outward

Build on your experience networking small groups, and gradually expand your view outward. Once you have successfully hooked up the individual locations, you can consider connections between locations on the same campus.

Here, you will probably encounter new problems like managing traffic flow. This is something like designing an interstate highway. You must provide for high overall speeds. You also must avoid congestion that renders the high speed useless.

Cross country

Only at the final step will your electronic expressway start to take you cross-country. Ideally, you have built on the needs you discovered at the local level to expand outward, meeting them with new ways to exchange information.

That should stay the same as you work your way outward to wider areas. You can expect to encounter some new technical challenges, though. Operating costs become a larger factor, particularly in the choice between public and private carriers. You must also take care in selecting the routes long-haul data will travel.

Is all this worth it?

The benefit you can gain from building an enterprise depends on your organization and its needs. You may find that you don't need a network at all.

More likely, your analysis will find ways you can profit by sharing more information. Then, your gains will depend on the degree to which the network you build responds directly to your organization's specific needs and opportunities.

Network integration checklist

1. What are your needs for LAN communication?
   - Routers
   - Hubs
   - Gateways
2. What are your needs for internetworked communication?
   - Backbones
   - Routers
   - Bridges
   - Gateways
   - Hubs
   - Mainframe access
3. Do any parts of the system require:
   - Fault tolerance?
   - Extra security?

12

Managing the Enterprise Network

*There's a simple way to manage networks. Or
maybe it's a way to manage simple networks.*

Not long ago, one of the organization's most valuable people was the
network whiz who could set up a Novell LAN and actually make it
work right. Today, the criteria for personal value are much tougher. A
LAN can include several types of systems. Then, that LAN can be part
of an enterprise network.

The enterprise network places new demands on the people who manage it. The focus shifts from managing individual networks to managing an enterprise network with multiple systems. You must take
charge of all these divergent systems. What's more, you must cope with
different layers of networks and network management. You may well
have one management system at a central point, supporting multiple
management systems in individual departments.

That demands not only good people, but good management tools.
Therein lies a problem. The ideal enterprise network tool kit would
make television's *Home Improvement* look underequipped. Such a tool
kit does not yet exist. It's being created, but if enterprise network managers have one common lament, it is the lack of tools to manage their
expanding areas of responsibility.

Needs to Be Met

You will have to make the best use of the resources that are available
and hope that the future brings better tools—quickly. It is almost
impossible to manage a large enterprise network without automated
help. The network product marketplace does offer much help. LAN
operating systems let you see performance statistics and account for

Network management tools

- You need a lot
- You have a few

Figure 12.1   Perhaps the biggest current obstacle to enterprise networking is a shortage of management tools.

the network's use. From a remote location you can control terminal servers and bridges; these too report traffic conditions and errors. Add-on equipment is available for existing networks that are short of management ability.

After all this, there is still a shortage of network management tools. Networking technology continues to expand beyond the ability of existing resources.

There are still plenty of needs a network management system must meet. They include these technical needs:

- *Chain reaction failures.*   You need to know how a failure in one part of the network might affect the total operation. Suppose there should be a bug in the database software that keeps track of network addresses. It could block access to critical services like backup systems, but at the same time it could hide this problem from the monitoring system. You need cross-checks and consistency checks to detect this kind of problem.

- *Traffic congestion.*   Even like a well-designed highway, a network can suffer from traffic jams. If several network elements fail simultaneously, the load of blocked and diverted traffic can bring the system to a halt. Adding to the congestion: the messages the network generates to report the problems.

- *The unexpected.*   A network hit by unexpected events must be able to help itself. It should manage and reroute traffic to avoid trouble spots. The system must also react properly to duplicate messages or

Burning technical issues

- Multiple failures
- Congestion
- Unexpected problems
- Local and central management
- Protocols
- Testing
- Growth
- Adaptability

Figure 12.2   These are only some of the needs you must meet through network management.

messages from questionable sources. Most systems use timeouts and retransmissions to deal with these problems. Another approach is to display a status flag that warns of impending problems.

- *Centralized and decentralized management.*   Central management can also create a central point of failure. Decentralized management can be a source of inconsistency. In an enterprise network, you are likely to have elements of both, with their combined drawbacks. You must decide who should be responsible for managing such things as database consistency, standby systems, and database updates. Another decision: who should receive status information and error messages? Often, a local group can take care of problems in its own system. There are other times when central management is more effective.

- *Protocol standards.*   The choice of a network management standard—or none at all—can either improve management or make it harder. If you base the system on standards, you must be sure the entire system follows them. Otherwise, it might interpret nonstandard messages in strange ways. You must also make sure you can support the standards you want to maintain. On the other hand, standards make it easier to integrate network management with the network as a whole.

- *Testing.*   The network management system should include test points, including interfaces, snapshots, and tracing.

- *Growth potential.*   The management system should adapt to traffic growth and the addition of new nodes and networks. It should also incorporate new technology as opportunities arise.

- *Adaptability.*   The network management system should adapt to system changes. It should accept new features and technology easily and with little disruption.

Management Issues

Those are the technical issues. Enterprise network management involves many management issues, too. These include:

- Software distribution and version control
- Error response and correction
- Management of the system's configuration
- Security and access control

Managing software distribution

There has always been one good reason to manage software distribution and to make sure everyone uses the same version. Even differing versions of the same title can clutter the network with different formats and commands.

There's another reason that has little to do with the software itself. Unlicensed software can bring warrant-wielding detectives to your door, demanding stiff penalties. Viruses are also threats.

Nontechnical issues

- Software distribution
- Error response
- System configuration
- Security

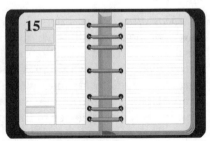

Figure 12.   Management includes problems like these as well.

You now can manage software upgrades from a central location. From this single distribution point, you can copy the software to remote file servers and local disks.

Like the old movie cliche of synchronizing watches, you can program the network to make the change at a preset time. If you are updating a distributed database, for example, install two copies—one old, one new—at each location. At the appointed time, the network will switch *en masse* from the old system to the new.

There is one big danger with this method. It presumes that every element will immediately make the switch. There are many reasons that may not happen. One server may lose its power at a critical moment, or its hard disk may be full when you try to load the new version. It will miss the mass upgrade, yet the system may assume that all went well. That single out-of-synch server can cause major disruptions.

To avoid this problem, take two steps. Distribute the software, and wait for confirmation that every node has received the transmission. Then trigger the simultaneous changeover.

The transition becomes tricker if you must upgrade transaction processing systems. A failure, or even a brief interruption, while a transaction is in progress could put parts of that transaction on the new and old databases. One solution is to include version information on all data transmissions. You can then program the system to reject transmissions based on outdated versions.

The dual software method can also help you fight off bugs and viruses. If you keep a previous version on the system, you can fall back on it should the new software develop a serious problem.

Shooting troubles

The largest bin in your management tool kit will contain tools to find and correct problems. All but the smallest networks require automated procedures to report errors, manage backups, and do other similar jobs. You will also need one or more qualified people to use these tools. On a small LAN this may be a part-time job for a single in-house expert. As the enterprise network grows, it will require more people, doing more specialized jobs.

Network management software can augment your staff and keep its numbers within reasonable limits. The jobs it can do include:

- Identifying and correcting problems
- Logging and reporting events
- Controlling operations

The software records problems as they arise. Depending on the type of problem, it may notify the network manager. Other types of problems, or those that exceed stated thresholds, are reported to central management.

The software may also have an echo mechanism or some other way to monitor resources like gateways and file servers. It notifies the appropriate manager when one of these resources fails.

When there is a problem, the software usually sounds an audible alarm. It puts up a display that describes the problem and its location. Management software can also point out the likely cause and suggest what the manager should do to isolate and correct the problem.

The system can collect these reports, creating a history file for each network element. The log can include information about the nature of the problem, how it was resolved, vendor contacts, and other information that might be helpful in the future.

Logging errors

Beyond these problem-solving messages, management software can report on other events that can affect the network and its performance. It can chart peak volume times and notify you when it detects new addresses on the system. It can direct this information to a printer or disk file.

The system should let you use this information to generate periodic reports, such as a log of network operations over the previous 24 hours.

Operator control

The system should respond to your queries about the status of any device attached to the network, including workstations, bridges, and gateways. Some of these elements may maintain their own records. For instance, a bridge can incorporate the Simple Network Management Protocol (SNMP). You then can use SNMP to query the bridge for its operating statistics on traffic, errors, and unusual events.

Another useful function tests the path between two workstations. This is particularly useful when there are repeaters or bridges between the stations.

Managing Configuration

Configuration management lets you learn and control what kind of software is on what systems. It helps you maintain an approved software list and look for exceptions, whether authorized or unauthorized.

Configuration management software also helps you keep track of how each element of the network is configured internally. You can use it, for example, to find out whether a PC on a department's LAN has the memory, processing power, and disk capacity to run a particular application.

Management and support checklist

1. What type of support do you now offer to network users?
2. What parts of this support is:
   - Centralized?
   - Decentralized at the department level?
   - Decentralized at an intermediate level?
3. What levels of support are available and appropriate at the departmental level?
4. What additional options are available for supporting the enterprise network?
   - Existing services
   - Outsourcing
5. Which networks are mission-critical? How do you provide for the necessary level of support?
6. What provisions should you make for:
   - Maintenance?
   - Disaster relief?

This information is particularly valuable to the technical support staff. You can solve many problems by analyzing and correcting a computer's configuration.

One decision you must make is where on the network to store user applications. Standard LAN practice is to place them on servers, where the connected workstations can share them. This is the easiest approach to manage, since it sharply reduces the number of software copies you must manage. The licenses for network software often assume this kind of configuration.

There is an alternative, but you might not want to consider it very seriously. This is a scrubber program that automatically erases unauthorized software, wherever on the network it may be. It eliminates much of the need to manage software installations by the simple expedient of eliminating the software.

This is like using a club when the appropriate instrument would be a scalpel. A scrubber indiscriminately wipes out all exceptions to the authorized list. It doesn't allow for flexibility in managing software installations. Ironically, while it restricts your flexibility, it is vulnerable to manipulation by a determined user.

SNMP: Simple Management?

You face enough challenges managing a diverse network. At the least, you can install a single network management system.

That isn't as easy as it might sound. Diverse networks come with diverse management systems. Network managers haven't been eager to fight these. Furthermore, as wiring hubs became popular, they also became logical sites for network control. They are the logical places to install a standardized network management system.

There are several candidates for that honor, including proprietary system IBM's Netview, and Digital Equipment's tool set. For a mixed environment, there is only one serious candidate: the Simple Network Management Protocol (SNMP).

First things first

SNMP has its roots in open systems and TCP/IP. True to its name, its designers set out to keep things simple. They started by responding to their customers' top priority in network management: fault isolation. SNMP can immediately flag a defective router, for example. This used to require repeated tests until you found the culprit.

This emphasis on fault detection dovetailed with the growing interest in network hubs. The hubs provide a logical administration point, and hub makers began to incorporate SNMP into their products.

This has been a key to the system's growing popularity. It is inexpensive. It does the most-needed jobs. It is easy to install and use. It is available in a growing number of products. At last count, more than 350 network products incorporated SNMP. These include most key network components like routers, intelligent hubs, bridges, and servers. You can choose from more than 50 network management stations that use SNMP to collect information about your network and display it on a central console.

For example, one user reports that he and 10 managers can use central consoles to view graphic representations of their network. They can communicate with SNMP-equipped routers and hubs to learn their performance and configuration. They can also receive warnings of network events.

Since SNMP is a nonproprietary standard, an SNMP management console can work with nearly any device, from any vendor, that also uses SNMP.

Networking and Security

Conventional wisdom holds that networks lack many security and data integrity features of large systems. Even on a mainframe with dozens of dumb terminals connected, all the processing takes place on one machine. All the screen handling, program logic, referential integrity checks, security checks, and similar functions are done on the mainframe. The terminal simply provides a view into that bigger machine.

Many developments are combining to change that picture. Ease of use has become important, illustrated by the spread of graphic interfaces. Databases that once lived on large systems are moving to network servers. There's a movement in the opposite direction, too, as stand-alone PC databases migrate into client/server architecture.

Are networks more vulnerable?

Confidential information could be reasonably well-protected when it resided on a single large system with its multiple built-in protective mechanisms. That information is much harder to protect now that PCs and networks have entered the picture. DOS, the prevailing PC operating system, has almost none of the technical checks and balances that large systems provide. Another serious problem is that desktop workstations are physically more accessible than their larger counterparts.

That does not prove the case for mainframe security. It just means that networks often lack built-in security measures. System administrators must provide them. You can't sit back and let a downsized system take care of its own security. You must actively provide it. But you can do that.

It's probably true that if you need ironclad protection for truly sensitive data, a LAN may not measure up to a well-protected mainframe. Still, it is possible to achieve a high degree of security, even in the open environment of an enterprise network. For example, Amoco maintains sensitive information on a Chicago-based network. That network must be available to dial-in access from employees across the country. Borrowing from mainframe technology, the company began a call-in system. An inbound caller cannot immediately gain access to the full network. The system accepts the caller's log-in information, hangs up, and redials a telephone number associated with that identification.

Network security challenges

- Physical protection
  - Servers
  - Connectors
- Access control
  - Passwords
  - Dialbacks
- Encryption

Figure 12.4   No system offers ironclad security, but even a far-flung network can come close.

Protect yourself

An enterprise network requires that you manage your own security. That kind of active self-protection would be necessary with any kind of system. A network whose managers want to control dial-in access is in much the same position as a large system that requires the same controls. Physical protection is another common concern for systems of all sizes. Just as large systems are located in secure, dedicated rooms, a LAN can also be physically isolated. You can place power supplies and hubs in locked closets; file servers can go in secure rooms. The networked PC workstations, then, present little more security risk than dumb terminals connected to a mainframe.

Selective security

The placement of your assets can also boost security. You might want to run application programs on desktop computers, but keep the data itself on a larger, better-protected system. In particular, large corporate databases are remaining on the main computers, with access provided by gateways and similar communication links. This pattern may have only a little to do with security. One small college, for example, is installing an extensive network system, but has left student grade and financial records on its mainframe. The main reason, officials explain, is the mainframe's ability to handle the sheer volume of data. Security is a secondary benefit.

System security

Network operating systems and allied utilities are increasingly providing security features the PC operating systems do not. There are programs to scan for viruses. There also are utilities that can restrict access to specified directories or files. Most network operating systems, including Netware and Vines, include account control features that restrict users to particular workstations and particular times.

You can use these features to keep people from logging in from home or after hours. For example, you can use an account control feature to permit logins to the finance department network only during normal working hours. This helps keep unauthorized users—from inside or outside the company—from looking at the corporate books.

In addition, most network operating systems let administrators set up different levels of access to files and data. While users may need access to certain types of corporate data, for instance, they won't need the ability to change or delete that data. Granting them read-only access to those files protects the data from both deliberate and accidental modification.

Unlike DOS, some computer system operating systems also have built-in security features. Unix and OS/2 control access and limit the permitted types of use of designated directories and files. OS/2 also can restrict the number of licensed application programs that operate on a network. This helps you prevent the use of pirated software.

The human factor

The real security challenge for a network administrator is how to manage the human factor. PC users constantly frustrate security professionals with their less-than-careful habits. These are people, for example, who use stick-on notes to post their passwords in plain sight. In particular, those who have come to regard PCs as truly personal tools may not understand that in a networked environment they may become responsible for corporate data that needs more protection.

For that reason, many security experts and PC managers say user education is a critical part of their security policies. Training is a high priority, concentrating on such subjects as how to recognize hazards and observe security procedures. One bank's security training program includes sessions in such subjects as managing change.

The idea behind this: a new network is a major change in the way an organization does business. A system is most vulnerable at times of change. It's a time when errors are frequent. A new program disk may contain a virus. Access controls may not yet be in place or may not work properly. The training is intended to help managers monitor and educate their employees more closely during this period. Says one PC manager, "Users need to understand that even transferring a file from a floppy disk to their hard drive is a significant change in their system."

That means there is a potential hazard they should be trained to recognize. This is one area where IS professionals can continue to use their talents in a networked environment. They can maintain the security, validity, and integrity of the data. This lets the users go about their own jobs.

The ease of use factor

This division of labor can help overcome another security problem. Maintaining a high degree of security in a networked environment can conflict with a major objective of downsizing: ease of use. Users often aren't receptive to institutional security procedures. There's more than personal preference involved here. Often, obtrusive security measures can keep people from doing their jobs effectively. The security features that keep out the bad people can be just as effective—and frustrating—at keeping out the good people. Some computer security professionals don't like to concede that point, but they must.

One solution is to carry out as many security measures as possible at the network level, rather than at individual workstations. This can include the use of a security-conscious operating system and keeping critical components within locked rooms.

Involve the users

Another important measure is to involve the users. To resolve conflicts between security and ease of use, many organizations have set up cooperative working arrangements. There, users can discuss their needs and problems with security and systems professionals. This process can break down resistance and build cooperation by helping each side understand the other. It also gives the participants a sense of ownership in the downsizing project. There's no better way to build enthusiasm and support.

Hackers and viruses

The two most heavily publicized types of security problems—hackers and viruses—are also among the least serious threats to most systems. Security experts estimate that the country holds only a handful of hackers that are the type who might cause deliberate damage to a system. The number of actual virus infections also does not match the apparent threat.

A Protection Strategy

People think of crimes as committed by mysterious strangers: shadowy muggers or scheming hackers. But whether in computers or other areas of life, most crimes are committed by somebody the victim knows. In business, that usually is an employee. The second most likely cause of data loss is the simple accident—the mispunched key at a critical moment or the cup of coffee spilled on a floppy disk.

Even so, when it comes to computer security, many corporations focus on protecting themselves from outsiders rather than insiders. Corporations spend much money on expensive security systems, when they might better spend their time more productively: making sure passwords are properly used, educating their employees on the need for security, and ensuring that backups are performed regularly.

The first question

How much security do you really need? That's the first question to ask when planning for network security. Its answer depends on the answer to another question: "What would the damage be if the most sensitive information on my LAN were compromised?"

If the answer is "Not much," you may need only to warn your workers not to write their passwords on stick-on notes. If the damage would be severe, you must do more to make sure your network is secure. What and how much you must do depends on several things: security features in the network operating system and applications, physical protection of the server and communications media, and the kinds of threats you face. Many users do not view all these items as a whole. In part, that's because vendors tend to offer piecemeal solutions. These products can respond to one security threat easily, but your system probably has holes somewhere else.

Rate your risks

Developing an effective protection strategy requires that you identify the specific risks you face. Classify your PCs and networks based on how they are used. Their use usually is an index of the security threats they present. You then can develop a security plan that responds to those risks. This could range from locked rooms for a network carrying a payroll application to regular virus detection on a PC used mainly for word processing. One company has developed a three-level system for classifying PCs and networks:

- Systems that handle highly confidential data such as client records and information on corporate strategy
- Mid-level systems handling information whose disclosure would not be a serious threat, but whose loss would cause problems
- Systems that hold only departmental files and personal work

In security, teamwork counts

- These must work together:
  - System features
  - Physical security
  - Threat analysis
  - Training and procedures

Figure 12.5 Security measures must work as a system, not as individual components.

Once it has established the security classification, the company institutes security measures to match. The top-category systems get a security package that includes passwords, data encryption, and audit trails. These systems are also physically secure and isolated from other networks. At the mid-level, where loss of data is the greatest threat, the company requires password access to sensitive files and limits transfers of files and programs. Regular backup is also a priority here. Bottom-level systems are often individual PCs, where the emphasis is on regular virus scanning. Some of these also require password access.

What you can do

Whatever the system, security problems tend to fall into the same few broad categories. Many problems of PC network security are just the same as those of mini and mainframe security. A few preventive measures will take care of most potential security problems. The major challenge is to make administrators and users aware of the potential problems and inform them of the tools available to solve them.

The two best steps an organization can take are to make regular backups and to set up a system of passwords. Take the time to make sure you have backups that are both available and safe. In particular, regular backups help with the small, everyday problems of lost files and data.

The password is probably the most important security measure you can take on any system: Says one security consultant, "Your system security is only as good as the password." But what makes a good password?

Most important, it should be hard to guess. That creates an immediate source of conflict with users, because they want passwords that are easy to remember. Even so, enforcing good password choice is a high-payoff security measure. Most outsiders who get into business systems do so by defeating password systems.

There are programs that will run through a password file looking for the most-used ones. Hackers use these programs to find passwords they can use to break into your system. System administrators can use the same programs to identify easy-to-guess choices within their own systems, and get them changed.

For high-security use, consider a program that forces users to change their passwords frequently. Some of these programs do so at preset intervals and issue new passwords to the users. These are generated at random and thus are harder to guess.

Depends on people

Whatever the protection plan, it ultimately will depend on people, not technology. User education will always be an important element of any security program. The most serious threat to your system comes from inside, not outside. That threat is much more likely to be accidental than deliberate. Problems involve acts like accidentally erasing a file— things that are preventable with proper precautions. Proper training can teach and motivate employees to take those precautions. For example, you can't back up all the files on individual systems from a central location. It's the users who must do that. Consider regular seminars on the personal aspect of computer security. Back them up with a regular newsletter, or with articles in other company publications.

Involve employees

These measures still won't work if they appear to the employees like edicts handed down from the mountain. Individual departments, and individual users, are intimately familiar with their operations, including the dimensions of any conflict between security and ease of use. Contrary to some managers' cynical expectations, most employees want to do their jobs effectively. They will resent any security measures, imposed from above, that keep them from doing it.

Involve employees in these discussions. Solicit their ideas for striking the balance. Not only will you have the benefit of their knowledge and understanding, but you will have the enthusiastic participation that comes from a sense of ownership in the results.

Don't overreact

There is a so-called "newspaper effect" that causes many system administrators to worry most about the most highly publicized external threats. This means they give too little attention to the basic measures, like backups and passwords, that can protect them from the more serious internal threats.

On a percentage basis, the threat from viruses is minuscule. An estimated 80 percent of all damage is caused internally. Still, the threat is real. It can become more serious when a networking project progresses from LANS to WANS. Departmental LANs are closed systems; many have no external gateways at all. Once you go through a gateway to an enterprise network, you've multiplied the number of people who can possibly gain access to your data.

Most hackers gain their access by discovering or guessing commonly used passwords. That means a well-managed password system that avoids such common terms is the best defense. Carelessness and ignorance by honest employees make up the largest menace to information security. A survey by the Executive Information Network showed that 55 percent of all computer security losses could be attributed to errors or omissions. Dishonest and disgruntled employees accounted for 25

Don't be fooled by publicity

- Major causes of loss:
  - Accidents
  - Dishonest employees
- Minor causes of loss:
  - Viruses
  - Hackers

Figure 12.6 For most organizations, the most highly publicized threats are really the least serious.

percent of losses. External threats, such as natural disasters, caused the remaining 20 percent. That leaves only 5 percent for all other causes, including invasions by outsiders.

Common-sense protection

Viruses are a case in point. They happen, but only a minority of all PC users have been victims. One generally recommended protective measure is to get software only from reputable vendors, buy it shrink-wrapped, and avoid public domain software and shareware. If you must download bulletin-board programs, try to limit yourself to those whose source code is available. This lets the system administrator examine the code for oddities.

Since even commercial software has been known to conceal viruses, users should run virus-scanning software at least once a month—more often if users are adding software or sharing a PC. One word of caution: virus scanning software works well and is constantly being improved, but it is not foolproof. Don't rely on this strategy alone.

Networking Products

This is a representative list of products available for downsizing products available at publication. It is subject to change, of course, as products are developed, modified, or dropped.

Network Operating Systems

LAN Manager
Microsoft Corp.
One Microsoft Way
Redmond, WA 98052-6399
(800)227-6444

NetWare
Novell, Inc.
122 East 1700 South
Provo, UT 84606
(800)453-1267

Vines
Banyan Systems Inc.
120 Flanders Rd.
Westboro, MA 01581
(800)828-2404 or (508) 898-1000
(508)898-1755 (fax)

Windows front ends

Access for Windows
Eicon Technology Corp.

2196 32nd Ave.
Montreal, Quebec H8T 3H7 Canada
(514)631-2592
(514)631-3092 (fax)

Dynacomm/Elite
Future Soft Engineering
1001 S. Dairy Ashford #101
Houston, TX 77077
(713)496-9400
(713)496-1090 (fax)

Extra for Windows
Attachmate Corp.
13231 S.E. 36th St.
Bellevue, WA 98006
(800)426-6283 or (206)644-4010
(206)747-9924 (fax)

Forest & Trees for Windows
Channel Computing Inc.
53 Main St.
Newmarket, NH 03857
(800)289-0053

I/F Builder
Viewpoint Systems
1900 S. Norfolk St. #310
San Mateo, CA 94403
(415)578-1591

IRMA WorkStation for Windows
DCA

1000 Alderman Dr.
Alpharetta, GA 30202
(800)241-4762

Lightship
Pilot Executive Software
40 Broad St.
Boston, MA 02109
(617)350-7035
(617)350-7118 (fax)

Lotus 1-2-3
Lotus Development Corp.
55 Cambridge Parkway
Cambridge, MA 02142
(617)577-8500

Paradox SQL Link
Borland International
1800 Green Hills Rd.
Scotts Valley, CA 95066
(408)438-8400

Relay Gold for Windows
Microcom Inc.
500 River Ridge Dr.
Nowood, MA 02062
(800)822-8224

Rumba
Wall Data Inc.
17769 N.E. 78th Pl.
Redmond, WA 98052

Internetworking

Interoperability

3Com Corp.
5400 Bayfront Plaza
Santa Clara, CA 95052
(800)638-3266 or (408)764-5000

Beame & Whiteside
Software, Ltd.
P.O Box 8130
Dundas, Ontario, Canada L9H 5E7
(416)648-6556
(416)648-6556 (fax)

Cayman Systems, Inc.
26 Lansdowne St.
Cambridge, MA 02139

(617)494-1999
(617)494-9270 (fax)

FTP Software, Inc.
26 Princess St.
Wakefield, MA 01880
(617)246-0900
(617)246-0901 (fax)

Information Presentation Technologies, Inc.
555 Chorro St., Suite C
San Luis Obispo, CA 93401
(800)233-9993 or (805)541-3000
(805)541-3037 (fax)

InterCon Systems Corp.
950 Merndon Pkwy., Suite 420
Herndon, VA 22070
(703)709-9890
(703)709-9896 (fax)

Locus Computing Corp.
9800 La Cienega Blvd.
Inglewood, CA 90301
(800)955-6287 or (213)670-6500
(213)670-2980 (fax)

Network Research Corp.
2380 North Rose Ave.
Oxnard, CA 93030
(800)541-9508 or (805)485-2700

Novell, Inc.
122 East 1700 South
Provo, UT 84606
(800)453-1267 or (801)429-5900

Shiva Corp
1 Cambridge Center
Cambridge, MA 02142
(800)458-3550 or (617)252-6300
(617)252-6852 (fax)

Sun Microsystems, Inc.
2 Federal St.
Billerica, MA 01821
(800)872-4786 or (508)667-0010

Wollongong Group, Inc.
1129 San Antonio Rd.
Palo Alto, CA 94303
(800)872-8649,   (800)962-8649,   or
(415)962-7100 in California

Bridges

3COM Corporation
3165 Kifer Road
Santa Clara, CA 95052-8145
(408)562-6400

Advanced Computer Communications
720 Santa Barbara Street
Santa Barbara, CA 93101
(805)963-9431

BICC Data Networks
1800 West Park Drive
Westborough, MA 01581
(508)898-2422

Cisco Systems, Inc.
1350 Willow Road
Menlo Park, CA 94025
(415)326-1941

Crosscomm Corporation
133 E. Main Street
Marlboro, MA 01752
(508)481-4060

Digital Equipment Corp. (DEC)
146 Main Street
Maynard, MA 01754-2571
(508)493-5111

Gateway Communications, Inc.
2941 Alton Avenue
Irvine, CA 92714
(714)553-1555

Halley Systems, Inc.
2730 Orchard Parkway
San Jose, CA 95134
(408)432-2600

IBM
Old Orchard Road
Armonk, NY 10504
(914)765-1900

Infotron Systems Corp.
9 N. Olney Ave.
Cherry Hill, NJ 08003
(609)424-9400

Microcom Corporation
500 River Ridge Drive
Norwood, MA 02062
(617)762-9310

Microwave Bypass
25 Braintree Hill Office Park
Braintree, MA 02184
(617)843-8260

Network Application Technology
21040 Homestead Road
Cupertino, CA 95014
(408)733-4530

Network Products Corporation
1111 S. Arroyo Pkwy, Suite 450
Pasadena, CA 91105
(818)441-6504

Novell, Inc., Comm Division
890 Ross Drive
Sunnyvale, CA 94089
(415)969-1999

Racal Interlan Corp.
155 Swanson Road
Boxborough, MA 01719
(508)263-9929

RAD Data Communications, Inc.
151 W. Passaic Street
Rochelle Park, NJ 07662
(201)568-1466

Retix
2644 30th Street
Santa Monica, CA 90405
(213)399-2200

TRW Information NEtworks
23800 Hawthorne Blvd.
Torrance, CA 90505
(213)373-9161

Ungermann-Bass, Inc.
2560 Mission College Blvd.
Santa Clara, CA 95050
(408)496-0111

Vitalink
6607 Kaiser Drive
Fremont, CA 94555
(415)794-1100

Wellfleet Communications
12 DeAngelo Drive
Bedford, MA 01730
(617)275-2400

Routers

3COM Corporation
3165 Kifer Road
Santa Clara, CA 95052-8145
(408)562-6400

Advanced Computer Communications
720 Santa Barbara Street
Santa Barbara, CA 93101
(805)963-9431

Banyan Systems
115 Flanders Road
Westborough, MA 01581
(508)898-1000

Cisco Systems, Inc.
1350 Willow Road
Menlo Park, CA 94025
(415)326-1941

Digital Equipment Corp. (DEC)
146 Main Street
Maynard, MA 01754-2571
(508)493-5111

Eicon Technology Corp.
2196 32nd Avenue
Lachine, Quebec, Canada H8T 3H7
(541)631-2592

IBM
Old Orchard Road
Armonk, NY 10504
(914)765-1900

Novell, Inc., Comm Division
890 Ross Drive
Sunnyvale, CA 94089
(415)969-1999

Proteon, Inc.
Two Technology Drive
Westborough, MA 01581
(508)898-2800

RAD Data Communications, Inc.
151 W. Passaic Street

Rochelle Park, NJ 07662
(201)568-1466

TRW Information Networks
23800 Hawthorne Blvd.
Torrance, CA 90505
(213)373-9161

Vitalink
6607 Kaiser Drive
Fremont, CA 94555
(415)794-1100

Wellfleet Communications
12 DeAngelo Drive
Bedford, MA 01730
(617)275-2400

Gateways

3COM Corporation
3165 Kifer Road
Santa Clara, CA 95052-8145
(408)562-6400

Advanced Computer Communications
720 Santa Barbara Street
Santa Barbara, CA 93101
(805)963-9431

AST Research, Inc.
2121 Alton Avenue
Irvine, CA 92714
(714)863-1333

Attachmate Corp.
13231 SE. 36th Street
Bellevue, WA 98006
(206)644-4010

Banyan Systems
115 Flanders Road
Westborough, MA 01581
(508)898-1000

Cisco Systems, Inc.
1350 Willow Road
Menlo Park, CA 94025
(415)326-1941

Crosscomm Corporation
133 E. Main Street
Marlboro, MA 01752
(508)481-4060

Digital Communications Associates (DCA)
1000 Alderman Drive
Alpharetta, GA 30201
(404)442-4000

Digital Equipment Corp. (DEC)
146 Main Street
Maynard, MA 01754-2571
(508)493-5111

Eicon Technology Corp.
2196 32nd Avenue
Lachine, Quebec Canada H8T 3H7
(541)631-2592

Gateway Communications, Inc.
2941 Alton Avenue
Irvine, CA 92714
(714)553-1555

IBM
Old Orchard Road
Armonk, NY 10504
(914)765-1900

ICOT Corporation
3801 Zanker Road
San Jose, CA 95150-5143
(800)227-8068

Ideassociates Inc.
29 Dunham Road
Billerica, MA 01821
(508)663-6878

Infotron Systems Corp.
9 N. Olney Ave.
Cherry Hill, NJ 08003
(609)424-9400

J&L Communications
9238 Deering Avenue
Chatsworth, CA 91311
(818)709-1778

Network Products Corporation
111 S. Arroyo Pkwy, Suite 450
Pasadena, CA 91105
(818)441-6504

Network Software Associates
39 Argonaut

Laguna Hills, CA 92656
(714)768-4013

Novell Inc., Comm DIvision
890 Ross Drive
Sunnyvale, CA 94089
(415)969-1999

Rabbit Software Corp.
Great Valley Corporate Center
7 Great Valley Parkway East
Malvern, PA 19355
(800)722-2482

Racal Interlan Corp.
155 Swanson Road
Boxborough, MA 01719
(508)263-9929

Retix
2644 30th Street
Santa Monica, CA 90405
(213)399-2200

The Santa Cruz Operation (SCO)
400 Encinal Street
Santa Cruz, CA 95061
(408)425-7222

TRW Information Networks
23800 Hawthorne Blvd.
Torrance, CA 90505
(213)373-9161

Ungermann-Bass, Inc.
2560 Mission College Blvd.
Santa Clara, CA 95050
(408)496-0111

Wollongong
1129 San Antonio Road
Palo Alto, CA 94303
(415)962-7100

TCP/IP

3Com TCP with DPA
3Com Corp.
(408)764-5000

Chameleon
Netmanage Inc.
(408)257-6004

Embedded TCP/IP
Venturcom Inc.
(617)661-1230

Fusion for DOS
Network Research Corp.
(805)485-2700

LAN Workplace for DOS
Novell Inc.
(801)429-7000 or (800)638-9273

LAN Workplace for Macintosh
Novell Inc.
(801)429-7000 or (800)638-9273

LAN Workplace for OS/2
Novell Inc.
(801)429-7000 or (800)638-9273

Net/One TCP
Ungerman-Bass Inc.
(408)496-0111 or (800)873-6381

Newt-SDK
Netmanage Inc.
(408)257-6004

Pathway Access for DOS
Pathway Access for Macintosh
Wollongong Group
(415)962-7100

PC/NFS
Sun Microsystems, Sunconnect division
(800)872-4786

RPC-SDK
Netmanage Inc.
(408)257-6004

SimPC
Simware Inc.
(613)727-1779

Smarterm 340
Persoft Inc.
(608)273-3000

TCP Connection
Walker, Richer & Quinn
(206)324-0407

TCP/IP
Venturcom Inc.
(617)661-1230

Client/Server

Server 290
Parallan Computer
(415)960-0288

Development environments

Access SQL
Software Products International
9920 Pacific Heights Blvd.
San Diego, CA 92121
(619)450-1526

ATxtract
Panttaja Consulting Group, Inc.
103 Plaza Street
Healdsburg, CA 95448
(707)433-2629

Bigtec SQL Object
Bigtec
P.O. Box 13242
Reading, PA 19612-3242
(215)478-9660

Choreographer
GUIdance Technologies
800 Vinial Street
Pittsburgh, PA 15212
(412)231-1300

DataEase SQL
DataEase International, Inc.
7 Cambridge Drive
Trumbull, CT 06611
(203)374-8000

dBASE IV Server Edition for DOS
Ashton-Tate Corporation
20101 Hamilton Avenue
Torrance, CA 90502
(213)329-9989

DEDE (Database Entity Development Environment)
Bigtec
P. O. Box 13242

Reading, PA 19612-3242
(215)478-9660

Easytrieve Plus
Pansophic Systems, Inc.
2400 Cabot Drive
Lisle, IL 60532
(708)505-6000

Enfin/2
Enfin Software
6920 Miramar Road, Suite 307
San Diego, CA 92121
(619)549-6606

Erwin/ERX
Logic Works, Inc.
601 Ewing Street Suite B7
Princeton, NJ 08540
(609)924-0029

Erwin/SQL
Logic Works, Inc.
601 Ewing Street Suite B7
Princeton, NJ 08540
(609)924-0029

GURU Version 3.0
Micro Data Base Systems, Inc.
Two Executive Drive
Lafayette, IN 47903
(800)344-5832

Nevisys
Nevis Technologies, Inc.
300 Corporate Pointe
Culver City, CA 90230
(213)338-0257

Nomad
MUST Software International
101 Merritt, No. 7
Norwalk, CT 06856
(203)845-5000

Omnis 5
Blyth Software
1065 E. Hillsdale Blvd., Suite 300
Foster City, CA 94404
(415)571-0222

PowerBuilder
Powersoft Corporation

70 Blanchard Road
Burlington, MA 01803
(617)229-2200

Q+E Database Library
Pioneer Software
5540 Centerview Drive, Suite 324
Raleigh, NC 27606
(919)859-2220

Quicksilver/SQL
Wordtech Systems, Inc.
21 Altarinda Road
Orinda, CA 94563
(415)254-0900

SQL Object Library for Object/1
Vanguard Business Solutions, Inc.
2401 Marinship, Suite 290
Sausalito, CA 94965
(415)331-3883

SQL Toolkit
SQL Solutions
New England Executive Park
Burlington, MA 01803
(617)270-4150

SQLWindows Developer's System
Gupta Technologies, Inc.
1040 Marsh Road
Menlo Park, CA 94025
(415)321-5471

SQLWindows for SQL Server
Client-Server Starter System
Gupta Technologies, Inc.
1040 Marsh Road
Menlo Park, CA 94025
(415)321-5471

Superbase 4 for Windows
Precision Software, Inc.
8404 Sterling Street
Irving, TX 75063
(214)929-4888

The SQLFile System
Vinzant, Inc.
4 Skyline Drive
Portage, IN 46368
(219)763-3881

Development tools

JAM/DBi
JYACC
116 John Street
New York, NY 10038
(212)267-7722

KnowledgeMan Version 3.0
Micro Data Base Systems, Inc.
Two Executive Drive
Lafayette, IN 47903
(800)344-5832

Object/1
Micro Data Base Systems, Inc.
Two Executive Drive
Lafayette, IN 47903
(800)344-5832

ObjectView
Matesys Corporation N.A.
900 Larkspur Landing Circle, Suite 175
Larkspur, CA 94939
(415)925-2900

PC/FOCUS SQL Server Interface
Information Builders
1250 Broadway
New York, NY 10001
(212)736-4433

SQL Server Toolkit for Presentation Manager
DataWiz International
1291 East Hillsdale Blvd., Suite 210
Foster City, CA 94404
(415)571-1300

SQL Server Toolkit for Windows
DataWiz International
1291 East Hillsdale Blvd., Suite 210
Foster City, CA 94404
(415)571-1300

SQLFile for Windows
Vinzant, Inc.
4 Skyline Drive
Portage, IN 46368
(219)763-3881

Visual Basic
Microsoft Corporation
One Microsoft Way
Redmond, WA 98052-6399
(800)227-4679

Server hardware

Superservers

Multiaccess Series 3000
Advanced Logic Research
(212)581-6770 or (800)289-7697

NCR 3445, 3450, 3550
NCR Corp.
(800)225-5627 or 513-445-5000

NF100, NF200, NF300, NF400
Netframe Systems
(408)944-0600

Omnisystem
Northgate Computer Systems
(612)943-8181

Powerframe
Tricord Systems
612/557-9005

Powerpro
Advanced Logic Research
(212)581-6770 or (800)289-7697

Server 290
Parallan Computer
(415)960-0288

Starserver E
AT&T Computer Systems
(800)247-1212

Systempro
Compaq Computer Corp.
(713)370-0670

Midrange systems

AT&T Computer Systems
(800)247-1212

Bull HN Information Systems
(508)294-6000

Concurrent Computer Corp.
(908)758-7000

Control Data Corp.
(612)853-5445

Data General Corp.
(509)366-8911 or (800)328-2436

Datapoint Corp.
(800)733-1500 ext. 7884

Encore Computer Corp.
(305)587-2900

IBM
(800)426-2468

MAI Systems Corp.
(212)730-5100

MIPS Computer Systems
(408)720-1700

Modcomp Inc.
(305)974-1380

NCR Corp.
(513)445-5000

Prime Computer Inc.
(508)620-2800

Pyramid Technology Corp.
(508)620-2800

Sequent Computer Systems
(800)854-0428

Sequoia Systems
(508)480-0800

Siemens Nixdorf Information Systems
(617)273-0480

Stratus Computer
(508)460-2000

Tandem Computers
(408)285-6000

Unisys Corp.
(215)986-4011

Glossary

10BaseT A popular version of Ethernet networking, using twisted wire instead of the usual coaxial cable.

API Application Program Interface. A means of connecting an application program with the network. It consists of software interrupts, calls, and data formats.

APPN Advanced Peer-to-Peer Networking. A networking system developed by IBM. It allows systems of all sizes to act as peers on the same network.

ATM Asynchronous Transfer Mode. A developing system of long-distance communication that features high speeds and the ability to handle multiple data streams.

asynchronous a transmission method in which the time periods between characters need not be equal. Start and stop bits coordinate the transmission.

back end The processing part of a client/server system. It is usually, but not always, the server.

backbone A network that connects several other networks, such as those within the same building.

bandwidth The range of frequencies a circuit will carry. Used informally to mean the amount of information a network can carry at one time.

batch processing A system which accumulates transactions over a period of time, then updates the database at the end of the period.

bridge A device used to connect two networks that use different physical media and protocols.

CASE Computer Aided Software Engineering. Software that automatically generates program code.

client/server An application in which a server computer maintains resources for one or more client computers.

coaxial A type of cable with a central core surrounded by an insulating layer.

concentrator A type of wiring hub.

database server A type of network server that manages a database for network clients.

DECnet A communication protocol and related products from Digital Equipment Corp. It is compatible with Ethernet and other systems.

distributed   A network resource, usually a database, split among multiple locations.

DOS   Disk operating system. The prevailing operating system for IBM-standard personal computers.

downsizing   Moving business applications from mainframes and minicomputers to networks of smaller systems.

e-mail   Electronic mail, a popular network application that lets employees exchange electronic messages.

EDI   Electronic Data Interchange. The use of networks between suppliers and their customers to transmit orders, payments, and other information electronically.

enterprise network   A system of interconnected networks that serve an entire organization.

Ethernet   A common protocol used in local area networks. It uses coaxial cable, except for the 10BaseT specification which uses twisted-pair wiring.

fault tolerance   The ability of a computer to perform when errors occur.

file server   A type of network server that maintains files for network clients.

frame relay   A long-distance network system that packages data into packets called frames. It's generally considered a successor to X.25.

front end   The user part of a client/server system. It is usually, but not always, the client.

FTP   File Transfer Protocol. A protocol that describes how computers can transfer files between each other. Users can see file directories of either computer and can do some file management tasks.

gateway   A device that connects a local area network to a larger network or system.

groupware   A class of software that uses electronic mail to serve multiple users at once.

GUI   Graphical User Interface. A system of screen presentation that uses graphics instead of text.

hub   A central connection point for network wiring.

internetworking   Linking multiple networks so they will operate together.

interoperability   The ability of two applications or systems to work with each other.

IPX   Internet Packet Exchange. The Netware communication protocol used to move data between servers and workstations.

ISDN   Integrated Services Digital Network. A system for combining voice and data transmission over long-distance lines.

ISO   International Standards Organization. An international organization that developed the Open Systems Interconnection (OSI) model.

LAN Manager   A network operating system developed by Microsoft and 3Com.

LAN Server   The IBM network operating system associated with OS/2.

LAN   Local area network. A small network, usually of personal computers, that serves a single department or workgroup.

legacy applications   Applications now running on larger systems, now candidates for migration to enterprise networks.

mail-enabled   Describes applications that have the built-in ability to use electronic mail.

media   The cable or wiring used to carry network signals. Plural of *medium*.

mission-critical   Describes major applications, often running on mainframes, that are essential to an organization's success.

NetBIOS   Network Basic Input/Output System. A software layer that links a network operating system with specific hardware.

Netview   IBM's network management and control architecture, incorporating both mainframes and PCs running OS/2.

Netware   The Novell network operating system, popular on PC networks.

NFS   Network File System. A distributed file sharing system developed by Sun Microsystems.

NLM   Netware Loadable Module. A facility for running applications under Netware. Without it, these applications might require dedicated PCs.

NOS   Network Operating System. A network's counterpart to the operating system of a single computer.

object orientation   A method of programming that uses objects, which can contain both information and program instructions.

open systems   a networking standard based on the use of widely used standards, rather than proprietary specifications.

OS/2   IBM's personal computer operating system, with multitasking and networking features.

OSF   Open Software Foundation. A combination of industry vendors working on standard versions of Unix and distributed computing technology.

OSI   Open Systems Interconnection. An internetworking protocol that links networks at seven distinct levels. These levels are often used to describe other kinds of networking systems.

peer-to-peer   A networking system that does not require a server. All connected systems can operate on an equal basis.

proprietary   Technical specifications unique to a single vendor.

RDBMS   Relational database management system. A method of database management which uses common elements to connect multiple data tables.

relational database   A type of database which uses common elements to connect multiple data tables.

rightsizing   Moving an application to a new, more efficient platform. Usually a synonym for downsizing.

RMF   Remote Management Facility. A Netware facility that provides for remote network management from a central location.

router   A device used to connect two networks that use different topologies, but share a common protocol.

RPC   Remote Procedure Call. A set of software tools developers can use to create distributed applications. These tools generate code for both the client and server sides.

server   A networked computer that provides services such as communication, printing, or database management for the network's clients.

smart hub   A hub that contains internetworking logic.

SNMP   Simple Network Management Protocol. A basic system for managing and overseeing networks.

SONET   Synchronous Optical Network. A network transmission system devised for fiber optics.

SQL   Structured Query Language. A specialized programming language used to manage and query relational databases.

Superserver   A high-capacity server used on local area networks.

TCP/IP   Transmission Control Protocol/Internet Protocol. A widely used pair of protocols used to link networks.

Telnet   A terminal emulation protocol, usually used with TCP/IP.

token ring   A network topology in which an electronic token circulates from node to node, picking up and delivering messages.

topology   The layout of the network, including the wiring layout and the message flow.

transaction processing   a system that records retail sales or other activity as it happens. Often called on-line transaction processing (OLTP).

transparency   The ability to retrieve and manage distributed data without knowing its source or location.

twisted pair   A type of network wiring which uses pairs of twisted wire, similar to telephone wire.

Unix   An operating system used widely for technical applications and in network servers and workstations.

Vines   A Unix-based network operating system from Banyan Systems.

WAN   Wide area network. A network that uses long-distance communication methods to operate over large areas.

workstations   Personal computers and other systems that serve individual users and are connected to networks.

X Window   A windowing system for networked workstations, usually under Unix.

X.25   A communication protocol used widely in wide area networks. It assembles material into packets for transmission.

X.400   A common transport standard for electronic mail.

X.500   A coming extension of the X.400 e-mail standard. It provides for directory services.

Xbase   A manufactured term, referring to database management systems similar to the dBASE product line.

Bibliography

Ambrosio, Johanna. "Data modeling: Tough but rewarding." *Computerworld*, Nov. 16, 1992, p. 127. Data modeling, in its essence, is defining what the business does and how, then figuring out what data is required to support those requirements.

———. "Mainframe Metamorphosis: Not a Disappearing Act." *Computerworld*, Aug. 17, 1992, p. 1. The mainframe may be wheezing a bit in its old age, but it is expected to survive into the next century, albeit in some new roles.

Angus, Kevin. "Windows, OS/2 and Alternate GUIs." *LAN Times*, Oct. 12, 1992, pp. 74–13. Aside from the GUI standards, Windows, and OS/2, there are other GUIs from which to choose.

Anthes, Gary H. "4GLs expected to ride client/server wave." *Computerworld*, Aug. 31, 1992, p. 85. Developers of client/server applications are forsaking third-generation languages such as COBOL and C in favor of a new breed of fourth-generation languages, which generate code, build interfaces, and connect to DBMSs.

———. "Newspaper takes step into the LAN age." *Computerworld*, May 20, 1991, p. 1. The solution: 700 IBM Personal System/2 workstations and servers running OS/2 and LAN Manager attached to a Tandem Nonstop TXP computer via IBM token ring networks. To avoid any more election night disasters, each hardware component will have a twin for backup.

———. "Small firms unite through net." *Computerworld*, Jan. 20, 1992, p. 59. A government, industry, and university partnership has set up a test network, linking South Carolina manufacturers and state colleges and universities. The goal is to help small and medium-sized firms compete in national markets.

———. "Smooth client/server takeoff at United." *Computerworld*, May 11, 1992, p. 68. Moving off a mainframe eases the scheduling of an airline's 8000 pilots and 17,000 flight attendants. United's model seeks to minimize the amount of paid time crews spend waiting for flights.

———. "Training biggest obstacle in client/server move, survey says." *Computerworld*, Dec. 14, 1992, p. 89. Companies find that mastering client/server technology is not as hard as the training issues.

Aranow, Eric and Tom Kehler. "Objects can set the stage." *Software Magazine*, Client/Server edition, May 1992, p. 43. Object technology is the software approach that greatly simplifies implementation and maintenance of large-scale distributed systems.

Aranow, Eric. "Object technology means object-oriented thinking." *Software Magazine*, March 1992, p. 41. Shifting to object-centered development requires adopting the new and discarding old ways. The race is on to embrace object technology and reap its benefits. Those who are successful will be those who make the paradigm shift.

Arnold, Geoff. "Opening Up to Open Systems Computing." *LAN Times*, July 8, 1991, p. 53. Powerful new "open systems" such as Unix workstations are being added to computing resources at a rapid rate, creating yet another category of system. The bigger issue is making use of existing resources—like DOS PCs—within today's heterogeneous networks.

Arrington, Joseph J. "Integrating LANs and Mainframes." *LAN Times*, May 20, 1991, p. 79. For years now, the workstation segment of the computer industry has been promoting the concept of downsizing, but most enterprises that operated mainframes in 1985 are still operating them today.

Arriola, John A. "Optimizing your Netware LAN." *Infoworld*, Oct. 12, 1992, p. 64. There are a number of performance enhancing tweaks that can get your network up to speed and buy time to evaluate future needs.

Asbrand, Deborah. "Users struggle with LAN licensing agreements." *Computerworld*, Dec. 2, 1991, p. 80. As LAN software has become increasingly varied and sophisticated, so have the licensing agreements that govern the software's use.

Autry, James A. "The truth about data." *Computerworld*, March 11, 1991, p. 25. Here are two big lies of the technological age: computers save on paperwork, and computer-generated data makes decision-making easier.

Ayre, Rick. "Looks like a form, feels like E-mail." *PC Magazine*, Feb. 25, 1992, p. 29. A new breed of software, variously called groupware, workflow management, mail-enabled applications, or smart forms, is coming into its own.

Baker, Steven. "Serving Up Netware." *LAN Magazine*, December 1992, p. 65. Unix products let SPARC workstations act as Netware clients to DOS, OS/2, and Macintosh clients.

———. "Just Holding Hands." *LAN Magazine*. Interoperability Supplement, Fall 1992, p. 6. New products are poised to ease the way between DOS and Unix, leaving the gritty details of the underlying network behind.

Ballou, Melinda-Carol and Kim S. Nash. "No rush to toss aside proprietary minis." *Computerworld*, Aug. 3, 1992, p. 1. While executives from DEC, DG, and Wang labor to restructure, many customers are quietly planning moves from proprietary mini-computers toward an open future.

Bancroft, Bruce. "Cancer Institute Builds Enterprise Network." *LAN Times*, Jan. 20, 1992, p. 21. Four key objectives shared the number one priority: uniform physical design and cabling, universal terminal and PC access, computer-to-computer communication using recognized standards, and standard file transfer utilities.

Bandrowski, Paul U. "Downsizing Decisions." *Computerworld*, March 11, 1991, p. S1. Downsizing is much more than the use of micros or minicomputers in an effort to reduce costs. It actually constitutes a major modification in business philosophy and the way a corporation uses the vast amount of data at its disposal.

Barker, Richard. "Repository Technologies: A Look Ahead." *Oracle Magazine*, Fall 1992, p. 51. The computer market will look for applications that are responsive, flexible, and appropriate to ever-changing needs. Issues include defining the essential components of CASE and repository technology.

Barry, Doug. "When to use object DBMSs." *Computerworld*, Oct. 26, 1992, p. 122. Object-oriented DBMSs support the use of complex data. How do you know your data is complex?

Barry, John and Martin L. W. Hall. "Computing In the Age of Connectivity." *LAN Times*, Sept. 14, 1992, p. 69. Finding solutions for integrating Unix and PC LANs means increased communication and resource sharing.

Barry, John. "Databases Everywhere." *DBMS*, April 1992, p. 8. With the advent of networks, the client/server model and the ability to digitally encode anything from customer records to video images, database has taken on extended meanings.

Bartholomew, Doug. "Business Alignment: The CEO's View." *Information Week*, Oct. 26, 1992, p. 12. Despite a difference of opinion among senior corporate executives about how to bring IS in line with corporate strategy, most agree that doing so is desirable, if not essential.

Baum, David. "GUI hooks key to Con Edison's EIS development." *Computerworld*, Sept. 28, 1992, p. 56. Strategic applications are found in every company, but rarely on the desks of executives. That's because important corporate information is often stored on inflexible systems.

———. "Interesting Developments." *Computerworld*, Feb. 1, 1993, p. 83. You can avoid the fear and loathing that come from client/server application development tools that don't do the job. Make your life easier by educating yourself on the types of tools available and what they're good for.

———. "Middleware." *Infoworld*, Nov. 30, 1992, p. 46. Even after a client/server application is up and running, tying other business functions to it can be an exercise in frustration. Developers need tools that will provide consistent and uniform access to system resources across all platforms.

———. "Moving from punch cards to object orientation: The evolution of application development." *Infoworld*, Sept. 7, 1992, p. 48. The client/server marketplace is evolving quickly. Roughly, it consists of three major segments: databases, networks, and application development tools.

———. Reducing the burden of software maintenance. *Infoworld*, July 6, 1992, p. 58. Software re-engineering is one of the leading issues confronting information executives. Is there hope? Fortunately, yes.

Becker, Pat. "Down or Out?" *LAN Magazine*, October 1992, p. 107. Should downsizing mean the demise of that data dinosaur, the mainframe?

———. "A Ghost of an OSI Chance." *LAN Magazine,* December 1992, p. 73. Issues surrounding the implementation of open systems await resolution.

———. "Share and Share alike." *LAN Magazine*, Interoperability supplement, Spring 1992, p. 6. By building interoperability among dissimilar PC network operating systems, users don't have to wish they had access to their neighbor's files and printers. Everyone can share.

Bell, Jon and Joan Frank. "A Classic Case of Success." *Oracle Magazine*, Summer 1992, p. 20. To support its worldwide soft drink business, the Coca-Cola Co. relies on a network of regional bottlers. One of the latest of these uses Oracle to manage its business over a client/server network.

Bergstrom, Jeff. "Extending Your Network to Remote Users." *LAN Times*, May 11, 1992, p. 33. One market segment is just beginning to establish itself: LON or LAN Outer Network. The new concept identifies an expanding group of users and rounds out the complete computing environment found in today's corporate structures.

Berst, Jesse. E-mail makes big strides. *Computerworld*, March 2, 1992, p. 42. E-mail is much more than a convenience. It is maturing into a core technology, thanks to four developments: mail-enabled products, message filtering, programming standards, and powerful e-mail engines.

———. "Focusing on client/server." *Computerworld*, Feb. 17, 1992, p. 38. This vague term has finally coming into clear focus. These days, the typical project uses Windows on the client and an SQL database engine on the server. Under this scheme, both sides do what they do best.

———. "The true cost of a GUI." *Computerworld*, Oct. 21, 1991, p. 64. Trying to figure out the cost of moving to Windows or Presentation Manager? Let me warn you of a few things you're likely to overlook.

———. "Worth the Pain." *Computerworld*, Jan. 6, 1992, p. 42. Networking Windows is a pain, but it is often worth the pain.

Betts, Mitch. "No shortcut to client/server." *Computerworld*, Oct. 12, 1992, p. 118. Client/server systems are actually complex webs of hardware and software that are inextricably linked to each other.

Biery, Roger. "Collapsed Backbones: Next Step in Premises Networks." *LAN Times,* Sept. 14, 1992, p. 47. Organizations are doing for their entire premises network infrastructures what the hub has done for their LAN connectivity: collapse the architecture into a more reliable and manageable system.

Bingham, Sanford. Hail, "Hail. Internetworking's Here." Network Testing (*Communications Week*), March 2, 1992, p. 10. Internetworking management has become a hot button. At stake is control over the design and implementation of the wide area connections needed to tie together the burgeoning class of local area networks.

Black, David. "The Squeaky Wheel." *LAN Magazine*, January 1993, p. 61. Workflow software may help your business turn into a well-oiled machine. This application is not a technology toy.

Bloom, Eric P. "Getting down." *Computerworld*, Aug. 10, 1992, p. 69. The decision to downsize to a smaller platform may seem like a tough one, but actually it's the easy part. The real killer is figuring out exactly how to do it. There are a bunch of possibilities.

Bloor, Robin. "Repository Technology." *DBMS*, December 1991, p. 17. CASE tools that use repository technology will provide significant increases to development productivity.

────. "Shells and Kernels. Graphical user interfaces on the client; Unix on the server." *DBMS*, February 1992, p. 12.

────. "Tactics for Downsizing." *DBMS*, December 1992, p. 14. A development environment can make or break a downsizing effort. Very few DP departments have constructed a development environment that has any orientation toward software migration.

────. "The End of Relational?" *DBMS*, July 1992, p. 8. The relational theory of data is unsuitable for managing data in object databases. The object-oriented view keeps the process and the attribute together. The relational view does not.

Bochenski, Barbara. "Access Method Complexity Daunting to Programmers." *Software Magazine*, November 1992, p. 75. Programs can intercommunicate using a variety of mechanisms, including RPCs, SQL, RDA, and DRDA. Microsoft recently added its Open Database Connectivity (ODBC) to the list. This article explores these mechanisms, with a serious look at RPCs.

────. "Database mix poses a sharing challenge." *Software Magazine*, March 1992, p. 63. IS execs build ties where none were available and find retrieval easier than distributed update. Users would like universal data access to the different systems and databases of departments within large organizations. That is difficult to achieve.

────. "Enterprise developers work to tap the internet." *Software Magazine*, February 1992, p. 66. If an application developer does not consider local area network interconnection when writing new programs, serious problems can result. The developer needs a basic understanding of networking concepts such as what an internet is.

────. "Internetworking 201." *Software Magazine*, February 1992, p. 75. The seven-layer Open Systems Interconnection (OSI) model established by the International Standards Organization (ISO) is a convenient tool for helping to understand networking concepts.

────. "Vendors address networking complexity." *Software Magazine*, February 1992, p. 76. One of the simplest explanations of bridges, routers, and gateways uses workers in a mail room as a networking analogy.

Bolt, Robert C. "Transaction Processing vs. Decision Support." *DBMS*, September 1992, p. 22. A three-tiered architecture provides a compromise between decision support and transaction processing.

Booker, Ellis. "Graphic interfaces need artful programmers." *Computerworld*, April 29, 1991, p. 41. GUI technologies, which many believe are the future core of user computing, are putting new demands on software developers. Those developers must now create systems and interfaces as aesthetically pleasing as they are functional.

────. Management: "The buck stops where?" *Computerworld*, Oct. 5, 1992, p. 83. As the IS team loses its iron grip on information technology spending, it tightens its hold on platform standards.

────. "New service a welcome guest at Hyatt." *Computerworld*, July 15, 1991, p. 51. Hyatt Hotels Corp. completed the most ambitious step in its migration to Unix: replacing its central IBM mainframe-based reservation system with a relational database management system on multiple Unix processors.

Borenfreund, Jesse. "Workspace Computing: Moving Beyond the Desktop." *Unix International Gazette*, September 1992, p. 1. Workspace computing expands the functional requirement from expanding personal productivity to a means of integrating groups of workers into the information resources of the enterprise.

Borsook, Paulina. "Eliminating the swivel factor." *Infoworld*, Feb. 17, 1992, p. 45. Netware Management System (NMS) provides a common platform for Novell and third-party management applications to handle everything from server CPU utilization to LAN equipment inventories.

────. "Harmonic convergence?" *Infoworld*, July 20, 1992, p. 55. Bridge and router market endures change and technological culture clash. Bridging and routing technology are constantly evolving, product categories are varied and blurred, and there are numerous options facing potential users.

────. "Putting Unix servers on the network." *Infoworld*, Sept. 21, 1992, p. 66. Unix has always been a good place to put a database. The network is now a good place to put Unix.

————. "Smooth Sailing with Unix." *Infoworld*, Sept. 21, 1992, p. 52. Users are finding Unix to be an industrial strength platform for client/server application processing.

————. "SNMP tools evolving to meet critical LAN needs." *Infoworld*, June 1, 1992, p. 48. The Simple Network Management Protocol is anything but simple. SNMP is growing in scope and importance with new features constantly being added to meet user demands. But some LAN managers say SNMP may soon run out of steam.

————. "When Simple Gets Complex." *Network Testing (Communications Week)*, March 2, 1992, p. 27. CMIP put complexity into the protocol so everything on the network had to be complex. SNMP started out simple, but the increased volume of remote monitoring has made it more complex.

Bowden, Eric J. "Configuring Macs on Novell Nets." *LAN Times*, Sept. 28, 1992, p. 51. It's easier to get your server talking Appletalk than your Mac client talking IPX.

————. "RAID: The Next Step in Disk Subsystems." *LAN Times*, May 25, 1992, p. 53. RAID is basically a method of spreading your data over multiple drives and introducing redundancy into a disk subsystem to improve reliability.

————. "So, What Is the Difference Between These RAID Levels?" *LAN Times*, May 25, 1992, p. 60. A RAID 5 solution is not necessarily better than a RAID 3 solution. It all depends on your system configuration.

Bozman, Jean S. "A new approach to data management catches on." *Computerworld*, Oct. 26, 1992, p. 28. Object-oriented databases are like cookie jars that can store a lot of goodies, but these handy receptacles still are relatively rare.

————. "Client/Server may not cost less." *Computerworld*, Feb. 17, 1992, p. 6. Users' hopes of saving money may be dashed once they realize the cost required to make each program work remains the same. Client/server doesn't really save you money. It really ends up making your end users more productive.

————. "GTE phones home with client/server." *Computerworld*, March 16, 1992, p. 1. GTE Telephone Operations has decided to encircle its IBM mainframes with an extensive Unix-based client/server network in hopes of shielding users from having to know where data is located.

————. "Independent tool sets catching on." *Computerworld*, Sept. 14, 1992, p. 87. Open systems should have open tools, say users as they map out distributed client/server applications, but more often they are picking the independent tool sets they like most, taking on only one database application at a time.

————. "Levi Strauss cuts client/server pattern." *Computerworld*, Nov. 16, 1992, p. 127. The company is in the final stages of a pilot project to prove that object-oriented programming, workstations, and Unix servers can be used in production systems.

————. "Mainframe to PC LAN shift taking hold." *Computerworld*, Aug. 31, 1992, p. 4. Downsizing was once the byword of missionary PC advocates. Now, true IS believers testify to 30 to 50 percent cost savings by moving mainframe applications to local area networks.

————. "New, tougher Garfield emerges." *Computerworld*, Feb. 17, 1992, p. 53. There is no warm fuzzy feeling for old-line MIS with its large staff and reliance on batch processing. The old system just took up space and slowed us down. It forced us to be a reactive company; this new system allows us to be a proactive company.

Brambert, Dave. "Manage Through Windows." *LAN Magazine*, November 1992, p. 101. Yes, Windows is being used today for network management. No, it's not perfect, but wait until you see what tomorrow brings.

————. "Support your users." *LAN Magazine*, September 1992, p. 34. Looking for network support? You might find it in your own back yard and other places you never thought to look.

————. "The Layered Look." *LAN Magazine*, October 1992, p. 85. Network management giants move, shake, and make easy-to-use software.

Brandel, William. "Is the World Ready for Unixware?" *LAN Times*, July 20, 1992, p. 1. Unixware, a 32-bit Unix-based operating system, is an attempt to get the best of both worlds, Netware and Unix.

————. "Lotus Notes Captures Attention." *LAN Times*, March 23, 1992, p. 1. Classifying it as client/server or as groupware would be an oversimplification.

————. "Messaging Vendors Flirt with Truce over Mail Standard." *LAN Times*, Nov. 23, 1992, p. 16. User requirements appear to be forcing some concessions from the two key proponents of competing messaging application program interfaces (APIs).

————. "Unix: Is It Finally Making the Move Into the Networking Mainstream?" *LAN Times*, July 6, 1992, p. 1. Like a circus that comes to town every year, Unix is back. But now it isn't just scientists and academics who praise the system, or the big-iron back-office folk. This time, PC LAN users are the target audience.

Breidenbach, Susan. "You never hear anyone 'upsizing.'" *LAN Times*, Sept. 14, 1992, p. 6. Downsizing is inevitable. At least four out of five companies have done it, are doing it, or are planning to do it. Some have tried to promote the politically correct term "rightsizing," but without a lot of effect.

Brenner, Aaron. "Integration Migration." *LAN Magazine*, Interoperability Supplement, Fall 1992, p. 39. Choosing the right enterprise network integration vendor can be a difficult decision. Follow the signs, and know exactly what you want.

Briere, Daniel and Christopher Finn. "Frame relay selection is no picnic." *Network World*, Feb. 1, 1993, p. 45. While frame relay has matured in the last year, service selection can be like walking through a minefield.

Briere, Daniel. "Public or Private?" *Network World*, July 20, 1992, p. 55. Making the choice between public and private networking gets tougher as carriers build more functionality into the public network.

Brindle, Dan. "Maintaining Windows 3.1 in a LAN environment." *Infoworld*, Aug. 17, 1992, p. 88. Windows' latest incarnation promises to relieve some of the burden of network user support from the IS professional.

Bristol, Doug. "DOS and Unix work great together." *Infoworld*, June 15, 1992, p. 64. Operating system decisions shouldn't come down to either/or choices between DOS and Unix. Combining the two isn't the technical or operational nightmare some vendors would have us believe. In fact, integrating the operating systems offers significant advantages.

Brown, Bob. "Client/server move may alter industry." *Network World*, July 20, 1992, p. 31. The move to client/server computing could result in a network industry power shuffle, depending on how established vendors adjust and emerging companies are embraced.

Brown, Ronald O. "Bridges and Routers: Network Traffic Cops." *Infoworld*, April 20, 1992, p. 48. Bridges and routers are supplying a vital piece of users' internetworking puzzle, allowing LAN administrators to design larger, more secure and efficient networks.

Burns, Nina. "E-mail software." *Computerworld*, Feb. 10, 1992, p. 83. LAN-based packages are selling fast, and they're being used for a lot more than just interpersonal messaging.

————. "It's In the Mail." *LAN Magazine*, March 1992, p. 45. Lotus, Microsoft, and Novell have outlined their strategies for building large corporate e-mail systems. But will they deliver on those promises?

————. "Mail-enabled apps deliver savings." *Communications Week*, Feb. 3, 1992, p. 32. E-mail becomes the transport for automating business work flow.

————. "Promises and Reality." *LAN Magazine*, Interoperability supplement, Spring 1992, p. 28. A well-integrated e-mail system pays off in productivity and lower costs. Less obvious is how to build a multi-vendor, integrated, and manageable system.

Busse, Torsten. "Enterprise network managers are waging an uphill battle." *Infoworld*, June 8, 1992, p. 55. As enterprise networks grow in size and complexity, they can become management nightmares without well-thought out administrative procedures and battlefield-hardened management tools.

Butler, Martin and Robin Bloor. "Database Functions." *DBMS*, November, 1991, p. 17. Today's DBMSs provide integrity checks, triggers, and stored procedures.

———— and ————. "Distributed Database." *DBMS*, September 1991, p. 16. The primary problem for network administration is not how to set up LANs, but how to interconnect them.

———— and ————. "SQL's Clouded Future." *DBMS*, August 1991, p. 17. SQL promotes interoperability between software products, and, as such, the level of support for it is encouraging and healthy for the industry. However, SQL is not without its problems, and potential users of SQL should be aware of them.

Butterline, Mark A. "Get thee to a PC." *Computerworld*, July 20, 1992, p. 83. Offloading application development from a mainframe to a PC promises cost and productivity benefits. But is it right for you?

Carr, Jim. "The Mac Moves to Ethernet." Data Communications, October 1992, p. 115. With new Ethernet hubs, management software and adapters, the Macintosh can become a full member of the corporate network.

Case, Loyd Jr. "Having it All." *LAN Magazine*, Interoperability supplement, Spring 1992, p. 13. When connecting PC LANs and Unix hosts, do you approach the integration plan from the desktop up or from the host down? Here are the pros and cons of having it all.

Cashin, Jerry. "Standards the Keynote in Network Management." *Software Magazine*, November 1992, p. 61. The key to the future of network control and the long-sought goal of enterprise-wide management remains standards. Certainly, SNMP will be pivotal, but CMIS/CMIP has government backing and will also find a niche.

Celko, Joe. "An introduction to Concurrency Control." *DBMS*, September 1992, p. 70. Concurrency control deals with sharing computer resources among many users at the same time.

Chowning, Dave. "Cleaning up the EPA." *DBMS*, August 1992, p. 3. How EPA developed a document management system that provides easy access to all its paperwork.

Coale, Kristi. "Network Printing: emerging from the labyrinth." *Infoworld*, March 3, 1992, p. 44. Printing is one of the most basic services provided by a LAN. It should be simple. But jobs often get garbled, are misrouted, or are lost altogether.

———. "Rightsizing moves power to corporate users." *Infoworld*, Jan. 20, 1992, p. 44. The term denotes shifting reliance for corporate data from mainframes to desktop PCs and LANs. Rightsizing doesn't have to mean the end of an IS professional's career, but can be a golden opportunity to acquire new skills and distinguish oneself.

Colwell, Nancy. "Sun's client/server evangelist." *DBMS*, February 1992, p. 40. How Nancy Colwell helped Sun Microsystems position itself as more than just a Unix workstation vendor.

Comaford, Christine. "Don't say the D word." *Computerworld*, Oct. 21, 1991, p. 94. Old pros aren't always thrilled at the opportunity to become young novices again. Change can be very threatening. Give the following methods a try.

———. "Graphical user interfaces: Keep them sleek and simple." *Computerworld*, April 22, 1991, p. 37. Know your users. Make frequent tasks easy. Adapt to users' work patterns. Consider multiple skill levels. Provide navigation help. Be consistent. Don't rely on users reading the manual. Don't get too cute.

Cooney, Michael and Maureen Molloy. "Forging the ties that bind." *Network World*, Sept. 28, 1992, p. S33. It isn't always pretty, but it is possible to link SNA, DECnet, and TCP/IP networks.

Coursey, David. "Frame Relay Bypasses WAN Bottlenecks." *Infoworld*, April 8, 1991, p. S1. Frame relay, an emerging international networking standard, gives witness to the virtue of simplicity. Frame relay . . . results in a protocol well suited for handling large amounts of "bursty" data.

Cox, John. "Oracle Refining DBMS." *Communications Week*, Feb. 1, 1993, p. 1. Oracle Corp. is working on a version of its database management system that will let users incorporate complex data types such as software objects, compound text, and digitized sound and video into their applications.

Cox, Tom. "Peer-to-Peer Computing." *Oracle Magazine*, Spring 1991, p. 43. There are at least four different areas of computing that are correctly identified by the phrase client-server. The computing areas that use this architecture include file sharing, database serving, computation engine sharing, and the X Window System display.

Cross, Thomas B. "ISDN: Under construction." *Infoworld*, Jan. 13, 1992, p. S64. Its promise remains largely unfulfilled as users may wait years for installation.

Cruikshank, F. Peter. "Setting Up a 'Combo' Network is Something Only Stephen King Could Have Dreamed Up." *LAN Times*, July 20, 1992, p. 51. To effectively network

Windows, you need to know some basic facts. Windows has files that are hardware-specific (System.Ini) and user-specific (Win.Ini).

Curcuru, Steve. "Sorry, I Don't Do Windows." *LAN Times*, Oct. 12, 1992, pp. 74–75. In the past, that has been the prevailing view of most network managers. But times are changing, and there are good reasons to install Windows on your network.

Currid, Cheryl. "Corporate computer illiteracy can be addressed by simply training users." *Infoworld*, Feb. 3, 1992, p. 52. In too many places, better business practices don't result from merely installing computers. Often, it's a case of computer illiteracy.

———. "Dirty data is dancing dollars out the door." *Infoworld*, Oct. 26, 1992, p. 73. Lots of companies are sitting on silos of useless stuff. Their data problems go way back to legacy systems that were built without a lot of business rules or error checking.

———. "LAN benefits being discovered." *Compaq Compass*, November/December 1991, p. 1. Until recently, however, LANs were only found in large corporations. Now, LANs are spreading to small-to-mid-size workgroups in large companies as well as small ones.

———. "Mainframe-only experts should begin to sharpen other skills." *Infoworld*, Jan. 27, 1992, p. 55. The job market for folks with mainframe-only skills is drying up.

———. "Some still think the universe revolves around the mainframe." *Infoworld*, Dec. 23, 1991, p. 30. Our society doesn't place IS professionals in jail for exposing new computing theory, but it does have ways of dealing with people who defy conventional wisdom.

Daly, James. "Apple lets loose with networking barrage." *Computerworld*, May 25, 1992, p. 20. Apple Computer extended its reach into the corporate enterprise by rolling out additional links to IBM, multi-platform, and open systems worlds.

Darling, Charles B. "Waiting for Distributed Database." *DBMS*, September 1991, p. 46. A geographic information system makes use of elements of distributed database. I'll measure it against each of Date's twelve rules of distributed databases.

Dauber, Steven. "Finding Fault." *Byte*, March 1991, p. 207. As networks become more widespread and important, fault management and performance monitoring become business necessities.

Davis, Tim. "The LAN as a Platform for Mission-Critical Apps." *LAN Times*, Sept. 9, 1992, p. 55. Using the LAN as a platform for mission-critical applications is not child's play. Companies that have taken a naive approach to this issue may be running into problems.

Day, Michael. "Nervous NLM Creators Need Not Fear." *LAN Times*, March 9, 1992, p. 26. Netware Loadable Modules, of NLMs, are server-based applications which run on the Netware 3.X operating system. To date, there are not as many commercial NLM products as many expected.

———. "The Muscle Behind Netware's TTS." *LAN Times*, June 17, 1991, p. 23. How file and record locking procedures generate implicit transactions.

———. "Network Printing: The Second Generation." *LAN Times*, Aug. 10, 1992, p. 45. No longer satisfied with merely sharing printers, network users are demanding faster, smarter printers.

Day, Rolland. "Novell's SMS: A Sensible Standard for Network Backup." *LAN Times*, July 6, 1992, p. 27. Now that networks are serving entire organizations, companies are realizing they need standardized network services. The most critical areas are network data backup and recovery.

Denny, Bob. "E-mail: Now Come the API Wars." *LAN Times*, Nov. 23, 1992, p. 60. Which electronic messaging standard will win out? Or will there be a collection of standards that fail to solve users' problems, but make some vendors very rich?

DePompa, Barbara. "Choosing a computing platform requires careful study." *MIS Week*, May 28, 1990, p. 30. Although the decision to buy networked microcomputers, a minicomputer, or a mainframe system is based on far more than the merits of these technologies, you should know the advantages and disadvantages of each before you buy.

———. "Lowering the Drawbridge." *Communications Week*, Feb. 1, 1993, p. 37. With APPN, IBM hopes to open up the fortress of SNA, but is it enough to entice software vendors and users to cross the moat?

Derfler, Frank J. Jr. and Kimberly J. Maxwell. "The Media Move the Message." *PC Magazine*, Sept. 10, 1991, p. 351. A guide to the options available for transmitting data between geographically separated local area networks is presented.

Defler, Frank J. Jr. and Steve Rigney. "Smart Links Between LAN Segments." *PC Magazine*, Sept. 10, 1991, p. 121. The real heart of LAN-to-LAN connectivity is perhaps found in the bridges and routers that establish connections over long-distance lines.

Derfler, Frank J. Jr. "Connecting LANs." *PC Magazine*, Jan. 14, 1992, p. 379. The best way to transfer data between LANs depends on how the networks are linked and the types of applications being used.

———. "Connectivity Simplified." *PC Magazine*, March 31, 1992, p. 251. Building a network means making choices. This overview explains the different options available for connecting computers in your office.

Dern, Daniel P. "Learn How E-Mail Works, and Put It to Work for You." *LAN Times*, Feb. 14, 1992, p. 37. Here are a few e-mail tips, thoughts, and dos and don't for network administrators, planners, and users.

———. "E-Mail Integration: Taking on new roles." *Infoworld*, Feb. 24, 1992, p. 41. As a result of corporate communication needs, E-mail is moving beyond its traditional role of interpersonal communication and is becoming a cross-network platform for transporting a variety of data.

DiDio, Laura. "IBM moves LAN to WAN Integration Close to Reality." *LAN Times*, April 20, 1992, p. 1. IBM Corp's recent Advanced Peer-to-Peer Networking (APPN) announcement, coupled with accompanying introductions from other vendors, are clear indications that the trend toward seamless integration of LAN and WAN technologies is accelerating rapidly.

———. "Medical College Melds Netware, Appleshare Nets." *LAN Times*, Jan. 25, 1993, p. 23. It's no secret there are obstacles and limitations with linking Macintosh and DOS-based LANs. Still, it doesn't take a brain surgeon to figure out how to connect these environments.

Dixon, Mark G. "Networks as '20th Century Shovels.'" *LAN Times*, Sept. 28, 1992, p. 29. The network management market is diverse, fragmented, and ill-defined. Many providers claim their products can solve all network management problems, but no single product can provide all the answers.

Dodge, Frank. "A winning client/server formula." *Computerworld*, Dec. 7, 1992, p. 85. Client/server applications can be developed quickly and economically. But you must develop the application from scratch, and you need top-notch senior people for the job.

Dohrmann, Kevin. "Driver Makes Network Switches a Breeze." *LAN Times*, July 6, 1992, p. 33. Stack managers are like telephone switches, making and managing communication connections between network transport protocols and network interface cards. Several network transport protocols can be loaded at the same time, allowing simultaneous access.

Dolan, Tom. "The Big Switch." *LAN Magazine,* March 1992, p. 83. A new class of internetworking devices delivers high throughput, graceful scalability, and easy installation. Do you need a switching bridge?

Doll, Dixon R. "The Spirit of Networking, Past, Present and Future." *Data Communications*, September 1992, p. 25. Just as networking technology has changed the way corporations do business, business has had profound effects on communication products and services.

Dortch, Michael. "Future Network Profiles: Transitions to Tomorrow." *Communications Week*, Nov. 9, 1992, p. 61. As technologies proliferate while budgets stay tight, planning for the long term has become a tough task.

———. "LAN OS Interoperability: Reaching Beyond Unix." *Communications Week*, March 2, 1992, p. 13. Progress toward interoperability continues, with vendors increasing their commitment to Unix as a common ground. Other technologies also may bring interoperability of diverse network environments even closer.

———. "Net Operating Systems Take Unix In." *Communications Week*, May 18, 1992, p. 13. As Unix software vendors try to bolster Unix in corporate networks, network operating system vendors are broadening users' options for LAN-to-Unix connectivity and interoperability, focusing on TCP/IP and related services.

————. "OS/2 Use Lags on Networked PCs." *Communications Week*, Aug. 24, 1992, p. 1. Of about 1.2 million copies of all OS/2 versions, analysts estimate that about 324,000 copies, or 27 percent, are being used on computers that are tied into networks. In comparison, about 3.6 million copies of Windows are running on networked computers.

————. "Unix Aids NOS Interoperability." *Communications Week*, Aug. 10, 1992, p. 13. A number of Unix-related features for peer-to-peer and server-based network operating systems have been unveiled recently that promise to bring greater interoperability among diverse LANs.

————. "Users Doubt Viability of OS/2 in Nets." *Communications Week*, Dec. 14, 1992, p. 17. Even rumored peer-to-peer enhancements to OS/2 are not likely to make the operating system any more popular among enterprise networkers.

Dostert, Michele. "Don't put your eggs in one LAN basket, research study advises." *Computerworld*, July 20, 1992, p. 45. Contrary to the belief that single operating systems make life simpler, a certain amount of chaos leaves corporate options open wider.

————. "Fax Servers Make Faxing Just Another LAN Service." *LAN Times*, March 9, 1992, p. 20. For most American office workers, the two really great inventions of the 1980s were stick-on notes and fax machines. As a third great technology, LANs, moves into the work place, it has to be integrated with the existing two.

————. "Integrating PC LANs with Unix Systems." *LAN Times*, May 25, 1992, p. 23. How can a PC LAN server find data on a Unix machine, and vice versa? There are three possible approaches to this compatibility problem.

————. "OS/2 faces Windows in the Netware world." *Computerworld*, Aug. 3, 1992, p. 55. As IBM and Microsoft struggle for the hearts and minds of PC users, both seem to realize that selling the best stand-alone operating system will not be enough. Both are looking at the networked world.

Dougherty, Elizabeth. "Many Hands Make Light Work." *LAN Magazine*, March 1992, p. 73. Network management: In the mystical world of LANs, extending updates from a central location is surpassing sneakernet as the way to update software.

Drummond, Rik. "Shopping for High-Speed WANs." *LAN Times*, Nov. 9, 1992, p. 46. Interconnecting LANs is a technology in constant change. To help get through the maze, several industry experts have offered some navigating tips.

Dryden, Patrick. "An Array of Hope for Servers." *LAN Times*, Dec. 30, 1991, p. 1. Drive arrays are here to stay, whether network managers seek fast storage or the insurance of data redundancy for disaster recovery.

————. "Users Cite RAID's Benefits and Concerns." *LAN Times*, May 25, 1992, p. 1. Redundant Array of Inexpensive Disks (RAID) systems have become vital tools to some network managers who have critical applications running on their LANs.

Duffy, Jim. "Seeking network management harmony." *Network World*, Sept. 28, 1992, p. S23. The quest for integrating SNMP, CMIP, DME, and other network management standards and technologies.

Duncanson, Jay. "Standing the Multiplexer on Its Head." *LAN Times*, Sept. 14, 1992, p. 47. Network managers are becoming aware of new options for interconnecting LANs. While bridges and routers have continued to improve, network service providers have introduced new and improved services.

Eckerson, Wayne and Ellen Messmer. "Is OSI Dead?" *Network World*, June 15, 1992, p. 1. There is a growing perception that the OSI movement is sputtering and will soon run out of gas. Meanwhile, TCP/IP, which OSI was supposed to make obsolete, has grown in functionality and surged in popularity.

Eckerson, Wayne. "People management skills vital to downsizing effort." *Network World*, June 8, 1992, p. 33. The most challenging aspect of downsizing is not implementing technology, but managing change and its impact on IS staff members.

————. "User downsizes in an off-the-shelf way." *Network World*, July 13, 1992, p. 19. Last year, Motorola Inc.'s Computer Group embarked on a two-year migration from IBM mainframes running applications developed in-house to distributed Unix processors using primarily packaged applications.

Edelstein, Herbert A. "Relational v. Object-oriented." *DBMS*, Nov. 1991, p. 68. Will the victor in the database wars of the 1991s be relational or object-oriented?

————. "Using Stored Procedures and Triggers." *DBMS*, Sept. 1992, p. 66. A comparison of stored procedures in Sybase SQL Server, Interbase, Rdb, Ingres, Informix, and Oracle.

————. "Document Image Management." *DBMS*, April 1992, p. 46. DBMS-based electronic file cabinets and workflow systems take a big step toward the paperless office.

————. "Software pricing undergoing shakeup." *Software Magazine*, July 1992, p. 52. Software is increasingly making up a higher percentage of information system costs. Accordingly, vendors have begun to answer customer demands that pricing and licensing reflect the value of the software itself.

Elizer, Lee. "Making Sense of Backup." *LAN Times*, Feb. 10, 1992, p. 76. The network perspective on backup becomes complex due to the number of independent users with direct access to data. Once you accept the fact that backup is a necessity and not a luxury, the choices really begin.

Engelbrecht, Ron. "Just One Disk Crash Could Pay for a RAID Solution." *LAN Times*, May 25, 1992, p. 21. In many cases, the cost of a single-disk failure is greater than the incremental cost required to protect the data by using a second, mirrored disk or a disk array.

English, Larry P. "Object Databases at Work." *DBMS*, Oct. 1992, p. 3. You've heard about object-oriented DBMSs, but what do you know about the technology. This article presents an overview of key concepts and a look at a handful of real-world applications.

Ernst, Martin L. "Return of the killer application." *Computerworld*, March 23, 1992, p. 99. The next big hit probably won't be a single application, but a set of powerful supports for users.

Ferris, David. "Count Hidden Elements in Cost of PC Network E-mail." *Infoworld*, Feb. 10, 1992, p. 69. Cost assessments are usually based on equipment and software product expenses. Hidden components such as technical support and communication links are ignored.

————. "Figuring the Real Cost of Operating a PC Network." *LAN Times*, May 20, 1991, p. 51. It's often thought that PCs come dirt cheap. The trouble with this analysis is that it doesn't include the hidden costs.

————. "Multiprocessing: The New LAN Architecture." *LAN Times*, June 3, 1991, p. 56. The designers of superservers seek to improve LAN performance by adding one or more processors. Where these processors are added and how they are used determine how much performance will improve.

————. "Security and PC Networks: Old Problems, New Cures." *LAN Times*, Aug. 5, 1991, p. 33. Computer security is a recognized issue with mainframe-based systems, but it's new to the world of PC networking. Many of the problems are similar, and some—such as viruses and software licensing—demand new solutions.

Fetterolf, Peter. "Connectivity: The sum of its parts." *Byte,* November 1991, p. 197. We are making headway connecting the worlds of wide area networks (WANS), LANs, and metropolitan area networks (MANs). Bridges, multiprotocol routers, and other devices are finally making the promise of network connectivity more than just a gleam in the eye.

Fincher, Kelvin. "Remote Dial-up Invaluable to Nomadic Employees." *LAN Times*, July 6, 1992, p. 33. For users, network managers and developers at Canada's Imperial Oil Ltd., full-bore remote access is the new reality of their workdays.

Finkelstein, Richard and Colin White. "The pluses and minuses of going distributed." *Computerworld*, June 3, 1991, p. 101. Most organizations are focusing their attention on client/server and cooperative processing. Both these distributed computing technologies offer several pluses . . . but these potential benefits come with unresolved questions.

Finkelstein, Richard. "Client/server Middleware: Making Connections Across the Enterprise." *DBMS*, January 1993, p. 46. What do you do when you need access to mainframe data? The answer is middleware, a new class of software that facilitates client/server connections and lets client applications transparently access and update remote data.

————. "Four Rules for Downsizing Databases." *Data Based Advisor*, April 1991, p. 67. But downsizing also has its costs and potential traps that you'll have to understand before undertaking any major project. How can you avoid the associated risks? Just follow a few rules.

————. "OS/2, Unix, More Stable than Netware." *Infoworld*, Feb. 10, 1992, p. S67. Along the way to client/server computing, Netware failed to address the need for operating system protection, preemptive scheduling, virtual paging and, with this, stability and predictability.

————. "SQL database servers run the gamut." *LAN Times*, June 17, 1991, p. 65. The popularity of OS/2 and Unix database servers continues to grow. Database servers offer greater price/performance, more scalability to various platforms, greater productivity, and greater support for distribution of data.

Fisher, Sharon. "A Working Definition," *Computerworld*, Oct. 7, 1991, p. 98. As the name implies, TCP/IP stands for two separate protocols.

————. "Data security experts say errors are greatest threat." *Infoworld*, Sept. 9, 1991, p. S74. When it comes to computer security, many corporations focus on protecting themselves from outsiders rather than insiders. But more often than not, crimes are inside jobs.

————. "Distributed Database Management Tools Scarce." *Communications Week*, April 27, 1992, p. 29. Despite the special problems of managing networks with distributed databases, few tools that specifically address these issues exist.

————. "Dueling Protocols." *Byte*, March 1991, p. 183. One of the hottest topics in networking today is network management. Much of the attention in managing heterogeneous networks has focused on two families of network management protocols.

————. "Five Ways Networks Pay Off." *PC World*, March 1991, p. 193. But despite the headaches, organizations of all sizes are installing networks at an amazing rate, anticipating enormous payoffs. Some firms are looking to PC LANs as flexible, cost-efficient alternatives to minicomputers and terminals; others want a way to exchange messages.

————. "Interfaces to Bring SNMP Support to Windows Alps." *Communications Week*, April 20, 1992, p. 1. Microsoft Corp. may be close to endorsing a standard set of programming interfaces that developers can use to build SNMP support into applications running under Windows or Windows N.

————. "Making SNMP a More Versatile Manager." *Communications Week*, April 13, 1992, p. 1. A movement is under way to increase the power of the Simple Network Management Protocol without adding greatly to its complexity.

————. "New Windows on Corporate Data." *PC World*, August 1991, p. 189. PCs will run an application developed with SQL Windows. It will allow executives to use a Windows front end to query an Oracle database on the VAX.

————. "Novell's Network Management System." *Communications Week*, Feb. 10, 1992, p. 1. Novell's Netware Management System will help users manage large, Netware-based LANs, but may make it more complicated for them to develop an enterprise-wide management system for heterogeneous networks.

————. "Software Distribution Not Yet Linked to Management." *Communications Week*, July 13, 1992, p. 37. Software distribution and network management, both increasingly important to enterprise networks, do not often work hand-in-hand today.

————. "Superman? No, superserver." *Computerworld*, May 6, 1991, p. 73. LAN server vendors are touting power and speed, but buyers need to decide how much is actually too much. Superservers are optimized from the get-go to handle either very large file sharing responsibilities or mission-critical applications.

————. "TCP/IP." *Computerworld*, Oct. 7, 1991, p. 97. Effective, yes. Well supported, definitely. But if you're looking for a graceful way to link PCs to hosts, you'd better wait a while.

————. "Unix, DOS and OS/2: There is no simple answer." *LAN Times*, Oct. 7, 1991, p. 145. The problem is deciding which PC operating system—DOS, OS/2, or Unix—is the best one on which to base your network. There's no simple answer, because it's not a simple question. A number of factors come into play.

Flynn, Laurie. "For most managers, Windows networking is still an oxymoron." *Infoworld*, Aug. 26, 1991, p. 35. Hearing that networking Windows was still such a sore subject among not only industry luminaries, but also the audience of business users was unnerving.

Flynn, Mary Kathleen. "E-mail API: Lotus v. Microsoft." *PC Magazine*, Feb. 25, 1992, p. 29. The X.400 standard was supposed to link various proprietary e-mail systems, but it is so complicated few vendors have bothered to implement it. Not surprisingly, software developers are rushing to try to create a de facto e-mail standard.

Forbus, John. "LAN security: don't let disaster strike your network system." *Infoworld*, Sept. 9, 1991, p. 2. How much local area network security do you need? First answer this question: "What would the damage be if the most sensitive information on my LAN were compromised?"

Forsythe, Jason. "LAN/WAN Tools Show Achilles Heel." *Network Testing (Communications Week)*, March 2, 1992, p. 9. As the LAN/WAN market and open systems movement continue to gather steam, proper network management is barely keeping up the pace. Effective management is the weak link of most networks.

Foshay, Laird. "Client/Server Computing: A State of Mind." *Personal Workstation*, March 1991, p. 80. Increased productivity depends on a broad, clear vision of the role of computing in our lives.

Foster, Ed. "WANs: Are They Too Big and Too Slow to Play with Your LANs?" *Infoworld*, April 8, 1991, p. S1. PC-LAN managers entering the realm of enterprise networking are often shocked by their first experiences with connectivity to wide area networks. WANs such as IBM's System Network Architecture (SNA) have been around, so they may seem slow.

Frank, Maurice. "CASE Tools for Xbase." *DBMS*, May 1992, p. 56. As the complexity of Xbase applications increases, so does the need for CASE tools that work with the Xbase language. To do so, they must be able to import existing files to develop a database model, use .dbf files for data dictionaries, and create .dbf files from the CASE-generated model.

Fratarcangeli, Claudio. "Locking and Referential Integrity in Oracle." *DBMS*, Dec. 1992, p. 81. Any discussion of integrity enforcement in a multi-user environment is incomplete if it does not take concurrency issues into account.

Frenkel, Garry. "NFS gives PC users a global vision." *Infoworld*, May 18, 1992, p. 51. One of the key tools being used to bridge PC and Unix environments is the Network File System, a distributed file sharing system developed by Sun Microsystems Inc.

Friedman, Norman. "APPN Rises to the Enterprise Architecture Challenge." *Data Communications*, Feb. 1993, p. 3. TCP/IP has built up an impressive early lead as the enterprise network architecture of the future, but APPN offers features TCP/IP can't match.

Frye, Colleen. "API Wars Stifle Growth of Mail-Enabled Applications." *Software Magazine*, Client/Server Edition, Jan. 1993, p. 48. Competing cross-platform APIs slow corporate development of applications that leverage mail transport systems.

Forger, Roberta. "The Ten Deadly Network Sins." *PC World*, March 1991, p. 201. Most of the troubles organizations encounter come down to unrealistic expectations about the commitment required in planning, installing, and managing the net.

Gallant, John and Joanne Cummings. "Users share concerns about network-based applications." *Network World*, Sept. 7, 1992, p. 1. Network executives face many challenges in helping their companies realize the promise of distributed applications.

Gantz, John. "The Hidden Costs of Downsizing." *Oracle Magazine*, Spring 1992, p. 4. As with any technological change, goblins lurk behind every door and trolls under every bridge. The unwary will find that there are hidden costs to downsizing, particularly in implementation and daily management.

Gareiss, Robin. "X.25's Popularity Remains High." *Communications Week*, Aug. 3, 1992, p. 21. New high-speed data services, such as frame relay, are turning users' heads, but applications for tried-and-true X.25 services aren't likely to disappear in the near future.

Garretson, Rob. "Piecing together your heterogeneous networking strategy." *Infoworld*, April 27, 1992, p. 50. For thousands of large organizations, multiplatform, multivendor networking is no longer an ambitious goal, but a daily necessity.

Garver, Mark. "Get the Most Out of RAID: Combine Levels 0 and 1." *LAN Times*, May 25, 1992, p. 20. There are six levels of RAND technology. In a transaction-oriented LAN server environment, the combination of levels zero and one offers a superior solution.

Gaw, Shannon. "Platform Politics." *LAN Magazine*, Interoperability Supplement, Fall 1992, p. 53. The shift to enterprise computing has created a battle for control between independent LAN managers and grand ol' corporate MIS.

Gerber, Cheryl. "Downsizing with Unix." *Infoworld*, Aug. 24, 1992, p. 46. IS managers looking to downsize operations are finding Unix to be a smart solution for a growing set of reasons. Chief among them are price, performance, a growing number of off-the-shelf applications, graphical interfaces, and development tools.

Germann, Christopher. "WANs: Conditions Count." *LAN Times*, 1991–92 Buyers Guide, p. 10. Mainframes and minis are not going to be shelved for LANs. Instead, important developments will center around internetworking.

Giancarlo, Charles. "ATM: Your Future Unlimited Network." *LAN Times*, Aug. 10, 1992, p. 29. The power of Asynchronous transfer mode lies in its ability to provide high-capacity switching, independent of protocol and distance. These characteristics are currently needed on customer premises today.

Gianforte, Greg. "Successfully Supporting Network Users." *LAN Times*, Feb. 10, 1992, p. 73. Proactive managers take steps to monitor and analyze LAN performance. This article will examine steps a manager can take to increase the reliability of a LAN system and to increase user satisfaction.

Gibson, Steve. "Developing Software for the Windows API is No Simple Task." *Infoworld*, June 10, 1991, p. 34. The Windows "difficulty dilemma" arises from the fact that the development and debugging tools we've had to work with have been inadequate for the task of managing the weirdness of Windows' programming.

Gill, Philip J. and John Desmond. "Unix nets an attractive development platform." *Software Magazine*, July 1992, p. 63. Some Unix database and tool players see an opportunity for a new market as a means for CASE tools to communicate.

Gill, Phillip J. "RAD Tools, Techniques Take Graphic Direction." *Software Magazine*, April 1992, p. 41. GUI-based computing brings new requirements to the application development table and new demands on programmers. CASE tools vendors are moving to adapt their products.

Gillespie, Kelly. "Secrets of Novell's NetWare requestor and Microsoft's SQL server." *Data Based Advisor*, July 1991, p. 92. Many networks use Novell's NetWare and want to run Microsoft Corp's OS/2-based SQL Server. One solution is to use Novell's NetWare Requestor for OS/2.

Gillooly, Caryn and Margie Wylie. "LAN users find you still can't get there from here." *Network World*, June 29, 1992, p. 1. Interoperability may be on the lips of the leading network operating system vendors, but it doesn't appear to be in their hearts. They simply are not doing enough to ensure their products work with one another.

Gillooly, Caryn. "Prepping peer NOSes for the enterprise." *Network World*, Aug. 17, 1992, p. 33. Vendors are beginning to accommodate user demands that the integrate peer-to-peer NOSes with corporate nets.

Girard, John E. "The more things change . . ." *Computerworld*, May 4, 1992, p. 83. Despite all the hoopla about client/server computing, the first wave of implementations are mostly going in as time-share systems. Their architectures resemble scaled-down mainframe environments rather than true distributed powerhouses.

Girishankar, Saroja. "Cards Will Elevate Hubs' Network Status." *Communications Week*, April 13, 1992, p. 1. The simple wiring hub is gaining sophistication as new add-on cards empower it with advanced networking features.

———. "Revised PPP Proposed as Routing Standard." *Communications Week*, Sept. 28, 1992, p. 19. Vendors are implementing an enhanced Point-to-Point Protocol that should let dissimilar routers closely interoperate when forwarding data over public networks.

———. "Routers Give User Power to Connect." *Communications Week*, March 9, 1992, p. 17. Router internetworks are by no means new, but when communication is vital and diverse LANs do not communicate, a multi-protocol router network can change the meaning of communication.

———. "Vendors Pushing PC-based Routers." *Communications Week*, March 2, 1992, p. 17. A spate of PC-based router products has hit the market in the last six months. The products are aimed at users of enterprise networks who have remote offices of up to 100 users.

Glass Brett. "Transactions prevent multi-user chaos." *Infoworld*, March 23, 1992, p. 65. In this tutorial, I'll cover the basics of transaction processing and concurrency, two concepts vitally important to client/server computing and database management.

————. "Database Tower of Babel: Portable SQL Still a Dream." *Infoworld*, March 11, 1991, p. S14. Database vendors frequently make inflated claims about the portability of database applications written in Structured Query Language, or SQL. Alas, while this "SQL Myth" might be so in an ideal world, it has little to do with reality.

————. "Relying on Netware NLMs." *Infoworld*, Oct. 12, 1992, p. S80. Originally designed to add functionality to Netware, server-based applications can supplant mainframes.

————. WANs require an enterprise-wide strategy. *Infoworld*, June 8, 1992, p. 62. If your company's networks grew up piecemeal rather than as a result of a cohesive strategy, you may already understand why these young entrepreneurs planned the network infrastructure before the first employee was hired.

————. "When it comes to protocols, TCP/IP is universal." *Infoworld*, Aug. 5, 1991, p. S63. TCP/IP is the most highly involved and widely used set of protocol standards for nonproprietary networks. The protocols of the TCP/IP suite, also called the Internet or DoD protocols, perform many useful functions.

————. "Windows 3.0 and Networks." *Byte*, April 1991, p. 343. What you don't know about Windows 3.0 and LANs can get you into a lot of trouble. Here are a few mistakes to avoid.

Goldberg, Cheryl and Jill Huntington-Lee. "Those *!@?#$ routers!" *Computerworld*, May 18, 1992, p. 104. IS workers complain of configuration problems, troubleshooting difficulties, and more. It's not really routers causing all of the headaches; the blame is more accurately pined on the complexity of internetworking.

Goldberg, Steven J. "LAN interoperability is the common goal." *Communications Week*, Dec. 2, 1991, p. IG1. Connectivity is no longer enough for users. They want interoperability and transparency between network operating systems, accompanied by adequate security and ease of management.

Gow, Kathleen A. "No thanks, I can do it by myself." *Computerworld*, May 20, 1991, p. 98. New tools and utilities are helping to turn passive end users into PC adventurers. Many personal computer users who could barely walk through a software program a few short seasons ago are starting to build their own applications.

Gratzer, Frank. "ATM and SMDS: A Good Match." *Communications Week*, Feb. 1, 1993, p. 35. There is confusion in the industry regarding the relationship between SMDS and ATM. Understanding the relationship requires a clear description of what each is.

Greenstein, Irwin. "Wideband for the 1990s: smarter, leaner, and cheaper." *Networking Management*, March 1991, p. 70. Wideband offerings are about to get smarter and more flexible. The technologies that are leading this wideband revolution are frame relay and SMDS.

Griendling, Paul. "The Bright Side of WANs." *California Lawyer*, Dec. 1991, p. 64. With a wide area network, every workstation in the firm has access to documents.

Guster, Dennis and Adam Amato. "Semaphores Signal Network Processes." *LAN Times*, Nov. 9, 1992, p. 29. A semaphore is a powerful programming tool. It provides a signal to a workstation that is used to coordinate the order of process execution in a network environment.

Gutterman, Jimmy. "Windows development tools." *Infoworld*, Sept. 14, 1992, p. 58. The popularity of Microsoft Windows has meant that long-time DOS programmers have had to adjust to an entirely new way of designing applications.

Hadden, Tom. "Net Backups: A New Perspective." *LAN Times*, Aug. 10, 1992, p. 25. As PC networks have gotten larger and more complex, less and less network data is being properly backed up. This comes at a time when downsizing companies need to allocate more resources to ensure that the data on their LANs is secure.

Hamilton, Rosemary. "Mission-critical tools aim at desktops." *Computerworld*, Feb. 3, 1992, p. 37. Users are installing core business applications on desktop platforms, with the goal of incorporating mainframe-class features such as reliability, integrity, and security.

————. "Teamwork key to workgroup success." *Computerworld*, Aug. 10, 1992, p. 1. Workgroup computing has been touted as the next savior of productivity, but IS executives say it will be a surefire dud unless companies first address the organizational challenges it presents.

Hammons, Jim. "Teaching minis new tricks." *Computerworld*, June 10, 1991, p. 63. Necessary changes lie ahead, but midrange machines are proving they can be right for server jobs.

Hanna, Mary Alice. "IBM pushes DRDA link to relational data." *Software Magazine*, November 1991, p. 49. With its latest Systems Application architecture (SAA) framework, Information Warehouse, IBM promises access to many third-party relational database management systems.

Hansch, Ed. "Transitioning to Open On-Line Transaction Processing." *Unix International Gazette*, Sept. 1992, p. 7. Today, the majority of the world's OLTP runs on proprietary mainframe computers, mainly performed by IMB's CICS system. There are signs that the huge CICS application base is accelerating its movement to more cost-effective platforms.

Harding, Elizabeth. "Distributed Opinions." *Software Magazine*, April 1992, p. 25. While many computer manufacturers claim to be offering distributed computing environments, a number of observers have expressed contrary views. The move from a hierarchical model to a distributed model remains a long-term goal, they say.

Hare, Curtis C. "Downsizing Changes Role of Help Desk." *LAN Times*, Aug. 24, 1992, p. 55. Network managers face new expectations of quality support and service.

Harper, Eric. "Imaging: Paperless or Just Less Paper?" *LAN Times*, Nov. 23, 1992, p. 81. The amount of new data acquisition being committed to electronic document storage, as opposed to physical storage, is growing, but it still has a long way to go.

Haverty, Jack. "Frame Relay and LANs: Look Before Your Link." *Data Communications*, May 21, 1992, p. 21. Frame relay, which is widely promoted for LAN interconnection, may well turn out to be ideal for that purpose—providing users know what they're getting into.

Held, Jeffrey, Marvin Chartoff, and Catherine McKee. "Distant Harvest Depends on Tools for Remote Sites." *Communications Week*, Oct. 12, 1992, p. IWP31. For individual workers, access to the enterprise network is no longer a luxury, but a requirement. Many organizations have yet to meet the needs of mobile and small-office workers.

Held, Jeffrey, Mike Rothman, and Paul Li. "Bringing Remote Users Back Home." *Communications Week*, Oct. 12, 1992, p. IWP41. The shift toward distributed processing has created fresh headaches for network managers who need to manage remote as well as locally attached users.

Herman, Edith. "Do You Need Frame Relay? Not Necessarily, Experts Say." *Communications Week*, May 18, 1992, p. 64. Corporate users should not be misled into thinking frame relay is a miracle technology. Some users may expect too much.

Herman, James. "Distributed Network Management: Time Runs Out for Mainframe-Based Systems." *Data Communications*, June 1992, p. 3.

———. "Object Orientation Bears Fruit." *Communications Week*, July 6, 1992, p. 35. Distributed objects on the network may well be the key to the future of distributed processing.

———. "Transaction Processing Opens Up." *Communications Week*, May 4, 1992, p. 43. A rainbow of options colors the OLTP market as proprietary systems give way to open architectures. OLTP transactions are the ultimate conquest for the open-systems movement.

Herndon, David. "DB2 does Client/Server." *DBMS*, Oct. 1992, p. 68. The state of Kentucky develops a client/server system that gives its social workers access to DB2 via Netware, SQLWindows, and SQLGateway.

Heywood, Peter. "Global Public Frame Relay: Risky Business." *Data Communications*, Nov. 1992, p. 85. Network managers thinking about placing their chips on international public frame relay services had better think again. Providers have ambitious goals, but track records have been spotty.

Higgins, Kelly Jackson. "Stuck in isolation." *Network World*, Sept. 28, 1992, p. S15. Users wait while vendors and carriers take a shot at providing interoperability among frame relay nets.

Hildebrand, Carol and Clinton Wilder. "Never fear—Re-engineering is here." *Computerworld*, Dec. 23, 1991, p. 8. A depressed economy, leaner budgets and tougher competition are forcing IS managers to re-evaluate their operations.

Hildebrand, Carol. "Bendix Notes push tied to quality initiative." *Computerworld*, July 20, 1992, p. 1. Bendix Automotive Systems Group has kicked off a downsizing process that could eventually move the firm's automotive sector onto a multiple-LAN platform anchored by Lotus Notes and CC:Mail.

———. "Managing the aftermath." *Computerworld*, Aug. 5, 1991, p. 58. The PC has made the world a different place for IS departments. From programming to organization to vendor relations, here's a look at its dramatic impact.

Hillegass, Jim. "Interconnecting DOS and Unix." *LAN Times*, Jan. 25, 1993, p. 31. The connection between DOS and Unix is actually a subtopic of interoperability, but it is one of the most important.

Hindin, Eric M. "Multiprotocol Routers: Small is Getting Big." *Data Communications*, May 21, 1992, p. 79. Downsizing has come to the multiprotocol router business, led by vendors who claim to have products that can bring internetworking to small, remote sites for which conventional routers are overkill.

———. "Netware Gears Up for the Enterprise." *Data Communications*, Sept. 21, 1992, p. 51. Most concepts of enterprise networking have one common thread: Any user can gain easy access to any other user or any resource at any geographic location in the network.

Hindus, Leonard A. "International conglomerate eyes OSF." *Computerworld*, July 13, 1992, p. 56. Unilever's 500 firms undergo migration, seeking gain in software portability and productivity.

Hoffman, Thomas. "Home Depot gets Unix renovation." *Computerworld*, Aug. 10, 1992, p. 20. Escalating transaction processing demands have led the nation's largest home improvements retailer to start swapping minicomputers at its 200 outlets with Unix-based midrange systems.

Horwitt, Elisabeth. "Caveat emptor on SNMP tools." *Computerworld*, April 27, 1992, p. 63. Purchasing a router, hub, or personal computer that supports the Simple Network Management Protocol standard may not guarantee that the device will be fully manageable by an SNMP management system.

———. "Diverse standards take step in unison." *Computerworld*, Sept. 14, 1992, p. 67. A consortium of users, vendors, and standards organizations has released Omnipoint 1, a treatise on how today's conflicting network management products and standards can live together in peaceful coexistence and interoperability.

———. "Kitchen sink approach out." *Computerworld*, Dec. 23, 1991, p. 38. The network supermanager is losing its high-priority status. Many organizations have gotten tired of waiting for the ultimate "manager of managers" to arrive and are looking at simpler, less far-ranging alternatives.

———. "Managers seek balance in LAN control." *Computerworld*, Feb. 17, 1992, p. 14. A large number of information systems managers seem to be struggling with the same dilemma:

———. "Organization, not tools, key to LAN management." *Computerworld*, Sept. 7, 1992, p. 8. Technology may well be the last thing a company needs to consider as it struggles to put a network management strategy together.

———. "Proprietary LAN managers still prevail." *Computerworld*, Aug. 24, 1992, p. 69. Local area network management is still extremely fragmented and based mainly on proprietary systems. Users are focusing on tools designed to manage a particular type of LAN, not on centralized, integrated systems.

———. "SDLC routing snags users." *Computerworld*, Nov. 16, 1992, p. 1. Bad user karma is overwhelming the idea that a router can handle Systems Network Architecture with the same ease with which it directs local area network traffic.

———. "SMP a rising star at Interop." *Computerworld*, Oct. 26, 1992, p. 83. A quiet revolution is going on to depose SNMP in favor of the more functional Simple Management Protocol (SMP).

———. "Users restless for LAN Management." *Computerworld*, Feb. 24, 1992, p. 50. Novell's Netware Management System may be the closest thing yet to a definitive local area network management platform. However, Novell's product will not be shipped for some time, and there are still user demands waiting for third-party solutions.

———. "Unix for Netware set for launch." *Computerworld*, Sept. 28, 1992, p. 4. Univel plans to announce its Unixware family of client/server products next week. The idea is for users to continue to use Netware while also making use of Unix.

Hubley, Mary. "Distributed Open Environments." *Byte*, Nov. 1991, p. 229. Open Software Foundation and Unix International pave the way toward interoperability. You once had only two ways to create an enterprise-wide distributed computing system. You could build your own or you could hand over the future of your company's computing to one vendor.

Hughes, Randy. "Meeting the Challenges of Unix, PC LAN Integration." *LAN Times*, Dec. 30, 1991, p. 20. File and print sharing is just the first step in joining the two worlds.

Huntington-Lee, Jill. "The latest in frame relay." *Computerworld*, Aug. 31, 1992, p. 87. Most implementers are experimenting with frame relay or are planning to use it in combination with faster methods in the future.

———. "Unearthing Router Management Treasure." *Communications Week*, Sept. 21, 1992, p. 64. The router is the great enabler of LAN/WAN connectivity and the chosen vehicle for ushering in asynchronous transfer mode networks. But when it comes to management, routers are a bit unruly.

Hylas, Robert E., Bruce Gordon, and Glenn R. Dinetz. "The Upside of Downsized Systems." *Best's Review*, Property/Casualty Insurance, December 1989, p. 78.

Inmon, William H. and Susan Osterflet. "Data patterns say the darndest things about your business." *Computerworld*, Feb. 3, 1992, p. 73. Most businesspeople will tell you it's not only the information you get, but also how you analyze and interpret it that makes a difference.

Jander, Mary. "SNMP 2: Coming Soon to a Network Near You." *Data Communications*, Nov. 1992, p. 66. A follow-up to SNMP will remain faithful to the successful original formula, while correcting some weaknesses in the original.

Janson, Jennifer L. "Smaller hardware can mean safer data, users say." *PC Week*, Sept. 10, 1990, p. 148. MIS managers seem to agree that data is more secure on LANs than on other networks, with benefits ranging from better data backup and data control to increased reliability of data over time.

Janusaitis, Robert. "LAN Management." *Computerworld*, Jan. 27, 1992, p. 91. There are thousands of things to be managed on interconnected LANs, from hardware to protocols to administrative tasks.

———. "Meeting the NOS selection challenge." *Network World*, Oct. 12, 1992, p. 77. A growing number of firms are favoring distributed processing across interconnected LANs over the centralized terminal-to-host architecture.

Jeane, Harvey. "PC Imaging: You no longer need a mainframe to do it." *LAN Times*, Sept. 14, 1992, p. 43. It's not easy, but with a lot of planning it can be done.

Johnson, Amy H. "Don't Play Your ATM Card Yet." *Corporate Computing*, Oct. 1992, p. 38. ATM is expensive and far from seamless, because the full spectrum of ATM-based network components doesn't exist yet.

Johnson, Jim and Sidnie Felt. "Open Security an Oxymoron?" *Software Magazine*, Aug. 1992, p. 71. MIS professionals fear that adding open systems such as Unix to the corporate network will leave the organization vulnerable to security breaches. But experts contend that Unix' bad reputation comes more from cultural than functional factors.

Johnson, Jim. "A survival guide for administrators." *Software Magazine*, Dec. 1992, p. 54. The suite of tools for managing centralized, mainframe-based production systems is rich and mature. Vendors now are trying to provide equivalent functionality on open platforms.

Johnson, Johana Till. "SMDS: Out of the Lab and Onto the Network." *Data Communications*, Oct. 1992, p. 71. Regional carriers say Switched Multimegabit Data Service is the technology ticket for high-volume data applications.

———. "Frame Relay Products." *Data Communications*, May 1992, p. 69. Despite frame relay's reputation as a simple technology, building networks is trickier than it sounds.

Product definitions are blurry, implementations vary widely, interoperability testing is rudimentary, and interaction with higher-level protocols can be a crapshoot.

Johnson, Maryfran and Thomas Hoffman. "Open systems growing pains." *Computerworld*, Oct. 5, 1992, p. 41. Pioneering users are running into new and unexpected problems as their open systems installations mature.

Johnson, Maryfran. "At what price open systems?" *Computerworld*, Dec. 14, 1992, p. 65. IS executives were asked, "During your company's migration to open systems, what have you found to be the hidden or unexpected costs?"

———. "New network cuts mainframe bills 90%." *Computerworld*, July 13, 1992, p. 53. American Airlines development unit reaps savings with distributed Unix-based system.

Johnson, Stuart J. "Standard software licensing API is just the beginning, groups say." *Computerworld*, May 25, 1992, p. 12. The LSAPI provides a standard interface for implementing concurrent software licenses on networks.

Jones, Bob. "Client/server development tools." *Computerworld*, March 9, 1992, p. 73. It's hard to tell which is more confusing: the term client/server or the mix of tools intended to develop these newfangled applications.

Juneau, Lucie. "End-user liberation forces change in IS mindset." *Computerworld*, Aug. 5, 1991, p. 59. Many users have learned not just computer jargon, but also how to program applications and make hardware and software selections.

———. "The Trials, tribulations and triumphs of TCP/IP." *Computerworld*, Oct. 7, 1991, p. 103. Despite compatibility snags and implementation glitches, users say TCP/IP is worth it.

Kafalas, John. "Two early converts keep on marching." *Computerworld*, May 11, 1992, p. 102. At DHL Worldwide Express and Hyatt Hotels Corp., the shift to open systems was hardly easy, but neither would turn back.

Kallman, Ernest A. and Sanford Sherizen. "Private Matters." *Computerworld*, Nov. 23, 1992, p. 85. E-mail privacy is a contentious issue. Here are some ideas for putting together a privacy policy that works.

Kalman, David M. "Mixing the Message." *DBMS*, Feb. 1992, p. 8. Client/server computing poses serious technical and managerial challenges. It also offers many benefits. Whether you perceive client/server computing as a waste, a windfall, or a wash depends on your computing background—PC or mainframe—and the specific needs of your organization.

———. "Roundtable Revisited." *DBMS*, Jan. 1991, p. 8. The client/server roundtable will act as a clearing house for information.

Kastner, Peter S. "Client/Server in the Real Enterprise." *Oracle Magazine*, Summer 1992, p. 88. The client/server model promises to harness the power of desktop computing while connecting an enterprise's information sources to its users. Yet IS management wants to know how good client/server computing is right now.

Keenan, Vernon. "Apples to VAX." *LAN Magazine*, June 1992, p. 73. Macintoshes give VAX resources a friendly face. Here's a look at what Mac-to-VAX connectivity can do for you.

———. "One From All, All From One." *LAN Magazine*, Interoperability supplement, Spring 1992, p. 34. As corporations move to LANs, IS departments must build interoperability among workgroup databases. Here's a look at the issues and challenges.

Kehler, Tom. "Users Discover Objects." *Software Magazine*, Client/Server Edition, Sept. 1992, p. 16. Early users pursue cost and time savings; others wait for products to embrace enterprise and team issues.

Kent, Paul and Rohan Mahy. "PC to Mac and Back." *LAN Magazine*, Dec. 1992, p. 50. How to connect your Macs to benefit from your Netware environment.

Keogh, Lee. "APPN: IBM's Bid for Multiprotocol Nets." *Data Communications*, May 1992, p. 55. Tomorrow's SNA/APPN is expected to be so well-engineered that it will easily outperform today's TCP/IP and OSI, making it the first choice on multiprotocol backbones for everything from low-speed transport to bandwidth-hungry multimedia applications.

Kernighan, R. Lynn. "Are You Ready for ODBC?" *DBMS*, Oct. 1992, p. 60. With its Open Database Connectivity application programming interface, Microsoft hopes to make universal access to data a reality.

————. "Downsizing with CASE." *DBMS*, Jan. 1991, p. 73. A new class of CASE tools simplifies the development of client/server applications.

————. "Hardware for DBMS Applications." *DBMS*, June 1992, p. 37. Choosing a midrange hardware platform designed to get the most out of your DBMS. Before assessing non-technical decision criteria you should understand and appreciate the technical merit of the various hardware platforms.

Keyes, Jessica. "CASE + GUI Tools = Access to Corporate Data Assets." *Software Magazine*, April 1992, p. 63. While GUI tools can help you get to the data, large firms may need control of a repository.

————. "Code Trapped Between Legacy, Object Worlds." *Software Magazine*, June 1992, p. 39. IS tries wrapping code with front ends until object tools can unlock legacies.

————. "The case for super CASE." *Corporate Computing*, Oct. 1992, p. 183. Providing a complete set of CASE tools has turned out to be too big a job for most tool vendors. Bringing together all the elements of a successful CASE portfolio is much more difficult than anyone anticipated.

Kine, Bill. "Options for Supporting Multiple Protocols." *LAN Times*, Dec. 30, 1991, p. 50. Gateways have traditionally been the means for interconnecting diverse network protocols.

————. "Understanding the Requirements of 10BaseT." *LAN Times*, May 11, 1992, p. 27. 10BaseT is designed to provide Ethernet connectivity at full 10Mbps speeds over common voice-grade telephone wires. It is often misunderstood.

King, Julia. "Apple's VITAL Strategy." *Infoworld*, July 27, 1992, p. 52. Apple has introduced a cookbook of ways to integrate its Macintosh with diverse enterprise computing environments. VITAL includes not only Apple products but those from other vendors.

————. "Linking LANS: Payoffs, pitfalls, pathways." *Computerworld*, April 11, 1991, p. 67. The Camp Hill, Pennsylvania-based health insurer has saved "hundreds of thousands" of dollars in mainframe upgrades. It has also achieved any-to-any connectivity across all of its diverse computing platforms.

————. "Still up in the air." *Computerworld*, May 27, 1991, p. 71. Despite vendors' claims to the contrary, integrated network management does not exist today. No single system can manage the entire sprawl of interconnected, multivendor, multitechnology LANs many companies are contending with.

Klein, Mark. "Front end techniques." *DBMS*, SQL Server supplement, Jan. 1992, p. 4. The traditional build-vs.-buy balance has shifted because of the modularity of the client/server environment and the application development tools available for it.

Klessig, Bob and George Prodan. "FDDI and ATM: No Sibling Rivalry." *LAN Times*, Nov. 9, 1992, p. 35. Compatible technologies will coexist after ATM costs drop.

Knight, Bob. "The data pollution problem." *Computerworld*, Sept. 28, 1992, p. 81. Missing, wrong, and otherwise rotten data costs U. S. firms billions each year.

Knox, A. W. and A. J. Aapraro. "Ways to Enhance Client/Server Performance." *LAN Times*, Dec. 9, 1991, p. 34. Building client/server applications seems relatively simple. But if performance is important to you, you've got to take a more active role.

Kondamoori, Bob Kesav. "The Challenge of Building Extended LANs." *LAN Times*, April 6, 1992, p. 29. Using existing technology can take the sting out of growing a network. Existing technology can be used to simplify the creation, maintenance, and expansion of enterprise-wide networks.

Korzeniowski, Paul. "Gateways Link Legacy, Distributed Databases." *Software Magazine*, Nov. 1992, p. 85. To take advantage of client/server architectures, organizations are looking to database gateways for better connectivity between distributed and legacy databases.

————. "Back to the mainframe for storage of LAN data." *Software Magazine*, July 1992, p. 73. In the first generation of LAN backup products, the server backed up the nodes separately from central storage management. As LANs have multiplied, IS professionals are seeking host-based LAN backup products.

————. "Building New Apps on E-mail." *Software Magazine*, Client/Server Edition, March 1992, p. 35. Mail-enabled applications help groups communicate and automate. Electronic-mail systems are emerging as building blocks for new applications. By themselves, electronic-mail systems move mail messages or documents among users.

———. "Computers geared for third parties." *Software Magazine*, Nov. 1991, p. 63. NCR phased out proprietary DBMS; AT&T merger raises some questions.

———. "E-Mail and Enabled-Application Futures Detailed at Networld." *Communications Week*, Feb. 17, 1992, p. 5. The leading PC network-based e-mail companies continued to lay the groundwork for mail-enabled applications, but many needed features are months or years away from general availability.

———. "E-mail Becoming Foundation for Networked Applications." *Software Magazine*, Jan. 1992, p. 95. LAN mailboxes doubled in the last two years; Boeing's 400 users like connectivity options. As LAN electronic-mail use has spread, new requirements have emerged. Once mail systems are connected and users have an infrastructure for moving information.

———. "Groupware: More Talk than Action." *Communications Week*, Feb. 24, 1992, p. 36. Despite a lot of hoopla about mail-enabled applications and groupware software, few vendors currently sell such products.

———. "LAN Capacity Planning Mostly a Black Art Today." *Software Magazine*, June 1992, p. 48. Vendors scramble to deliver tools, but users who can't wait find answers.

———. "LANs a weak link in security chain." *Software Magazine*, Oct. 1992, p. 96. Until centralized LAN security becomes a reality, users must make do with add-on products. These create integration problems that challenge IS professionals.

———. "Mail-enabled Applications Slow to Catch On." *Communications Week*, July 6, 1992, p. 29. LAN electronic mail products and their users have only scratched the surface of the mail-enabled features available in Windows. Mail-enabled describes the integration of e-mail capabilities with stand-alone applications.

———. "More features overlapping between DBMS, OLTP monitors." *Software Magazine*, Sept. 1992, p. 75. As Unix is used more as an OLTP platform, developers face difficult choices between similar features offered by DBMS and OLTP products.

———. "Object-Oriented DBMSs Strive to Differentiate." *Software Magazine*, May 1992, p. 68. The market for a new generation of object-oriented databases is in its early stages. The dozen or so suppliers vary from established hardware firms to software startups. Growth estimates differ widely.

———. "Shielding Developers from Net Complexities." *Software Magazine*, June 1992, p. 61. Developing client/server applications is fundamentally different than building traditional mainframe programs, or even PC applications. To ease network programming, developers are using remote procedure calls (RPCs and message queuing systems).

———. "Shifting access to users." *Software Magazine*, Client/Server Edition, Sept. 1992, p. 32. Data integrity and security are at issue as users gain wider access to data. Coors' solution is a read-only EIS.

———. "SNMP: From Underdog to de Facto Standard." *Software Magazine*, Aug. 1992, p. 65. Many companies have turned to wiring hubs, which provide a logical data control point, to control networks. As the hubs work with equipment from a variety of vendors, a standard protocol link was needed—and found.

———. "The New Flavors of Data Access." *Communications Week*, Sept. 28, 1992, p. 52. As carriers augment their basic offerings with new services like frame relay and switched data, finding the right data communication service is no longer a simple choice between dial-up and leased lines. New services have created a wide range of options.

———. "Unix winning over the bean counters." *Software Magazine*, Oct. 1992, p. 121. Belt-tightening companies, seeking better price/performance ratios, are considering financial applications based on Unix.

———. "Windows and TCP/IP tie the knot." *Infoworld*, Oct. 26, 1992, p. 64. Skyrocketing PC and LAN use have made the microcomputer the portal to enterprise systems. Companies are turning toe TCP/IP to build these enterprise networks, and Windows is increasingly being called upon to put a new fact on TCP/IP.

Kosiur, Dave. "Macintosh: The universal client?" *Infoworld*, Aug. 5, 1991, p. S1. The trend toward heterogeneous networks and multiple computing platforms makes it harder for customers to settle on only one computer as the perfect client. Apple Computer would like the Macintosh to step into this morass as the ideal universal client.

Krivda, Cheryl. "Enterprising Hubs." *LAN Magazine*, Interoperability Supplement, Fall 1992, p. 17. As vendors integrate bridging, routing, and management, the superhub is quickly becoming essential equipment in the interoperable network.

———. "The Hub of the Matter." *LAN Magazine*, Dec. 1992, p. 127. Vendor competitiveness, user demand, and developments in integrated circuit technology have helped make wiring hubs a truly simple solution.

Krol, Natasha. "Restoring the Original Enterprise Perspective with Objects." *Oracle Magazine*, Fall 1992, p. 5. Few companies can afford to throw away their legacy applications. Most will look for ways to enable better analysis and evolve their old systems. Object technology can play a significant role here.

LaMotte, Jack. "Successful Network Managers Emphasize End-User Empathy." *LAN Times*, Sept. 28, 1992, p. 70. The network lets the organization capitalize on the dynamic relationship among people, information, and technology. The network professional's challenge is to provide a system where users are more productive and effective.

LaPlante, Alice. "Downsizing Difficulty." *Infoworld*, March 11, 1991, p. S6. Downsizing makes a lot of sense in some situations, but that's no guarantee it will be easy.

———. "Downsizing With Superservers: Experts Urge Caution." *Infoworld*, March 11, 1991, p. S11. The superserver is becoming a key strategic tool in the eyes of many corporate IS managers. But those on the cutting edge of this technology warn that it can be dangerously sharp.

———. "Guarding their turf." *Infoworld*, Sept. 9, 1991, p. S59. The move to corporate-wide networking is causing IS managers to focus on security. LANs are more vulnerable to security risks than their larger system components.

———. "LAN-based DBMSes gaining momentum." *Infoworld*, March 23, 1992, p. S57. In this article, we examine the implementation efforts of three organizations who put mission-critical DBMSes on LANs.

———. "Leaving MIS Standards Behind." *PC World*, Nov. 1991, p. 71. Standards are the mainstay of most MIS departments, but if the PC users in your department are confined to particular programs, they may feel limited when more attractive alternatives beckon.

———. "Preaching the benefits of client/server computing throughout TI." *Computerworld*, Sept. 28, 1992, p. 57. Syd Limerick spends most of his time spreading the word about client/server computing throughout the worldwide operations of Texas Instruments.

———. "Resistance to Change Can Obstruct Computing Strategy." *Infoworld*, June 10, 1991, p. S59. Many companies developing enterprise computing strategies find that the most important hurdle is getting employees to understand and buy off on the changes it may require in the way they work.

———. "Retraining staff is crucial to a shift to information management." *Infoworld*, Feb. 17, 1992, p. 52. Dorothy Yetter is completing a five-year strategic plan that will help shift emphasis away from mainframe development to the desktop. Her main challenge is retraining her staff.

———. "The Tamperproof Office." *PC World*, July 1991, p. 238. Guarding against security threats requires a strategy that involves all levels of users and management. Here's how one company protects its most important asset: data.

Layland, Robin. "Do you believe in magic?" *Data Communications*, July 1992, p. 31. When frame relay hopefuls find out that the technology doesn't do what they expect, they're more than a little disappointed. They needn't be. The real advantage to public frame relay services is the savings they afford to large mesh networks.

———. "For routing, 'Ships in the night' Should Stay at the Dock." *Data Communications*, May 1992, p. 31. Despite the sea change toward router-based internetworks, it doesn't appear that any single routing protocol will rule the saves anytime soon.

Leibs, Scott. "The Culture Trap." *Information Week*, Nov. 2, 1992, p. 42. Many executives are now waking up to the fact that corporate culture goes far beyond whether employees wear jeans to work.

————. "We're All In This Together." *Information Week*, Oct. 26, 1992 supplement, p. 8. Business alignment may be a nebulous term, but it's no fly-by-night consultant's fantasy.

Leinfuss, Emily. "Distributed DB2 proving difficult." *Software Magazine*, Sept. 1992, p. 63. Lacking cross-platform referential integrity, development in a DB2 environment must implement RI within applications. Careful data modeling is the key.

————. "Security managed one DBMS at a time." *Software Magazine*, Oct. 1992, p. 77. Data transparency to the end user is the promise of a new generation of data access products. However, each operating system and each database usually requires its own security clearance. The two are in conflict.

Letson, Russell. "OLTP migrates to PC LANs." *Systems Integration*, May, 1990, p. 40. On-line transaction processing (OLTP) has not traditionally been considered a job for the personal computer (PC) local area network (LAN) area, although nothing in the basic idea of a transaction exceeds the capacity of a DOS-based PC.

Liebing, Edward. "A to Z: Networking basics." *LAN Times*, 1991–92 Buyers Guide, p. 14. The best place to start is with good initial planning and laying out what you will accomplish.

Lifton, Ron. "Selecting Bridges, Routers." *LAN Times*, Oct. 7, 1991, p. 99. Network administrators must decipher the type of technology, evaluate the features of benefits, and investigate the manufacturer's position in the industry, commitment to standards, R&D activities, reference installations, and support policies.

Lindquist, Christopher. "Windows, client/server versions ahead." *Computerworld*, Dec. 23, 1991, p. 42. Move over, stand-alone, DOS-based database management systems. The shirt to client/server systems is slower than anyone expected, largely because the transition is difficult and presents new problems no one expected.

Livingston, Dennis. "Pilgrims progress on the open road(s)." *Computerworld*, May 11, 1992, p. 97. The nirvana of open systems is being sought fervently by companies large and small. But as in any search for paradise, the best way to get there is subject to much debate.

————. "Unix emerges as unexpected net treasure." *Network World*, July 27, 1992, p. 33. Users are rethinking the mad world of mainframe computing and discovering that Unix-based computers are ideal servers for supporting network applications on distributed LANs.

MacAskill, Skip. "ATM emerging as LAN hub alternative." *Network World*, July 20, 1992, p. 21. The move by major hub vendors to fine-tune their Asynchronous Transfer Mode (ATM) strategies may be an indication intelligent hubs will soon be challenged by more powerful ATM switches.

————. "ATM threatens to usurp FDDI as backbone choice." *Network World*, July 13, 1992, p. 1. Long touted as the next-generation local area network, FDDI may be leapfrogged by Asynchronous Transfer Mode (ATM).

Mace, Scott. "ODBC kit lacks back ends." *Infoworld*, Oct. 5, 1992, p. 3. Windows developers say the lack of back-end support is slowing their initial acceptance of Microsoft's Open Database Connectivity (ODBC) developer's kit.

Maloy, A. Cory. "DOS and Macintosh Overcome Barriers." *LAN Times*, April 6, 1992, p. 31. What's left to address? Inaccessibility of data and incompatibility of software.

Manson, Carl and J. Scott Haugdahl. "Dynamic and Distributed." *Byte*, March 1991, p. 167. Unless you want a system manager at each distributed site, you need automated network management tools.

Mantelman, Lee. "Workflow: Improving the flow of corporate data." *Infoworld*, June 29, 1992, p. 46. Workflow systems are designed to automate business procedures using computers, networks, databases, and messaging systems. This emerging technology builds on the concept of groupware by adding distributed processing and client/server computing.

Mardeisch, Jodi. "Windows Front Ends Tame Mainframe Data Access." *Infoworld*, May 20, 1991, p. S75. Information systems' managers are attempting to ease the process of accessing important data by using Windows as a front end to the host.

————. "Meeting Halfway." *Infoworld*, April 22, 1991, p. 48. The Mac and the PC may finally be on course, but the work isn't over yet.

Margolis, Nell. "N.Y. Life moves back to the future." *Computerworld*, Feb. 24, 1992, p. 89. Insurer forsakes quest for flashy technology and refocuses on customer service.

Martin, James. "Reskilling the IT professional." *Software Magazine*, Oct. 1992, p. 140. Successful retooling of the information technology organization not only depends on changing methods, but also requires enabling people to handle the process of change.

Matthes, Lynne. "Moving Forward." *DBMS*, Dec. 1991, p. 12. After a long wait and a lot of promises, client/server has emerged from its cocoon. We define client/server most basically as a technology that increases productivity by logically dividing data processing between back-end servers and front-end clients.

Maxwell, Kimberly. "Remote access networking: riding the wave of portability." *Infoworld*, Oct. 5, 1992, p. 58. While just about everyone travels with a notebook computer these days, plugging into corporate LAN resources continues to frustrate many users.

McCarthy, Vance. "Novell thinks big with WAN APIs." *Infoworld*, June 8, 1992, p. 1. Novell has taken an important step in assuring Netware support for wide area network needs with the release of a Netware WAN interface specification.

———. "Peer-to-peer poised to battle Netware." *Infoworld*, Aug. 17, 1992, p. 1. Peer-to-peer networking vendors, long thought of as providers of entry-level products, are poised for an aggressive assault on Netware.

McClanahan, David R. "Conceptual design." *DBMS*, Jan. 1992, p. 66. Database design is essentially the identification of each data element and its function in the system. Database design is very concerned with planning for the future.

———. "Hands-on design." *DBMS*, Feb. 1992, p. 62. Part V: Creating an entity-relationship diagram for a small business conceptual database model.

———. "Physical Database Design." *DBMS*, April 1992, p. 62. A discussion of the SQL statements that will implement your database design.

———. "Relational database design." *DBMS*, Oct. 1991, p. 63. A series of articles on database design begins with this article on relational architecture.

———. "Relational Operations." *DBMS*, Dec. 1991, p. 70. Part 3 of the series on database design is a discussion of the relational operators: selection, projection, binary operators, and joins.

———. "Database design: relational rules." *DBMS*, Nov. 1991, p. 54. This second part of a series on database design covers using the rules of normalization to provide relational integrity.

McCullough, Thomas J. "Don't Forget Repeaters for Connectivity." *LAN Times*, June 22, 1992, p. 31. An increasing number of departmental Ethernet networks are being connected together by bridges or routers. There is another choice which is often overlooked: the repeater.

McGoveran, David. "Online Complex Processing." *DBMS*, Oct. 1992, p. 85. Traditional desktop applications involve a way of working that is different from large multiuser systems. RDBMSs must support relatively unconstrained workloads. Something more than OLTP is needed.

McIntosh, Thomas F. "How to Engineer an FDDI Network." *LAN Times*, Sept. 29, 1992, p. 43. Bell Labs' briefing on ways to lay out dual, counter-rotating ring.

McLarnon, Scott. "4GLs Getting New Spin." *Software Magazine*, Client/Server Edition, March 1992, p. 11. Application developers can choose from several partitioning options. Today, there are few tools that support multiple models, forcing trade-offs, but allowing a gradual shift to wider distribution of data and functions.

McMullen, Melanie. "A Late Arrival of a Faster Train." *LAN Magazine*, June 1992, p. 50. Chugging along with only slight growth, Microsoft's LAN Manager, even with improved features and speed, still hasn't hit the big leagues.

———. "Token Ring Tales." *LAN Magazine*, Sept. 1992, p. 87. The sluggish token ring market may get a much-needed boost with the emergence of smarter MAUs and CAUs, and IBM's blessing of 16MBps over UTP.

———. "Wireless Network Security." *LAN Magazine*, Nov. 1992, p. 21. Doubt and worry about security is one of the biggest hurdles facing wireless network vendors and has contributed to slow growth in the market.

Mehler, Mark. "Mac network acceptance slow but steady." *Computerworld*, March 16, 1992, p. 69. Hard feelings die hard. That's a big reason why the Macintosh still has a long way to go to become an everyday fixture in enterprise-wide, multi-vendor corporate environments.

Mehler, Mark. "Maytag: No more lonely employees." *Computerworld*, Feb. 1, 1993, p. 81. Maytag Corp. is using downsizing as an occasion to improve communication. As part of the conversion, the appliance manufacturer is trying to link its nine domestic divisions via a wide area token ring.

———. "Tiny dynamos advance the faith." *Computerworld*, May 11, 1992, p. 97. Small integrators are leading the open systems crusade and are earning attention from users and big foes.

Merenbloom, Paul. "Supporting remote users of your LAN." *Infoworld*, Nov. 2, 1992, p. 44. The issues of remote network access are plentiful. Here are some ideas to consider when implementing remote access computing on your LAN.

Metcalfe, Robert. "Networks Are Not the Bottlenecks Most Think." *Communications Week*, Dec. 23, 1991, p. 11. A startling number of network owners is considering a premature switch to very fast fiber optic networks. Most would be amazed to learn that their networks are nearly empty.

———. "Frame relay is now able and ready to internetwork LANs." *Infoworld*, July 13, 1992, p. 45. I have good news about the telephone companies. They are taking a step in the right direction with a new service called frame relay.

Metz, Sandy. "Network Hubs: The Evolution Continues." *LAN Times*, Oct. 12, 1992, p. 89. From basic repeaters to third-generation intelligent hubs, hub development keeps pace with network needs.

Mier, Edwin E. and Betsy Nocom. "Is Fiber Cabling the Future?" *Communications Week*, Aug. 17, 1992, p. 35. Users face a conundrum: invest today in expensive fiber or wait for cheaper copper alternatives.

Mier, Edwin E. "Lineup: A product guide to bridges/routers." *Communications Week*, Dec. 9, 1991, p. 22. Buyers of bridge/routers have moved their focus from questions of throughput to those of interoperability.

———. "The Cell Switching Revolution." *Communications Week*, Dec. 14, 1992, p. 61. It may take a decade or more, but the hot new cell switching technology called ATM will eventually replace the hodgepodge of switching techniques that now permeate data and telecommunication networks.

———. "Blocking the e-mail Gateway." *Communications Week*, Feb. 10, 1992, p. 41. While future electronic-mail challenges and rewards are expected to stem from windowed interfaces, today's intermediate user challenge is primarily one of making e-mail work across multiple protocols and network operating systems.

———. "Dropping the Mail in the Window." *Communications Week*, Feb. 10, 1992, p. 41. PC Windows and electronic-mail growth aren't necessarily symbiotic. Vendors are eying ways for the two technologies to interact more effectively, and perhaps eventually even to merge.

———. "Hubs: An Embarrassment of Riches." *Communications Week*, May 25, 1992, p. 49. Users face a plethora of choices, some of which seem to promise interoperability, but deliver only connectivity.

———. "SNMP, From Counters to Clocks." *Communications Week*, Jan. 27, 1992, p. 57. The Simple Network Management Protocol has entered the commercial networking world and has begun to supplant proprietary network management schemes and to make inroads into the future once thought to be reserved for Open Systems Interconnection-based management.

———. "SNMP Version 2: Will It Be a Box Office Boom or Bomb?" *Communications Week*, Feb. 1, 1993, p. 25. It isn't the SMP (Simple Management Protocol) any more. It has been formally renamed SNMP Version 2.

Miley, Michael. "Integrating e-mail across enterprise LANs." *Infoworld*, May 11, 1992, p. S47. Six years into the LAN e-mail revolution, users and vendors alike are struggling to integrate their e-mail systems, across multiple servers and platforms, between private and public systems, and between e-mail and other workgroup applications.

———. "X.400 pushes the envelope." *Infoworld*, July 20, 1992, p. 42. Messaging tools still insufficient for the task of building enterprise e-mail.

Millikin, Michael D. "A Client/Server Success Story." *Data Communications*, July 1992, p. 39. For all the unfulfilled promises, some tangible progress is being made in the great client/server quest. Particularly encouraging is a new type of product known as the mail-enabled application.

―――. "Apple Serves up a VITAL Networking Approach." *Data Communications*, May 1992, p. 35. The new architecture can help users integrate PC LANs with enterprise network applications.

―――. "Why Smart Users are Taking Notes." *Data Communications*, May 21, 1992, p. 33. With Notes, Lotus has prevailed by exploiting the power of open hardware platforms and the client/server model for networked applications. Users deciding on operating systems, applications, and hardware are advised to look for Notes' paradigm.

Millman, Howard. "There's something for all in application generators." *Computerworld*, Jan. 13, 1992, p. 68. Whatever your level of expertise, degree of commitment, or performance objective, you can find a Windows-based application generator to meet your needs.

Mitchell, Tracy A. "TV Station Gives Practical Advice for Network Security." *LAN Times*, Sept. 14, 1992, p. 16. After establishing reliability, the biggest obstacle in selling management on networking is usually providing security. But security means different things to network administrators and to top management.

Mohan, Surichi. "Roadmap guides users down path of open systems." *Infoworld*, April 27, 1992, p. 55. Unix International, the consortium spearheaded by AT&T to advance the cause of open systems, recently released the third edition of the Unix System V Roadmap.

Monash, Curt. "Application Software in the 1990s." *Oracle Magazine*, Fall 1992, p. 88. The application development industry will undergo many changes in the 1990s. Almost every application category will be transformed by three major trends: ease of use, flexibility, and distributed information.

Morris, Larry. "Integrated Services Digital Network Defined." *LAN Times*, Jan. 20, 1992, p. 29. Despite claims of its demise, ISDN is alive, well, and evolving.

Morris, Michelle D. "Manufacturing Firm Succeeds with E-Mail." *LAN Times*, Feb. 14, 1992, p. 37. E-mail can delivery information, but it can carry a hefty price: capital outlay, complexity, memory requirements, and user training. Reliability Inc. has found a solution.

Mulqueen, John T. "Distributed Database: A Dream?" *Communications Week*, March 23, 1992, p. 43. Even if distributed database access were available today, users would need to take extreme care in designing and justifying such systems.

―――. "Enterprise Design Tools in the Works." *Communications Week*, Aug. 17, 1992, p. 5. Modeling costs and predicting performance for enterprise networks have been a murky black art, but software tools are starting to appear that will help planners rationalize network planning.

―――. "Is Collapse in Networks' Future?" *Communications Week*, Aug. 31, 1992, p. 20. Is the collapsed backbone the future of the enterprise network? According to this theory, the traditional bus or ring backbone that connects multiple LANs is being collapsed into a single high-end router or switch.

―――. "Will Hubs Become Center of Net Universe?" *Communications Week*, Sept. 7, 1992, p. 19. The concept of a single device becoming the central switching point for enterprise networks is controversial. Once simple wiring connectors, hubs are evolving to include internetworking, switching, and multimedia.

Nance, Barry. "Interoperability Today." *Byte*, Nov. 1991, p. 187. The OSI stack provides a blueprint for interoperability and shows that our reach still exceeds our grasp. Getting applications to work together seamlessly across a heterogeneous network is not yet commercially feasible.

―――. "Managing Big Blue." *Byte*, March 1991, p. 197. IBM provides some serious network management tools for serious networks.

Nash, Jim. "Niagara Mohawk looks to tap the power of networking." *Computerworld*, Feb. 25, 1991, p. 52.

―――. "Users expect modular network pieces." *Computerworld*, March 2, 1992, p. 20. Looking just over the horizon, network managers see a gradual industry-wide shift in the use of network operating systems, from sharing resources toward connecting multiple vendors' equipment and applications.

————. "Vendors standardize on software license interface." *Computerworld*, May 25, 1992, p. 4. Users seeking relief from multiple conflicting software licensing policies got a break when 20 key developers announced they would standardize on the Software Publisher's Association's License Service application programming interface.

Nastier, Daniel J. "Understanding a Network's Life Cycles." *LAN Times*, March 9, 1992, p. 25; April 6, 1992, p. 24. Effectively managing an internetwork environment requires a thorough understanding of a company's network life cycle. This cycle consists of the phases a network undergoes from inception and design through implementation and support.

Nitzsche, Kyle. "The elusive illusion." *Network World*, Nov. 30, 1992, p. 43. Many users are fascinated by distributed database management that provides the illusion that data stored at multiple sites is local. Well, right now, that's just what it is: an illusion.

Norman, Carol A. and Robert A. Zawacki. "Teamwork takes work." *Computerworld*, April 1, 1991, p. 77. Self-directed IS groups can collapse management layers and increase staff effectiveness, but they can also rock the boat if not eased in correctly.

O'Brien, Timothy. "E-mail to be foundation of new information highways." *Network World*, May 25, 1992, p. 23. Corporations are looking to move e-mail beyond its traditional role to that of a transport mechanism for a variety of evolving multimedia technologies.

————. "Getting messaging in line." *Network World*, Sept. 28, 1992, p. S19. Users are pushing messaging suppliers to overcome the interoperability woes that make it hard to communicate.

————. "Looking for the best net-building strategy." *Network World*, Dec. 7, 1992, p. 27. Some analysts suggest the best approach is to use a combination of leading network products, instead of relying on a single vendor.

————. "Users trudge along client/server path." *Network World*, June 15, 1992, p. 35. A Dun & Bradstreet (D&B) survey finds firms implementing the technology, but still having a tough time of it.

Olsen, Marshall. "The Real Power Behind the Network." *LAN Times*, Nov. 9, 1992, p. 55. The biggest mistake companies make is not training one or more individuals as network administrators.

Olympia, P. L. "LAN Data Security." *DBMS*, Aug. 1992, p. 97. Today, anyone engaged in LAN application development seems forever changed by the data security paranoia that comes with the job. Isn't it ironic that we installed LANs to share data, then decided we didn't really want to?

Panza, Robert. "Keep the Peace." *LAN Magazine*, Oct. 1992, p. 53. How to use Windows to assemble an armada of allied protocols for enterprise interoperability.

————. "The Maltese Packets." *LAN Magazine*, Sept. 1992, p. 53. By sleuthing through a traffic analysis, one network designer uncovered slow performance, and optimized the network for packet size and speed.

————. "War of the Protocols." *LAN Magazine*, Oct. 1992, p. 38. The multi-protocol Windows workstation is positioned to satisfy interoperability requirements.

————. "Welcome to RDAville." *LAN Magazine*, Dec. 1992, p. 81. The remote database access specification may be the ultimate solution to database interoperability, if vendors accept ISO's forthcoming standard.

Pascal, Fabian. "OS/2: Quirks & fixes." *Computerworld*, Aug. 31, 1992, p. 93. Version 2.0 has much to recommend it, but there are some things you need to know before you try to install it in a mixed-vendor environment.

————. "SQL in perspective." *Infoworld*, July 8, 1991, p. S48. Viewed in the proper perspective, SQL is much better than what we had, but worse than what it should and could have been. Unfortunately, there are some entrenched misconceptions about both positive aspects and flaws.

Patch, Kimberly. "Net Advantage?" *Communications Week*, Jan. 6, 1992, p. 24. Digital Equipment Corp.'s DECNet Phase V, renamed Advantage-Networks, has the reputation for being a pipe dream that never quite materialized. But many users and analysts are beginning to take a fresh look at DEC's architecture, vision, and products.

Pepper, John. "The Horizontal Organization." *Information Week*, Aug. 17, 1992, p. 33. Call it what you will—the horizontal organization, the flattened organization, the empowered team approach—the idea that there's a new and better way for companies to organize is one of the most fundamental changes in American business in years.

———. "The Bigger the Network, the Scarier." *Information Week*, Sept. 7, 1992, p. 41. The LAN boom has increased the need for security. Surprisingly, the biggest problem is accidental misuse.

Perschke, Susan. "Xbase Enters the Modern Age." *DBMS*, May 1992, p. 3. Since its humble debut 10 years ago, the Xbase language has become an important player in corporate computing. Now, Xbase developers look to the decade of client/server.

Peterson, Cornelius. "Windows Changes Network Printing." *LAN Times*, July 20, 1992, p. 26. Users embrace Windows software for font selection and graphics capabilities.

Petreley, Nicholas. "How to pick a winning DBMS platform." *Infoworld*, March 23, 1992, p. S53. Choosing the right products for implementing a client/server database is not a simple matter. Here is a list of some of the most important issues to consider.

———. "What we have here is a failure to communicate." *Infoworld*, Oct. 12, 1992, p. 85. If your organization depends on a high level of reliability and seamless interoperability between mail users, the best route may be to standardize on a single e-mail product.

———. "X.400 addressing with gateways: an attempt at simplicity." *Infoworld*, Oct. 12, 1992, p. 96. One of the ideas of X.400 was to establish an e-mail addressing standard. In practice, the gateways usually demand a more complex addressing scheme.

Petursson, Ingvar. "Object orientation: more than meets the eye." *Computerworld*, Oct. 12, 1992, p. 33. Object modeling does not apply only to software engineering. It also applies to how we model organizational structures.

Pfrenzinger, Stephen. "Reengineering goals shift toward analysis, transition." *Software Magazine*, Oct. 1992, p. 44. Re-engineering existing systems and engineering new systems are not mutually exclusive. There recently has been a dramatic shift in the technology, focusing on current systems analysis, new systems transition, and maintenance.

Pieper, Karl and Karen Leonard. "The backbone of choice." *Network World*, Sept. 28, 1992, p. S11. FDDI has been around for some time now, but users still should evaluate each FDDI product for interoperability, to ensure that different product bands work together.

Plotkin, Steve. "Determining Management Issues is Vital." *LAN Times*, Oct. 7, 1991, p. 45. As LANs grow and change, a constant goal of MIS and Information Center management is to isolate the critical success factors and vital issues that need attention. One challenge is to focus on significant mission issues while deflecting technical trivia.

Pooley, Mike. "Blue Coup." *LAN Magazine*, Oct. 1992, p. 75. To combat mainframe tyranny and PC anarchy, team up OS/2, LAN Server, and CICS for distributed computing.

Porter, Blair. "Offloading development to the PC pays off for CGI." *Computing Canada*, Sept. 27, 1990, p. 47. Processing one million database transactions daily in a multi-user, database server environment, a major Canadian consultancy is using a PC database management system to prototype, develop, and test mainframe applications for a government agency.

Pratt, Fred. "Intelligent Concentrators Deliver Control." *LAN Times*, May 11, 1992, p. 31. Network managers confronted with sprawling LANs know the value of intelligent hubs.

Prince, E. Ted and David R. Kniefel. "What's the objective?" *Computerworld*, Oct. 5, 1992, p. 81. Object-oriented technology is actually a shift in a way people think about and approach systems development.

———. "What's the Objective?" *Computerworld*, Oct. 5, 1992, p. 81. You've heard all the hoopla about object-oriented technology. Now find out what's really going on.

Pulaski, Eric. "Choosing the Right Audit/Inventory Product." *LAN Times*, July 6, 1992, p. 37. As networks grow in size and complexity, network administrators must not only keep track of server data, but they must also analyze workstation information. LAN-based inventory and auditing packages do this far better than stand-alone versions.

Radding, Alan. "A Forest of APIs." *Infoworld*, May 4, 1992, p. 47. Digital Equipment's Network Application Support (NAS) is a multifaceted computer architecture that will allow applications to run across a variety of operating systems, hardware platforms, and networks.

———. "Dirty downsizing." *Computerworld*, Aug. 10, 1992, p. 65. Forget what zealots tell you. Here's some straight talk on the grubby political, technical, and money issues at the front lines.

———. "Downsizing without the fuss." *Computerworld*, Nov. 30, 1992, p. 81. Not ready for client/server, but need to cut data center costs? Consider rehosting on midrange systems.

———. "Five Types of Tools Get Data from Legacy Systems." *Software Magazine*, Client/Server edition, Jan. 1993, p. 31. Three types of gateways, APIs, and 4GLs offer middleware solutions. Each has benefits and drawbacks.

———. "Linking databases: many paths." *Computerworld*, June 3, 1991, p. 93. Users don't care where data resides, or whether its scattered among mainframes, minicomputers, personal computers, or local area networks. They just want transparent, real-time, on-line access and update capabilities. Now.

———. "Superservers to the rescue." *Infoworld*, Nov. 9, 1992, p. 73. As LANs get larger and more complex, superservers are taking on more of the heavy work.

———. "Superservers waiting in the wings." *Infoworld*, April 6, 1992, p. 46. Superservers, a special class of PC LAN server, are just now finding their way into corporations.

Rajput, Wasim E. "Effective client/server systems should not keep end users in the dark." *Infoworld*, Oct. 12, 1992, p. 57. Although most users don't need to see their transaction happening, they do need to know the status of their requests.

Rao, Anand. "Face the Risks." *LAN Magazine*, June 1992, p. 91. Don't let fear of the unknown keep you from installing a network. Here's how to analyze the inherent risks to minimize their effects.

———. "Right on Target." *LAN Magazine*, Jan. 1993, p. 89. Take aim at network management problems by thinking through your troubleshooting methods before you find yourself in crisis.

———. "Team Players." *LAN Magazine*, Nov. 1992, p. 87. Building a team that can balance the technology and people sides of the network management equation demands a new game plan. Here are some coaching tips for building your offense.

———. "You Ought to Audit." *LAN Magazine*, Sept. 1992, p. 4. Do you know your network? An audit helps review its performance and its contributions to your business goals.

Ray, Garry. "Object orientation catching corporate eye." *Computerworld*, June 15, 1992, p. 77. Object-oriented technology is moving beyond the testing stage and appearing on corporate development plans. But it will be two to three years before object-based systems graduate from today's plans to tomorrow's enterprise-wide applications.

Rebman, Kevin. "ATM—A Wolf in Sheep's Clothing?" *LAN Times*, Oct. 26, 1992, p. 43. On paper, Asynchronous Transfer Mode may seem like the ultimate solution, but only specific networks will realize benefits by adopting ATM.

Reinhold, Bob and Allen Harris. "Imaging makes its mark on nets." *Network World*, June 8, 1992, p. 43. With proper design, users can reap the benefits of imaging without placing an undue burden on the network.

Rhodes, David. "Fitting LANs into enterprise management." *Network World*, Oct. 12, 1992, p. 65. The majority of network administrators say their companies lack an overall strategy for managing LANs.

Rinaldi, Damian. "Case Study: Should 'Big Brother' be Watching?" *Software Magazine*, Client/Server Edition, September 1992, p. 55. A corporation has concerns about traffic volume on its 'open form' e-mail network. Should the company police the service, at a possible loss of morale, or should it support electronic freedom of speech?

———. "Client/Server Economics: Balancing the Equation." *Software Magazine*, Jan. 1992, p. 79. Care and feeding of Client/Server may cost more than development. The trade-off between low unit costs for clients and servers versus an additional mainframe system is only part of the cost/benefit equation.

———. "Plotting Recovery Routes." *Software Magazine*, Client/Server Edition, March 1992, p. 21. As corporate data is distributed, MIS may find itself inheriting backup control from LAN managers.

————. "Software updating Hiccups." *Software Magazine*, Client/Server Edition, Sept. 1992, p. 24. If client/server is the better mousetrap, electronic software distribution will help customers make a beaten path toward successful implementation.

Rizzi, John. " 'Mail-enabled' Applications Demonstrate Power of E-mail." *LAN Times*, May 25, 1992, p. 37. Person-to-person e-mail is powerful, but many experts believe other forms of e-mail can have a more powerful effect on productivity. Here are some examples of currently available mail-enabled applications.

Rodriguez, Karen. "RISC brings new horizons into view for business." *Infoworld*, June 15, 1992, p. 57. RISC workstations and servers are increasingly finding their way into mainstream business environments. RISC is challenging PC technology in commercial markets.

Rosarie, Carol. "FDDI: The Promised LAN." *Infoworld*, Aug. 10, 1992, p. 42. Fiber Distributed Data Interface (FDDI) represents the next plateau in high-speed networking.

Rose, Marshall. "Making the transition from TCP/IP to OSI." *Computerworld*, Oct. 7, 1991, p. 99. It's questionable when—and if—OSI will achieve dominance over TCP/IP, but it's still a good idea to plan for coexistence or an eventual transition.

Rosen, David. "Keeping LANs in control." *Software Magazine*, Client/Server edition, May 1992, p. 21. Network management grows in importance as multivendor networks increase.

Roti, Steve. "Serving up Servers." *DBMS*, September 1992, p. 82. Organizations that are considering client/server database computing have a variety of reasons. One thing they need to be clear about: client/server is not inexpensive. Although PC hardware has become a commodity, client/server software has not.

Rounds, Martha. "Is your LAN data secure?" *Software Magazine*, Client/Server edition, May 1992, p. 27. LAN security is now a free-for-all of DBMS, OS, and third-party options. "The root of the security problem in the client/server environment is that these machines were never designed to be secure."

Roy, Mark R. "Now the real network challenge is managing your management systems." *Infoworld*, June 8, 1992, p. 53. As corporate networks continue to expand, the population of management systems is quickly reaching critical mass. Now, a new problem is arising: how do you manage the management systems?

Ryan, Alan J. "Cigna re-engineers itself." *Computerworld*, July 8, 1991, p. 79. What does a reinsurance firm get when it replaces 85 percent of its systems and organizes itself along team lines? Annual savings of $1.5 million and quick delivery of information to line staff.

Ryan, Bob. "On the Fast Track." *Byte*, Nov. 1991, p. 361. Frame relay is an adaptation of packet switching technology developed for ISDN. The exciting aspect of frame relay for LAN users and administrators is its ability to connect geographically distant LANs at high-transmission speeds and to allocate bandwidth as needed.

Rhymer, John. "Joining the Seams." *Communications Week*, Oct. 12, 1992, p. IWP7. Users today can indeed build a distributed database access framework, but only by making sacrifices when it comes to openness, flexibility, functionality, and cost. Users must put aside the binders that separate communication from applications.

————. "Managing Distributed Data: This Upside-Down, Backwards World." *Communications Week*, Oct. 12, 1992, p. IWP26. The promise of easy access to data remains elusive. The reason has much to do with the fact that corporate data is organized in multiple databases and in a fashion that is both upside down and backward.

Sammartino, Fred. "The ATM Forum: A Year in Review." *Data Communications*, Oct. 1992, p. 123. Once merely an obscure switching technology behind future telephone networks, ATM is now expected to be at the heart of a revolution in communication.

Sandwen, Cecile. "Protocols Provide a Wealth of Important Information." *LAN Times*, June 8, 1992, p. 37. Data by itself does not constitute total communication. Other important information is found in the protocols, the languages through which networks converse.

Saunders, Stephen and Peter Heywood. "X.400's Last Windows of Opportunity." *Data Communications*, May 21, 1992, p. 73. The X.400 electronic messaging standard has a solid reputation for linking proprietary e-mail packages.

Sautter, William. "Improving LAN Performance." *Oracle Magazine*, Fall 1991, p. 78. Over the past year, two trends have emerged that are garnering significant attention in the computer industry: the need to increase local area network (LAN) performance and the desire to "rightsize" applications from minicomputers and mainframes to PC-based LANs.

Sayles, Jonathan. "Building an Application Development Workbench." *DBMS*, Sept. 1992, p. 48. If you develop large databases, chances are you use an application development workbench (ADW). If you're not using an ADW, here's why you might want to look into one, whether you're developing mainframe, mini, or client/server applications.

———. "Building an ADW." *DBMS*, Oct. 1992, p. 74. A detailed discussion of 12 steps for designing and implementing a customer application development workbench.

Schatz, Willie. "What is re-engineering, anyway?" *Computerworld*, Aug. 31, 1992, p. 97. Companies define the term as they redefine the way they do business.

Schnaidt, Patricia and Dave Brambert. "The Netware Express." *LAN Magazine*, June 1992, p. 36. Netware, the network operating system with the staggering installed base and the wide variety of services, is the express train of NOSs.

Schnaidt, Patricia. "Banyan Accelerates." *LAN Magazine*, June 1992, p. 43. Fueled by open systems and sparked by new manufacturing flint, Banyan Vines ascends the grade of enterprise network operating systems.

———. "Security." *LAN Magazine*, March 1992, p. 19. Information security entails making sure that the right people have access to the right information, that the information is correct, and that the system is available. These aspects are referred to as confidentiality, integrity, and availability.

———. "Tutorial: ATM." *LAN Magazine*, Oct. 1992, p. 21. While ATM was envisioned as a technology for public network carriers, its application has been recast. You can expect to see ATM deployed in private as well as public networks.

———. "X.400 Messaging." *LAN Magazine*, June 1992, p. 19. As corporations build enterprise networks, dissimilar e-mail systems must be connected via a common transport. Very often, that platform is X.400.

Schnapp, Marc. "Windows DBMS's, GUI Applications." *DBMS*, Jan. 1991, p. 46. Custom database applications operating on tree-like hierarchical menu systems are nearing their retirement dates. Event-driven environments present an easier way for users to approach their databases.

Schultz, Beth. "Frame Relay Reality Clashes with Users' Expectations." *Communications Week*, March 9, 1992, p. 1. Providers of frame relay products and services are finding that a number of users have inflated expectations about exactly what the technology can do for them.

Schussel, George. "Distributed DBMS decisions." *Computerworld*, May 6, 1991, p. 81. Will you go with a client/server DBMS or a true distributed DBMS?

Schwartz, Jeffrey. "Unisys: More for Client/Server." *Communications Week*, Feb. 17, 1992, p. 4. Unisys corp. has extended its client/server computing architecture across its A Series product line and has announced a new mid-range computer.

Scott, Karyl. "Asynchronous Transfer Mode." *Infoworld*, Dec. 7, 1992, p. 68. ATM is an emerging technology that promises to change the fabric of local and wide area communication.

———. "Internetwork routing enhancements planned for Netware." *Infoworld*, July 13, 1992, p. 46. A key ingredient of an enterprise network is the ability to link multiple and disparate systems into a coherent whole. Internetworking and multi-protocol routing are essential building blocks.

———. "LAN interconnection demands on the rise." *Infoworld*, Feb. 3, 1992, p. 43. Frame relay, SMDS, and ATM services emerge as strategic LAN/WAN integration solutions.

———. "Linking up the enterprise." *Infoworld*, Dec. 23, 1991, p. 32. Novell is positioning Netware as a unifying force in corporate enterprises. Novell hopes to move into larger and more complex environments. Its goal is to establish Netware as a key enterprise integration platform.

———. "Netware on Downsizing Fast Track." *Infoworld*, Feb. 10, 1992, p. S61. The Netware operating system is one of a handful of platforms being implemented for client/server application development.

————. "Network hubs evolving to tackle enterprise management." *Infoworld*, March 30, 1992, p. 48. Today, hubs are the central point of control and management for the physical plant that comprises departmental and enterprise networks.

————. "Parlez-vous TCP/IP?" *Infoworld*, Oct. 7, 1991, p. 45. Internetworks, once the exclusive preserve of government and university researchers armed with sophisticated Unix workstations and supercomputers, are now widespread. And the main reason is the TCP/IP protocol suite.

Scott, Mary E. "A downside to downsizing." *Computerworld*, Sept. 30, 1991, p. 62. Are you frustrated by the skills gap—or gulf—that's stalling your company's ability to leverage new technology fully? Many large companies that are downsizing from a mainframe environment are staffed with hundreds or thousands of COBOL programmers.

Semilof, Margie. "Can LAN 'Kits' Solve Enterprise-Net Problems?" *Communications Week*, Jan. 27, 1992, p. 11. LAN "starter kits" marketed by several vendors would appear to be ideal solutions for enterprise networkers seeking to support remote offices within their overall networking and management strategies.

————. "LAN Adapters Are Gaining More Features, Lower Prices." *Communications Week*, March 9, 1992, p. 11. Adapter vendors are working to make their products unique, adding network management features, multiple media connections, FDDI connections, and other enhancements.

————. "Servers: Consolidate or Distribute?" *Communications Week*, Jan. 13, 1992, p. 9. Users must ask whether it's smarter to consolidate multiple functions on a single server or to distribute these functions across several servers.

————. "Users Bypass Minis in Favor of PC Servers." *Communications Week*, Jan. 13, 1992, p. 9. Networkers are not interested in turning their minicomputers into LAN servers. They are opting to combine PC-based servers with links to needed data and applications residing on minis.

————. "Users Unsure of Need for LAN Superservers." *Communications Week*, Feb. 24, 1992, p. 1. Powerful superservers, which have held out the promise of widely supplanting mainframes, are suffering an identity crisis. Superserver vendors, some of which are startup companies, are having a tough time explaining to users just how the products

Senne, Lynn. "Strategies for Handling Today's Vast LANs." *LAN Times*, Oct. 7, 1991, p. 123. In addition to the original "shared resources in a segment" concept of a LAN, we now see many new paradigms emerging: distributed computing, workgroup/collaborative computing, and enterprise computing.

Shafer, Les. "Connecting Unix and DOS." *LAN Times*, Oct. 7, 1991, p. 154. What to look for when choosing software connectivity. Unix is a protected OS, offering better performance and greater capacities than DOS, and is available on a range of systems.

Shah, Kumar. "Interconnectivity Services in the Corporate Network." *LAN Times*, Aug. 19, 1991, p. 53. By assembling basic levels of internetworking building blocks, such as Netware 3.11, to connect workgroups, you can begin to build an effective corporation-wide internetwork.

Shaw, Richard Hale. "C++ and Client/Server." *DBMS*, July 1992, p. 43. The client/server revolution has changed the way we think about database applications, but it hasn't changed the way most programmers work.

Shipley, Buddy. "Routers." *Computerworld*, May 18, 1992, p. 99. They may not be the most elegant of solutions; they definitely require lots of care. But routers will get your data from one LAN to another.

Shirk, Gary. "Building a Superserver." *LAN Times*, June 3, 1991, p. 61. Processing on a file server is I/O intensive. The applications server gives the CPU much more work. Today, the most obvious need for multiple CPUs is in database management applications.

Sinnreich, Henry. "Any-to-Any Networking: Getting There from Here." *Data Communications*, Sept. 1992, p. 69. The foundation for tomorrow's all-inclusive global network is likely to be made up of several competing technologies.

Sjogren, Sam. "A Bite out of LAN Crime." *LAN Magazine*, Interoperability Supplement, Spring 1992, p. 21. It's great to have a heterogeneous environment, but connecting different platforms presents a unique set of security problems.

Sloman, Jeffrey. "Control Central." *Byte*, March 1991, p. 175. Tools, techniques, and advice for managing centralized network services.

Smalley, Eric. "Making applications fit your network." *Computerworld*, Dec. 2, 1991, p. 77. Managers dealing with LAN applications face two unique challenges: matching their setup to what the application developer expects and addressing user expectations.

Snell, Ned. "Scaling Future in View." *Software Magazine*, Client/Server Edition, March 1992, p. 27. The goal is to grow LANs to WANs and tie into existing systems. Many DBAs will be dealing with the scalability question. This sticky task of choosing client/server components can easily grow along with the client/server environment.

————. "Training to build GUI apps." *Software Magazine*, Client/Server Edition, May 1992, p. 14. Shift to graphical front ends requires gradual retraining.

Snyder, Joel. "Painting Apples Blue." *LAN Magazine*, Dec. 1992, p. 38. Connecting an IBM mainframe to Macintoshes sounds hard, but it's not.

————. "TCP/IP for the Mac." *LAN Magazine*, May 1992, p. 93. TCP/IP networking on the Macintosh can be divided into three parts: the network hardware, the network software, and the applications that sit on top of both.

Spence, Chris. "Downsizing with Netware." *Infoworld*, Oct. 12, 1992, p. S73. IS managers can let go of the mainframe mindset and downsize critical applications to the LAN. Really.

Sprung, Lance. "With SNMP, No LAN is an Island." *LAN Times*, Aug. 24, 1992, p. 29. Although today's networks consist of multiple technologies and equipment from a variety of vendors, the challenge is to manage it as a single entity. This calls for a standard framework for network management.

St. Clair, Melanie. "Beyond Batteries." *LAN Magazine*, Nov. 1992, p. 137. An uninterruptible Power Supply (UPS) used to be a battery in a box. Now, with advanced capabilities, UPS is becoming an integrated network component, not just something hanging on the network.

————. "Broadening the Scope of Bridges." *LAN Times*, April 6, 1992, p. 49. Much of the networking marketplace has been grouping bridges and routers into a single category called internetworking devices. It is important to distinguish between these technologies, because they have different functions and capabilities and divergent futures.

Stahl, Stephanie. "Matters of Protocol." *Information Week*, Oct. 26, 1992, p. 42. Network administration has become more crucial as networks get more complex. For relief, users are turning to the Simple Network Management Protocol, which encompass everything from LANs to public frame relay services.

Stallings, William. "Improving the LAN Escape." *LAN Magazine*, Interoperability Supplement, Fall 1992, p. 27. Speedy switching services such as Frame Relay, SMDS, ATM, and Sonet will soon become wide-area rivals. Which one will be right for your network?

Stephenson, Peter. "LAN bridges: connecting your LAN to a world of information." *Government Computer News*, Aug. 15, 1988, p. 63. Each type of internet has its own set of communications parameters. The solutions are by no means obvious.

————. "Mixing and Matching LANs." *Byte*, March 1991, p. 157. The primary problem for network administration is not how to set up LANs, but how to interconnect them.

Sterling, J. Mark. "Downsizing marks change in industry direction." *Canadian Data Systems*, Feb. 1988, p. 69. The convergence of technology trends and prospects of economic turmoil has users looking more closely at the risks of implementing new technology.

Strehlo, Christine. "SQL Server and Netware." *DBMS*, SQL Server supplement, Jan. 1992, p. 8. Netware is architecturally different from LAN manager; there are differences in the way SQL Server is installed and used.

————. "The Unix invasion." *Infoworld*, Sept. 21, 1992, p. 61. Unix was once the operating system most closely identified with the proprietary minicomputer, but it now meets industry criteria for open systems.

Syed, Rehan and Sam S. Gill. "A CASE for Rightsizing Applications." *Oracle Magazine*, Fall 1991, p. 82. With an integrated set of strategies and tools, users can build applications quickly and cost effectively.

Tash, Jeffrey B. and Paul Korzenioski. "Theory Meets Reality for New Breed of Apps." *Software Magazine*, May 1992, p. 78. MIS faces new management, maintenance, and training issues when scaling client/server applications from pilot stages to wide deployment. Developers must learn new techniques, and the corporate infrastructure may need retooling.

Tate, Paul. "Exploring New Fields of IT." *Information Week*, July 6, 1992, p. 24. British Petroleum is pioneering a comprehensive information strategy, leveraging everything from client/server to outsourcing and re-engineering, while challenging some of the basic assumptions of managing such an expansive IT infrastructure.

Taylor, Allen G. "How vendors have and have not met criticism." *Computerworld*, Feb. 25, 1991, p. 73. Since relational databases were unleashed on the world, people have voiced frequent complaints about them. Here's what vendors have and have not done to meet user criticism.

———. "The next standard for SQL and what it will mean to you." *Computerworld*, Feb. 25, 1991, p. 72. The next SQL standard will be big and extremely complex. No one is anywhere near in compliance with it. As a result, there are major incompatibilities among different vendors' products, though they may all claim to meet the standard.

———. "Windows Tools for Client/Server." *DBMS*, Aug. 1992, p. 61. Client/server database tools are just part of the booming Windows-oriented software market, and how that segment is itself devising. Categories include database tools, application development products, query and reporting packages, and tools for nonprogrammers.

Tittel, Ed and Paul Burch. "Tape backup provides a safety net for corporate LANs." *Infoworld*, Aug. 3, 1992, p. 52. The job of protecting LAN-based data is time consuming and often unpredictable, but to ignore this important part of network management is to tempt fate.

Tolly, Kevin. "Gateway Vendors: It's Time to Wake Up to SNMP." *Data Communications*, May 1992, p. 39. Gateway vendors need to wake up to SNMP. The industry has failed to converge on even a base set of local gateway management features, let alone a distributed model.

———. "Grading Smart Hubs for Corporate Networking." *Data Communications*, Nov. 21, 1992, p. 57. Smart hubs already make it possible to structure wiring so reliability is part of network design. But if they're going to grow into their internetworking reputations, they'll have to do more.

———. "Testing the New SNA." *Data Communications*, May 21, 1992, p. 58. The first SDLC transport products are here—internetworking equipment that can merge traditional SNA backbones with bridge/router internetworks.

Tomlinson, Gary B. "Redefining Interoperability in the 90's." *LAN Times*, Aug. 19, 1991, p. 50. A completely new approach to network computing was taken in the early '80s. This concept has evolved into the modern network operating systems, but are now becoming more commonplace on enterprise-wide internetworks of LANs and WANs.

Trutna, Rick. "SQL: An idea whose time has come." *LAN Times*, June 17, 1991, p. 64. In the information age, a company's database is one of its most valuable assets. As downsizing becomes a business reality, users will need to access this database through their PC LANs.

Turner, Mary Johnston. "A good support strategy yields distributed computing benefits." *Network World*, Dec. 14, 1992, p. 45. Users won't gain the long-awaited benefits of distributed computing until they settle staffing and support issues.

Udell, John, Tom Thompson, and Tom Yager. "Mix 'n match LAN." *Byte*, Nov. 1991, p. 272. The Byte Lab puts together a LAN for Unix, Mac, and Netware clients.

Ullman, Ellen. "You can't run on everything." *Byte*, Nov. 1991, p. 255. How to choose a portability toolkit or decide on a long-term portability strategy. Ideally, you should be able to write portable applications, but you might find it more practical to rewrite the software for specific applications. Portability is a goal, not an edict.

Vacca, John. "Modest Progress." *LAN Magazine*, July 1992, p. 77. Tools for developing true distributed computing applications are coming along, but the usefulness of the tool and the experience level of the programmer must rise.

———. "The Bottom Line." *LAN Magazine*, Jan. 1993, p. 49. To fulfill your goals of keeping the user up and running, you must analyze your network management requirements.

Van Kirk, Doug. "Client/server tips popularity scales." *Infoworld*, June 1, 1992, p. 50. This is a good time to be involved with enterprise computing. Budget pressures are forcing corporations to explore downsizing.

———. "IS staff, end users: a failure to communicate." *Infoworld*, Dec. 7, 1992, p. 72. Even after reorganizations, team-building exercises and customer awareness training, many IS shops pay no more attention to user issues than they have in the past.

———. "LAN Security." *Infoworld*, Nov. 23, 1992, p. 43. As PC LANs become home to mission-critical applications, the integrity and security of these networks becomes increasingly important. Network security policies and technologies are receiving increased scrutiny.

———. "Messaging wars revisited: standardizing APIs." *Infoworld*, Oct. 26, 1992, p. 68. Competing attempts by several electronic mail vendors to establish a single, common API for messaging systems has pitted Lotus against Microsoft.

———. "Pioneering companies are unplugging mainframes." *Infoworld*, Aug. 3, 1992, p. 56. While some companies are studying the possibilities of client/server computing, and others are beginning a slow migration to distributed processing, a few brave organizations have jumped in with both feet.

———. "Rewards outweigh risks of cross-platform development." *Infoworld*, Sept. 7, 1992, p. 56. Although client/server applications can reduce computing costs and provide users with more sophisticated programs, it can be hard to develop distributed applications across several different hardware platforms.

Varin, Thomas A. "Workgroup Hub Puts Flexible UTP to Work." *LAN Times*, Jan. 20, 1992, p. 21. Allows both centralized control and distributed processing.

Vaughan-Nichols, Steven J. "Transparent Data Exchange." *Byte*, Nov. 1991, p. 211. Data transparency refers to being able to use data residing on different types of systems connected by a network. We have made progress in transferring the data between systems, but mere access to files located on systems with different architectures isn't enough.

Verma, Umesh. "Defining Network Managers' and Administrators' Functions." *LAN Times*, June 22, 1992, p. 27. In the past, network management was a catch-all category. The industry just recently began defining network management as network and administrative operations above a user level.

Vinzant, David. "Getting Started with Your Own Data." *Oracle News*, June 1991, p. 6. So, you've decided to try using an Oracle Server for your database needs. But one big question still looms in your head: how will it behave with our data?

———. "Netware: Choice Platform for Downsizing." *Infoworld*, Feb. 10, 1992, p. S66. The network operating system and transport protocols are the glue that hold client/server systems together. Without the network, the clients and server can't communicate.

Violino, Bob and Chuck Appleby. "The Down Side of Downsizing." *Information Week*, July 20, 1992, p. 31. Winds of change are carrying client/server computing, and IS is bracing itself for the turbulence.

Volino, Judd and Chris Chance. "Hidden costs in using a LAN operating system." *Computerworld*, Dec. 2, 1991, p. 76. Many managers soon find out that it takes more than what comes in a shrink-wrapped package. While these additional costs are rarely prohibitive, they are significant.

Volino, Judd. "LAN operating systems." *Computerworld*, Dec. 2, 1991, p. 75. Choosing the right one might not be as easy as you think; potential buyers must match capacity limitations and application needs.

Watt, Peggy, Bill Soper, and Dave Berry. "Deciding on Downsizing." *DBMS*, Dec. 1991, p. 52. When an aging mainframe couldn't cut it, Chevron Canada turned to a client/server system. It became clear early on that a new system would be a culture shock.

Watterson, Karen. "Banking on EIS." *DBMS*, SQL Server supplement, Jan. 1992, p. 19. Microsoft Consulting Services aids First Interstate Bank in implementing a SQL Server-based executive information system.

———. "ODBC." *Microsoft SQL Server Connection*, July 1992, p. 13. Microsoft's ODBC for interoperable database access is a superset of the SQL Access Group's Call Level Interface. Microsoft took a middle route, selecting core functionality as the least common denominator, but providing support for other optional features.

———. "The importance of WOSA." *Infoworld*, Aug. 17, 1992, p. S60. Microsoft's plan for mix-and-match clients and servers makes Windows well-behaved and network-aware.

Weinman, Eliot D. "Software's Fountain of Youth." *Information Week*, Aug. 31, 1992, p. 24. New re-engineering tools can help protect investments in legacy software, improve customer service, respond to opportunities, and prepare for client/server computing.

Weitz, Lori. "Code Generators Gain Versatility." *Software Magazine*, Aug. 1992, p. 38. CASE code generators promise gains in the quality of code produced, ease of maintenance, standardization, performance, and portability. Vendors are now moving to better integrate generators with existing CASE tools.

Wexler, Joanie M. "CC:Mail yanks Unix desktops onto the net." *Computerworld*, Sept. 14, 1992, p. 4. User enthusiasm for a Unix version of CC:Mail is in step with industry reports that Unix systems sales are largely outpacing overall hardware growth.

———. "Distributed computing drives support costs." *Computerworld*, July 27, 1992, p. 55. The proliferation of distributed computing environments and client/server applications is making organizations increasingly dependent on enterprise networks. Managers are now investing heavily in internal and external network support.

———. "FDDI prices plunge toward affordability." *Computerworld*, May 25, 1992, p. 20. The price of 100M bit/sec local area networking nosedived toward the vicinity of user budgets, when aggressively priced Fiber Distributed Data Interface products emerged.

———. "Growth of networks nurtured at EPA." *Computerworld*, June 3, 1991, p. 59. We're shifting mainframe applications to LANs because of the diversity of what people are doing and because it's cheaper to add [computing power] to LANs.

———. "Hospital Consolidates LANs." *Computerworld*, Sept. 16, 1991, p. 81. A major integration effort is underway at Children's Hospital, where the foundation is in place for an organization-wide network aimed at blending an assortment of local area networks and computers that have sprung up.

———. "Hub routing modules address growing networks." *Computerworld*, July 8, 1991, p. 50. Routing is intended to make efficient use of the network by sending data over the most available and direct route between nodes. It also allows the partitioning of networks for tighter access control by eliminating the "broadcast" nature of bridges.

———. "Internetworking product demand booms." *Computerworld*, Jan. 20, 1992, p. 59. Once users made the commitment to LANs, they found they needed to move on and connect different environments.

———. "LAN security marching to smart hubs." *Computerworld*, Feb. 17, 1992, p. 1. Smart-hub vendors have begun to attack the growing vulnerability of information traveling across LANs. Hubs are likely homes for security because they are becoming the focal point of network management and, unlike local area network servers, are generally secure.

———. "Micros could save Knight-Ridder $1.7 million." *Computerworld*, July 20, 1992, p. 1. After running its services on Tandem computers, Knight-Ridder Financial is seriously considering a migration onto high-end personal computers. Boulderstone said he is willing to live with networked PCs because "fault tolerance is a bit of a myth."

———. "Network systems becoming redundant with rise of Unix." *Computerworld*, Feb. 24, 1992, p. 14. As companies migrate to Unix and other operating systems that contain robust communication capabilities, the benefits of network operating software such as Netware and LAN Manager will probably diminish.

———. "Remedies here for melding SNA nets, LANs." *Computerworld*, March 23, 1992, p. 65. As IBM nears completion of its advanced peer-to-peer networking (APPN) project for migrating host-centered computing environments to LAN internetworks, other vendors are falling in line to help users cost-effectively collapse their parallel networks.

———. "Router software IQ as important as nuts, bolts." *Computerworld*, Oct. 5, 1992, p. 49. Router purchasing decisions are growing more strategic as companies become increasingly dependent on LANs. Reliability and performance are being folded into the buying equation.

———. "Slow migration to ATM expected." *Computerworld*, July 27, 1992, p. 55. ATM is a high-speed technology that is expected to expand and to eventually eliminate the boundaries between LANs and wide area networks.

———. "Turbo Ethernet on way." *Computerworld*, Oct. 5, 1992, p. 1. Startup pumps network speed to 100 Mbit/sec.

White, Colin J. "Dr. Codd's Rules Revisited." *Oracle Magazine*, Winter 1992, p. 45. The relational database field has come a long way since 1985, when Dr. E. F. Codd published his well-known 12 rules for evaluating relational products. Although product support for Dr. Codd's 12 rules still varies, most of the differences remain confined.

White, David W. "Lineup: A product guide to remote LAN analyzers." *Communications Week*, Dec. 2, 1991, p. 36. Most problems can be solved before they become problems by keeping a pulse on the network.

———. "Networking with OS/2, Windows." *Communications Week*, Aug. 10, 1992, p. 43. There are pros and cons to building networks with today's leading operating systems.

Wilkinson, Stephanie and Tracey Capen. "Remote Control." *Corporate Computing*, Oct. 1992, p. 101. SNMP is neither the only standard for managing networks remotely nor the best, but it is the most common.

Williams, Dennis and Blaine Homer. "Routers: LAN Shakers and Movers." *LAN Times*, Oct. 26, 1992, p. 69. Hub-based routers are the key to centralized station and routing connections—at a reasonable cost.

Williams, Dennis. "Bridges + Routers = Brouters?" *LAN Times*, Oct. 26, 1992, p. 82. The differences between a bridge and a router are fuzzier now than ever before.

Winkler, Connie. "Users support OS/2 for development." *Infoworld*, Aug. 17, 1992, p. 62. In-house developers cite security, stability, and versatile tools as keys to creating innovative applications.

Winship, Sally. "Buyers applaud rapid application development SQL front ends provide." *PC Week*, Nov. 12, 1990, p. 155. While Structural Query Language (SQL) front ends afford developers a number of benefits, paramount among them is the ability to develop complex applications quickly.

Wylie, Margie. "Apple cultivates a magnanimous net strategy." *Network World*, Sept. 28, 1992, p. S7. Thanks to Appletalk, Macintoshes can be networked using a variety of network technologies with many different operating systems. However, Appletalk networks tend to be excluded from the mainstream.

Yager, Tom and Ben Smith. "Is Unix Dead?" *Byte*, September 1992, p. 134. Despite its problems, Unix is not dead. It is the only operating system to offer multitasking, graphics, and cross-platform compatibility in one package. Sales totaled $18.2 billion in 1991 and should climb to $44.7 billion in 1996.

Zachmann, William F. "Upsizing: the other half of the equation." *PC Magazine*, Dec. 11, 1990, p. 95. Upon further reflection I've realized that downsizing, important as it may be, is only part of the picture. Another, equally important aspect is what I've chosen to label "upsizing."

Zeile, Mike. "Expanding the Enterprise by Collapsing the Backbone." *Data Communications*, Nov. 21, 1992, p. 71. Collapsed backbones combine hubs and routers to boost throughput and simplify net management. They improve performance and transfers between network types and they offer easy access to WANs.

Ziff, Robert. "No Magic Here." *Corporate Computing*, Oct. 1992, p. 53. Mainframes claim I/O superiority over PCs, but the miraculous power just isn't there.

Zornes, Aaron. "Downsizing Dividends via Distributed Data Access." *Oracle Magazine*, Summer 1992, p. 4. Downsizing represents a fundamental shift in the way organizations use computers. Distributed DBMS, remote procedure calls, and object technology will emerge to dramatically simplify client/server application development.

———. "Relational DBMS: Making peace with the past." *Computerworld*, Feb. 25, 1991, p. 65. The walls that separate nonrelational and relational database management systems are gradually starting to crumble.

Index

10BaseT, 229, 231, 232, 256, 258, 292, 329, 330, 354
3Com, 235, 248, 331
3M, 213

Aberdeen Group, 81
Access control, 220, 228, 229, 231, 233, 259, 306, 370
Access units, 195
Action Technologies, 190, 192
Adapters, network, 228
Advanced Peer-to-Peer Network (APPN), 259
Advantage, competitive, 19
AIX, 214
Alisa Systems, 187, 188
All-in-one, 175, 184–186, 188, 194
American Airlines, 213, 353
American Express, 217
American National Standards Institute (ANSI), 134, 136
Amoco Production Co., 166
Andersen Consulting, 46
Andrew file system (AFS), 216
Apache, 179
Apple, 3, 191, 234, 342, 354, 356, 360, 371
Appleshare, 237, 238, 343
Appletalk, 237, 238, 242, 248, 250, 257, 339, 371
Appletalk filing protocol (AFP), 238
Application
    client/server, 43
    e-mail, 180
    selection guidelines, 22
Application Control Architecture (ACA), 161

Application developer, 44, 103, 104, 338, 367
    training, 45
Application development, 7, 10, 11, 15, 26, 45, 74, 81, 83, 91, 109, 113, 133, 171, 191, 205, 210, 262, 336, 337, 341, 348, 354, 360, 361, 365, 368, 371
    employees, 113
    tools, 91
Application environment specification (AES), 213
Application program interface (API), 104, 137, 143, 152–155, 169, 353, 361
    e-mail, 181
    Middleware, 263
Approved software, 16, 17, 308
Architecture, 72, 74, 82, 96, 101–103, 119, 134, 153, 155, 159, 161, 177, 187, 202, 211, 213, 214, 217, 220, 226, 232, 248, 249, 261, 272, 290, 310, 331, 337, 338, 341, 345, 347, 350–352, 358, 360–362, 365
Arcnet, 228, 231, 233, 256
Asynchronous, 194, 267, 270, 290, 297, 329, 348, 352, 357, 363, 365
Asynchronous Transfer Mode (ATM), 267, 270, 329, 348, 352, 357, 363, 365
    evaluation, 272, 273
    uses, 272
AT&T, 185, 192, 236, 244, 355, 360
AT&T Mail, 185
Atlas, 213–216, 218, 219
    definition, 218
    specifications, 219
Atomic, 119, 120, 123
Attribute, 124, 338

ABOUT THE AUTHOR

Dick Baker is a knowledgeable professional writer who combines technical information with tested strategies for implementing and managing new technologies. He is the author of 15 computer books, including the *Computer Security Handbook, EDI*; *What Managers Need to Know About the Revolution in Business Communications*; and *Downsizing: How to Get Big Gains from Smaller Computer Systems*, all published by McGraw-Hill.